INDIA *and* SOUTH ASIA

INDIA *and* SOUTH ASIA

ECONOMIC DEVELOPMENTS
IN THE AGE OF GLOBALIZATION

ANJUM SIDDIQUI, EDITOR

M.E.Sharpe
Armonk, New York
London, England

Library of Congress Cataloging-in-Publication Data

India and South Asia: economic developments in the age of globalization / Anjum Siddiqui,
editor.
    p.cm.
Includes bibliographical references and index.
ISBN-13: 978-0-7656-1452-0
1. South Asia—Economic conditions. 2. South Asia—Economic policy. 3. Investments,
Foreign—South Asia. 4. Globalization—South Asia. I. Siddiqui, Anjum, 1954–

HC430.6.I55 2006
338.954—dc22   2006010855

Printed in the United States of America

The paper used in this publication meets the minimum requirements of
American National Standard for Information Sciences
Permanence of Paper for Printed Library Materials,
ANSI Z 39.48-1984.

∞

BM (c)   10   9   8   7   6   5   4   3   2   1

To the loving memory of my parents
who inspired me to learn and speak the truth

Contents

Tables and Figures

Tables

Figures

Acknowledgments

This book has benefited from the comments of many associates. I am particularly thankful to the University of Ontario Institute of Technology for providing me with a sizable research grant that allowed me to meet various expenditures associated with the research and writing of this book.

Excellent research assistance was provided by Sadat Reza and Benjamin Mandel who helped in the completion of certain chapters. Comments from the contributors to this volume of readings are also gratefully acknowledged.

Seminar participants at Monash University (Malaysia campus), International Islamic University Malaysia, and University of Malaysia, and the Applied Economics Research Center (AERC), University of Karachi, Pakistan, provided valuable comments. All remaining errors are my responsibility.

Introduction

South Asia in World Focus

Amid the euphoria over China's phenomenal growth rates and the growth experience of the Asian Tigers in the Association of Southeast Asian Nations (ASEAN) region, South Asia was relegated to the background by international investors and ASEAN and China were at center stage. However, the political developments in Asia, particularly after the September 11 terrorist attacks on the World Trade Center in New York and in Washington, DC, and Pennsylvania, and the swift U.S. reprisals on Afghanistan, have catapulted the region into the international media headlines. The interest in South Asia is now both political and economic.

Another reason South Asia is now being viewed with more interest in the European Union (EU) and the United States is that India has become a regional economic and political power (quasi-power if not yet a superpower) and it has also succeeded in thawing its political standoff with China, which began in 1962 with the war in Sikkim and lasted for a good three decades or more. India officially recognized China's sovereignty over Tibet in 2003 and trade between the two regional powers has doubled from its pre-2003 levels. The information technology (IT) industry is a good example of this new alliance. India's new policy is based on cooperation with China rather than on competition in order to become a potent IT force in the world. India wants to expand the market for its $17.2 billion exports (2004–5) software industry in China and subsequently in Japan, as the Chinese market would be a springboard because Chinese characters form the basis of Japanese script.

Not only has India changed its foreign policy to improve economic relations with China, another significant development has been economic inroads into ASEAN through a host of initiatives. First of all China has emerged as India's second largest trading partner, its share being 5.6 percent of India's total foreign trade. United Arab Emirates, with a 5.5 percent share in India's total trade, was at number three—slightly behind China. The United States continues to lead with a total share of 11.1 percent in 2004–5 (April–October). With ASEAN, India has evoked an "open skies policy," established training facilities for ASEAN members in India, and signed a Joint Declaration on Terrorism and the Framework Agreements. A free trade agreement between India and ASEAN is expected to be concluded within ten years. In 2003 India joined the ten-nation ASEAN security pact. Significantly, China, which like India is a dialogue partner of the grouping, is also a member of the 1976 treaty (ASEAN security pact), under which members pledge respect for the independence, sovereignty, and territorial integrity of all countries, noninterference in the internal affairs of one another, and peaceful settlement of intraregional disputes. The treaty was amended in 1998 to allow countries outside ASEAN to join it with the consent of all ten member nations—Brunei, Cambodia, Indonesia, Laos, Malaysia, Myanmar, Philippines, Singapore, Thailand, and Vietnam.

With China threatening the EU and the United States as a mini economic power in its own right and expanding its investment base to a number of countries in South and Southeast Asia, the United States is taking on a more proactive role in South Asia. After Mauritius,[1] the United States was the second largest source of foreign direct investment (FDI) in India, accounting for $3 billion (16 percent of FDI) between 1991 and 2001, and the U.S. trade deficit with India was approximately $11 billion (Morrison and Kronstadt 2005). Foreign investors are eyeing a sizable Indian market, where the number of affluent consumers varies widely, depending on whether India or the United States is calculating the size of the middle class. While the Indians estimate their middle class at approximately 300 million, the U.S. Commerce Department estimates that India has 20 million consumers with annual incomes exceeding $13,000, another 80 million with incomes exceeding $3,500 and about 100 million with incomes in excess of $2,800. Thus the United States does not wish to leave the large Indian market to China, and, in a sense, the United States and China have competing economic interests in South Asia. This observation is supported by the fact that Sino-Indian trade has increased almost 95 percent since 2002, and in 2004 India's trade surplus with China exceeded $1.78 billion. While China may be a cheaper supplier of raw materials and labor to the developed countries, India ranks close to China, and the Indian trade surplus with China partially explains this observation.

The United States is currently pursuing a trade strategy to open up the Indian and Chinese markets for its goods and services. The United States is devoting more enforcement resources to pressure China and India into rescinding their "discriminatory" technology trade policies (Mark 2004). Specifically, the United States is concerned because China has imposed a proprietary encryption scheme for wireless local area networks within Chinese borders. Furthermore, Beijing has levied a controversial 17 percent value-added tax (VAT) on sales of imported and domestically produced semiconductors, but it has granted a 6 percent rebate for integrated circuits both designed and built in China. The United States claims that China's VAT policy is a violation of

World Trade Organization (WTO) rules that prohibit member countries from treating domestic products more favorably than imported goods.

Similarly, India is under increasing U.S. criticism for benefiting from the offshoring of U.S. service industry jobs while returning little in trade incentives to the United States. The United States is also concerned about lost retail revenues to India due to software piracy. It is claimed that the United States has lost approximately $342 million in retail revenues due to India's lack of enforcement of intellectual property rights despite being a signatory to WTO agreements. While there is certainly merit in ensuring compliance with the WTO to open up world trade, the United States itself is guilty of improprieties in its own policies—the WTO ruled in 2004 that the annual $5 billion tax break given to U.S. exporters amounts to an illegal export subsidy. It set a deadline for Washington to change its tax code or be penalized.

So while the United States watches both China and India, and strives to open their markets for its goods and services, it also fears the pervasive Islamic fundamentalism in Afghanistan and Pakistan and is watchful of similar developments in Central Asia and Iran and the activities of Hezbollah in Lebanon and Palestine. The threat of Al-Qaeda will not subside for the foreseeable future, and, consequently, Pakistan will continue to be wooed by the United States, although not with the same ardor by other G-8 countries. While U.S. interest in Pakistan is driven largely by its foreign policy, especially that pertaining to arresting insurgencies and terrorism, its interest in India is driven more by economic factors.

South Asia's Development Challenges

Notwithstanding these recent political and economic developments of the Indian subcontinent, there is a commonality of economic issues faced by South Asia. Mass poverty, poor infrastructure, misgovernance, rampant corruption, political uncertainty, and war are age-old problems of this region. Add to this the economic effects of a post-WTO world and we have economic problems associated with the liberalization of trade and capital flows. Bring in the International Monetary Fund (IMF) and the World Bank, and we have the economic effects of (sometimes) rigid conditionalities and structural adjustment programs (Stiglitz 2002). Antagonists of the World Bank and the IMF and the antiglobalization activists may have a case against some harmful effects of conditionalities (Chossudovsky 2003), but they cannot blame the multilateral agencies for demanding repayment of the money they loan out. If that requires conditionalities like balancing budgets and improving the environment for trade, then the spirit of such an enabling economic environment for the return of debt cannot be faulted. The anticonditionalities and antiglobalization camps are also most vocal in demands for incessant loans and grants from the multilateral organizations and G-8 countries. They fail to see two crucial flaws in their position. First, financial and physical capital does not flow on demand but toward its highest rate of return. Economic planners would thus have to make their economies vibrant enough to attract badly needed FDI. Second, the history of loans and grants shows that countries whose debts were forgiven or who received the largest grants were the ones that piled up further deficits and showed little economic growth (Easterly 2002).

Against this backdrop, what are South Asia's core economic problems and where do we begin to study them? One could argue that the problems and issues of population and fertility should be the foremost concerns of inquiry for understanding the economies of this region of 1.3 billion people. This understanding of the population bomb is important as the region will explode in further poverty if the more than 2 percent population growth rate is not arrested and reversed immediately. Others can make a convincing case for relegating economic issues and giving primary importance to political developments in the region, in the belief that all economic activity is the fallout of political decisions and power sharing among the factors of production, particularly owners of land and capital, with labor marginalized. Still another argument can be made that the region's poor economic performance is due to public corruption and misgovernance, and that governance must be fixed first, or there can be no development. Antiglobalization critics blame all of South Asia's woes on the globalization of product and capital markets. In their minds anticapitalism is associated with antiglobalization, laments Bhagwati (2004). In support they cite the ASEAN currency crisis of the late 1970s and the post-WTO order. The list can be expanded to include many different explanations for the underdevelopment of South Asia.

The answer to South Asia's poor economic and human development does not lie in any single factor. Underdevelopment is a multifaceted disease that cannot be cured with a magic vaccine. If it were that simple, economists would be a happy lot and it would be easy to shift all blame to the much-maligned politicians.

The chapters of this book represent an attempt to study and understand selected economic issues that are crucial to the development and growth of South Asia. While there is no universal agreement among economists concerning the list of development issues facing third world countries, or the sequence in which they have to be addressed, I have arbitrarily selected some core macro issues to be addressed in this volume on South Asia. This does not imply a downplaying of the micro issues pertaining to labor markets or decisions on fertility. While those issues merit serious attention, they are too voluminous to be accommodated in this book. In summary, the selected issues of this volume are largely macro in nature, for example, the economic effects of national debt, fiscal deficits, capital flows, international trade and globalization, corruption, and governance and militarization.

Another relevant question concerns why this book focuses on this self-selected range of issues and not others that characterize the region such as poverty. Poverty is the fallout and consequence of the macroeconomic governance (read misgovernance) of an economy. In other words it is endogenous to the socioeconomic and political decisions of the policymakers. Hence, in discussing these issues in the book, we address the core problems and the root causes of mass poverty, at least in the case of South Asia. For example, government fiscal deficits, debt, current account deficits, and the saving and investment behavior of domestic residents are all interrelated. Because an irresponsible and unaccountable government overspends and misallocates spending, its policies are associated with both internal and external deficits and debt. Furthermore, when they spend more on nondevelopment than on investment-related development projects, governments can be accused of crowding out domestic investment and exports and worsening the payments balances through a depreciating currency, as well as contributing to stagnant economic growth—we have witnessed all these phenomena in South Asia over the past four decades.

South Asia's future is in its own hands and it is quite naive to believe that factors such as debt forgiveness and more access to developed country markets will be a panacea for the region's economic problems. It is correct that in a globalized world with increasing current and capital account convertibility, external shocks cannot be ignored and may have destabilizing effects on domestic markets and currency. However, it is folly and an easy refuge for policymakers to shift the blame for economic malaise on adverse supply shocks (such as war and oil price hikes) and denial of market access by developed countries. While fair access to international markets will no doubt improve economic outcomes in developing countries, market access is not a sufficient condition for development, better allocation of resources, economic efficiency, or, for that matter, equality of opportunity.

Given this knowledge of poverty from the development experience of developing countries, one is inclined to conclude that the heart of the problem is *governance* as manifested in fiscal and monetary prudence, which cannot be achieved without accountability, transparency, democracy, and the rule of law. India's record in managing a democracy that has extremely heterogeneous socioeconomic groups is a model for South Asia. Based on this model, other countries in the region, namely, Pakistan and Bangladesh, can take some lessons. Endless structural adjustment programs, debt write offs, and eternal promises of growth budgets have not changed the economic and institutional fundamentals in South Asia. Domestic savings rates remain the lowest in the world, poverty rates are among the highest, population growth rates have not come down to levels of confidence, corruption indexes rank South Asia as the most corrupt, governments continue to spend unwisely, squandering billions in military expenditures, and institutions continue to be run by subsidies—vestiges of economic rents as patronized by the governments.

The South Asian countries as a whole do not have a great track record in privatization. While some measure of privatization has taken place, it is not wrong to generalize that in South Asia the state continues to engage in the production of goods and services. For example, the government has a significant role in the provision of energy, banking, and defense production. The government also continues to be a major employer. Free market economists, including this author, believe that it is not the business of the government to be in business; therefore, speedy privatization is essential for economic efficiency. Moreover, the smaller the size of the government, the less corruption. One should be careful in noting that privatization can be misused by governments to obtain foreign exchange for financing their current expenditures and trade deficits. In fact, we are witnessing such a phenomenon recently in Pakistan whose trade deficit was $12.112 billion in fiscal year 2005–2006, almost 10 percent of the gross domestic product (GDP), due to its high import bill and the domestic inflation. In cases such as the Pakistani economy of the 2000s the root causes of trade and fiscal deficits must be addressed without recourse to easy privatization proceeds. The danger in not controlling these twin deficits is that the currency will be periodically devalued and the vicious cycle of deficits, devaluation, and poverty will not be broken.

Those who are either despondent or skeptical about South Asia's future can point to the corrupt bureaucratic and political status quo over the past six decades. They may see no signs of South Asian growth and might well question who will bell the cat and where the process of recovery and growth will begin.

It is no secret that economic recovery is dependent on a sustainable, transparent, and credible rule of law and democratic institutions. Institutional failures can be a serious impediment to sustained economic growth (Temple 2003) and uncertainty in governance rules and regimes can negate any positive effects of institutional improvements on growth (Pritchet 2003). No wonder that the thinking on development economics has changed from the narrow saving–investment–growth focus to a multidimensional approach involving transparent and democratic institutions that will churn the wheels of the economy and be representative of the preferences and welfare of the governed. Multilateral institutions entrusted with the task of eradicating global poverty have now also embraced an interdisciplinary and multifaceted approach to development. This is because there is no linear sequential ordering of policies that can take a developing economy toward sustainable growth. While this is correct, there are indeed some core areas of policymaking that must be put on track for development to succeed—some of these "core areas" or "fundamentals" are discussed in this volume.

Author Contributions to This Book

Given the nature of the beast (underdevelopment), the issues addressed in this volume are diverse in scope. Consequently, the book is divided into four parts: Part 1 presents an introduction to South Asia. Part 2 deals with macroeconomic issues focusing on the twin budgetary and trade deficits, foreign direct investment, investment in human capital, capital flows and their effects on domestic saving, and the consequent impact on economic growth. Part 3 examines the South Asian Free Trade Agreement (SAFTA) in the South Asian Association for Regional Cooperation (SAARC) and whether globalization has improved economic development in the region. We also examine poverty in South Asia and assess whether structural adjustment has adjusted anything and what has been achieved by IMF/World Bank programs in the region. Part 4 examines governance and corruption and also looks at the 'wisdom' of military spending in the region.

We now briefly summarize the findings and observations of the individual chapters in the four parts of the book. The first chapter in Part 1, "South Asia at a Glance: A Taxonomy of Growth Challenges," by the editor of the book, Anjum Siddiqui, provides a general overview of South Asia's political economy and compares its performance to other regions. Using comparative data, the chapter briefly examines the region's history, human development status, economic and trade structure, and sets a context for regional development challenges. The stylized facts of this chapter highlight an immediate need for action by respective South Asian governments and a call to move beyond lip service, rhetoric, and dressed-up statistics to address both literacy and health along with improving the investment climate, and, most important, substantially improving governance indicators.

The truism that a region's economic development is the fallout of political decisions is equally applicable to South Asia. In "The Political Economy of South Asia," Edelgard Mahant, a political scientist, explores the foreign policy of the European Union and the United States toward the region as well as the policies of India, the largest trading partner and an emerging power in Asia along with China. The author concludes that true socioeconomic integration is still far from being achieved, and she suggests that territorial issues be set aside and trade and commerce take center stage, as is already being demonstrated in Sino-Indian relations.

The chapters in Part 2 examine selected macroeconomic issues and their implications for economic growth and development, focusing largely on the economics of fiscal and current account deficits and the consequences of national debt and capital flows for investment and growth of GDP.

In the opening chapter, "India's Economic Growth Miracle in a Global Economy: Past and Future," Baldev Raj examines India's economic growth in historical context and observes that India's performance since the 1980s is the direct result of investments in human capital and the accumulation of physical capital and infrastructure. The past high level of savings in the country and some development loans have helped to finance these investments. India is no longer afraid of international competition and is a worthy regional challenger to China.

A key issue in South Asia has always been the growth of the twin deficits: current account deficits and trade deficits. Ahmed M. Khalid examines this issue in "Twin Deficits in South Asian Economies: Observations and Empirical Evidence," to determine whether fiscal deficits have led to external imbalances. He uses econometric tests to investigate any causal relationship between the two deficits as well as to identify the direction of causality. He concludes that due to the absence of developed domestic capital markets, fiscal deficits have to be financed from capital inflows (current account deficits). Evidence also indicates that current account deficits have caused fiscal deficits in some South Asian countries. Geoff Harris's chapter in Part 4 of the book sheds light on how the arms race may be an important factor in the persistence of these deficits.

Focusing on India and South Asia, in "Emergence, Severity, and Contours of the Fiscal Deficit in India and South Asia," Raghbendra Jha concludes that fiscal deficits in most South Asian countries are unsustainable. The high levels of fiscal deficits are exacting a toll on these economies and immediate corrective action needs to be taken to prevent further negative consequences on the region.

Focusing solely on public capital and ignoring private capital flows in his chapter, Abdul Waheed studies the interrelationship of "Foreign Public Capital and Economic Growth of Developing Countries: A Selected Survey." He examines various theoretical approaches addressing the impact of foreign public capital (concessional and nonconcessional) on the economic progress of a developing country. The review shows that no single theory or perspective has emerged with anything nearing a consensus regarding the macroeconomic effects of foreign public capital.

As domestic savings are never enough to finance development and growth, FDI becomes an important source of foreign private capital flows. Sajid Anwar and Parikshit K. Basu examine "Foreign Investment and Economic Growth:

A Case Study of India" and find that the impact of FDI inflows in India can be described as mixed, at best. They contend that while FDI is important for a capital-starved economy, its undesirable impact is worth considering.

In "Human Capital Investment and Development in South Asia," Anjum Siddiqui examines some statistics on the state of education and human development and concludes that among South Asian countries, India has taken the lead in developing human capital, due to its educational policies. He further observes that the causes of low literacy are not high dropout rates and gender inequality in access to education, but a response to the poor socioeconomic policies of the regional governments which includes inadequate spending on education. A key finding is that poverty and illiteracy are interrelated in a long-term vicious circle, and the fight against illiteracy is facilitated by economic development. Moreover, service delivery in social services and education rests crucially on governance and community empowerment.

Umer Khalid looks at measuring poverty in South Asia in "Poverty in Pakistan and South Asia: Concept, Measurement, and Analysis." The comparison of South Asia with other world regions reveals that the proportion of the world's poor living in South Asia increased between 1987 and 1998. The author concludes that globalization as manifested by the increasing integration of South Asian economies into the global economy has brought about an increase in South Asian poverty levels relative to other regions of the world.

Part 3 studies the impact of globalization and international trade on the countries of the region and the impact of the WTO and the Doha Round of trade negotiations is examined. The opening piece by Ann Weston, "South Asia's Trade and Commercial Relations with Canada," reviews the direction and magnitude of South Asian trade. The author notes that India rose to the rank of tenth largest exporter of services in the world and used those earnings to finance its growing trade deficits. However, trade within the South Asian region is less than 5 percent of the total trade of South Asia, which is much lower than that of any other regional grouping in the world. The region remains one of the most protected, whether in terms of tariffs or other types of policies restraining imports. The author notes that East and Southeast Asia, which are included in the Asia-Pacific Economic Cooperation (APEC) grouping, provide benefits to their economies through various types of cooperation within the Asia-Pacific region and with the European Union and the United States. The same benefits of cooperation are not available to major South Asian countries because they do not have any special bilateral or regional preferential trade arrangements in either the EU or U.S. markets.

Dushni Weerakoon's chapter, "Regional Economic Cooperation Under SAARC: Possibilities and Constraints," is timely and most relevant to the current thaw in relations between India and Pakistan. SAARC has experienced many roadblocks and received much lip service from politicians and bureaucrats across the divide. Stumbling blocks in implementing a free trade agreement (FTA) in the region were the Indo-Pakistani conflicts and periodic wars. In the event that current peace initiatives are formalized in confidence-building measures, one can expect SAARC to make progress. One is tempted to conclude that SAARC will remain a failure with endless ifs and buts unless India and Pakistan move beyond their current confidence-building measures and sign a peace pact. A constant complaint by India is that Pakistan should not support cross-border terrorism and should prevent any terrorists from crossing into India, especially through the long and porous border along Kashmir. A general comment applies that the proliferation of regional trade blocs is the consequence of slow progress on WTO recommendations for free trade. Some trade blocs were inspired by political motives (e.g., ASEAN), though that was not the motivation for forming SAARC.

In "Repositioning SAFTA in the Regionalism Debate," Saman Kelegama and Ratnakar Adhikari discuss the literature on regional trade agreements and conclude that SAFTA should move beyond borders and strive for pan-Asian cooperation.

Using data on Sri Lanka's exports in his chapter, "Market-Oriented Policy Reforms and Export-Led Industrialization: The Sri Lankan Experience," Premachandra Athukorala observes that Sri Lanka has improved its economic performance despite local insurgency. This happened as Sri Lanka followed export-oriented policies in its labor surplus economy and gained a comparative cost advantage among trading partners.

Part 4 of the book studies the role of governance and institutions in economic development—factors for which there is a growing body of evidence indicating that these are key enabling factors for the success of any economic programs. Currently, the World Bank actively supports devolution programs for political governance in South Asia. Following recent elections to local bodies in Pakistan, municipal governance has come under the jurisdiction of the local *nazim* (administrator), representing a radical move away from the colonial structure in which the government's deputy commissioner was the all-powerful ruling bureaucrat. Whether this devolution structure will work to enhance social and human development and improvement in the administration of municipalities is dependent on the accountability of the nazims and the various checks and balances in place. It is too early to gauge whether the new system is an improvement or old wine in new bottles.

In the opening chapter, "Decentralization of Governance and Development," Pranab Bardhan identifies problems of monitoring and enforcement in a decentralized governance structure, such as that being currently legislated in Pakistan. Another issue involves inferring the wrong causation due to the problem of simultaneity. For example, better beneficiary participation due to decentralization may cause improved project performance, but improved project performance often also encourages higher participation. In addition, Bardhan suggests that governments should not jump to quick conclusions regarding gains from decentralization. The gains themselves may be the result of other policies that were in place prior to decentralization.

Elaborating further in "Governance Issues in India," Desh Gupta and Bhagwan Dahiya observe that India, which recognizes the independence of the judiciary from the executive and parliament, is much more successful than China in terms of rule of law. While the regulatory quality of both countries is poor, China, with its stronger commitment to reforms since 1979, has better indicators of government effectiveness.

Corruption is the consequence of poor governance and hence a discussion of corruption issues is an integral part of the explanation for poor socioeconomic development and the growth of poverty in South Asia. In his chapter, "Corruption in South Asia: Causes and Consequences," Johann Graf Lambsdorff points out that while attracting foreign capital is important for South Asia, the corrupt bureaucratic structure is an impediment to attracting FDI. He observes that South Asian countries have a poor record with respect to law and order and is a promising avenue for reform. He suggests that attracting foreign capital would be possible only if the politicians' hands are tied by the rule of law so as to avoid corruption.

Finally in "Military Expenditure in South Asia: A Case Study of Economic Irrationality," Geoff Harris concludes that the military is not particularly effective in providing a number of noncore activities such as running businesses or corporations for which it is a high-cost provider. It might be argued that while the military is waiting for an external threat it should be gainfully employed in "socially useful activities." Harris argues that the role of the government is only useful if it is cost effective and that is the only way that their usefulness should be ascertained. Harris agrees with Dumas (2002, 16–17) that military expenditures have a zero social rate of return. While military expenditure may offer other value such as providing security in times of external threat, it has no *economic* value because it does not affect the "material standard of living." Regarding South Asia the author concludes clearly that "countries that engage in arms races do not become more secure, but they do become poorer."[2]

The chapters in this book arrive at many conclusions. Emphasizing the fundamentals of economic growth and demonstrating the dependency of economic progress on fiscal prudence, saving, and human capital, we reaffirm the importance of these traditional factors in economic growth. Emphasizing governance, we warn against the harmful effects on the region of fiscal deficits and military spending. While there is much to be disillusioned about, the book reveals optimism concerning South Asia's future provided the region seriously starts being attentive to, and improving, its core fundamentals. Globalization of financial and goods markets leave South Asia no choice but to compete and innovate (Siddiqui 2005). Membership in the WTO and the end of the Multifiber Arrangement now call for strategic local and global partnerships as have been successfully practiced by Korean and Japanese firms in their quest to capture a share of the lucrative EU and U.S. markets.

Notes

1. Many foreign firms investing in India are registered in Mauritius for tax purposes, thus making Mauritius the largest source of FDI for India.

2. The hostility between India and Pakistan is believed to have led to an arms race between the two countries, which might have contributed to their retarded economic growth. *Jülide Yildirim and Nadir Öcal* investigate this twin problem of arms race and economic growth for the time period 1949–2003. The empirical results suggest that there is a mutual causal relationship between the military expenditures of India and Pakistan. Even though military expenditure does not cause economic growth in Pakistan, there is causality from military expenditure to economic growth in India. A VAR analysis revealed that military expenditure hinders economic growth in India in the long run, but it has a growth promoting effect in the short run.

References

Bhagwati, Jagdish. 2004. *In Defense of Globalization.* Oxford: Oxford University Press.

Chossudovsky, Michel. 2003. *The Globalisation of Poverty and the New World Order.* 2d ed. Shanty Bay, Ontario: Global Outlook.

Dumas, L. 2002. "The Role of Demilitarization in Promoting Democracy and Prosperity in Africa." In *Arming the South: The Economics of Military Expenditure, Arms Production and Arms Trade in Developing Countries,* ed. J. Brauer and J. Dunne, 15–34. London: Macmillan.

Easterly, William. 2002. *The Elusive Quest for Growth: Economists' Adventures and Misadventures in the Tropics.* Cambridge, MA: MIT Press.

Mark, Roy. 2004. "U.S. Increasing Trade Pressure on China, India." March 9, www.internetnews.com.

Morrison, Wayne, and Alan Kronstadt. 2005. *Indo-US Economic Relations, CRS Report for Congress.* February 10.

Pritchet, Lant. 2003. "A Toy Collection, a Socialist Star, and a Democratic Dud?" In *In Search of Prosperity: Analytic Narratives on Economic Growth,* ed. Dani Rodrik, Princeton, NJ: Princeton University Press.

Siddiqui, Anjum. 2005. "Global Challenges and Strategies for South Asian Business." Paper presented at the South Asia Management Conference, Karachi, Pakistan, November 9–10.

Stiglitz, Joseph E. 2002. *Globalization and Its Discontents.* New York: Norton.

Temple, Jonathon. 2003. "Growing into Trouble." In *In Search of Prosperity: Analytic Narratives on Economic Growth,* ed. Dani Rodrik. Princeton, NJ: Princeton University Press.

Part I

Introduction

1

South Asia at a Glance

A Taxonomy of Growth Challenges

Anjum Siddiqui

South Asia, a region of 1.3 billion people or one-fifth of the world's population, comprises Afghanistan, Pakistan, India, Nepal, Bangladesh, Sri Lanka, Bhutan, and the Maldives. These countries are members of the South Asian Association for Regional Cooperation (SAARC) (Figure 1.1).[1] The region accounts for about 3 percent of the world's gross domestic product (GDP) and approximately 1 percent of total world export volume, with strong market positions in sugar, cotton, manufacturing, and textiles, and, more recently, information technology. At the same time, South Asia has the largest concentration of poverty in the world, with human development indicators ranked among the lowest, and with five of its eight countries currently classified by the United Nations among the world's least developed countries (LDCs). With the emergence of India as a regional economic and military power and with Pakistan acting as a frontline state for U.S. interests in the region, South Asia has taken on new prominence for the West since the terrorist attacks on the United States on September 11, 2001 (9/11).

Regardless of their political differences and disparate resource base, South Asian countries share common concerns and exigent needs with the rest of the developing world. However, South Asia is distinguished from other developing regions by its huge population and military conflicts, with drastic consequences for its political economy, as well as its society and institutions. Another striking feature of South Asian economies is the endemic institutional, bureaucratic, and political corruption that is widely recognized as an impediment to socioeconomic progress.

This chapter provides an overview of South Asia's human development status and a snapshot of the South Asian economy, to set the stage for a discussion

Figure 1.1   **Political Map of South Asia**

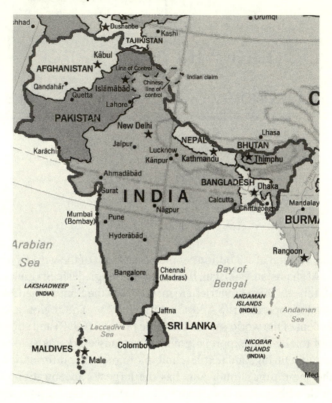

of the region's development challenges in a globalized world connected by trade, capital flows, and international labor mobility.

The Development Challenges of South Asia

Some stylized common characteristics of developing nations around the world include low standards of living, low per capita national income, high rates of population growth and dependency burdens of the nonworking population, high and rising levels of unemployment and underemployment, substantial dependence on agricultural production and primary product exports, a prevalence of imperfect markets and limited information, and dependence, and vulnerability in international relations.[2] Certainly, all of these characteristics are present to some extent in South Asia, but some more than others.

This section will address some pressing development challenges in South Asia: large population and population growth, and corresponding low per capita income measures; low levels of human development, that is, low levels of living standards and quality of life, and poor opportunities; and a high degree of dependence on agriculture as a source of livelihood. In addition, several other major impediments to development in South Asia are identified, including low savings and capital accumulation ratios, large and unsustainable debt burdens, rampant and pervasive corruption, and a high incidence of political instability.

Large Population and Population Growth

Many of South Asia's problems are exacerbated by the region's large population and high population growth rate. In aggregate, with at least twice as many people as each of the members of the Association of Southeast Asian Nations (ASEAN), Latin America, and sub-Saharan Africa, South Asia's population has grown 2.2 percent annually (since 1960) compared to 1.6 percent population growth in the rest of the world and 0.8 percent population growth in the high-income countries of the Organization for Economic Cooperation and Development (OECD). Among other factors, South Asia's economic development is clearly hampered by the sheer number of people to whom it is home. As a case in point, compare the astounding population density in Bangladesh of 1,007 people per square kilometer to a mere 26 people on average in Latin America. More pertinently, population density per square kilometer of arable, cultivatable land is extremely high in South Asia, which raises issues of food security.

Population was and remains a challenge and bottleneck to growth and quality of life for teeming millions in South Asia. The annual world population growth rate is 1.3 percent, at about 77 million people a year. Six countries—India, China, Pakistan, Nigeria, Bangladesh, and Indonesia—account for half of that total. The population control record of various governments in the region has been mixed and the population growth rate remains around 2.6–3 percent, which is clearly unsustainable. Free condom distribution by itself has had mixed results, at best, and has not proved to be very successful in arresting the high rates of fertility among married couples.[3] The battle against high population growth rates can be won only through increasing literacy rates—a case in point is the lower number of children per family in educated middle-class households of South Asia.

South Asia's huge population has created a slew of problems, including lower capital intensity of production, reduced labor productivity, thinly spread land and food resources, growing gender inequality due to increased dependency ratios, and lower savings and investment due to less productive

Table 1.1

Population Growth vs. GDP Growth, 1990–2000
(compound annual growth rate, %)

	GDP growth	Population growth	Per capita GDP growth
Afghanistan	NA	4.1	NA
Bangladesh	4.8	1.7	3.0
Bhutan	6.3	3.0	3.2
India	5.5	1.8	3.6
Maldives	7.4	2.6	4.6
Nepal	5.0	2.1	2.5
Pakistan	4.0	2.5	1.4
Sri Lanka	5.2	1.3	3.9
South Asia	*5.2*	*1.9*	*3.2*
ASEAN	4.9	1.7	3.2
Other			
China	10.1	1.1	9.0
United States	3.3	1.2	2.0

Source: World Bank, *World Development Indicators, 2002.*

consumption expenditure. The other obvious impact of high population growth is that it lowers per capita GDP and increases poverty.

South Asia's 1.9 percent annual population growth between 1990 and 2000 decreased per capita GDP growth by exactly 1.9 percent (see Table 1.1). ASEAN's GDP over the same period grew by 0.3 percent less than SAARC's GDP, but in per capita terms the two regions are equal. Conversely, high GDP growth in countries like China is amplified in per capita terms by corresponding low population growth.

An additional perspective on the population of South Asia is that a high dependency ratio implies a drag or inefficiency of the working economy, potentially due to high birthrates without corresponding growth in the economy, or perhaps a high degree of age dispersion with large concentrations of the population incapable of working. Moreover, high dependency implicitly suggests a high degree of "momentum" for the population growth rate . This means that even if fertility rates diminish significantly, as the large number of dependent youths mature and have children of their own, substantial population growth will continue until a time when both fertility and dependency rates are low.

In South Asia (see Table 1.2), there has been a gradual decline in dependents per worker over the past five decades, although the dependency ratio remains higher than in any other region, with the exception of sub-Saharan

Table 1.2

Dependency Ratio (dependents to working-age population)

	1970	1980	1990	2000
Afghanistan	0.82	0.84	0.89	0.89
Bangladesh	0.96	0.98	0.90	0.70
Bhutan	0.80	0.81	0.85	0.89
India	0.79	0.74	0.69	0.63
Maldives	0.85	0.87	1.00	0.85
Nepal	0.81	0.85	0.87	0.80
Pakistan	0.98	0.90	0.85	0.82
Sri Lanka	0.84	0.66	0.61	0.48
South Asia	*0.82*	*0.78*	*0.73*	*0.66*
ASEAN*	0.87	0.75	0.67	0.60
Latin America and Caribbean	0.88	0.79	0.69	0.59
Sub-Saharan Africa	0.91	0.94	0.94	0.89
European Monetary Union	0.59	0.55	0.48	0.48
North America*	0.75	0.65	0.58	0.53
World	0.77	0.71	0.64	0.59

Source: World Bank, *World Development Indicators, 2002.*
  *Unweighted average across countries.

Africa. South Asia's dependency ratio of 0.66 is about equidistant between high-income OECD countries at 0.48 and the United Nations list of LDCs at 0.85.

Low Growth of Human Capital and Poor Human Development Indicators

The United Nations Development Programme (UNDP) definition of human development goes beyond per capita income. It includes such variables as education, which creates human capital, longevity (health), and civil rights, which reflect noneconomic aspects of the quality of life. The economic relevance of these variables, simply put, is that just as health can potentially increase earnings opportunities (in addition to its direct benefits in terms of quality of life), so can increases in levels of education and freedom (UNDP 2004).

Countries in South Asia typically rank among the lower and middle countries out of the 175 ranked in terms of human development (Table 1.3). The dispersion of rankings in South Asia ranges from Pakistan at 144 (the worst in South Asia), with an index value of 0.499 in 2001, to the Maldives ranked 86, with an index value of 0.751. Despite relatively low rankings, however, each country has shown a gradual increase in index value since

Table 1.3

Human Development Index (HDI; ranking among 175 countries and index value)

Country	HDI rank 2001	1975*	1985	1995	2001
Maldives	86	NA	NA	NA	0.751
Sri Lanka	99	0.609	0.644	0.715	0.730
India	127	0.416	0.443	0.553	0.590
Bhutan	136	NA	NA	NA	0.511
Bangladesh	139	0.336	0.352	0.443	0.502
Nepal	143	0.287	0.326	0.451	0.499
Pakistan	144	0.334	0.370	0.472	0.499

Sources: Calculated on the basis of data on life expectancy from the United Nations); data on adult literacy rates from the United Nations Educational Scientific and Cultural Organization (UNESCO); data on combined gross enrollment ratios from UNESCO; and data on GDP at market prices (constant 1995 US$), population and GDP per capita (PPP US$) from the World Bank.

*The numbers for 1975–2001 show the HDI index values. The HDI rank is for 2001 within a sample of 175 countries.

1975, reflecting slow income per capita growth and gradual but very slow translation into enhanced welfare and services.

Literacy and Education

A key component of human development index (HDI) rankings is attainment in education as measured by literacy rates and enrollment ratios. South Asia's aggregate illiteracy rate remains among the highest in the developing world, with approximately one in two people unable to read. While the aggregate regional statistics are heavily weighted by India's enormous population, of note are countries such as Afghanistan, Bangladesh, Nepal, and Pakistan, where total illiteracy rates soared above 70 percent and up to 95 percent for women in 1980, improving to only about 60 percent in 2000. This improvement is less significant in view of regional comparisons that show illiteracy rates less than 40 percent in sub-Saharan Africa and less than 20 percent in Latin American and ASEAN countries.

Relative illiteracy rates between males and females also show a similar trend. While female illiteracy has decreased over the 1980–2000 period, it has remained fairly constant proportionally at twice that of male illiteracy. Similarly, recent school enrollment statistics show a significant level of gender inequality with female to male ratios averaging approximately 0.8 in South Asia and as low as 0.55 in Pakistan in 2001.

From 1960 to 1990, the world's median primary gross educational enroll-ment rate increased from 80 percent to 99 percent. In 1990, South Asia's primary enrollment rate was 90 percent, and only 77 percent among females. With the exception of sub-Saharan Africa, this places South Asia among the worst regions in the provision of primary education, and this disparity further increases at secondary and tertiary (postsecondary) levels.

Policymakers and academics in South Asia are still on the learning curve to a full understanding of why human development programs in educa-tion and literacy have met with little success, and why these efforts have not translated into economic growth.[4] One explanation is that in countries with high levels of government intervention, and even more so in countries with high incidences of corruption, returns from lobbying the government for favors are higher than investments in education. In other words, schooling is worthwhile only when government actions create opportunities for growth as opposed to opportunities for redistribution. Another finding from South Asia is that merely setting administrative targets for primary school enrollment does little if the quality of education attained remains low, and the infrastructure, teachers, and community support are lacking. For example, a recent survey found approximately one-third of teachers in Uttar Pradesh, India, absent.[5]

Moreover, in economies where there is a direct link between schooling attained and earning potential, parents are more apt to send their children to school as opposed to engaging them in child labor. It is a known fact that cor-ruption, low salaries for teachers, and low public spending on school supplies have severely diminished the quality of education in developing countries. For instance, in Pakistan teacher positions in government-run schools are dispensed on a large scale by politicians as patronage, leading to low-quality instructors who teach in Urdu as opposed to English, and disproportionate emphasis on religious learning. These factors potentially diminish the eco-nomic returns to education from the public school system.

Health

Another factor that determines the HDI rankings pertains to health and access to medical care. Despite some improvement in access to doctors, substandard housing, lack of dependable water supply, poor sanitation, and malnutrition continue to contribute to the widespread proliferation of disease in South Asia. This is manifested in increased incidence of infant and maternal mortality relative to developed nations, lower life expectancy, and the prevalence of diseases.[6]

Table 1.4 shows several common measures of health conditions in South Asia relative to other developing regions. Although currently projected to be

Table 1.4

Life Expectancy and Infant Mortality (as %, unless noted otherwise)

	Life expectancy at birth (years)		Infant mortality rate (per 1,000 live births)		Under-five mortality rate (per 1,000 live births)		Probability of survival to sixty-five	
	1970–1975	2000–2005	1970	2001	1970	2001	Female 2000–2005	Male 2000–2005
Bangladesh	45.2	61.4	145	51	239	77	61.1	57.9
Bhutan	43.2	63.2	156	74	267	95	66.1	61.1
India	50.3	63.9	127	67	202	93	67.5	61.9
Maldives	51.4	67.4	157	58	255	77	69.5	69.5
Nepal	43.3	59.9	165	66	250	91	57.6	56.4
Pakistan	49.0	61.0	117	84	181	109	61.9	60.0
Sri Lanka	65.1	72.6	65	17	100	19	84.6	73.5
South Asia	*49.6*	*64.2*	*133*	*60*	*213*	*80*	*66.9*	*62.9*
ASEAN*	55.5	67.0	79	40	116	53	73.5	64.6
Latin America and Caribbean	61.0	70.4	86	28	123	34	78.7	66.5
Sub-Saharan Africa	43.9	26.9	136	107	223	172	36.1	32.0

Source: United Nations Development Programme, *World Development Reports, 2003.*
*Excludes Vietnam.

Table 1.5

Poor Population: Regional Distribution
(number of people in millions and % of population, respectively)

Regions	Pop.[a] (%)	No. of people living on less than $1/day (millions)[b]		Headcount index[c] (%)	
		1987	1998	1987	1998
East Asia and Pacific	91	418	267	27	15
(excluding China)	71	114	54	24	9
Eastern Europe and Central Asia	82	1	18	—	4
Latin America and Caribbean	88	64	61	15	12
Middle East and North Africa	53	9	6	4	2
South Asia	98	474	522	45	40
Sub-Saharan Africa	73	217	302	47	48
	88	*1,183*	*1,175*	*28*	*23*

Source: World Bank, *Global Economic Prospects and the Developing World 2001.*
[a]Percentage of population covered in survey.
[b]The $1 a day is in 1983 purchasing power parity terms.
[c]The headcount index is the percentage of the population below the poverty line.

lower than in Latin America and ASEAN countries, life expectancy in South Asia has improved significantly from fifty years to sixty-four in the past thirty years. Moreover, and encouragingly, infant and under-five mortality rates have halved over the same time period. However, these levels fall well short of health indicators in the developed world.

Poverty

In 1998, according to the World Bank, over half of the world's 6 billion people lived on less than $2 per day. Absolute poverty is defined to correspond roughly to consumption levels of $1 per day. With 522 million people in poverty as of 1998, South Asia constituted approximately 40 percent of the world's poor, which is substantially higher than for other regions with the exception of sub-Saharan Africa (Table 1.5).

Such high levels of poverty indicate that South Asia's steady economic growth of around 5 percent per annum has not been accompanied by corresponding increases in the quality of life of the poorest people in the region. A view of development that focuses on improving conditions for the poorest of the poor, popularized in the 1970s, is called the basic human needs (BHN) approach.[7] Its proponents claim that BHN is more effective in improving growth than focusing on aggregate income alone (Streeton 1981). Moreover, because measures of income inequality are not highly correlated with measures of absolute poverty (a measure that reflects the number of poor living without basic needs) (Tendulkar and Jain 1995), BHN proponents argue that policies geared toward improving aggregate income inequality alone do little to help those in "true" poverty. Clearly, little has been done to help the poorest of the poor in South Asia.

A key element to the BHN approach is the improved distribution of assets and income, referred to as reduced asset and income inequality. Studies have shown a link between relative equality in key assets such as land and rapid economic growth, but the "jury remains out" on the larger question of whether lower income inequality necessarily complements growth (Deininger and Squire 1998; Forbes 2000). According to the World Bank, income inequality within countries has not changed significantly over the past thirty years, but intercountry income disparities have increased. As a result, the average income of the richest twenty countries is approximately thirty times that of the twenty poorest countries, as compared with approximately fifteen times forty years ago. Therefore, in addition to nonexistent increases in equality within countries, the poorest countries are relatively worse off than they were almost half a century ago.

By the above criteria, South Asia is among the poorest, if not the poorest, region in the world. As a result, the World Bank's strategy for South Asia focuses (broadly) on both strengthening the economic environment for growth and on "pro-poor" interventions in health and education, rural development, infrastructure and capacity building, and the expansion of access to economic opportunities.

Continued Dependence on Low Productivity Agriculture

> God forbid that India should ever take to industrialism after the manner of the west . . . keeping the world in chains. If [our nation] took to similar economic exploitation, it would strip the world bare like locusts.
>
> —Mahatma Gandhi

Despite a steady decrease in reliance on agriculture just under a third of South Asia's GDP still comes from crop production. That figure is relatively high in comparison with 15 percent and below for the rest of the developing world, and much lower than percentages in high-income OECD countries.

Employing approximately two-thirds of South Asians, the agricultural sector is notably less productive than either manufacturing or the services industry. This high level of dependency on primarily subsistence agriculture is indicative of low investments in agricultural productivity as well as low investments in capital and technology-intensive sectors, resulting in a very slow structural shift away from subsistence farming. The fact that agriculture provides employment to more than 50 percent of the workforce in densely populated economies invariably gives the sector lower productivity per worker than the average productivity per worker for the economy as a whole. Thus, a rise in productivity per worker in agriculture is critical to raising the economy-wide labor productivity and hence per capita real income.

Pakistan's agricultural sector has in general declined as a percentage of national income since the 1950s when it constituted approximately half of GDP. Today, agriculture accounts for about 23 percent of GDP and employs about 44 percent of the labor force. Sri Lanka has made the greatest strides in reducing dependency on agriculture and its share in GDP is only 17 percent, but its share in total employment is 36 percent. However, 75 percent of the population is classified as rural due to linkages to the agricultural sector. In India, between 1980 and 1998, while the share of the agriculture sector in GDP has declined from 35 percent to 25 percent, it employs roughly two-thirds of the population. These statistics reveal that while the shares of agriculture in total GDP are declining in various South Asian economies, the sector supports almost two-thirds of the population of the region. Hence, improvements in rural labor productivity, access to credit and water, and reduced rural illiteracy will remain the key issues over the next few decades.

Low Rates of Capital Formation and Savings

An important caveat of South Asia's economy has been the slow accumulation of capital stock, a widespread measure of industrialization and development. As Table 1.6 shows, South Asia's gross capital stock, while growing faster than that of Latin America and sub-Saharan Africa since 1960, lags behind Latin America and ASEAN in magnitude.

Since the deficiency in physical capital relative to labor can be viewed as a basic *cause* of low labor productivity and hence low per capita income in land-scarce, labor-abundant economies, rapid capital accumulation and its efficient utilization become key to economic growth.

Capital investments, in turn, depend on the region's rate of savings, which are characteristically low in South Asia. Table 1.7 shows gross domestic savings as a percentage of GDP. Over the past decade, the average savings rate in South Asia has been stagnant at just under 20 percent of GDP and Pakistan's saving rate is the lowest in the region. The region's savings rates are slightly

Table 1.6

Gross Capital Formation (constant 1995 US$ millions)

	1970	1980	1990	2000	Growth/ yr. (%)
Bangladesh	3,597	4,703	5,241	11,773	6
Bhutan	NA	42	79	NA	NA
India	21,446	32,462	64,060	122,920	5
Maldives	NA	NA	NA	165	NA
Nepal	NA	393	629	1,353	NA
Pakistan	3,652	5,111	9,209	11,148	5
Sri Lanka	726	2,489	2,439	4,649	7
South Asia	*30,049*	*45,879*	*82,884*	*154,320*	*5*
ASEAN*	25,626	67,412	135,359	161,343	8
Latin America and Caribbean	166,160	324,330	266,970	421,060	4
Sub-Saharan Africa	54,170	74,226	50,708	68,589	3

Source: World Bank, *World Development Indicators Database, 2002.*
*Data not available for Myanmar, Brunei, Cambodia, and Laos.

Table 1.7

Gross Domestic Savings (% of GDP)

	1980	1990	2000
Bangladesh	2.1	9.7	17.8
Bhutan	8.0	32.1	18.5
India	17.3	22.5	21.4
Maldives	4.6	25.2	44.6
Nepal	11.1	7.9	16.1
Pakistan	6.9	11.1	12.1
Sri Lanka	11.1	13.8	17.2
South Asia	*14.6*	*19.7*	*19.7*
ASEAN*	29.8	30.8	33.5
Latin America and Caribbean	22.3	21.5	19.0
Sub-Saharan Africa	23.5	16.3	16.6

Source: World Bank, *World Development Indicators Database, 2002.*
*Weighted by GDP. Excludes Brunei and Laos.

higher than sub-Saharan Africa and far below ASEAN. In fact, to match the gross domestic savings rate of ASEAN, South Asian countries would have to save on average 14 percent more of their GDP.

Large Debt Burden

With all eight South Asian countries among the debtors of the International Monetary Fund (IMF) program, it is not surprising that large debt burdens factor into their economic flexibility and development concerns. To illustrate the severity of the debt problem we briefly examine some commonly used debt-related ratios. A country's debt can be analyzed from the debt–GDP ratio, short-term debt–reserves ratio, and debt-service ratio. Below we briefly examine these ratios for Bangladesh, India, Pakistan, and Sri Lanka.

The debt–GDP ratio measures the economy's ability to pay its debt. During 2000–2003 Sri Lanka had the highest average debt–GDP ratio in the region at 56 percent with Pakistan closely behind at 50 percent. India has the lowest regional average debt–GDP ratio at 20.5 percent. The short-term debt–reserve ratio is an indicator of a country's capacity to meet its payment obligations in terms of foreign currency reserves held by the central bank. This ratio ranged from less than 7 percent in India to 29 percent in Sri Lanka. Pakistan saw a dramatic improvement in the ratio from 100 percent in 2000 to less than 17 percent in 2003. This was due to significant aid inflows from the United States and G-8 countries, and debt rescheduling. Another factor was the increase in remittances through official banking channels which increased reserves and reduced the debt-reserve ratio. The debt-service ratio is the ratio of interest and principal payments on debt to the exports of goods and services. It is an important measure of country risk assessment by rating agencies and lenders. Over the period 2000–2003 this ratio has improved for Bangladesh, Pakistan, and Sri Lanka but India has seen an increase from 14.4 percent in 2000 to 18.8 percent in 2003.

One harmful consequence of aggressive aid to developing countries is their being saddled with unsustainable debt. Many developing countries have foreign debts so large that their interest payments have become a crushing burden. The Republic of the Congo, for example, has annual debt service payments equal to 50 percent of its export earnings; Uganda's debt service equals 44 percent of its exports. With such high interest payments on debt servicing, the hope of paying off the principal remains far-fetched. In South Asia, the most extreme example of this is in Pakistan. Carrying an external debt of US$28 billion, debt service consumed nearly a third of Pakistan's export earnings in 2001. The combined domestic and external debt burden of Pakistan is US$65 billion, for which debt-service payments constitute a major part of government spending and are associated with persistent fiscal deficits. As a result, development spending has lost out in the competition for resources. In Pakistan, social spending has been at less than 4 percent of GDP since the 1980s, with development spending only slightly higher. It is predicted that South Asia will continue to experience high debts and debt-service payments unless it addresses the root causes of these deficits: persistent fiscal and current account imbalances. The causes of South Asian debt are discussed in more detail below.

Corruption

> When buying and selling are controlled by legislation, the first things to be bought and sold are legislators.
>
> —P.J. O'Rourke

Corruption remains a major siphon of productivity and resources in most South Asian countries. It influenced the dismissal of two prime ministers in Pakistan and Indian premier Atal Behari Vajpayee's offer to resign in July 2001, after the outbreak of the Tehelka.com and Unit Trust of India scandals, and led to widespread cries of corruption in the wake of parliamentary elections in Bangladesh and Sri Lanka in 2001.

Transparency International's Corruption Perceptions index ranked Sri Lanka 66, India 83, Pakistan 92, and Bangladesh as *the most* corrupt country of the 133 countries surveyed, which takes into account both government and private sector corruption and mismanagement.[8] In November 2001, every country in the region except Sri Lanka and Afghanistan signed the ADB-OECD Anti-Corruption Initiative for Asia-Pacific, committing each signatory to create an action plan and to evaluate implemented reforms within eighteen months. Each action plan was required to address the "three pillars" of anticorruption activity: improvements in the civil service, the reduction of bribery, and the closer involvement of civil society. However, difficulties in measuring corruption reduction goals and pervasive skepticism that such action plans were only lip service, have called into question the effectiveness of such initiatives. The National Accountability Bureau (NAB) in Pakistan has been entrusted with the task of arresting corruption. However, the NAB lets off politicians and corrupt government officials if they pay part of the fraudulent money for which they are accountable. Others have accused the NAB of discriminating against the opposition of a sitting government. More recently in 2006, the NAB did not apprehend parliamentarians in the sugar scandal in Pakistan. Bangladesh's ranking as the most corrupt country surveyed in 2001 was widely perceived as an international indictment of Sheikh Hasina's Awami League government and most certainly played a role in its defeat by the Bangladesh National

Party (BNP) in 2002. However, once the BNP came to power, it did little to change the status quo, as corruption cases pending against BNP politicians were abruptly withdrawn.

What have we learned about the causes of corruption? The main cause is related to the structure and quality of a country's government and institutions. It has been shown that centralized corruption, wherein one leader seeks to maximize the take from the system as a whole, is less damaging than decentralized corruption, wherein there are many bribe takers but no coordination among them. In basic terms, each bribe taker in the decentralized system is incentivized to take as much as he possibly can from each bribe giver, in turn causing people to seek better ways to avoid giving bribes, and subsequently lowering the aggregate collection of bribes (Shleifer and Vishny 1993). Moreover, a strong dictator's corruption "tax rate" will not significantly harm growth because the size of the aggregate take is directly linked to the size of the economy. As such, on a relative scale, decentralized corruption is worse than centralized corruption for the growth prospects of an economy. A key point which merits attention is that institutional corruption in private and public sector organizations can persist irrespective of democratic rule or dictatorship. This corruption manifests itself first in leadership failures and poor human resource policies and then financial corruption (Siddiqui 2003b).

The poor quality of institutions is also strongly correlated with the perception of corruption (Easterly 2002). In its ratings of country credit, the *International Credit Risk Guide* rates four aspects of institutional quality: rule of law, quality of bureaucracy, freedom from government repudiation of contracts, and freedom from expropriation. Intuitively, deficiencies in any of the above will create incentives for corrupt behavior. As such, it is these measures linked to corruption—for example, poor quality decentralized institutions, high black market premiums (Mauro 1996), military spending (Gupta, de Mello, and Sharan 2000), and even high barriers to international trade (Ades and Di Tella 1994)—that need to be addressed first by the multilateral institutions striving to stem corruption. Going a step further, international donor agencies have themselves been the subject of criticism for lack of transparency and lack of coherent strategy to quell corruption in recipient countries. It is worrisome that the World Bank, despite its intimate knowledge of the extent of corruption in South Asia, has not pressed the respective governments in the region to reduce and arrest corruption—it has merely expressed concern. If the World Bank is serious about being engaged as a partner in the economic prosperity of South Asia, it will have to stop praising the South Asian governments for their "performance" in its annual country reports, and start tying all financial assistance to an improvement in the corruption ratings.

Political Instability

Finally, a key factor impeding development in South Asia is the ongoing political instability that has resulted in three wars between India and Pakistan, the separatist movement of Tamil Tigers in Sri Lanka, the renouncing of democracy in Nepal, and political instability in Bangladesh. The war on terrorism in Afghanistan and in the North–West Frontier Province of Pakistan, and the continued unrest in Kashmir have all contributed to a turbulent and politically unstable South Asia.

Perhaps the most direct measure of the cost of political instability is the proportion of the economy devoted to the military. In South Asia, military spending accounts for approximately 2.7 percent of GDP versus 1.0 percent for health and 3.7 percent for education. Pakistan, by far the biggest spender on defense (proportionally to GDP), has a military budget that exceeds its combined health and education budget by a factor of two (UNDP 2003). According to the World Bank, 29 percent of Pakistan's budget is spent on military expenditures.[9] In 1999, as a proportion of GDP, Pakistan spent 4.6 percent on defense and only 1.8 percent on education, whereas India spent 2.3 percent on defense and 4.1 percent on education in the same year. In 2001, Pakistan increased its defense outlays to 4.5 percent of GDP while India slightly reduced its military expenditures to 2.1 percent of GDP. An Indian nuclear weaponization program would cost 0.5 percent of GDP per year and is equivalent to the cost of providing universal elementary education in India (Reddy 2004). While both countries blatantly hide defense expenditures in the name of secrecy, according to one Indian estimate more than 3,000 public housing units could be built for the price of one nuclear warhead, and expenditures required to develop India's "minimum" deterrent could meet 25 percent of the yearly costs of sending every Indian child to school. Nearly all Pakistani children could be educated and fed for the cost of the nuclear and missile arsenal that is being created for their "protection" (Lavoy 1999).

While the arms race continues, peace efforts have also picked up momentum. Over 2004, confidence-building measures (CBMs) are being elaborated by India and Pakistan. These efforts have included two visits by Pakistan's President General Pervez Musharraf to India in 2004–5, the resumption of cricket ties between the two countries after a twelve-year hiatus, and the initiation of a bus route from Pakistan to Indian-occupied Jammu and Kashmir in 2005. Progress on peace has been slow and the remaining stumbling block is an equitable solution to the Kashmir problem. India has stressed that it would like Pakistan to cease cross-border support of the Kashmir movement, and that progress on peace will come after India is satisfied that all such support has stopped. As the CBMs move forward, peace in the region will facilitate economic expansion through decreased diversion of resources for defense and increased regional trade.

Industry, Trade, and Aid: Stylized Features of South Asia's Economy

With the exception of India, Pakistan, and Sri Lanka, all of the South Asian countries can be found on the United Nations list of the world's forty-nine LDCs, denoting low aggregate income and income growth, weak human resources, and a low level of economic diversification.

Structure of the Economy

The farming sector accounts for approximately one-third of GDP and over two-thirds of employment in the region. South Asia's manufacturing sector remains dominated by clothing and textiles, but also has major ongoing operations in steel, aluminum, petrochemicals, and utilities. Services represent a large and growing share of the South Asian economy, including high-growth industries such as information technology, particularly in India.

Generally speaking, economic structure refers to the various means by which national income is produced, which breaks down into three broad sectors: agriculture, manufacturing, and services. There are several intuitive truisms about the structure of an economy: a high and nondecreasing dependency on agricultural production at a subsistence level represents stagnant industrialization; increased manufacturing output of high value-added goods represents advances in technology; and productivity and increased reliance on services generally reflect a shift away from a resource-based economy. South Asia as a whole has shown signs of improvement in the past fifty years according to these criteria. Agriculture has diminished by approximately 20 percent as a proportion of GDP; services have increased by approximately 10 percent; and manufacturing has remained approximately the same, but has begun to diversify into higher value-added goods.

With approximately 16 percent of GDP coming from value-added manufacturing, Sri Lanka, India, Pakistan, and Bangladesh are the most manufacturing-oriented economies in South Asia, roughly comparable to sub-Saharan Africa, but below Latin America and ASEAN by 5 percent and 10 percent, respectively.

In Sri Lanka, manufacturing is concentrated in low-tech consumer goods industries, specifically garments and textiles. Bangladesh's primary manufactures are mainly of a comparable technology caliber, including jute manufactures, ready-made garments, cotton textiles, seafood processing, and more recently, pharmaceuticals. In India, while clothing, textiles, steel, aluminum, and fertilizers remain key sectors, other higher technology industries have emerged in petrochemicals, specialty pharmaceuticals, electronics, and motor vehicles. In Pakistan, manufacturing has seen growth in utilities, mining, and textiles. In contrast to manufacturing, the services sector continues to be a large and increasing proportion of the South Asian economy, representing approximately half of GDP.

Trade Challenges in SAARC

South Asia's exports in 1996 were $50 billion, which was 1 percent of the world's exports, one-third of the exports of China, and less than Thailand's exports, but trade within SAARC remains low at only $4 billion. To address this problem, a South Asian Free Trade Agreement was signed in 2004 under which Pakistan and India would reduce their tariffs to 0–5 percent within seven years beginning in 2006, and the least developed countries are to reduce their tariffs to 0–5 percent within ten years beginning in 2006. Each member state of the SAARC was to maintain a sensitive list of products for which tariffs will not be reduced. This is expected to increase the current US$4 billion trade to around US$14 billion (*Asia Times Online* 2004).

India has a trade surplus with all countries of the region and also has significant informal trade with both Pakistan and Bangladesh, facilitated by third-party countries through which Indian goods are smuggled. India's exports to SAARC countries increased from $622 million in 1991 to $2 billion in 2000, indicating 9 percent growth during this period, whereas India's imports from SAARC were only $182 million in 1995. India's trade with SAARC countries is around 3 percent of its total trade and amounts to a trade surplus of $2.2 billion. This trade imbalance is a matter of concern for SAARC countries. The surplus may be due partially to subsidies for Indian industry in the form of subsidized energy rates. Finally, SAARC trade has not picked up over the past decade due to the conflict between its two largest members, India and Pakistan. The future of SAARC rests crucially on peace and stability in the region. SAARC trade should be used as a confidence-building measure in the process of peace and the Kashmir issue should be totally delinked from trade promotion issues.

Multifibre Arrangement

On December 31, 2004, the thirty-year-old Multifiber Arrangement (MFA) expired. The agreement had regulated the multibillion-dollar annual world trade in garments through export quotas. India is buoyant about its post–MFA trade prospects. According to "DHL-McKinsey Apparel and Textile Trade Report," the value of the global textile and apparel industry is likely to go up to US$248 billion by 2008 with China, India and Pakistan expected to be the "Clear Winners." The report forecasts that India has the potential to increase her share from the current 4 percent to 6.5 percent valued at US$16 billion by 2008. The Indian Cotton Mills Federation also expects that Indian textile exports will rise to $40 billion from the present $12 billion by 2010. The textile industry employs 35 million people and accounts for nearly one-quarter of India's exports. Pakistan too is upgrading its textile machinery to benefit from the expiration of the MFA. The share of textiles in overall manufacturing activity in Pakistan is 46 percent, its share in export earnings is 68 percent, value addition is 9 percent of GDP, and it provides about 38 percent of the total employment in the country.

After the MFA's expiration it is expected that the United States and the European Union (EU) will demand better market access for their products in South Asia. They would also apply pressure for compliance with WTO policies on tariff liberalization (in LDCs) and intellectual property rights, and they are expected to enforce strict rules of origin on South Asian exports. U.S. and EU buyers are expected to demand higher quality products that meet industry standards for developed countries. As outlined in the Textile Vision 2005, Pakistani exporters will have to ensure compliance on labor and environmental issues (Baig 2004).

The expiration of MFA quotas does not mean automatic free and open market access for South Asian goods in markets of the EU and other developed countries. The European Commission (EC) has recently levied antidumping duties of 13.1 percent on bed linen exports by Pakistan. One can only hope that this EU duty is an isolated measure and not part of a general policy on nontariff barriers to restrict exports from identified countries. Recently, Bangladesh has also been subjected to antidumping trade remedial measures (TRMs) by India, the United States, and Brazil resulting in a loss of US$50 million in exports in 2004. The WTO countervailing measures can be enforced when foreign products are dumped, marketed at a price less than production cost, or subsidized, and their import causes or threatens to cause "material injury" to domestic industry. South Asian businesses fear that the incidence of TRMs will increase in a quota-free trade regime if domestic industries are perceived to suffer competition from imported products. In 2004 a total of 1,511 antidumping measures were imposed worldwide, mainly by India, the United States, the EU, Argentina, and South Africa. Due to the high volume of export subsidies, particularly in developed countries in agricultural industries, developing countries dependent on primary exports are often at a disadvantage in trade. Moreover, despite a general lowering of average tariff rates in the past decade, there has been only marginal improvement in tariff dispersion (peaks and escalation), specific tariffs, and tariff rate quotas.[10]

In manufactures, South Asian exporters face similar tariff and nontariff barriers to trade. Higher tariffs on manufactured goods than on primary exports act as a significant disincentive for local entrepreneurs to move up the processing chain in primary and merchandise markets. Table 1.8 compares South Asia's exports in primary goods with manufactures as a percentage of total merchandise exports. In general, South Asia's predominant exports are labor-intensive manufactures, and there has been an increasing trend toward manufactures relative to primary exports since 1990. South Asian countries still rely heavily on agriculture for approximately one-third of the region's export volume, but notably less so than Latin America and Sub-Saharan Africa.

An interesting question is what sort of goods—capital- or labor-intensive —will South Asia be exporting in this post–MFA era? As the literacy level and availability of skilled workers is low, and also because there is a scarcity of natural resources (land), it is expected that South Asia's exports over the next two decades or so will be less-skill-intensive (labor-intensive) manufactured goods (Mayer and Wood 2001). The availability of a skilled workforce thus becomes an important determinant of the structure of exports. A case in point is Indian software exports of $12.5 billion in 2003–4, which were possible only due to the availability of skilled software developers. The comparative advantage in labor-intensive manufactures will continue for the foreseeable future, changing only if the skill level of South Asian workers changes faster than that of its competitors.

This comparative advantage would result in more exports after the expiration of the Multifiber Arrangement. With abolishment of the stringent MFA quotas, an increase in labor-intensive exports of textiles and cotton is now possible. However, a large increase in such exports requires the reduction of official barriers to trade. In the case of India, it is expected that in this nonquota environment, the share of manufacturing employment could rise by about 5 percent, and employment in primary goods exports will fall as the share of primary goods in exports falls (Mayer and Wood 2001).

WTO Readiness

How ready is South Asia to deal with the post–MFA world of competition? Almost 70 percent of the export activity in the textile industry is generated by small and medium enterprises (SMEs), and their competitiveness is crucial to their survivability. Compliance with WTO standards on environment, child labor, and quality necessitates improvement of the management and production skills in which they are deficient. The high price of electricity in Pakistan cuts into the competitiveness of these manufacturing units, which are not large enough to reap any economies of scale by spreading their fixed costs. Constant

Table 1.8.

Trade Structure

	Import of goods and services (as % of GDP)		Export of goods and services (as % of GDP)		Primary exports (as % of merchandise exports)		Manufactured exports (as % of merchandise exports)	
	1990	2001	1990	2001	1990	2001	1990	2001
Bangladesh	14	22	6	15	NA	NA	77	NA
Bhutan	32	60	28	30	NA	60	NA	40
India	10	15	7	114	28	21	71	77
Maldives	64	76	24	93	NA	NA	NA	42
Nepal	21	32	11	22	NA	23	83	67
Pakistan	23	19	16	18	21	15	79	85
Sri Lanka	38	44	29	37	42	23	54	77
South Asia	29	38	17	33	30	28	73	65
ASEAN*	49	75	46	83	51	21	52	77
Latin America and Caribbean	12	19	14	18	65	40	34	49
Sub-Saharan Africa	26	33	27	32	NA	NA	NA	33

Source: United Nations Development Programme, *World Development Reports, 2003.*
*Excludes Vietnam.

innovations in products, processes, and marketing are required. It is expected that fierce competition from China and India will reduce exports that SMEs in Pakistan have traditionally enjoyed.

The World Economic Forum's Global Competitiveness Report, 2004–5, has examined the readiness of 133 developing countries to deal with the competitive environment of the post–WTO world. It shows that in terms of technological readiness, India's rank is 26, Pakistan's is 84; in firm-level technology absorption, India is listed at 18, Pakistan at 44; and in quality of scientific research readiness, India is ranked 17 while Pakistan is 94. In terms of the availability of scientists and engineers, India tops the list while Pakistan is down at 61. Some possible causes of Pakistan's low rankings are very low research and development expenditures by both firms and the government, poor attainment in higher education, and poor quality and quantity of scientific research.

The Economics of Aid and Debt

At the Earth Summit at Rio de Janeiro in 1992, the twenty-two OECD countries agreed to contribute 0.7 percent of their GDP toward developing country assistance. However, all countries have failed to meet their commitment and are contributing not more than 0.2–0.4 percent. If aid were to flow at the agreed level of commitment, official development assistance (ODA) would increase by another US$175 billion (Heller and Gupta 2002). According to the World Bank, the ODA to developing countries has been decreasing by about 20 percent since 1990. Aid as a proportion of central government spending in OECD countries has fallen from 0.82 percent a decade ago to the current level of 0.58 percent. This means that the LDCs are left short of funds to meet the UN Millennium Development Goals, and as a consequence, it is most likely that these goals may not be achieved. It is also interesting to note that although in 2000, 31 percent of the ODA commitments were for social sectors, only 1.5 percent was allocated to education and 2 percent to health (Reality of Aid). This does not speak well of the priorities of donor countries.

ODA spending is also dependent on donor interests and priorities (largely political). For example, South Asia and sub-Saharan Africa, which are home to the poorest people in the world, received only 40 percent of the total ODA. Thus, the poorest of the poor are not the major recipients of aid. Moreover, aid has been tied either to conditions such as reduction in fiscal deficits and privatization or to the demand that consultants and supplies from donor countries be used by aid recipients. While reduction in deficits as a condition for aid is not bad, per se, this condition has not been properly implemented, and the World Bank/IMF have allowed the LDCs to cut back social spending in education and health as long as they meet the conditions of reductions in budget deficits. The more sensible conditionality would have been to reduce administrative and defense expenditures and not development funding. Thus the World Bank/IMF is partly responsible for the decline in social spending in South Asia, and especially in Pakistan.

There has been much media attention clamoring that South Asia, like other LDCs, will not be able to experience economic growth or pursue human development projects if it continues to pay high debt-service costs. While this may be true, the solution is not as simplistic as writing off all LDC debt. Debt write-offs will not incentivize fiscally irresponsible governments to cut back nondevelopment and administrative spending, including defense expenditures. It is feared that if all debt of India and Pakistan were written off, these countries will engage in enhanced spending on the arms race.

Aid in itself is not an engine of growth. Not all LDCs can experience similar benefits with an equivalent amount of aid. Many factors are cited as necessary for aid to have real effects. Among these, good governance and lack of corruption occupy central importance. A case in point is the banking sector reform loan of US$300 million taken by the Pakistan government from the World Bank in 2001. The primary interest of the Pakistan government was to acquire this money for shoring up its acute balance of payment difficulties and shortages of foreign exchange reserves, and not so much to reform the banks. However, the World Bank did ensure some compliance with respect to the closure of loss-making bank branches and some staff retrenchment, though not as much as was desirable, given the huge head office and salary costs of domestic public sector banks (Siddiqui 2003a). As is typical when it comes to implementation, the World Bank failed to ensure and monitor compliance at a level that would have generated further efficiencies in the banking sector—efficiencies commensurate with the financing that was provided.

Capital flows to LDCs may also have detrimental effects, especially if the transfers are large relative to the size of the economy and the inflows are spent primarily on nontraded goods in the domestic market. This would increase aggregate demand, which would be partly satisfied through an increase in imports, thereby worsening the trade balance. The domestic price level would also rise due to higher demand in the domestic market. If the country is on a fully flexible exchange rate system or on a managed float, the increased supply of foreign exchange (due to capital inflows) not matched by a large increase in imports (by the domestic country) would lead to an appreciation in both the nominal and real exchange rates. Indeed, this is what was observed in the wake of post–9/11 capital flows into Pakistan where the rupee appreciated by 8 percent in 2002.

In the event that the central banks of the LDCs are maintaining a fixed exchange rate or even crawling pegs, the nominal exchange rate would by definition remain unchanged. However, the increase in the money supply caused by capital inflows would increase domestic demand and prices, and the currency would appreciate in real terms (i.e., the real exchange rate would appreciate). The net impact of large capital inflows on a developing country would be adverse due to both higher inflation and an overvalued currency. Higher prices would largely hurt the lower- and middle-income population and an appreciated currency would reduce exports and jobs in the export-related industries. Thus capital inflows can contribute to poverty in aid recipient countries. Causal empiricism suggests that this is indeed being observed in some aid-receiving South Asian countries, such as Pakistan. Despite billions of dollars in capital inflows through the Asian Development Bank, World Bank, and G-8 countries, poverty has increased. The beneficiaries have been the rent-seeking bureaucrats and politicians entrusted with managing and governing capital inflows.

In 2001 South Asia was the recipient of approximately $5.5 billion dollars in ODA. Despite the fact that aid as a percentage of GDP is higher, aid per capita in South Asia is lower than in its developing country counterparts, perhaps indicating a basis for the disbursement of aid that does not favor South Asia and its large population.

Causes of Debt: The Case of Pakistan

What are the possible causes of debt in South Asia? South Asian countries have experienced some common causes of debt accumulation. For example, most of the governments in this region have been running fiscal deficits and current account deficits that have had to be financed through debt. They have also experienced currency devaluations that have increased domestic currency debt-servicing costs, hence leading to budgetary deficits and resulting in further debt. Below we discuss in greater detail the causes of Pakistan's debt accumulation in the 1980s and 1990s to gain insights about South Asia in general.[11]

1. *Low national savings:* National savings are composed of private and public (government) savings. If the government is dissaving, that is, incurring budget deficits, the national savings will be low. During the period 1997–2000, negative public savings averaged approximately 3.2 percent of GDP.

2. *Fiscal indiscipline:* Fiscal spending on the noninterest component of total spending was 11.7 percent of GDP in 1990 to 12.8 percent of GDP in 2000. Coupled with this, a low tax base led to fiscal deficits that resulted in

debt financing. At one time, the tax base benefited from high customs duties on imports, which fetched on average 35–40 percent of total government tax revenues. However, when Pakistan subscribed to the IMF structural adjustment program, it had to progressively reduce customs tariffs from a high of 225 percent in the 1980s to 25 percent in 2002. This resulted in tariff revenue that accounted for only 12 percent of total revenue collection.

3. *Loss-making public sector corporations:* The government either bailed out these loss-making corporations or extended guarantees toward their contingent liabilities. In 2002, the support amounted to a colossal 3.2 percent of GDP (117.6 billion rupees), which is more than the government's spending on the education sector. The bulk of the spending was to the two utility companies: the Water and Power Development Authority and the Karachi Electric Supply Organization. In addition to annual financial support for operations and salaries, contingent liabilities take an immense chunk of the fiscal resources. Contingent liabilities only kick in when a corporation defaults. In 2000 the outstanding stock of such liabilities amounted to 337 billion rupees or 10 percent of GDP.

4. *Declining capital inflows:* During the 1990s, capital inflows had decreased without any corresponding increase in FDI. The government had to resort to short-term commercial debt and foreign currency liabilities, thereby adding to the debt burden, and more expensively.

5. *Current account deficits:* The 1990s was also a period of stagnant exports and low remittances. In 2001 the noninterest current account deficit was 3.2 percent of GDP. The financing of this deficit led to further debt accumulation.

6. *Rising interest rates:* The increase in interest rates led to a tripling of debt-service payments and reached 5.8 percent of GDP in 1994.

7. *Reduced bank borrowing:* Because the government agreed with the IMF to reduce its borrowings from the central bank, it resorted to nonbank borrowing mainly through savings certificates of the national saving scheme, and these carried a much higher interest rate (10 percent interest on Defense Savings Certificates) than the government's short-term paper, such as treasury bills.

8. *Capital flight:* While there are no clear calculations of capital flight, it is estimated that through overinvoicing of imported machinery, billions of dollars have been deposited in foreign banks.

The solution to the debt problems is a multipronged approach, as has indeed been proposed by the government of Pakistan. The pillars of that approach are: fiscal control of spending, using privatization proceeds for debt retirement, and obtaining debt write-offs and rescheduling from international financial institutions and G-8 countries. However, debt will not be reduced if the government fails to address the fundamental cause of high indebtedness, the fiscal and current account deficits. These deficits have been caused and exacerbated by the expensive regional arms race between India and Pakistan. Money saved on defense can release billions of dollars to cure the twin deficits (fiscal and current account).

There are no quick or easy solutions for Pakistan or South Asia to reduce high debts and debt-service payments. Nevertheless, results could be seen within the decade if governance and corruption indicators are appreciably improved, and the government concentrates on promoting higher education for training the engineers, technicians, and scientists who can develop comparative advantages in products, processes, and marketing to deal with the challenges of a global marketplace. At the same time, the region will have to drastically reduce its population growth rate; otherwise, per capita GDP will not improve and poverty will persist unchecked indefinitely.

Summary

South Asia is facing a huge challenge in the task of providing food, shelter, clothing, education, health, and jobs to its 1.3 billion-plus population. Healthy growth rates over the past five years have provided the region with some financial resources. However, the task is enormous and requires the support of G-8 countries in meeting the ODA obligations they agreed to in Rio de Janeiro in 1992. Developing countries and South Asia have not been given a level playing field by developed countries with respect to access to their markets. If the EU and the United States continue to resort to nontariff barriers and antidumping duties on one pretext or another, the fruits of globalization will be denied to South Asia. The World Bank and IMF programs in South Asia will not be successful in achieving the Millennium Development Goals if aid is not tied to reducing corruption, and to commitments from South Asian governments to increase their own funding of the social sector programs in education and health. Implementation of programs through good governance and reduced corruption are critical factors for success in South Asia's march into the post–9/11, globalized world.

Notes

1. The South Asian Association for Regional Cooperation was established in 1985 to accelerate economic growth, social progress, and cultural development in the region. Member countries include Bangladesh, Bhutan, India, the Maldives, Nepal, Pakistan, and Sri Lanka. Although Afghanistan is not an official member of SAARC, we have included it in South Asia because of its centuries-old cultural, political, and trade links to neighboring Pakistan and India.

2. See Todaro (1997) for a good discussion of the characteristics of a developing country.

3. In a report on the use of condoms in sub-Saharan Africa and Asia, it was found that less than 7 percent of women in Africa had used condoms in the previous instance of sexual intercourse with their regular partners, and less than 50 percent used them for casual sex partners (London School of Hygiene and Tropical Medicine, November 2003).

4. Stern (2001) found that an additional year of education could improve productivity by 10 percent. However, Pritchet (2001) found little or a weak relationship between growth in education and growth in output per worker.

5. On any given day, 36 percent of Punjab's government primary school teachers are absent. This rate is well above the 25 percent rate for India as a whole. The report points out that absenteeism among school teachers in the state is the third highest in the country after Bihar and Jharkhand, which top the list. Compounding the problem is the finding that even when teachers are present, only half (49.8 percent) are teaching. This is below the all-India average of 59.5 percent (see World Bank 2004).

6. These are most commonly gastroenteritis, respiratory infection, malaria, leprosy, cholera, pneumonic plague, tuberculosis, typhoid, trachoma, goiter, and HIV/AIDS.

7. The BHN approach takes into account food, clothing, shelter, basic health services, and provision of basic education.

8. The Transparency International Corruption Perceptions index ranked 133 countries in terms of the degree to which corruption among public officials and politicians was perceived. It is a composite index drawing on seventeen different polls and surveys from thirteen independent institutions, carried out among business people and country analysts, including surveys of residents, both local and expatriate (Transparency International 2003).

9. On the connection between high levels of military spending and corruption, see Gupta, de Mello, and Sharan (2000).

10. Specific tariffs (an absolute dollar amount of duty per unit of import) are generally viewed as less transparent and more distorting to prices than ad valorem tariffs. Tariff-rate quotas (in which tariff rates are dependent on the quantity imported) emerged from the Uruguay round of WTO multilateral trade negotiations in an attempt to minimize market access for certain sensitive products. The result, however, was prohibitive out-of-quota rates and in-quota rates that remained high. Specific tariffs and tariff-rate quotas are also punitive to developing countries in particular, as they are most frequently utilized to protect domestic agricultural products.

11. For a detailed analysis of Pakistan's debt, see Asian Development Bank (2002).

References

Ades, Alberto, and Rafael Di Tella. 1994. "Competition and Corruption." Oxford University Institute of Economics and Statistics Discussion, Paper 169.

Asia Times Online, January 13, 2004. www.atimes.com/atimes/archive/1_13_2004.html.

Asian Development Bank, Resident Mission in Pakistan. 2002. "Escaping the Debt Trap." Working Paper no. 1 (December).

Baig, Mirza I. 2004. "Global Scenario of Textiles and Position of Pakistan." *Pakistan Textile Journal* (March). www.ptj.com.pk/Web%202004/03-2004/global.html.

Deininger, Klaus, and Lyn Squire. 1998. "New Ways of Looking at Old Issues: Inequality and Growth." *Journal of Development Economics* 57, no. 2: 259–87.

DHL Mackinsey "Apparel and Textile Trade Report." 2004. www.domain-b.com/compa-nies/companies_d/dhl_worldwide/20040319_McKinsey_study.html.

Easterly, William. 2002. *The Elusive Quest for Growth: Economists' Adventures and Misadventures in the Tropics*. Cambridge, MA: MIT Press.

Forbes, Kristen J. 2000. "A Reassessment of the Relationship Between Inequality and Growth." *American Economic Review* 90, no. 4: 869–87.

Gupta, Sanjeev; Luiz de Mello; and Raju Sharan. 2000. "Corruption and Military Spending." International Monetary Fund working paper 00/23 (February). Washington, DC.

Heller, Peter S., and Sanjeev Gupta. 2002. "Challenges in Expanding Aid Flows." *Finance & Development* 39, no. 2 (June). www.imf.org/external/pubs/ft/fandd/2002/06/heller.htm.

Lavoy, Peter. 1999. "The Costs of Nuclear Weapons in South Asia." USIA-U.S. Foreign Policy Agenda, Responding to the Change of Proliferation, September. www.nti.org/e_research/official_docs/dos/999PL.DOS.pdf.

London School of Hygiene and Tropical Medicine. November 2003. "Are People Using Condoms: Current Evidence from Sub Saharan Africa and Asia and the Implications for Microbicides."

Mauro, Paulo. 1996. "The Effects on Growth, Investment and Government Expenditures." International Monetary Fund Working Paper 96/98 (September). Washington, D.C.

Mayer, J. and A. Wood 2001. "South Asia's Export Structure in a Comparative Perspective." *Oxford Development Studies* 29, no. 1: 5–29.

Pritchet, Lant. 2001. "Where Has All the Education Gone?" *World Bank Economic Review* 15: 367–91.

Pritchet, Lant, and Deon Filmer. 1999. "What Educational Production Functions Really Show: A Positive Theory of Education Spending." *Economics of Education Review* 18, no. 2 (April): 223–39.

Reality of Aid. 2002. www.devinit.org/realityofaid/kintro.htm.

Reddy, Rammanohar C. 2004. "Indo-Pak Defense Spending." *South Asian Journal*, no. 3 (January–March). www.southasianmedia.net/Magazine/Journal/indopak_defence.htm.

Shleifer, Andrei, and Robert Vishny. 1993. "Corruption." *Quarterly Journal of Economics* 108 (August): 599–617.

Siddiqui, Anjum. 2003a. "Institutional Corruption in Pakistani Banks." *South Asia Tribune* 47 (June 22–28). www.satribune.com—the online newspaper is now closed.

Siddiqui, Anjum. 2003b. "Leadership Failures Change Management and Institutional Corruption" in *Collaborative Leadership*, ed. B. Schell. New York: McGraw Hill.

Stern, Nicholas. 2001. "Investing in Education and Institutions: The Path to Growth and Poverty Reduction in Pakistan." Paper presented at the National Workshop on Pakistan's Poverty Reduction Program, Islamabad, April 12.

Streeton, Paul, et al. 1981. *First Things First: Meeting Basic Human Needs in Developing Countries*. New York: Oxford University Press.

Tendulkar, Suresh D., and L.R. Jain. 1995. "Economic Growth, Relative Inequality, and Equity: The Case of India." *Asian Development Review* 13, no. 2: 138–68.

Todaro, Michael P. 1997. *Economic Development*. 6th ed. New York: Addison Wesley.

Transparency International. 2003. *Global Corruption Report 2003*. Berlin.

United Nations Development Programme. 2003. *Human Development Report 2003*. Geneva.

———. 2004. *Human Development Report 2004*. Geneva.

University of Texas. Perry-Castaneda Library Map Collection, www.lib.utexas.edu/maps/asia.html.

World Bank. 2002. *Global Economic Prospects and the Developing Countries 2002*. Washington, DC.

World Bank. 2002. *World Development Indicators CD-ROM*. Washington, DC.

———. 2003. *World Development Report 2003*. Washington, DC.

———. 2004. "Resuming Punjab's Prosperity." Poverty Reduction and Economic Management Sector Unit, South Asia.

Additional Works Consulted

Dawn: The Internet Edition. 2001 and 2002. dawn.com.

Tanzi, Vito. "Corruption Around the World: Causes, Consequences, Scope and Cures." International Monetary Fund working paper 98/63 (May 1998). Washington, DC.

United Nations Conference on Trade and Development (UNCTAD). *The Least Developed Countries Report 2002*. Geneva, 2002.

United Nations Development Programme (UNDP). *Regional Human Development Report: HIV/AIDS and Development in South Asia*. Geneva, 2003.

United Nations Educational, Scientific and Cultural Organization (UNESCO). *World Education Report 2000*. Paris, 2000.

United Nations Population Fund. "Experience of 20 Years: Achievements and Challenges." *Population Policies and Programmes* (2000): 96.

Verspoor, Adriaan. "Educational Development: Priorities for the Nineties." *Finance and Development* 27 (March 20–23, 1990): 20–23.

World Bank. "Population and the World Bank: Implications from Eight Case Studies." Washington, DC, 1992.

———. "Poverty in Pakistan: Vulnerabilities, Social Gaps and Rural Dynamics." Paper presented in Islamabad, January 8, 2003. Washington, DC, 2002.

———. *The World Bank Annual Report*. Washington, DC, 2002.

———. *The World Bank's Operational Trade Agenda*. Washington, DC, 2003.

World Bank et al. *Global Poverty Report 2000*. G8 Okinawa Summit (July 2000).

2

The Political Economy of South Asia

Edelgard Mahant

When the states of South Asia[1] emerged from the retreating British Empire, their dominant ideology was one of soft socialism. The system of government these states initially adopted was a Westminster-style political democracy (though Pakistan did not hold its first parliamentary elections until 1973),[2] and governments were expected to play a leading role in the economic development of the new countries.[3] As for foreign policy, India's Prime Minister Jawaharlal Nehru began with idealistic notions of Third World solidarity, peace, and goodwill toward other countries (Pakistan, of course, excepted).[4] The new government of Pakistan began with no such ideals. Born in war, its foreign policy since 1947 has been dominated by the military and the attendant crude version of European and North American neorealism. India inherited neorealism from the British but did not return to it until 1962.

By the 1990s, the picture had changed. Among foreign policy elites, neorealism was still dominant. But on economic issues, India had begun to adopt some elements of the neoliberalism that Prime Minister Margaret Thatcher and President Ronald Reagan had preached during the previous decade. In Pakistan, Westminster-style democracy was but a memory, whereas India had adapted the model to suit its own culture and traditions. India and Japan are the only Asian states that have been democratic for a significant period of time.

This chapter discusses the political and economic policies adopted by one of the governments within South Asia (India) and two of the governments outside it (China and the United States) with respect to that region. What kind of political and economic objectives have these three powers pursued in their relations with South Asia? Have the economic policies supported the political objectives, or have economic objectives predominated? To what extent have the three great powers achieved the objectives they pursued with respect to South Asia?

India's Policies Toward the Subcontinent: The Political Dimension

Except for hostility toward Pakistan, the foreign policy of newly independent India was focused on other parts of the Third World and the Commonwealth as much as it was on the subcontinent.[5] The Nehru government, along with the governments of Indonesia and China, was a proud sponsor of the 1955 Bandung Conference, a meeting of twenty-two heads of state and government, which ultimately led to the 1962 founding of the Nonaligned Movement. That same government, along with the governments of Pakistan and Sri Lanka, was an active participant in the newly refurbished British Commonwealth. The Commonwealth-sponsored Colombo Plan was designed to promote the economic development of the subcontinent. This foreign policy of goodwill and cooperation lasted until China attacked India in 1962, at which time India's foreign policy became one of hard-nosed realism.[6] Pakistan, unlike India and Sri Lanka, did not aspire to nonalignment. In 1954, its government made the decision to align itself with the United States, an alliance that with varying degrees of formality has survived to this day.[7]

For India's governing elites the division of British India into several sovereign states[8] denied them the country to which they believed themselves entitled. So the Indian government took two types of measures to establish its hegemony over the subcontinent. The first consisted of the absorption into India of the princely states and European colonies that had not become part of India at the time of independence. The first to go were Junagadh and Hyderabad, which Indian troops occupied in 1948. Next was the French colony of Pondicherry in 1954. Then came Goa, which Indian troops occupied in December 1961. Last to be incorporated was Sikkim, an Indian protectorate from 1950 to 1974. After contested elections, the Indian army intervened and in April 1974, new elections were held under Indian supervision. The resulting assembly voted to join India, and in September 1974, Sikkim became a state of the Indian Union.[9] This completed the expansion of India—so far.

The expansion of India did not include Kashmir. Kashmir is a much larger territory than the others, and it borders on Pakistan. In 1948, when Indian troops attempted to occupy Kashmir, they encountered resistance from Pakistani forces. After the two nations, with United Nations (UN) assistance, negotiated a cease-fire, the territory of this former princely state (Jammu and Kashmir) was divided. About one-third is controlled by Pakistan, the rest by India. The boundary between the two parts is known as the Line of Control or LOC, by which terminology both governments emphasize that this is not an international boundary, but rather a temporary line, subject to further negotiations and definition. Since 1949, the LOC has been the scene of a war (in 1965) and a military action (the Kargil crisis of 1999). Both governments claim the territory of Jammu and Kashmir, and as of 2005, no resolution of this dispute was in sight.

The issue of Kashmir is illustrative of the state of relations among the states of South Asia. Territorial disputes are difficult to resolve in that they tend to become issues of national prestige and because control over territory is a zero-sum game: only one government can own it. Public opinion in both India and Pakistan would not allow either government to make major concessions with respect to Kashmir, and only major concessions from both sides could lead to a solution. It is hoped that the recent adoption of economic liberalism and the consequent rise in prosperity in India, but not in Pakistan, will reduce nationalistic sensitivities.

Just as the Indian and Pakistani governments' policies on Kashmir reflect the priorities of an earlier age, Indian foreign policy with respect to neighboring states resembles that of the age of imperialism. The British had a policy of controlling the subcontinent by playing favorites among the various states and their rulers. The Indian government, in spite of its expressed Third World idealism, assumed from the day of independence that India had a right to be the dominant power in South Asia. India even has its own versions of the Monroe Doctrine. The Indira Doctrine (1980) stipulates that problems with neighboring states must be solved bilaterally and that external powers should have no role in the region. The more elaborate, and some say more moderate, Gujral Doctrine of 1996 added that India does not expect reciprocity from neighboring states and enjoined them not to interfere in each other's internal affairs and to respect each other's territorial integrity.[10] In short, the regional superpower has taken on the role of regional policeman.

The government of independent India has signed treaties with Bhutan, Nepal, and Sri Lanka. A 1949 treaty with Bhutan gave the Indian government the right to advise Bhutan on its foreign policy. After the 1959 Chinese takeover of Tibet, and the consequent economic loss to Bhutan of its trade with China, the Indian government stepped in with technical assistance, including the construction of a road to India. When Bhutan tried to assert its independence by applying to join the UN, India reluctantly agreed. Bhutan joined the UN in 1971, after a UN investigation decided that it was indeed a sovereign state.[11]

India and Nepal signed a treaty of everlasting friendship and consultations on foreign policy issues in 1950; within months the Indian government was interfering in Nepalese domestic affairs. India offered Nepal unsolicited advice on a new constitution, and when that advice was not immediately accepted, Nehru warned that the longer the Nepalese took to make their decision, the greater the threat to their security.[12] In 1960, after the king of Nepal dismissed a pro-Indian prime minister, the Indian government imposed a blockade on the landlocked country. When Sino-Indian relations deteriorated in 1962, the Indian government lifted the blockade. In 1969 India withdrew its military observers from Nepal. By the 1980s, when the government of Nepal was showing signs of an independent foreign policy by buying arms from China and allowing the Chinese to build a road within Nepal, the Indian government reimposed the blockade in 1989, including petroleum shipments for which Nepal had no other source. Though the blockade was lifted in 1990, Indo-Nepalese relations have continued to be uneasy, with the Nepalese government negotiating with China as India exerts economic and political pressure on the country. Nepal has also sought revision of the 1950 Friendship Treaty, but so far the negotiations have been inconclusive.[13]

Though Ceylon was a part of British India, independent India regarded Sri Lanka as an ally rather than a vassal. The relationship, however, did not remain problem free. The British had favored the island's Tamil minority. The government of independent Sri Lanka retaliated by restricting the political and cultural rights of the Tamils. By the 1970s, the Tamil areas of Sri Lanka were seething with unrest, and by 1983, armed revolt had broken out. In India, Tamil-speakers, their political parties, and their state government pressured the government of India to help their oppressed brethren across the strait. Sri Lankan Tamil groups opened offices in India. Indian Tamils secretly shipped supplies and even arms to Sri Lanka, and Indian authorities tolerated these illegal actions. The Sri Lankan government hinted that it might need to buy arms from Pakistan or the United States, a clear challenge to Indian dominance of the subcontinent.[14]

In 1985, India's new prime minister, Rajiv Gandhi, ordered that Indian forces were no longer to tolerate or facilitate the sending of supplies to the Sri Lankan Tamils. However, his efforts to mediate between the Sri Lankan government and the Tamils came to naught; the extremism of the Liberation Tigers of Tamil Eelam (LTTE) was so intense that even India's Tamils kept their distance. With the problem of domestic support resolved, in 1987, Rajiv Gandhi's government came to an agreement that invited Indian troops to Sri Lanka in support of the Sri Lankan government's war against the LTTE. India would play the role of regional policeman. The military operation was a disaster. India lost hundreds of the 70,000 troops it sent. The Sri Lankan government did not give the Indian troops the support it had promised. And in 1989, the Sri Lankan government and the LTTE began talks. They asked the Indian troops to leave, which they did. After a brief cease-fire, the civil war in Sri Lanka continued.[15] And shortly after that, a Tamil extremist suicide bomber killed Rajiv Gandhi. By the 1990s, the situation was back to what it had been before the Indian intervention. The civil war continued and the Sri Lankan government threatened to seek help from Pakistan or the United

States. The great majority of Indian Tamils seem to have relinquished the idea of an independent homeland, for themselves or the Tamils in Sri Lanka, though suspicions about their sympathy for the LTTE remain.[16] In 2003, a fragile truce halted the civil war.

The relationship between India and Pakistan is different. Pakistan is the second largest country on the subcontinent (see Table 2.1). India cannot dominate it.[17] In 1947, Pakistan was a country separated by India: West Pakistan (the current country) and East Pakistan (now Bangladesh). Relations between the two/three countries have varied from outright war to cautious reconciliation. They have seldom been cordial.

Indian attitudes toward Pakistan have been almost uniformly negative. The first generation of Indian leaders saw Pakistan as a country that had deprived India of a large part of its territory and population. They also looked down on Pakistan, a state that owed its identity to Islam; they saw India's secular and multireligious state as more in tune with the modern world. And as it became obvious that Pakistan would not be a democracy (the first elections were held ten years after independence, the first parliamentary election in 1973), Indians had one more reason to look down on Pakistan. When Pakistan allied itself with the United States, both directly and through the Central Treaty Organization (CENTO) and the Southeast Asia Treaty Organization (SEATO), both shadowy organizations of little real effect, Indians had one more reason to feel superior. Nonalignment, even if it was with a tilt toward the Soviet Union, was considered morally superior to alliance with a superpower.[18] Last, and worst of all for bilateral relations, many Indians believed that Pakistan had no right to exist, or at the least would and should dissolve into its constituent parts. The 1971 division of Pakistan into two sovereign states confirmed many Indians' expectations in this respect. While officially no Indian leader would express such a view, Hindu fundamentalists and some other Indians still espouse a second breakup of Pakistan.[19]

Pakistan's first political leaders held their own ideals. They envisioned an Islamic state that would be modern, economically developed, and moderately secular, a state that could be a model for other Islamic states and one that could protect India's Muslims from the bigotry of the Hindu majority. Over the years, however, these ideals have faded. Any move by Pakistan to offer direct aid to India's large Muslim minority (10 percent of India's population) risks backlash and endangers that community. The degree to which Pakistan should be Islamic or secular remains a hotly debated issue within Pakistan. Survival of the state of Pakistan has become the government's primary preoccupation as its control over its northern territories fades, Islamic fundamentalism rears its head in the countryside, and violence infects the major cities (notably Karachi).[20] Pakistan has a powerful military establishment, well-equipped

Table 2.1

South Asia: Basic Economic and Social Indicators, 2003 (US$)

	India	Pakistan	Bangladesh	Sri Lanka	Nepal	Bhutan
Population	1,065,070,607	159,196,336	141,340,476	19,905,165	27,070,666	2,185,569
Area	3,287,590 sq km	803,940 sq km	144,000 sq km	65,610 sq km	140,800 sq km	47,000 sq km
GDP	$3.022 trillion	$317.7 billion	$258.8 billion	$73.49 billion	$38.07 billion	$2.7 billion
GDP per capita	$2,900	$2,100	$1,900	$3,700	$1,400	$1,300
GDP composition by sectors						
Agriculture	23.6%	23.6%	24.0%	19.2%	40.0%	45.0%
Industry	28.4%	25.1%	26.7%	25.3%	20.0%	10.0%
Services	48.0%	51.3%	49.3%	55.5%	40.0%	45.0%
Literacy rate						
Male	70.2%	59.8%	53.9%	94.8%	62.7%	56.2%
Female	48.3%	30.6%	31.8%	90.0%	27.6%	28.1%

Source: CIA World Factbook, www.cia.gov/cia/publications/factbook/ (July 22, 2004).

with weapons supplied by the United States, China, and others. It is not a negligible factor in the politics of South Asia, and it is not likely to break up into its constituent units, but it is in no position to embark on an assertive foreign policy to protect South Asia's Muslims.[21]

India–Pakistan relations began with the violence that accompanied the partition of British India and continued with the war that divided Kashmir in 1948. Since 1948, India–Pakistan relations have consisted of a series of military encounters separated by times of rapprochement and apparent reconciliation. The war of 1965 led to a brief detente. In 1971, the bloody repression by the Pakistani army of the secessionist movement in East Pakistan equaled anything seen during the partition of 1947.[22] When millions of East Pakistanis fled to India to escape the repression, the Indian army intervened, creating the independent state of Bangladesh. This Indo-Pakistan war was followed by the 1972 Simla Agreement, which formally ended the war and settled some other bilateral disputes.[23] A long period of detente came to an end in 1987, when a large Indian military exercise (Exercise Brasstacks) in and around Kashmir appeared to threaten Pakistan. The crisis ended with another era of detente, as Pakistan's president flew to India to attend a cricket match.[24] Gradual improvement, even the opening of the border to land traffic, suffered a serious setback in 1998 as both governments tested nuclear weapons, and ended in 1999, when the Kargil crisis erupted: A large-scale infiltration of Pakistan-supported militants in Kashmir was repulsed by the Indian army. Even though there have been other incidents of Pakistan-based terrorism within India (for example, the attack on the Indian parliament in December 2001), the time since Kargil has been one of renewed detente, with a summit meeting of President Pervez Musharraf and Prime Minister Atal Behari Vajpayee in Agra in July 2002, intensified high-level diplomacy after the South Asian Association for Regional Cooperation (SAARC) summit of January 2004, and a summit between the president and Prime Minister Manmohan Singh in April 2005.[25] India's policy has been to engage Pakistan, so as to induce its government to combat terrorism. By 2004, the Indian government began to liberalize Indian rule over Kashmir, in the hope that the Kashmiris would become loyal citizens of India.

Bangladesh, like Bhutan, began its existence as a client state of India. India provided the administrative support as well as economic assistance, which enabled the new and desperately poor state to function. In 1972, a bilateral treaty between India and Bangladesh committed both governments to respect for territorial integrity and sovereignty. But the same treaty also obligated the two governments not to allow their territories to be used for any threat to the security of the other and to maintain regular contacts with respect to major international problems affecting the interests of both states, wording once again reminiscent of the age of imperialism.[26] A second agreement, two years later, settled most of the outstanding boundary issues between the two countries.[27]

In 1975, after Bangladesh experienced its first military coup, Indo-Bangladesh relations began to deteriorate. Besides the resentment of the smaller against the larger state, there were issues such as the sharing of the Ganga River waters (on which see below) and illegal immigration from Bangladesh to India. In an effort to assert its independence, the government of Bangladesh began to improve its relations with other states, notably the United States, China, and even Pakistan. In 1991, when the United States and Bangladesh began a series of joint military exercises, it was India's turn to feel threatened.[28] By 2001, when sixteen Indian soldiers died in a border clash, Bangladeshis were burning effigies of the Indian prime minister. Though relations have improved since, and the Bangladesh government has expressed a willingness to negotiate outstanding issues, relations between India and its poorer neighbor continue to be precarious.[29] Bangladeshis accuse Indians of having a big brother attitude. They refuse to give India transit rights to deal with tribal areas on the east side of Bangladesh. The Indian government tries to outflank the Bangladeshis by building roads in Myanmar.[30]

India's Policies Toward the Subcontinent: The Economic Dimension

At the time of independence and for forty years thereafter, India and its neighbors treated economic issues primarily as issues of national concern. There was a consensus that governments would play the predominant role in economic development, governments would control international trade, and foreign investment would be guided and controlled in accordance with nationally formulated economic plans. As a result, India's economic policies with respect to its neighbors were largely driven by political imperatives. With the end of the Cold War, economic imperatives for a time became dominant in world politics. Indeed, it was possible for specialists in international relations to perceive an evolution from political to economic to cultural and communication issues. So in assessing India's foreign economic policies within South Asia, one can trace an evolution from the primarily political motives of the first forty years to the increasing importance of economic motives from 1991 to the appearance, by the end of the century, of cultural diplomacy and an interest in the Indian diaspora.[31]

Accordingly, India's foreign economic policy toward the subcontinent for the first four decades consisted primarily of economic measures in support of political aims. After the Sino-American reconciliation, when the United States cut aid to Nepal, India became Nepal's principal aid donor, lest that government turn to China for help.[32] When India blockaded Nepal in 1989, it was to punish that government for allowing China to build a road in Nepal. When India gave major economic assistance to Bhutan and to the new state of Bangladesh, it was in support of client states.

This pattern changed dramatically with the Indian economic liberalization of 1991.[33] India now needed both markets and foreign investment, and to that end it looked to its neighbors (and other countries). In 1985, the governments of Bangladesh and Pakistan had successfully advocated the creation of a regional organization, SAARC. At that time, India had been a reluctant participant, seeing the scheme as one whereby the smaller powers could combine to offset its natural dominance.

But once it began to liberalize its economy, India turned to SAARC. The first step was a South Asian Preferential Trading Arrangement, which was intended to establish free trade on a product-by-product basis. Implemented in 1995, it did not have much effect.[34] However, at their January 2004 meeting in Islamabad, the seven heads of government signed a treaty envisaging the creation of a South Asian Free Trade Area, which was to be implemented gradually as of 2006, with the three larger more developed economies (India, Pakistan, and Bangladesh) liberalizing trade at a somewhat faster pace than the others (Nepal, Bhutan, and the Maldives), with Sri Lanka occupying an intermediate position.

In the years before 1991, the one area where Indian economic policy toward its neighbors was driven by economic rather than political motives was in the sharing of natural resources. By way of illustration, I will discuss three such resources: the waters of the rivers that flow through the subcontinent, the hydroelectric power produced by the water in the mountains north of India, and the natural gas found in the territorial waters of Bangladesh.

In a subcontinent where reliance on monsoons has often led to disaster and where a majority of the population relies on agriculture for its daily bread (see Table 2.1), water for irrigation is a priceless natural resource. India and Bangladesh both use the water of the Ganga River for irrigation and transportation. A 1996 treaty between the two countries establishes a formula for sharing the river's water. While most observers agree that this treaty is fair to Bangladesh as well as to India, it was negotiated under pressure. Between 1971 and 1975, India built a dam at Farakka and diverted some water to the Hoogly River so as to increase the flow to the point where it was strong enough to reduce the silting of the port of Calcutta. India then negotiated the first water-sharing agreement with Bangladesh, and it was this treaty that the current treaty has replaced. Thus, if the treaty is fair, it is due to the political good sense of the Indian government, which chose not to exploit the physical advantage it had gained by building the dam.[35]

The story is similar for the Indus River system on the India–Pakistan border. While the rivers of this system, for the most part, originate in Indian-held territory, they are crucial to the agriculture of Pakistan. India began by cutting the flow to Pakistan in April 1948, and then restored some of the supply within a month. Long hard negotiations mediated by the World Bank began in 1952 and resulted in a 1960 treaty on sharing the water and setting conditions for its use. There have been problems with respect to the implementation of this treaty, notably from 1984 to 1987 when India began to build a dam that could have had the effect of keeping a portion of the water on India's side of the border, but overall the sharing of the water system has worked reasonably well.[36]

All of the South Asian states are in desperate need of energy. They have next to no oil supplies of their own, which makes the hydroelectric power and potential, of Nepal, Bhutan, and northern India a precious resource. According to one Indian estimate, Nepal has a hydroelectric potential of 83,000 MW of which only 591 MW has been developed. Yet less than a quarter of its own people have access to electricity. India and Nepal signed the first agreement for the Indian construction of hydroelectric projects in 1958, but for years progress in construction was hampered by Indian suspicions of foreign investment and Nepali suspicions of Indian motives. In 1997, the two governments signed the Makhali treaty, which provided for joint construction of hydroelectric projects with the participation of private investors from India and elsewhere. However disputes about details have delayed the actual construction of the projects, and by the end of 2003, only a few were in operation.[37]

In 1997, multinational firms found natural gas off the coast of Bangladesh. Though not huge by North American standards (369 billion cubic meters), this find represents a considerable source of wealth for a poor country. But few Bangladeshis have benefited from it. Before multinational firms or the Asian Development Bank will finance a pipeline to eastern Bangladesh, they want the government to make an agreement to export some gas to India and to use the proceeds to pay for the pipeline. However, no Bangladesh government has dared to make such a decision lest it be accused of selling the country's only natural resource to the greedy big brother. Bangladeshis want to make sure that there is enough gas to last them a long time, but they cannot agree on how long is long enough. By the spring of 2005, the decision was still pending. In 2002, Indian firms found natural gas under the Indian-controlled part of the Bay of Bengal, so Indians say they can wait for the Bangladeshi decision.[38]

India is the dominant economic power on the subcontinent. In the case of the two landlocked countries to the North, India is the predominant trading partner for Bhutan, and the most important trading partner for Nepal. China has now overtaken India as the most important supplier for Bangladesh, and Bangladesh sells little to India. The European Union does more trade with Sri Lanka than it does with India.[39] There are three Indian firms on the Fortune 500 list of major multinationals (ranked 461, 462, and 482), but India's investment in neighboring states has been mainly in the form of aid or government-sponsored investment, as in the hydroelectric projects in Bhutan.[40] Indian multinationals prefer to invest in wealthier countries. Indian firms have invested in the Sri Lankan rubber industry, but then Sri Lanka is the only country in South Asia that is wealthier than India.[41]

Any generalizations about India's economic relationship with its neighbors do not apply to Pakistan. In the first year after partition, 56 percent of Pakistan's exports went to India and one-third of its imports came from there.[42] By 2002, India–Pakistan trade was negligible,[43] as was most other legitimate movement across the border, a good illustration of the fact that when political end economic forces clash head-on, the former usually win out. The India–Pakistan border has been opened to land traffic several times over the past twenty years (most recently in early 2004), only to be closed again as political tensions escalated. In 2004, some Indian analysts detected a significant increase in India–Pakistan trade, but this was from a very narrow base.[44]

A policy of trade liberalization on the subcontinent should be particularly profitable for Pakistan, which is otherwise isolated in its part of the world, and perhaps as a result, Pakistan's economy has "flat-lined" over the past decade.[45] Afghanistan is not likely to become a significant trading partner, and much wealthier Iran is also not a good bet as a trading partner as long as its government is dominated by a conservative theocracy. At the time of the break with Bangladesh, West Pakistan was wealthier than India in terms of GDP per capita. India has now overtaken Pakistan by a margin of $2,900 to $2,100 (purchasing power parity) (see Table 2.1). India's gradual liberalization of its economy has led to accelerated economic growth. Pakistan can hope to share in that prosperity by trading with India, and Indian businesses are already calculating which goods they could sell to Pakistan if trade were liberalized.[46] Another scheme, favored by the Pakistani government, calls for the construction of a natural gas pipeline from Iran to India. India would receive much-needed energy, and Pakistan would earn foreign exchange on the transit fee. This scheme has not been blessed by the Indian government, which rightly fears the instability of the source and the route.[47]

The India–Pakistan relationship provides a good case study of the interaction of economic and political factors in international relations—under the most difficult of circumstances. In the 1950s, when West Europeans began to integrate their economies, they did so in the hope of preventing future wars on the continent, but in fact economic integration was possible because war between France and Germany was already highly unlikely. Now, some Pakistanis are asking for movement on the Kashmir issue before economic liberalization with India; the Indian foreign minister is calling on Pakistan to curb terrorism, while others, on both sides of the border, expect political benefits from economic contacts.[48] As in Europe, this situation calls for a compromise. Extreme political tensions will need to be defused before there can be any hope of economic integration, which, after all, calls for some degree of trust. But if economic integration and the resultant contacts, including the movement of people and cultural goods, do occur, the prospects for further confidence building and a peaceful future for the subcontinent are good.

U.S. Policy Toward the Subcontinent: Political Aspects

For the most part, the United States has not had a South Asian policy but rather separate policies toward India and Pakistan. Beginning with India, it is hard to imagine now the degree of goodwill toward former colonies that emanated from Washington for the first decade after World War II. The Truman administration gave foreign aid to help the new country develop, and in 1949, India and the United States together helped to negotiate an exit strategy for the Dutch in Indonesia.[49]

However, the bloom came off the rose before long. After the communist victory in the Chinese civil war (1949) and the North Korean attack on South Korea (1950), apparently with Soviet collusion, most of official Washington began to see a world divided between two forces, good and evil. Between good and evil there is little room for compromise, and India's policy of nonalignment appeared to be an attempt to compromise with evil. Worse yet, from an American point of view, India's leaders admired the socialist economies of China and the Soviet Union and attempted to adapt them for India.[50]

Pakistan, with an Islamist military government, would not appear to be a natural ally for the United States. But Pakistan's first governor general, Muhammad Ali Jinnah, opined that an Islamic state could not really ally itself with a communist one.[51] In February 1954, Pakistan requested American military assistance and in May the two governments signed a mutual defense assistance agreement.[52] Within a year, Pakistan joined both the British-inspired CENTO and the American-inspired SEATO.

The United States and Pakistan have been de facto allies ever since. Whenever a U.S. administration seemed inclined to follow a more evenhanded policy with respect to Pakistan and India, events conspired to heighten the importance of Pakistan. In 1957, the Americans built secret facilities in Pakistan, which enabled them to spy on Soviet Central Asia, and the American air force began to use Pakistani airports to make reconnaissance flights over the Soviet Union.[53] Relations deteriorated somewhat as the United States sent troops to Vietnam. There was also American resentment about Pakistan's advances to China while China was supporting the North Vietnamese. In an unrelated development, the United States briefly suspended military aid after the India–Pakistan war of 1965.

When the Nixon–Kissinger team took control of American foreign policy, Kissinger's geopolitics led to a rapprochement with China as a logical component of American policy in a bipolar world. Because Pakistan had good relations with China, Kissinger turned to Pakistan and asked its assistance in a secret approach to the People's Republic of China (PRC). It took more than two years, but in 1971, Kissinger secretly flew from Pakistan to China, and by 1972, China and the United States announced their rapprochement.[54] In 1971, when the Pakistani army was slaughtering civilians in East Pakistan, and India and Pakistan once again went to war, the United States, though ostensibly neutral, leaned toward Pakistan—so as not to endanger the greater geopolitical scheme.

After the end of the Vietnam War and during the era of Soviet-American detente, there seemed less need of an alliance with Pakistan. Indeed, in 1979, Pakistan left CENTO (it had left SEATO in 1972) and joined the Nonaligned Movement.[55] However, within months, Pakistan was back in the arms of its American friend. In December 1979, Soviet troops invaded Afghanistan. American help to the Afghan opposition was possible only through Pakistan, and the Reagan administration also prepared a generous military aid package.[56]

By the mid-1990s it became obvious that Pakistan was making nuclear weapons, and in 1998 both India and Pakistan held a series of nuclear tests, thereby unleashing automatic American sanctions.[57] Pakistan's economy was not growing, its educational system was collapsing, and its politics were in turmoil, with the army once again replacing an elected government in 1999. Official Washington classified Pakistan as a "failed state." However, September 11, 2001, quickly converted the "failed state" into a "frontline state," as American attention was once again focused not only on Afghanistan but also on its border region with Pakistan.[58] Pakistan has become an essential component of the American security architecture,[59] while the growth of Islamic terrorism in Pakistan itself is conveniently ignored.[60]

Whereas the American alliance with Pakistan has been continuous, relations with India have fluctuated from fairly good to not so good to fairly bad. Americans, especially John Foster Dulles, were disappointed in India's failure to support the United States during the Cold War. The American alliance with Pakistan was followed by an Indian approach to the Soviet Union. In 1955, Soviet leaders Nikita Khrushchev and Nikolai Bulganin visited India and expressed sympathy for the Indian position on Kashmir.[61] By the later years of the Eisenhower administration, U.S. policy toward South Asia became more evenhanded as Americans began to perceive India's potential as a major power. This trend accelerated when Kennedy replaced Eisenhower. Kennedy admired Nehru's idealism and appointed a well-known academic, John Kenneth Galbraith, as ambassador to India, thereby signaling a wish to upgrade and improve relations.[62] Goodwill led to support and military assistance when China attacked India in 1962.

The improvement in relations was, however, short-lived. As the United States became embroiled in Vietnam, India's refusal to support the United States led to hostility from Washington. India moved closer to the Soviet orbit, buying Soviet arms and selling consumer goods to the Soviet Union.[63] The 1971 war that broke up Pakistan brought a new low point in Indo-American relations. While ostensibly neutral, the Nixon administration sent an aircraft carrier to the Bay of Bengal and demonstrated its support for the government of West Pakistan, even as the American consul in East Pakistan sent graphic descriptions of the bloody West Pakistan oppression of the Bengalis.[64] In August 1971, the Soviet Union and India signed a treaty of friendship. When India moved into East Pakistan in support of the independence movement there, the Nixon administration cut aid to India.[65] India won the war and prevented a second humanitarian tragedy among the refugees, all without major direct outside assistance.

In 1974, India exploded a "nuclear device," and the United States imposed sanctions. Three years later, the Carter administration (1977–81) tried to improve relations with India. In 1990, tensions rose on the India–Pakistan border as India massed troops there. President George H.W. Bush sent his deputy national security adviser, Robert Gates, to mediate, and he found India more receptive than Pakistan.[66] In January 1995, India and the United States signed Agreed Minutes on Defense Relations between the United States and India, an agreement that provides for civilian as well as defense cooperation and cooperation in defense production and research.[67] President Bill Clinton visited India in March 2000, only tacking on a visit to Pakistan as an afterthought.[68]

Since September 11, 2001, the Indian government has been emphasizing what it has said for years, that terrorism inspired by Islamic fundamentalism is a danger to many countries, notably India and the United States. The two countries also share an interest in maintaining access to Middle East oil and in protecting the sea-lanes of the Indian Ocean. The second Bush administration has now accepted this argument in favor of common interests between the two states.[69] Indo-American relations are good. Americans are willing to work with India with one exception: they will not offend Pakistan to the point where Pakistan would no longer be willing to cooperate in the U.S. war on terrorism.

U.S. Policy Toward South Asia: The Economic Dimension

Some left-wing critics would have U.S. foreign policy dominated by a military-industrial complex that stops at nothing to promote its arms and related industries, or at best they see U.S. foreign policy as the tool of large multinational corporations that want to invest in and make money from poor countries, regardless of the human cost. While there may be some elements of truth in both of these characterizations, the reality is much more complex.

With the success of the Marshall Plan for Europe (1947–52), there was tremendous optimism in the United States about the miracles to be achieved by foreign aid. The United States embarked on an aid program for both newly independent India and Pakistan.[70] Even in 1951, when Indo-American relations had begun to deteriorate, the Truman administration responded generously when India needed food aid to tide it over a crisis.[71] Throughout the 1950s and into the 1960s, as American disappointment over India's friendliness to the Soviet Union grew, the United States continued to supply half of India's foreign aid.[72] By the 1960s, the optimism about the possibilities of foreign aid had waned. After the 1965 and 1971 wars with Pakistan, Indo-U.S. relations deteriorated. Aid was suspended and then restored only partially. Washington was particularly leery of selling India technology that might then fall into Soviet hands.[73]

Under President Lyndon Johnson (1963–69) a new factor entered into Indo-American relations. Johnson believed fervently that for the Indian economy to grow and increase agricultural production to the point that India could feed its own people, India should loosen some of the controls the government had imposed on the economy and should also accept more foreign investments.[74] Johnson succeeded in the first, but not the second aim. In 1965, he sent a team of economic experts to study the Indian economy. To preserve secrecy and avoid the appearance that the Indian government was giving in to U.S. pressure, Johnson had the U.S. representative to the UN Food and Agricultural Organization send the plans for Indian agricultural reform to him personally. As soon as the Indian government announced the agreed-upon reforms, Johnson increased food aid to tide the Indians over until production increased. While India needed food aid for several more years, the reforms Johnson and his teams negotiated with like-minded people in the Indian government freed Indian agriculture to grow, to the extent that, by the turn of the century, India was exporting food grains. Indeed this "Johnson" liberalization was one of the crucial steps on the way to the success of the green revolution.[75]

After the improvement in Indo-American political relations that followed the Soviet invasion of Afghanistan, the Reagan and Gandhi administrations (1982–84) negotiated a Memorandum of Understanding on the transfer of

Table 2.2

United States: Total Two-Way Merchandise Trade with Selected Countries, 2002 (US$ millions)

Country	Total value of two-way trade
Canada	370,010
China	147,210
South Korea	48,148
Netherlands	28,160
India	15,919
Indonesia	12,199
Pakistan	2,999

Source: Statistical Abstract of the United States, 2003, 816–19.

sensitive military technologies to India. The agreement was of limited significance, however, because the United States was not willing to transfer the technologies, such as supercomputers, that India most wanted.[76]

With the collapse of the Soviet Union, India had lost is principal economic ally. In 1991, Prime Minister Narasimha Rao and Finance Minister Manmohan Singh decided that they could save the faltering Indian economy only by gambling on economic liberalization. The results have been excellent. India's economic growth has accelerated, growing at a rate of at least 6 percent, and as of 2003, at 8 percent a year.[77]

With such rapid economic growth and development, Indo-U.S. economic relations are taking on a new dimension, and Indo-American trade has been growing rapidly (see Table 2.2 for more details). Newly prospering India presents economic opportunities. Now when Americans ask Indians to open their markets, protect intellectual property, and accept foreign investment, it is as much economic interest as ideology that drives American policy. At the same time, a growing Indian economy needs access to the American market, although Indians resent American lectures about child labor or safety or environmental standards and are also unhappy about American restrictions on imports of agricultural products and textiles.

The United States wants India to phase out quantitative restrictions on imports and buy more American agricultural products. India wants the Americans to allow the import of Indian-made textiles. The United States claims dissatisfaction with India's protection of intellectual property, especially patents. The Indian government complains of the difficulty Indians have in traveling to the United States.[78] However, most of these disputes take place within the multilateral context of the World Trade Organization (WTO), which India joined in

1995. India has also been the target of American protectionist legislation. Under the so-called Super 301 provisions of the American Trade Act (first enacted in 1988 and revived in 1999), the U.S. government has given itself the right to name entire countries, not just specific companies or industries, as unfair traders. The first list, published in 1989, named three countries, Japan, Brazil, and India. India was accused of requiring government approval for foreign investment and of allowing no foreign investment in the insurance industry. A second list, announced on May 1, 2001, lists sixteen countries, including India, as unfair traders. The specific charges against India are that it requires foreign companies to use specified levels of local content as a condition of investment in the rapidly growing Indian auto sector and that there are 2,700 kinds of goods barred from India altogether. India is also cited under a special 301 provision accusing it (and fifteen other governments) of not adhering to the WTO agreement on Trade Related Intellectual Property Rights. Neither announcement appears to have led to retaliatory measures.[79]

As for Bangladesh, American firms are anxious to begin drilling for oil and natural gas in Bangladesh's territorial waters and they want to build a pipeline to India so that sales to wealthier India can finance construction costs. Bangladesh has resisted these pressures.[80]

American economic policy in Pakistan has been dominated by political considerations. Pakistan has long been one of the principal recipients of U.S. aid. By 2003, the American government was providing debt relief as well as budgetary support. Strangely, the 2003 listing of aid recipients in the *Statistical Abstract of the United States* does not list Pakistan at all. The official figures show Israel as receiving $4.7 billion in economic and military aid in 2000, and Egypt $2 billion. That contrasts with $72 million to Bangladesh and $168 million to India. An American think-tank estimates annual U.S. aid to Pakistan as of 2003 to be about $720 million, but that amount does not include debt relief or the F16 fighter planes that Pakistan was twice denied by the U.S. Congress and that, as of March 2005, the administration was still trying to sell. Interestingly, Pakistan has been promised $60 million worth of white flour to compensate for the delay in the delivery of the F16s, suggesting that the country is not yet self-sufficient in food. Official and semiofficial numbers on aid almost certainly underestimate the true amount of American aid; various kinds of security cooperation in conjunction with the war on terror bring significant amounts of American money into Pakistan.[81]

Like India, Pakistan has been the object of U.S. pressure to liberalize its economy. In 1965, President Johnson also tried to persuade Pakistan to reform its agricultural sector, but with less success. Pakistan has been somewhat more receptive than India to pressure with respect to intellectual property and foreign investment, but to little avail. As Table 2.2 shows, U.S. trade with Pakistan is negligible, and because of the uncertain political situation and corruption, American investment has not increased.[82]

In spite of the alliance between the two countries, Pakistan, like India, has been the target of U.S. trade protection. There were quotas on imports of textiles from Pakistan, even though Pakistan depends on textiles for 70 percent of its export earnings. Under the WTO, the United States agreed to eliminate textile quotas by January 1, 2004, but there is growing pressure to reimpose them.

In terms of economic relations with South Asia, there has thus been a gradual evolution in U.S. policies, from one dominated by geopolitical considerations during the Cold War to one based on economic as well as political motivations. This is true of policies toward India as well as Bangladesh. In the case of Pakistan, geopolitical factors continue to drive American policy (political and economic). In 2002, for example, the U.S. government announced a series of quota increases for Pakistani textiles, "granted as part of the U.S. commitment to Pakistan for its help in the 'war on terror.'"[83] I could not have said it better myself.

China's Policies Toward South Asia: Political Factors

China's relations with the subcontinent can be traced to ancient times, indeed to the time of the Buddha who hailed from India but had a profound influence on China. During the age of colonialism, there was some contact between Indian and Chinese leaders opposed to the European domination of their continent, but these contacts were not a major factor in the success of India's independence movement or the Chinese civil war.[84] After the Chinese Communists had won the civil war, they feared that counterrevolutionary remnants might seek to reenter China from the south.[85] Remnants of the Nationalist forces survived in northern Burma (now Myanmar) for two decades or more.

Sino-Indian political contacts became important when Nehru and Zhou Enlai cooperated in the founding of the nonaligned movement (which, ironically China was not allowed to join because of its nuclear weapons). However, the cooperation between the two anticolonial brothers (*bhai-bhai*) as expressed in the five principles of nonalignment (*pansheel*) was short-lived. Even as Nehru and Zhou Enlai were being photographed, the government of the PRC began to assert its control over Tibet (1951). By 1959, Chinese repression had persuaded the Tibetan political and spiritual leaders, the Dalai Lama and many of his followers to flee to northern India, where they and their descendants remain to this day. In 1962, the Chinese government used military force to occupy some territory in India's Ladakh region. The Indian army was unprepared for a mountain war, and China had no difficulty in holding the territory it claimed.

On the principle that my enemy's enemy is my friend, Pakistan–China military contacts began in 1963. Ironically, Chinese and Pakistani leaders had first met at the Bandung conference. In 1956, Pakistan's prime minister visited China, and Zhou Enlai, Pakistan.[86] In 1963, China and Pakistan settled their boundary disputes, and military contacts began that same year, culminating in a military agreement in 1965, the year of an Indo-Pakistan war. Military cooperation continued apace from then, with the signing of a defense production agreement in 1974. Indeed, China is one of Pakistan's principal suppliers of arms.[87]

The government of Pakistan decided to manufacture nuclear weapons after the breakup of Pakistan in 1971, and it would appear that China pledged assistance as early as 1972, two years before the first Indian nuclear explosion. In 1995, China sold Pakistan ring magnets, which were vital to the construction of nuclear weapons and which other governments had refused to sell.[88]

China and India resumed diplomatic relations in 1976, but relations remained touchy.[89] A decade later, Prime Minister Rajiv Gandhi tried to improve relations with China. He visited Beijing in 1988 and initiated a program of confidence-building measures. Negotiations to settle outstanding border issues began in 1989 and have continued to the present. While various parts of the border have been agreed upon, much remains to be done.[90] Negotiations resumed in 2004, at which time Indian negotiators noticed that China had quietly dropped its claim to Sikkim by omitting Sikkim from the official yearbook of Chinese territories. Confidence-building measures reached a new high point in 2003, when the two navies conducted joint exercises off the coast of China, near Shanghai.[91] China shares a Muslim population with the states of the former Soviet Union, and seeks cooperation in countering Islamic movements. This is yet one more reason for China not to support the Kashmiris against the Indians.[92]

China maintains good relations with Nepal because Nepal provides China with a hinterland and supply bases that it can use to secure Tibet. China has also provided Nepal with a substantial mount of economic aid, building roads, factories, hydroelectric projects, and sports complexes in Nepal. Since 1989, China has stopped openly supporting Nepal against India.

The story is similar concerning the other South Asian states. While at one time China supported Bangladesh against India with respect to the Ganga waters, China now sees South Asia as a potential market for Chinese goods.[93]

China's Policies Toward South Asia: Economic Factors

China's interest in South Asia was almost exclusively geopolitical until the 1990s. China gave aid to several South Asian countries, notably Nepal and Sri Lanka. In 1952, it signed an agreement in which it agreed to buy Sri Lankan rubber in exchange for Chinese rice.[94] And of course, it became a major arms supplier to Pakistan. But this activity was for the purpose of countering India, not to make money for China. Until the economic reforms instituted under Deng Xiaoping, China's economic policies had been almost autarchic, and in any case, the South Asian countries had little of the technology or raw materials that China needed.

By the 1990s, China's economic reforms required it to engage in international trade, and the economies of South Asia provided promising markets. China is an important trading partner for Nepal (both as supplier and as purchaser), and it is an important supplier to both Bangladesh and India. China is not a major trading partner of either Pakistan or Sri Lanka, though it has increased its aid to the latter country in recent years. China is also an important supplier of small arms to Pakistan, Sri Lanka, Bangladesh, and Myanmar. Trade with China is more important to the South Asians than it is to China.[95]

China has been much more successful than India in attracting foreign investment. In 2002, China attracted $52.7 billion, as against India's $5.5 billion.[96] The two countries are thus in competition with respect to foreign investment. In 2000, China made the so-called Kumming proposals for closer economic cooperation between eastern India, Bangladesh, southern China, and Myanmar. While the Indian government suspected the Chinese of wishing to interfere in the subcontinent, the proposal could also be explained in economic terms.[97] Both India and China have an interest in maintaining the economic progress they have made, a factor that, sabre-rattling to the contrary, augurs well for the future peaceful development of the entire continent.[98]

Concluding Comments: A Political Economy of South Asia?

One of the questions posed at the beginning of this chapter concerned the degree to which the three powers have in fact achieved their economic and political objectives with respect to South Asia. Briefly, the answer is: to a very limited degree. India is not the dominant power, economically or politically, that its leaders had hoped it would be. Only Bhutan is India's client state. Nepal, Sri Lanka, Bangladesh, and, of course, Pakistan have followed independent foreign policies. Economically, India may become dominant in the subcontinent, but that is not yet certain. The United States has only one ally on the Indian subcontinent, and that ally, Pakistan, has been regressing with respect to its ability to fulfill the basic functions of a state, a fact that reduces its usefulness as an ally. China has begun to make some progress as a supplier to the subcontinent (notably to Bangladesh and Nepal), but it has little political influence, even over Pakistan whom it has helped so much. Thus, in traditional terms of influence via foreign policy, the three powers have not achieved much in South Asia.

Politics, rather than economics, has undermined the relations of the South Asian states with one another and the relations of those states with the United States and China for most of the time since World War II. However, since 1990, there has been a significant departure from this dominance of geopolitics. China is seeking markets for its growing economy. As the Indian economy grows, the Indian government is seeking to promote trade and other economic contacts with neighboring states. It appears that India and China are entering the age of the trading state in their relations with South Asia. It is worth noting that it is not the foreign policy and foreign economic policy of poor states that is determined by economic factors. It is as economies grow and expand that economic factors take on greater importance. In the case of South Asia, much remains to be achieved before the entire subcontinent arrives at the age of the trading state. Pakistan's economy and foreign policy are still dominated by politics, though some of this domination is imposed by the American super-power. Before the subcontinent can become a trading subcontinent, India and Pakistan will need to begin once again to trade with one another. Further measures of economic integration will have to follow. While Nepalese work-ers now have the right to move to India, the only other significant movement of peoples is illegal immigration, for example, of Bangladeshis into eastern India. True economic integration will mean not only the implementation of the South Asian Free Trade Agreement (SAFTA), but also some movement of people, investment, and cultural goods.

Cultural and intellectual contacts are also important. Granted that the entire subcontinent watches "made-in-India" movies, further integration requires free access to television programming and various other kinds of cultural, including academic, exchanges. Nepalese, Bhutanese, and Bangladeshi students already come to India in considerable numbers. Sri Lankan and Pakistani students should do the same. As geopolitics fades, and economic and cultural contacts grow, it is even possible to envisage a solution to the last major geopolitical controversy of the subcontinent, Kashmir. As economies develop and become interdependent, territory should become less significant. As contacts between peoples increase, belonging to one nation or another should also becomes less significant. In this way, France has reconciled itself to the fact that Germany owns the Saar, while Germany has accepted that Alsace and Lorraine belong to France, Austria has accepted that southern Tyrol is a part of Italy, and Hun-gary that Transylvania belongs to Romania. They are, after all, all members or potential members of the European Union. This is not to say that Asians need to adopt European values. Asian economic integration, if it happens, will be based on Asian values, such as a degree of respect for sovereignty and "open regionalism," meaning that common markets and free trade areas will have fluid boundaries, not the confederal rules and structures of the European

Union. If SAFTA and related measures can lead to a reconciliation of the peoples of South Asia based on Asian concepts and values, then economics will have triumphed over politics, rather than politics over economics as has been the case for many of the past fifty years.

Notes

1. For the purposes of this chapter, South Asia includes India, Pakistan, Bangladesh, Nepal, Sri Lanka, and Bhutan. Sikkim is treated as a part of India, and Myanmar (under the name of Burma once also part of the British Empire) as a member of the Association of Southeast Asian Nations now belongs to Southeast, rather than South, Asia. Some Indian commentators include Afghanistan in South Asia, but it is not so included here. Stephen Philip Cohen, *India: Emerging Power* (Washington: Brookings Institution Press, 2001), 249.

2. Dennis Kux, *The United States and Pakistan, 1947–2000* (Baltimore: Johns Hopkins University Press, 2001), 209.

3. C. Raja Mohan, *Crossing the Rubicon. The Shaping of India's New Foreign Policy* (New Delhi: Viking, 2003), 247.

4. Cohen, *India: Emerging Power*, 38, 41–42; S.H. Patil, "Collapse of Communism and Emergence of Global Economy: India's Experiment with New Economic Policy," in *India and the New World Order*, ed. Annpurna Nautiyal (New Delhi: South Asian Publishers, 1996), 215–25.

5. Cohen, *India: Emerging Power*, 230.

6. Ibid., 41.

7. Kux, *The United States*, 63; Cohen, *India: Emerging Power*, 131.

8. Just how many states emerged from British India depends on definitions that need not concern us here. Burma (Myanmar), for example, was under British control, but governed separately.

9. On the annexation of Sikkim, see A. Appadorai and M.S. Rajan, *India's Foreign Policy and Relations* (New Delhi: South Asian Publishers, 1985), 582–84.

10. Mohan, *Crossing the Rubicon*, 239–41; Cohen, *India. Emerging Power*, 75; C. Raja Mohan, *The Hindu*, January 2, 2003, www.medes.nic.in/opn/23003jan/2hin1.htm (accessed July 1, 2003).

11. Cohen, *India: Emerging Power*, 130; Mohan, *Crossing the Rubicon*, 257.

12. *Keesing's Contemporary Archives*, January 13–20, 1951, vol. 8, 11211.

13. *Keesing's Contemporary Archives*, vol. 35, no. 10, 1989, 37008; *Facts on File*, 1989, 904; J.N. Dixit, *India's Foreign Policy 1947–2003* (New Delhi: Picus, 2003), 200–201, 371–72; Cohen, *India: Emerging Power*, 233–34; www.country-data.com/cgi-bib/query/r-9159.html (accessed July 1, 2004).

14. Martha Crenshaw, "India and the Sri Lankan Dilemma," www.wesleyan.edu/gov/india_and_the_sri_lankan_dilemma.htm (accessed July 1, 2004); Dixit, *India's Foreign Policy*, 90, 239.

15. Crenshaw, "India and the Sri Lankan Dilemma."

16. Dixit, *India's Foreign Policy*, 235.

17. Cohen, *India: Emerging Power*, 32.

18. Ibid., 202.

19. Ibid., 46, 200, 206–7, 214.

20. Milind Thakar, "Coping with Insecurity: the Pakistan Variable in Indo-U.S. Relations," in *Engaging India. U.S. Strategic Relations with the World's Largest Democracy*, ed. Gary Bertsch, Seema Gahlaut, and Anupam Srivastava (New York: Routledge, 1999), 223–37.

21. Stephen Philip Cohen, "The Nation and the State of Pakistan," *Washington Quarterly* 25 (Summer 2002): 109–22; Mohan, *Crossing the Rubicon*, 187.

22. For graphic descriptions of the 1971 violence in East Pakistan, see the recently released reports of the American consul in Dhaka. National Security Archive, www.gwu.edu/nsarchiv/NSAEB/NSAEB79/

23. Dixit, *India's Foreign Policy*, 111; Cohen, *India: Emerging Power*, 219.

24. Cohen, *India: Emerging Power*, 146–48.

25. Mohan, *Crossing the Rubicon*, 173–84.

26. For a summary of the 1972 treaty, see M.R. Biju, *India's Foreign Policy. Towards a New Millennium* (Jaipur: National Publishing House, 2000), 365–68.

27. Ibid., 373–76.

28. On the joint military exercises, see ibid., 391–93.

29. Maqbool Ahmd Bhatty, "Growing India-Bangladesh Tensions," *Dawn*, May 7, 2001; reprinted at www.dawn.com/2001/05/07/op.htm+allinte (accessed July 1, 2004); "Khaleda Tells JS: Problems with Neighbours to Be Resolved Peacefully," New Nation Online Edition; available at http://nation.ittefaq.com/artman/publish/printer_9809.shtml (accessed June 10, 2004).

30. Mohan, *Crossing the Rubicon*, 240; C.S. Kuppuswamy, "India-Myanmar: Flourishing Ties," South Asia Analysis Group, Paper 902; available at www.saag.org/papers10/paper902.html (accessed July 21, 2004).

31. On the general evolution from political to trade factors in foreign policy, see Richard Rosencrance, *The Rise of the Trading State* (New York: Basic Books, 1986); Tom Travis, "Advantages and Disadvantages for India and the United States in the Emerging World Order," in *India and the New World Order*, ed. Annpurna Nautiyal (New Delhi: South Asian Publishers, 1996), 60–71; and B. Bhattatcharyya, "India's Foreign Economic Policy" in *Indian Foreign Policy. Agenda for the 21st Century*, ed. Lalit Mansingh et al. (New Delhi: Konarch Publishers, 1997), vol. 1, 210–21. On the progression toward cultural objectives in foreign policy, see the classic Samuel Huntington, "The Clash of Civilizations," *Foreign Affairs* 72, no. 3 (Summer 1993): 22–49; Utpal Banerjee, "Role of Cultural Diplomacy," vol. 1, 397–417, and J.N. Dixit, "Culture as an Instrument of Diplomacy," vol. 1, 418–28, both in *Indian Foreign Policy. Agenda for the 21st Century*, ed. Lalit Mansingh et al. (New Delhi: Konarch Publishers, 1997) and Cohen, *India: Emerging Power*, 45.

32. Narayan Khadka, "Foreign Aid to Nepal: Donor Motivations in the Cold Post-War Period," *Asian Survey* 37, no. 11 (November 1997): 1044–61.

33. This liberalization was to some extent a direct result of the collapse of the Soviet Union, which had supplied India with arms and some capital goods and bought Indian consumer goods. See Cohen, *India: Emerging Power*, 54.

34. Nancy Jetley, "SAARC: Looking Ahead" in *Indian Foreign Policy. Agenda for the 21st Century*, ed. Lalit Mansingh et al. (New Delhi: Konarch Publishers, 1997), vol. 2, 1–13, and Dixit, *India's Foreign Policy*, 149–50, 241–42. It is worth noting that the two most successful contemporary regional free trade arrangements began with sectoral free trade. The European Economic Community was preceded by the European Coal and

Steel Community, and the Canadian-American free trade agreement was preceded by the Trudeau government's proposals for sectoral free trade.

35. On the Ganga River Treaty and the background to it, see Ramaswamy Iyer, "Dispute Resolution: The Ganga Waters Treaty," in *Indian Foreign Policy. Agenda for the 21st Century*, ed. Lalit Mansingh et al. (New Delhi: Konarch Publishers, 1997), vol. 2, 124–38; Philippe Sands, "Introductory Note, Bangladesh Treaty on Sharing of the Ganges Water at Farakka"; available at www.asil.org/ilm/india.htm (accessed July 22, 2004); Anil Prakash, "Farraka Barrage: Cause for Concern"; available at www.asienhaus. org/wasser/farakka.htm (accessed July 23, 2004); "India's Farakka Barrage Is a Disaster for Bangladesh," posted December 9, 1995, www.cyberbangladesh.org/disastr.html (accessed July 23, 2004).

36. On the Indus Water Treaty, see Biju, *India's Foreign Policy*, 102–4; Indus Water Treaty is at http://wrmin.nic.in/international/industreaty.htm (accessed July 22, 2004).

37. S.D. Muni, "India and Nepal: Toward the Next Century," in *Indian Foreign Policy. Agenda for the 21st Century*, ed. Lalit Mansingh et al. (New Delhi: Konarch Publishers, 1997), vol. 2, 141–60; U.S. Department of State, Bureau of South Asian Affairs, "Background Note: Nepal," January 2004; available at www.state.gov/r/pa/ei/bgn/5283.hgtm (accessed July 22, 2004); "Nepal Asking India for More Power to Meet Shortage," *Alexander's Gas & Oil Connections* 33, no. 2 (January 22, 1998); available at www.gasandoil. com/goc/news/nts80403.htm (accessed July 22, 2004); "Indo-Nepal Agreement on Trisuli Hydro-electric Project, Katmandu," November 20, 1958; available at www.nepaldemocracy.org/documents/treaties_agreements/indo-nepal_treaty_trisuli . . . (accessed July 22, 2004); "India, Nepal Sign Major Deal in Power Sector, June 5, 1997," Rediff on the Net Business News, June 5, 1997, www.rediff.com/business/jun/05nepal.htm (accessed July 21, 2004); Embassy of India, Kathmandu, Nepal, "Nepal–India Relations," www. south-asia.com/Embassy-India/indneprel.htm (accessed July 21, 2004).

38. "Banglaldeshi Row over Gas Exports," BBC News, August 28, 2002, http://news. bbc.co.uk/1/hi/business/2220980.stm (accessed July 21, 2004); "India Loses Interest in Bangladesh Gas?" *The Hindu*, November 11, 2002; available at www.hinduonnet. com/thehindu/thescrip/print.pl?file=2002111204391200.htm (accessed July 21, 2004); "Bangla Keen to Export Natural Gas," *Telegraph*, March 4, 2004; available at www.telegraphindia.com/1040304/asp.others/print.html (accessed July 21, 2004); "Bangladesh to Export Gas to India If There Is Surplus," *ClariNews*, November 12, 2003, http://quickstart.clari.net/qs_se/webnewswed/at/Qbangladesh-india-gas.R40M_DNC.html (accessed July 21, 2004).

39. http://stat.wto.org/CountryProfiles (accessed July 2, 2004); www.saarcnet.org/ newsaarcnet/countryprofile /bhutan/foreigntrade.htm (accessed July 2, 2004).

40. "BPCL, HPCL, Reliance Among Fortune's Big Guns," *Tribune*, July 14, 2004; available at www.iocl.com/print.asp?fol_name=media&file_name=med510&p_title=News percent2 (accessed July 22, 2004).

41. Joe Thomas K [sic], "A Subcontinental Free Trade Utopia," *HIMAL South Asian*, January 2004, www.himalmag.com/2004/january/perspective.htm (accessed July 24, 2004).

42. Kavita Sangani and Teresita Schaffer, "India-Pakistan Trade," *South Asia Monitor*, no. 56 (March 2004), no pagination.

43. Chadha, SAFTA, January 5, 2004; "Pakistan-Foreign Economic Relations," http:// countrystudies.us/pakistan/47.htm (accessed June 11, 2004).

44. "Pakistan–India Trade Improves," Indo-Asian News Service, July 9, 2004, www.keralanext.com/business/readnews.asp?id=41401 (accessed July 23, 2004).

45. Cohen, "The Nation and the State of Pakistan."

46. "India-Pakistan Trade May Boom with Easing Tension," *Daily Times*, undated; available at www.dailytimes,com.pk/default.asp?page=story_8–1-2004_pg5_11 (accessed July 23, 2004).

47. Reza, HIMAL.

48. "Kashmir 'Focal Point' in Relations with India, Asserts Pakistan," *Indo-Link*, July 20, 2004, www.indolink.com/printArticleS,php?id=071904071147 (accessed July 20, 2004); "Pakistan Wants Resolution of Kashmir, Other Disputes," *GEO Pakistan News*, www.geo.tv/main_files/pakistan.aspx?id_30937 (accessed July 23, 2004); Rafique Goraya, "Pakistan Urges India to Take Cue from the I.C.'s Ruling," *Pakistan Times*, July 13, 2004, www.pakistantimes.net/2004/07/13/top5.htm (accessed July 19, 2004); Rafiqy Goraya, and Azka Jameel, "India-Pakistan Diplomats to Meet on Sidelines of SAARC," *Pakistan Times*, July 19, 2004, www.pakistantimes.net/2004/07/19/top1.htm (accessed July 23, 2004); "Terrorism Blocks Free Trade," *Daily Times*, July 21, 2004, www.dai;ytimes.com.pk/default.asp?page=story_21–7-2004-pag2_2 (accessed July 23, 2004).

49. Cohen, *India: Emerging Power*, 93.

50. Ibid., 40–45.

51. Kux, *The United States*, 20.

52. Ibid., 63–67.

53. Ibid., 91–92.

54. Ibid., 182–88, 202–3; Dixit, *India's Foreign Policy*, 75.

55. Kux, *The United States*, 88, 207, 237, 248–57.

56. Ibid., 248, 256–57.

57. Ibid., 248–57, 308–10, 318, 346; Virginia Foran, "Indo-U.S. Relations After the 1998 Tests," in *Engaging India. U.S. Strategic Relations with the World's Largest Democracy*, ed. Gary Bertsch, Seema Gahlaut, and Anupam Srivastava (New York: Routledge, 1999), 40–69.

58. *Washington Quarterly* 25, no. 3 (Summer 2002) included an article on Pakistan in a special issue on failed states. See Cohen "The Nation and the State of Pakistan." See also Stephen Philip Cohen, "The United States and South Asia: Core Interests and Policies and Their Impact on Regional Countries," paper presented at the conference on Major Powers and South Asia, Islamabad, August 11–13, 2003.

59. Cohen, "The Nation and the State of Pakistan."

60. Kux, *The United States*, 78.

61. Ibid., 86, 94, 106, 115–19.

62. Ibid., 161; Foran, "Indo-U.S. Relations," 45.

63. Dixit, *India's Foreign Policy*, 92; Jyotika Saksena and Suzette Grillet, "The Emergence of India-U.S. Defence Cooperation," in *Engaging India. U.S. Strategic Relations with the World's Largest Democracy*, ed. Gary Bertsch, Seema Gahlaut, and Anupam Srivastava (New York: Routledge, 1999), 144–168.

64. Kux, *The United States*, 182–88, 202–3; Dixit, *India's Foreign Policy*, 75 and 105.

65. Kux, *The United States*, 200.

66. Ibid., *The United States*, 306.

67. Saksena and Grillet, "The Emergence of India-U.S. Defence," 158.

68. Kux, *The United States*, 356–57.

69. Kanti Bajpai, "Coping with Insecurity: the Pakistan Variable in Indo-U.S. Relations," in *Engaging India. U.S. Strategic Relations with the World's Largest Democracy*, ed. Gary Bertsch, Seema Gahlaut, and Anupam Srivastava (New York: Routledge, 1999), 193–212; Christina Rocca, Assistant Secretary of State for South Asian Affairs. Testimony Before the House International Relations Committee Subcommittee on Asia and the Pacific, March 20, 2003, www.state.gov/p/sa/rls/rm/18893.htm (accessed June 9, 2004).

70. Cohen, "The Nation and the State of Pakistan."

71. Cohen, *India: Emerging Power*, 282.

72. Biju, *India's Foreign Policy*, 279.

73. Foran, "Indo-U.S. Relations," 43–44; Cohen, *India: Emerging Power*, 282.

74. Saksena and Grillet, "The Emergence of India-U.S. Defence," 151–52.

75. Foran, "Indo-U.S. Relations," 44.

76. Dennis Kux, *Estranged Democracies. India and the United States* (New Delhi: Sage, 1993), 240–49.

77. "Can India Work?" *Economist* (North American edition), June 12, 2004, 67–69; Rollie Lal, "China's Economic and Political Impact on South Asia," Testimony to the U.S.-China Economic and Security Review, Rand Corporation, December 4, 2003.

78. Foran, "Indo-U.S. Relations," 50–51; Jairan Ramesh, "Yankee Go Home but Take Me with You. Yet Another Perspective on Indo-American Relations. 2000." www.asia society.org/publications/ynakeegohome_content.html (accessed March 14, 2004).

79. Arvind Panagarriya, "India as Scapegoat: U.S. Action Under Super 301," *Economic Times* (University of Maryland), June 23, 1989; available at www.bsos.umd.edu/econ/panagariya/apecon/ET/TOI1-Section-301-India percent20as20 percent . . . (accessed July 30, 2004); USTR Press Release on WTO Actions, Special 301 Decisions, United States Mission to the European Union, May 1, 2000; available at http://www.useu.be/ISSUES/wt00501.html (accessed July 30, 2004).

80. Biju, *India's Foreign Policy*, 390–91; Rocca, Testimony.

81. *Statistical Abstract of the United States*, 2003, 812; "Bush Offers Pakistan $3 Billion in Aid," www.foreignaidwatch.org/modules.php?op=modload&name=Newsfile=index&catid=&topic=15 (accessed July 24, 2004); Ambassador Nancy Powell, Remarks, Business Council of Pakistan, January 23, 2003; available at http://usembassy.state/gov/islamabad/wwwhamb03022101.html (accessed August 2, 2004); U.S. Embassy Islamabad, Fact Sheet: U.S. Assistance to Pakistan, June 23, 2003; available at http://usem-bassy.state.gov/islamabad/wwwhusvisit030601.html (accessed August 2, 2004).

82. Center for International Development at Harvard University, Global Trade Negotiations Home Page, Pakistan Summary, http://www.ic.harvard,edu/cidtrade/gob/pakistangov.html (accessed August 2, 2004); Powell, Remarks.

83. Rocca, Testimony; Cohen, "The United States and South Asia"; "Dispute Settlement Update; U.S.-Pakistan Textiles; Anti-dumping," *ICTSD Bridges Weekly Trade News Digest* 5, no. 16 (May 1, 2001); available at www.ictsd.org.html/weekly/01–05–01/story4.htm (accessed August 2, 2004); "Can Pakistan Cash in on the New World Order in Textiles?" *Daily Times*, August 2, 2004, www.dailytimes.com.pk/print.asp?page=story_19–1-2003_pg5_18&ndate=08/02/2004 (accessed August 2, 2004); Office of the United States Trade Representative, Press Release, October 1, 1997, "USTR Announces Annual "Super 301" Review."

84. Swaran Singh, *China–South Asia: Issues, Equations, Policies* (New Delhi: Lancer Books, 2003), 1–141.

85. Ibid., 311–12.

86. Dixit, *India's Foreign Policy*, 62.

87. Singh, *China–South Asia*, 172; Cohen, *India: Emerging Power*, 259; Kux, *The United States*, 88.

88. Singh, *China–South Asia*, 177–78; Thakar, "Coping with Insecurity," 231–32; V.P. Dutt, "India-China: Promise and Limitation," in *Indian Foreign Policy. Agenda for the 21st Century*, ed. Lalit Mansingh et al. (New Delhi: Konarch Publishers, 1997), vol. 2, 236–37; Kux, *The United States*, 163.

89. Singh, *China–South Asia*, 179–88.

90. Ibid., 188–193; Amitabh Mattoo, "Shadow of the Dragon: Indo-U.S. Relations and China," in *Engaging India. U.S. Strategic Relations with the World's Largest Democracy*, ed. Gary Bertsch, Seema Gahlaut, and Anupam Srivastava (New York: Routledge, 1999), 219–20; Kux, *The United States*, 332–33.

91. Singh, *China–South Asia*, 71–99; Cohen, *India: Emerging Power*, 209, 260.

92. Shanghai Cooperation Organization, www.fmprc.gov.cn/eng/topics/sco/t57970.htm (accessed August 3, 2004); C.V. Ranganathan, "India-China Relations-Retrospect and Prospects," in *Indian Foreign Policy. Agenda for the 21st Century*, ed. Lalit Mansingh et al. (New Delhi: Konarch Publishers, 1997), vol. 2, 253.

93. Singh, *China–South Asia*, 129–39; Mohan, *Crossing the Rubicon*, 144; J.N. Dixit, "India–China Boundary Solution Should Reflect Ground Realities," *Hindustan Times*, January 25, 2004; available at www.hindusantimes.com/onlineCDA/PFVersion.jsp?article= . . . /181_547039,00008.htm (accessed January 26, 2004); Jyoti Malhotra, "Sino-India Talks Round 3 on Border in March. Sikkim Falls off China Yearbook," *Indian Express*, February 3, 2004; available at www.indianexpress.com/print.php?content_id=40341 (accessed March 16, 2004).

94. Cohen, *India: Emerging Power*, 179.

95. Trade statistics from http://stat.wto.org/CountryProfiles (accessed July 2, 2004). See also Singh, *China–South Asia*, 239, 319; Cohen, *India: Emerging Power*, 257–59.

96. Lal, "China's Economic and Political Impact"; Mohan, *Crossing the Rubicon*, 156–57.

97. Cohen, *India: Emerging Power*, 260.

98. Singh, *China–South Asia*, 210–27, 338; Mohan, *Crossing the Rubicon*, 230–31; V.P. Dutt, "India-China: Promise and Limitation," in *Indian Foreign Policy. Agenda for the 21st Century*, ed. Lalit Mansingh et al. (New Delhi: Konarch Publishers, 1997), vol. 2, 236–37.

Part II

Macroeconomic Performance and Issues in Economic Growth

3

India's Economic Growth Miracle in a Global Economy

Past and Future

Baldev Raj

India has had the second fastest-growing emerging economy in the world since the 1990s. This sterling growth performance for a large democratic developing country is welcome news not only for its people but also for the South Asia region. According to the conventional view, the sources of India's recent acceleration of economic growth may be traced to policy reforms at the beginning of the 1990s under the government of Prime Minister P. V. Narasimha Rao. His government liberalized the economy by eliminating import controls and reducing custom duties, devaluing the currency, eliminating controls on private investment, and breaking the public-sector business monopoly of the key industries. However, a careful review of growth performance in earlier decades, based on the analytical narratives of economic growth, revealed that it was actually the "transitional policy reforms," introduced immediately before 1985 by the government of Rajiv Gandhi, that created the first major growth surge in India (De Long 2003). These earlier policy reforms produced a structural break in the growth trend rate in 1985 by adding almost three percentage points to the growth rate per year because of their high benefits to costs ratio, or strategic value. During his administration, economic liberalization and policy reforms became ideologically acceptable for the first time. Another achievement of his government was that a few competent industry executives were appointed as cabinet ministers. Nevertheless, it is reasonable to accept the viewpoint that the second wave of reforms of the early 1990s solidified and sustained the country's earlier growth acceleration of the 1980s and improved the country's growth rate by more than one percentage point.

The aim of this chapter is to provide a broad-based system of analysis for assessing the acceleration of India's growth since 1985. This framework, we contend, is sufficient to arrive at an informed judgment about the central question: will the high growth trend be sustained for at least several decades? The framework examines the question from three perspectives: first, a century of historical experience is used to distill the common factors known to have contributed to or retarded the growth rate of countries in the past. The list of factors common to many countries includes major shocks or episodes that create an opening for needed reform, the presence of a popular ideology at the time of change, initial conditions, and traditions. The second perspective, that of unified economic growth and development theory, adapts the modern or neoclassical theory of growth developed by Solow (1956) to explain factors that have produced the sustained growth in the industrialized countries in the 1950s and 1960s. The new theory of growth and development adapts modern growth theory to discern the determinants of growth and development in both developed and developing countries. Above all, it stresses the importance of creating a society that nurtures and supports the vision of a bright future for the majority of families and their children. This perspective focuses on the following three issues: how to create a sustained growth in a country for several decades; how to create growth surge by using the trade and growth linkages in order to access more advanced technological knowledge and business know-how for creating "growth miracle"; and how to implement "demographic transition" by raising the return on investment in human capital by providing incentives for households to make choices about how many children to bear and how much capital to accumulate of different kinds as a simultaneous decision instead of viewing each choice as a separate decision.

The central idea of these three mechanisms of development and growth in a country is that human capital is an invisible force characterized by a "stock of common knowledge," although considerable visible effects may be discerned upon careful examination. The human capital has not only private effects but in addition has large social or external effects on the level of production. The third perspective concerns two practical issues under the heading of "growth strategies." The first issue involves the question of how to kick-start the growth in the short run by choosing economic policies suited to growth surges. The second issue involves the question of how to improve the structure and functioning of capital, credit, labor, and product markets and how to improve the country's institutions, including governance. Good governance is concerned with two goals: (1) to seek the improved allocation of capital, and (2) to encourage innovations in the country. This means solving the twin problems arising from "moral hazard" and "debt financing."

India's growth miracle is valuable as a benchmark for other developing countries that are experiencing significant growth shortcomings and looking for strategies to achieve high growth rates.[1] India's growth miracle has contributed to raising the overall growth rate of the South Asia region from 1.2 percent in 1960–80 to 3.3 percent per annum in 1980–2000. There are a number of reasons for optimism that India's growth take-off and surges of the past two decades will be sustained over several decades for a number of reasons. One reason is that India's ongoing gradual policy and institutional reform programs have remained on track despite changes in governments that have involved quite different political and social values. Second, the reform agenda continues to enjoy the support of major interest groups or stakeholders: politicians and public officials, family business and business groups, organized labor, the expanding middle class, and civil societies. Third, India's social capital of a large, educated, English-proficient middle class of about three hundred million not only has purchasing power but also is ready and eager to create the opportunities for business networking and career advancement necessary to succeed in today's global economy.

Historical Perspectives

One of the lessons of economic history is that one or more catastrophic events create an opening for change in the existing dysfunctional economic system. The Great Depression of the 1930s and World War II created an opening for change in the 1950s in Canada and the countries of continental Europe. These countries chose a variant of *state capitalism*, meaning that the government or its public officials made decisions on the allocation of capital and/or monitored the managers of major corporations. The motivation for this change was that the major private corporations under the existing *market capitalist* system were not fulfilling their social responsibilities. In the new economic system the corporations were to maximize the public welfare instead of the private profits of a few people who controlled or owned public corporations under the *market capitalism* system. These public officials were to make use of state knowledge and industrial policy to achieve the social goals of full employment and a high growth rate in the country based on innovation. This economic system delivered three decades of prosperity in most countries. Eventually, state capitalism failed because of several hidden flaws. One key flaw of this system was its inability to anticipate that once public managers (insiders) became entrenched there would be a tendency to form a tacit alliance with political insiders, thus sowing the seeds of political opportunism. Another flaw was the assumption that state knowledge is superior to market knowledge. The dual problems of high unemployment and high inflation that emerged were in part the result of entrenchment and the assumption that the state has a knowledge advantage. Experience has shown that in order to make the transition from the old economic regime to the new one, there must be a popular ideology waiting in the wings to be adopted at the critical moment (see Yergin and Stanislaw 2002).

Influenced by a variant of *state capitalism* ideology, Prime Minister Jawarharlal Nehru led India down the socialist path in the 1960s. *Fabian socialism* found its way from Britain to India via India's elite link with the London School of Economics. Nehru's government implemented broad regulation and bureaucratic oversight of the economy, which came to known as *Permit Raj.* According to the consensus view, this stifled economic growth or growth got "stuck at a drastically low level" during the first three decades.[2] This rhetoric suggests that India suffered a unique series of disasters caused by bad choices. However, the availability and use of comparable data on national income and growth rates for a cross-section of eighty-five countries made it possible for De Long (2003) to examine this consensus view using data from 1960–92. One of his surprising findings based on his study of comparative growth is that India's growth performance during this period from 1960 to 1992 was "average," and not disastrous as the rhetoric had claimed.[3]

Traditions and Opportunities

Recent research has focused on why some countries get trapped in a regime of poor institutions with a low level of property rights for outsiders while the insiders enjoy the benefit of a high level of property rights. This situation has been termed "entrenchment" by Morck, Wolfenzon, and Yeung (2004), although it is known as the "great reversal" in the financial economics literature (see Rajan and Zingales 2003). One explanation is that the deep factors driving economic entrenchment are historically rooted and hence are exogenously determined. Several researchers have persuasively argued that initial conditions that previously contributed to a country's poor growth rate performance are usually responsible for subsequent poor growth (Acemoglu, Johnson, and Robinson 2001; Acemoglu, Aghion, and Zilibotti 2002). For example, in British North America where the climate was not conducive to large-scale farming and the human capital of the majority of the population was uniformly high, the colonizers created more egalitarian distributions of political power. This political institution in turn created equal treatment for all and provided good opportunities for investment by the country's new entrepreneurs. Moreover, the state spent more public finances on education, and created institutions such as the land grant colleges to make new ideas available to farmers, and the economy prospered. In countries such as India where the climatic conditions led to high mortality among the European settlers, the preference was to make use of exploitative institutions, including high taxes and monopoly rights, to a select number of firms for importing machinery. This practice persisted even after the political ending of the colonial age. Monopoly control over imports of capital goods persisted because it was equally important to the local businesses. The policies of government monopoly of heavy industries, import duties, and other forms of import restrictions helped to preserve monopoly power of the existing business groups in line with the practice in the colonial years.

Recent research on corporate governance has shown that a high level of political influence of a small group of oligarchs on policies relative to larger diverse groups of people who have higher transaction costs for lobbying can produce entrenchment. Other forms of bad policies include high corporate taxes, high deficits and debt, inflation, and inflated exchange rates. Such policies are chosen and adopted by the government as a result of effective lobbying efforts by self-serving organized interest groups, such as business groups, organized labor, and bureaucrats (see Morck, Wolfenzon, and Yeung 2004). Accordingly, some researchers have argued in favor of treating policy choice in a country as an endogenous rather than an exogenous variable (e.g., see Olsen 1982).

Another explanation for entrenchment is the natural tendency toward it as entrepreneurs grow older and more inclined to become less dynamic in pursuing value-creating ideas that benefit outside shareholders. In other words, entrenched corporate insiders come to appreciate the advantage of weak shareholder rights for the larger group of outsiders. However, according to the modern law and economics literature, common law traditions are more likely to prevent the emergence of entrenchment in a country. The reason is that, given the uncertainty of positive outcomes under a common law regime, insiders have low incentive to use legal means to try to tilt outcomes in their favor.

Sometimes even less quantifiable institutions such as social capital can serve to deter insiders' natural propensity toward economic entrenchment. For instance, in countries that have a strong cultural tradition of formal public education, there is a strong possibility that a large portion of the educated middle class will have skills and intelligence to participate in policy debates. This type of policy activism could contribute to reducing outsiders' lobbying costs. Hence, the natural advantage of better-organized and well-financed insiders in influencing policies in their favor would be neutralized to some extent (see Putnam 1995).

Globalization

In the 1970s to 1980s, crises of confidence in the capabilities of governments to manage their economies emerged worldwide. Then, in 1991, came the breakdown of the Soviet Union into separate states. These events created an opening for broad support of free-market ideology in its improved form by many countries. Increased confidence in market knowledge was due in large part due to well-articulated global criticisms of the mixed economy approach in economic management. Support and articulation of this viewpoint can be found, for example, in the 1991 annual *World Development Report*. This report stated emphatically that the invisible hand of free markets is more powerful than the visible hand of governments not only from the perspective of economic theory but also based on historical experience and empirical evidence. Hence, free-market ideology became the consensus among economists and policy specialists.

The key question became how to make a transition from state capitalism to market capitalism. One strategy advocated by some development experts was to adopt the shock therapy approach. The Russian government chose this strategy of reform because it suited their autocratic approach to rule. The government announced deep cuts in defense outlays and other state-financed investments and existing subsidies to consumers and industries. This announcement was made by the leaders with no due process of consultation with the public either directly or indirectly through the Supreme Soviet. Shock therapy failed perhaps in part due to the inexperience of the political leadership, which failed to make a strong case to the public by articulating the merits of the change. In addition, leaders did not apply the proven political strategy of engaging stakeholders in some form of give-and-take compromise in order to enlist their support for change. A second strategy recommended by economists, the adoption of a gradual reforms approach, was used by India to implement the reforms in a finite number of small steps. The use of this strategy avoided the potential for escalating rifts between those who favored reform and those who did not. Of course, the undecided middle group, as expected, could move between the two extreme groups depending on the outcome of the initial reforms. China also used this second strategy in its own dual approach to reforms, with very good results, rather than using the more risky shock therapy approach. The success of policy reforms requires some complementary measures, for example, institutional reforms. This issue will be discussed later in the chapter.

International Governance Reform

The existing international institutional structure is a half-century old and viewed as dysfunctional by both insider and outsider country groups. These institutions are in need of reforms that address new challenges concerning development and provision and the financing of public goods in the new global environment. A related issue concerns how to deal with failed states where threats such as terrorism originate. Another issue is how to handle democratic deficits in various international institutions. There is no shortage of blueprints for reform of international governance institutions developed by various policy institutes and thinks tanks around the world, including the G-20/L-20 proposal of the Centre for International Governance Innovation, Waterloo, Ontario, Canada. While such reform proposals are readily available, a consensus view on the reforms with a broad support of majority stakeholders has not emerged.

Theory of Economic Growth and Development

Three theoretical models of economic growth and development, which adopt the modern theory of growth, serve as the second perspective of our assessment. To make modern growth theory more consistent with the stylized facts of recent growth history, it was necessary to adapt it into a unified theory of growth and development. The first two models to be discussed below are based on the simple assumption that the industrial revolution occurred in some societies as an unexplained given. The first model asks how to attain sustainable growth in the country. The second model asks what sort of economic relationship should exist between countries in which sustained growth is under way and countries that remain economically stagnant. The third model is an attempt to explain the historical fact that, based on data since 1800, demographic transition has already occurred in all countries of the world when they are grouped according to their growth experience into five categories. This model also uses the fact, based on an observed behavioral cross-section, that most high income families prefer to have fewer children and to spend more resources (time and money) on their acquisition of skills. Low-income families, on the other hand, prefer to have more children and spend fewer resources on their acquisition of marketable skills. These three adaptations of modern growth theory are successful in the sense that the new unified theory of growth and development provides an improved theoretical understanding of several key behavioral characteristics we observe in today's world.

The modern theory of growth that originated in the mid-1950s provides a successful empirical account of twentieth-century growth in the United States and of post–World War II growth in Japan and much of Europe. However, the balanced path of this theory, assuming an absence of population pressures and constant income growth, hardly fits the growth experience and behavior we observe worldwide. Our presentation of three models below is aimed at providing a nontechnical summary of the key development mechanisms that is compatible with the length constraints of this chapter. For a more detailed and complete treatment of these models and several other models, see Lucas (2002).

Model I: Human Capital and Growth

This model adapts modern theory for use as a theory of economic development by focusing on one of the key mechanisms of investing in general skills levels by a majority of the population. This mechanism has a long and successful research tradition in microeconomics theory and policy analyses. The strategy of this model is to take the occurrence of an industrial revolution as a given and ask: why does capital r of all kinds (physical and human) not move in sufficient quantity from developed countries to developing countries? How do we reconcile the fact that while the law of diminishing returns is a helpful construct in explaining the allocation of labor per unit of land in pre-industrial societies, it becomes less helpful in explaining allocation of labor per unit of capital in the modern industrial world? It is true that there has been some diffusion of knowledge through imitation of ideas, that we have seen an enormous flow of people and capital around the world in the past, and that these flows continue even today. But such flows in the past were clearly not large enough to distribute the transfer of productivity gains arising from the industrial revolution in the industrialized countries to the developing countries. Hence, the growing inequalities that have been observed in capital accumulation of all kinds (physical and human) suggest that increasing returns to scale are quite important. This in turn raises the question of what makes certain kinds of investments yield higher returns for factors of production when more investment has already occurred. How do we simultaneously square increasing returns to capital with diminishing returns of factors?

By human capital we mean the stock of general skills of the worker. We further assume that all workers have identical skills initially and that they spend a portion of their nonleisure time on current production and the remaining time in accumulating skills. Another assumption is that a worker's productivity depends not only on his productivity (internal effect) but also on the productivity of his coworkers (external effect). The average skill level of coworkers is assumed to contribute equally to the productivity of all workers (external effect). The purpose of this growth theory is to assess the effect of a worker's decision to acquire skills and the consequence of such decisions for the productivity of both the worker and the coworkers, and hence the growth rate of the economy. This model uses a closed economic system with competitive markets and identical rational economic agents (consumers and producers). Finally, it is assumed that constant return-to-scale technology conditions apply.

This model assumes that firms make use of physical and human capital in production but their returns, private and social, depend on the ratio of physical capital to human capital. This model has a constant asymptotic growth rate, making it easier to analyze in comparison with Romer's (1986) growth model, which assumes increasing returns to scale. This model offers new possibilities for understanding why increasing income inequality across countries occurs in a manner similar to that of Romer's model. That is, if we refer to a world with two Model I-type economies, it must be that the richer economy has higher human capital than the higher level of knowledge capital in Romer's model. Another feature of this model is that the external effects of human capital are not needed to ensure the existence of competitive equilibrium.

One prediction of this model is that each country's relative income is dictated by its initial situation. Thus, initial inequality persists, and balanced paths exist in this model. Also, the first prediction survives even when trade in capital goods is introduced. Supposing that there are no external effects in this model, a second prediction emerges: the return to labor at a given skill level would be equalized, which follows directly from the assumption of constant returns to scale. The final prediction of this model is that a given combination of capital and skilled labor will produce more in a rich country than in a poor country.

The external effects associated with human capital are very important, even though they are not directly observable. Notwithstanding this problem, we do know from ordinary experience that group interactions are central to individual productivity involving a group larger than the family but smaller than the human race as a whole. We benefit from interaction with our colleagues and they benefit from us. We also know that this kind of external effect is common to all the sciences and arts (creative subjects). In much the same way as in arts and science, external effects are equally important and present in the day-to-day economic life of the city as illustrated in Jacobs, *The Economy of Cities* (1969). Major cities such as New York, London, Toronto, Sydney, Bangalore, and Mumbai all have a financial district, diamond district, advertising district, and garment district, which confirms the existence of external effects. Moreover, we know that individuals have to pay high rents or high housing costs if they want to live in these cities. The willingness of individuals to pay the high cost of accommodation has to be balanced against the benefits of the external effects of human capital these cities provide them.

Model II: Human Capital and International Trade—Rapid Growth or Growth Miracle?

The aim of this model is to explain the observed fact that most growth miracles of the postwar period have been associated with trade and growth linkages.[4] This is one of the most compelling empirical regularities that strikes those trying to understand growth catch-up during the 1950s. A prominent feature of the spectacular growth successes of countries like Japan, South Korea, Singapore, Taiwan, and Hong Kong has been that these countries began to produce goods they had not made before. Furthermore, they began exporting products to the United States, successfully competing with it and with other European countries. In contrast, India chose to create tariffs as barriers to protect its inefficient domestic producers from foreign competition. This contrasting policy choice yielded average growth rate performance in India at least until the early 1980s when a policy shift came into effect. The empirical regularity concerning positive linkages of trade and growth supports the usual economic arguments favoring trade that were first articulated by David Hume and Adam Smith in describing the principle of comparative advantage. But classical trade theory has been unsuccessful in providing a good understanding of trade and growth linkages consistent with the growth miracles that have been observed since the postwar period. One difficulty in developing a good understanding is that whereas countries such as Taiwan and Hong Kong achieved successful growth miracles by means of a liberal trade policy, other countries like Japan, Korea, and Singapore achieved their growth miracles by means of a heavily managed trade policy environment. In the absence of counterfactual evidence, the issue is whether these countries would have achieved even better growth outcomes had they not used mercantilist policies. Another difficulty is that the application of the classical theory of gains from trade has so far failed to produce benefits from known trade models. None of these trade models has attained a magnitude of benefits anywhere close to that achieved by the trade-led growth miracle countries. Even Model I had no room for the catch-up growth miracle, perhaps because it was constructed primarily to explain the persistence of increasing income inequality. Similarly, the strategic trade model, which uses a two-goods structure with the production of one of the two goods involved in trade activity, failed to produce catch-up growth. This trade strategic model is not presented here but its details along with some other failed attempts to successfully produce trade-related growth miracles are provided by Lucas (2002: ch.1, sec. 5).

This is a human capital model but here skills are accumulated in the course of producing goods. This type of learning on the job appears to be most important for understanding growth miracles, although little is known about the relative importance of different forms of human capital accumulation of skills. This model replaces the assumption that production is deterministic by allowing for the possibility of random shocks to the production. The assumption of stochastic production draws inspiration from Parente and Prescott's (1993) observation that the prediction of the human-capital-based models with constant returns to scale can be interpreted as the constant instead of increasing inequality across countries. Once production is subject to random shocks, it follows that each country's income would depict random-walk-type behavior. Hence, income variance across countries would grow boundlessly. This prediction is a direct outcome of the assumption that the engine of growth of each country is not only its own human capital but also the external effects from the higher average level of human capital of the foreign business partners that accrue to producers of the country. One difficulty with this assumption is that it runs counter to the known fact that the growth in world productivity is largely because of an increase in the worldwide "stock of useful knowledge." To solve this problem, we have assumed in this model that some of the spillover effects of the countries are indeed worldwide. Another assumption of this model is that the labor factor is immobile while capital input is perfectly mobile.

In this model the growth miracle is achieved through knowledge accumulation in the form of on-the-job training in either an industrial or a related organizational setting. This type of knowledge accumulation is capable of producing a growth miracle. The premise of this theory is that the use of trade and growth linkages, as outlined in this model, can create one or more high growth periods in a country. But in order to sustain these high growth periods, the country must explore entering into long-term economic and technological alliances with a few technologically advanced countries for the following reason. The acquisition of skills by workers, managers, and entrepreneurs requires that the average level of human capital of workers and managers for the partner is higher than the knowledge of similar personnel in the home country. Moreover, in order to sustain a high growth rate, workers and mangers must continue to undertake the production of goods that are new to them. This model uses a learning-by-doing mechanism so that it can generate miraculously high growth rates that were realized earlier by several East Asian countries. The learning technology is treated such that everyone benefits from it for the simple reason that it has large external effects. This formulation is convenient for obtaining the competitive industry equilibrium. In addition, firms in the home country must strive to become large-scale exporters of products or services in order to realize large-scale production efficiency.

Another key prediction of this model is that the growth rate of physical capital will be equal to the growth rate of human capital. This prediction fails to capture the convergence that has been observed in a subset of countries or regions where incentives to accumulate both types of capital are present and financed by high savings rates and allocation of time to human capital accumulation. For the world as a whole, income divergence has been increasing, which is inconsistent with the model.

Model III: Demographic and Industrial Transition[5]

Income per capita in 1800 differed by a factor of two between the richest and poorest countries. The problem of explaining differences of this size in income levels was the objective of Adam Smith in his book *The Wealth of Nations*. The central theoretical problem for classical economists was to explain the tendency of per capita income to be at a stable constant level in the presence of improvements in technology. They did allow for the possibility that a stable level of income might differ among countries. They sought a theory that attributed such income differences to differing preferences and not to technology or available resources. The observed differences in ability to produce would induce differences only in population or fertility. Average incomes in the United States in 1997 were about twelve times the average income in India, while both countries grew at annual rates between 1.4 and 2.3 percent during 1960–1997. The possibility of this magnitude of difference in human conditions among countries was never addressed in the writings of classical economists. Modern theories of economic growth built upon the idea of the positive rates of technological change represented by industrial revolution also failed to deal adequately with a change in human conditions of this magnitude. These models assumed that technology either grows at an assumed constant rate or is generated as an equilibrium outcome by the assumption of constant or increasing returns to scale. They further assumed that technological change affects only income and not population rates. The predictions of both the classical theory of growth of Malthus and Ricardo, and the modern growth theory conflict sharply with the following two facts: (1) Output expansion has outpaced population growth for the past two hundred years; and (2) Different countries have remained on distinct growth paths even for relative long periods of time. These two conflicting theories must be unified if we are to understand a world where some countries have joined the industrial revolution and others have not. A general theory was needed that allows to make a transition from the situation of constant and stable per capita income in the face of technological improvements that existed through most of world history until the sustained growth of the past two centuries was realized, at least the OECD and the Asian NIC's countries. Moreover, modern growth theory and its recent descendent theories assume that the population growth rate is an assumed known. The central idea of Model III is that the industrial revolution and the associated reduction in fertility levels, also known as demographic transition, are different aspects of a single economic event. This model provides an integrative treatment of fertility and savings decisions by individuals for the purpose of explaining the transition from Malthusian stagnation to sustained growth. It requires two-state variables: human capital and population per unit of land.

This model has two types of long-run steady-state possibilities of this two-state growth model. One state is a Malthusian-type steady state with a constant income level. The second type is a perpetually growing economic state driven by the accumulation of human capital. The industrial revolution was not even a technological event insofar as changes in technology have occurred throughout history, but sustained growth in living standards is an event of the past 200 years. Major inventions in agriculture, the domestication of animals, the invention of language, writing, mathematics, and so on have all led to increased abilities in producing more goods and services. But these and many other inventions have also made it possible to increase population growth.

Discussion and Remarks

The ability to create new technology in the seventeenth century enabled Europeans to conquer the world and yet this did not increase the standards of living of ordinary people either in Europe or elsewhere. The theory of the classical economists Malthus and Ricardo explicitly predicted such changes as they were designed to explain events up to the past two centuries. Similarly, this was not even an institutional change event that gave legal rights to property and capital owners to transfer or sell such rights, creating another source of income, often far in access of subsistence raising their standards of living. The existence and persistence of wealthy landlords and inheritable property do not conflict with Malthusian or Ricardian fertility theory. These landlords also faced a quality–quantity trade-off. Common sense tells us that this type of change cannot generate sustained income growth because it affects only a few in the country. Also the redistribution of land can reduce fertility for some families while increasing fertility for others. The accumulation of reproducible physical capital adds new possibilities, but it cannot affect a country's long-run growth rate.

The accumulation of human capital can serve as an engine of sustained growth but human capital theories can be little more than older theories of growth that focus on technology. In Model III, a fertility decision is included in the theory of growth and we identify what type of human capital investment can affect the mass of households facing quantity–quality trade-offs, and which type of trade-off is essential for growth. A small group of political elites or aristocrats can produce Greek philosophy, but this is insufficient for starting an industrial revolution in a country. Industrial revolutions can start only when a mass of households in a society faces quantity and quality (utility) trade-offs.

The key idea in these three models of economic development and growth is that a successful transformation from a conventional agricultural economy to a modern growth economy requires an increase in the rate of accumulation of human capital, called "the stock of useful knowledge" by Simon Kuznets. While this point is indisputable, the growth of useful knowledge does not generate sustained growth in an economy unless it raises the return to investing in human capital for most families. More centrally, in order for sustained growth to occur in a society, a large portion of people must experience positive change in the lives that they envision for themselves and their children. Furthermore, their visions of the future must have sufficient force to inspire them to embrace changes in their behavior and attitude. This includes decisions to have fewer children and to prepare their children to exploit the opportunities of the modern world in such a manner that a larger percentage of the next generation will contribute to inventing new and better ways of doing things. In the words of V.S. Naipaul's award-winning novel of economic development, *A House for Mr. Biswas*, development requires "a million mutinies" (Lucas 2002, 15–18).

The Deeper Determinants of Growth[6]

The central issue of our time is the large gap between the world's rich and poor countries. Therefore, it is not surprising that the economics of growth occupied a central position in economics in the mid-1980s. In their standard way of thinking, economists view resource endowments (land, labor, physical capital, and human capital) and the productivity of these endowments, which are deployed to produce flow of goods and services (GDP). Accordingly the growth rate of output per capita is expressed as a function of deepening physical capital, human capital accumulation, and productivity growth. These determinants of growth are endogenous in the sense they are shaped by the development of technology, allocation and technical efficiencies, and incentives and constraints shaped by political, social, and cultural institutions. According to a popular threefold taxonomy, integration (trade), institutions, and geography are viewed as the "deeper" determinants of the growth rate but there is no shortage of other candidates. The role of "trade" as a driver of growth has long been a theme of economic history, development economics, and international policymakers from the World Bank, International Monetary Fund, and World Trade Organization. Trade, or the integration mechanism, plays a key role in creating the growth miracle in Model II. Similarly, institutional economists have long argued about the primacy of institutions in the growth process on the grounds that both higher income and trade require good institutions (see Coase 1998). Moreover, there are good reasons to think that as countries get richer they will need to acquire even higher-quality institutions and will trade more. It is therefore not surprising to find that much of the empirical work on the role of institutions is riddled with endogeneity of the institutional quality variable found in most cross-sectional studies. Moreover, there is good reason to think that there is a two-way interaction between trade and institutions; that is, openness to trade fosters good institutions and better institutions beget more trade. Finally, geography plays a role in determining income because the quality of resources and human health depends on geography. In-depth case studies can highlight various interactions among "deeper" determinants better than cross-sectional empirical studies. Notwithstanding these complications, transition countries like India and China have managed to produce remarkable transformations by developing their unique set of "transitional institutions," that conform to their country-specific circumstances concerning growth strategies discussed later in this chapter, while other countries have failed (cf. Rodrik 2004).

Innovation-Based Economic Growth

Economists' thinking about the long-term or "trend" movement of per capita income, since the middle of the 1950s, has been dominated by the idea that technology is the engine of economic growth (see Solow 1956). However, attention remained focused on capital accumulation because technology is embodied in capital. All other aspects of technological progress were treated as unexplained givens. A newer approach to economic growth theory in the 1980s refocused attention on technological development either through "knowledge" or "human skills" accumulation as the additional factor of production. This approach was motivated by the desire to find a solution to two tensions of the existing growth theory. One tension is that technology advances have continued to occur even though the reasons for technology progress remained unanalyzed. The second tension is that the convergence of both in the growth rates and the income levels of the growth-laggard countries that is conditional on saving rates and technology levels has not occurred. The approach was to include one more factor of production that can be accumulated but where this factor earns not only private returns but also societal or external returns. The incorporation of either "knowledge capital' or "human capital" as the additional factor of production not only helped to resolve the two tensions stated above but provided a newer mechanism for growth and development.

The inclusion of this new factor of production helped to compensate for the diminishing returns of capital with the large positive external effects of the new factor of production to obtain sustainable growth in the long run.

A newer but complementary approach to growth modeling proposed by Romer (1990) has provided one more mechanism of growth and development, which produces perpetual growth based on industrial innovations though intentional investment of resources by profits seeking firms or entrepreneurs. This approach has incorporated two additional stylized facts into the modern theory of growth. One stylized fact is that while the discovery at the individual level is mostly exogenous since the success rate of discovery is dominated by chance at that level. In other words, all valuable discoveries are beyond the control of an individual. At the aggregate level when large numbers of individuals or firms are involved in the discovery effort, the chances of discovering a valuable idea or product increases. The second fact is that many individuals and business firms have market power on many valuable discoveries, and they earn monopoly rent on them. The newer approach to growth theory begins with the postulate that knowledge (or human capital) accumulation takes place in business firms. All discoveries that have high economic value have both private and social returns just as knowledge or human capital has. Moreover, there are many kinds of distinct activities associated with the research and development (R&D) activities carried out by business firms through their focused effort for discovering new ideas of economic value or a new technique. The production of the "blueprints" is one kind of activity with external returns unless they do not have enforceable monopoly rights to produce goods using these ideas. Another type of activity is the production of goods for which the returns are largely private, even though the possibility of imitations of ideas or products cannot be prevented.

A short list of authors who have contributed to this approach include Grossman and Helpman (1991), who extended this approach for a closed economy to a world of international trade, and Aghion and Howitt (1992), who modeled the vague notions of "creative distruction" of Schumpeter. One feature of these models is that they tend to focus on describing activities of inventions and imitations in detail; another feature is that they provide an analysis of distribution of the returns from discoveries. Business firms in this setup are assumed to operate in monopolistically competitive market environments.

This newer approach, known as neo-Schumpeterian growth theory, has enhanced understanding of the economics of firm-based knowledge creation and diffusion processes. The innovation may involve production of new products or organizational change to improve productivity but ultimately such innovations will be supplanted by others through the process of creative destruction.

Moreover, the innovation-based international trade model has uncovered the role of history in the "dynamic comparative advantage" of trade (see Grossman and Helpman 1991, Chapter 8) because technology-leadership tends to be commutative. In broader terms this approach has uncovered connections between (1) trade and growth, (2) market size and growth, and (3) geography and growth. The international trade theoretical model tends to work on the rate of change rather than at the level of technological change.

The empirical support for this newer growth theory is available in the form of evidence from business cases as well as industry-based historical studies. A number of business cases have documented that the interactions among producers and users of capital or intermediate goods have been very helpful for improving the output per unit of all factors of production (or total productivity) in the user industry without making any payment for the improvements. Similarly, a number of historical industry studies for the machine tools, chemicals, semiconductors industries, and others have provided confirmation that firms tend to invest in new technologies whenever there have been opportunities to earn profits from such innovations. Such empirical evidence, however, tends to be less precise, leading to the criticism for its failure to provide some direct empirical evidence at the aggregate level. Caballerlo and Jaffe (1993) have produced some encouraging findings by estimating and calibrating a full general equilibrium model to account for the trends in aggregate productivity growth in the United States.

There are several policy implications of this newer theory of growth but only a select few are stated here. One policy implication is that the competitive markets structure assumed in the neoclassical growth models is unlikely to deliver public welfare automatically. This means that the *invisible hand* requires additional institutional support to deal with economic development problems associated with growth and welfare linkages.

Lastly, the innovations-based economic growth models do not cover all factors that are believed to contribute to intermediate or long-run growth since organization structures or management practices (such as quality circles, just-in-time inventory management) are deemed very important sources of higher Japanese total factor productivity levels prior to 1973 (see Nelson, 1984). The role of organizational change is stressed by Stiglitz (1988) in the context of asymmetric information problems of hidden knowledge and hidden action; these problems are not only an important source of market failures but they are equally central to the source of government (public) failures. One implication is that organizational ability is very important to take full advantage of innovation-based growth as emphasized by Alfred Chandler (1977).

Growth Strategies

The perspective of growth strategy is concerned with two practical questions: (1) what policies are needed to stimulate growth in the economy in the short run, and (2) what types of institutions are needed for sustaining growth momentum in the medium to long run. The two questions in turn are related to the two pillars of growth strategy. The first pillar utilizes a policy reform strategy to stimulate investment drive in the country involving either the private sector alone or private and public partnerships to boost investment in the economy's physical, human, and infrastructure capitals. The second pillar utilizes the institutional reform strategy to acquire missing institutions such as financial institutions and to reform other market-supporting institutions for sustaining a high growth rate in the economy. Together, these two pillars are concerned with the practical aspects of the economics and governance of the development and growth processes.

One sensible way to stimulate growth in the economy in the short run is to motivate entrepreneurs to invest in the economy by expanding the existing productive capacity, producing new goods, employing new technology, searching for new markets, and so on. There are two commonly used approaches to set this process in motion. The first approach views economic growth as the natural order of things in the economy, in the sense of the classical growth economist, Adam Smith, and in the neoclassical setting of Chicago's free market school. Hence, policy reform is needed to set up a fair and level playing field for all, with the objective of spurring productive dynamism in the economy by removing the most egregious forms of impediments to investment in the economy created by the state. According to this view, if the economy is not performing, it is usually because of government or institution failures. These failures may be due to high licensing requirements for investment or other forms of regulatory barriers to investment. Alternatively, failure can take the form of weak-enforcement of property rights or insufficient contract enforcement or some real and perceived biases toward politically connected firms that create dualistic economic structures, and so on. The aim of this approach is to remove some, if not all, of the real and perceived impediments to investment in the economy in order to create a surge of investment activity by private investors. In the early to mid-1980s Rajiv Gandhi's government successfully used this approach for accelerating growth in India with modest transitional policy reforms. Another approach to stimulating investment in the economy is based on the belief that the private drive to invest in the economy does not occur naturally. In order to stimulate private investment one always requires proactive leadership and direct state involvement. Such a hands-on approach is in the tradition of the development economists' strategic approach as articulated by Hirschman (1958), among others. In this approach, the role of the government is either to actively crowd in investment made by the government or to work in conjunction or partnership with private investors by providing incentives in the form of subsidies or tax breaks to stimulate investment in the economy. This approach is based on the market failure view, especially involving imperfection arising from the low-income environment that prevails in many developing countries. One primary type of market failure that prevents private investors from investing is seen as a lack of investment in the nontraditional sectors/industries that are viewed as key to development. Such investment has high social value for the economy. Another important source of market failure is associated with the presence of large-scale economies in some industries. Private investors are less inclined to invest in such industries either because of uncertainty about payoff or a lack of information about its cost structure or the perceived or real inability to raise sufficient financial capital. India used this approach during the period from 1950 to 1980 by directly investing in heavy industries. The choice of approach to be used would depend on a variety of factors; which type of market imperfection is viewed as important; how good the abilities of the government are in designing and implementing an appropriate policy choice; and the nature of existing institutional and administrative capabilities for implementing the planned outlays successfully. Given the history of a low success to failure ratio of the state system versus the market system the second choice is preferred, although this conclusion is at best context-specific. The use of this strategy appears to have achieved only average growth performance in India according to the recent analytical country study using cross-country data from 1950 to 1992 (see De Long 2003).

The issue of what policy approach to use to create a growth surge depends on the conditions prevailing in the economy, including fads and fashions. During the 1950s and 1960s, the most popular choice was to use national planning and import-substituting industrialization to kick start growth in the developing countries. Then, in the 1970s, the growth strategies shifted toward the use of the price system and outward orientation, which was aimed at giving "the markets" a larger role. By the late 1980s, the policy reforms converged to a form of policy advice grouped into higher-order economic principles such as fiscal discipline, competitive currencies, trade and financial liberalization, deregulation, and privatization. By the end of the 1990s, the focus began to shift again, adding more economic principles to the above list, now including three more economic principles: anticorruption and corporate governance, social safety nets, and targeted antipoverty programs. Accordingly, these second-generation reforms were institutional in nature, and hence were labeled "good governance" principles. Moreover, the combined policy reforms-cum-institutional reforms as a package were labeled "growth strategies." The ultimate goal of the strategic growth approach was to acquire good quality institutions that do not violate high-order economic principles. A short list of high-order economic principles included the protection of property rights, contract enforcement, market-based competition, appropriate incentives, sound money, and debt sustainability. These economic principles are aimed at solving the known problems of both markets and government failures that lie at the heart of the Washington Consensus on the policy reform agenda. The long list of economic principles added to the above short list of high-order principles is needed to meet the challenges that arise with the major shift from the state system to the market system. This major shift usually creates opportunities for powerful, politically connected groups, and other opportunistic unlawful people to exploit ordinary citizens. Principles such as anticorruption and good corporate governance, the need for social safety nets, and an antipoverty program take on high priority. The form of good governance may vary from country to country. Growth strategies are deemed to be a set of policies and institutional arrangements aimed at convergence with the standard of living prevailing in advanced countries. These growth strategies are distillations of the operational lessons of long history or experience. They can be viewed as the contours of successful strategies observed based on growth experiences (for details, see Dixit 2004, ch.4).

We now turn to the question of what has been learned from the policy approach to economic development and growth. One of the key lessons based on experience with development policy of the past few decades is that the effect of policy on observed growth is short-lived. The simple answer to this negative finding is that most successful growth spurts in various countries have tended to be context specific. The second lesson is that policy reforms require minimal institutional reforms, and growth spurts tend to be associated with a combination of both standard and nonstandard practices. For instance, a growth spurt in India was attained in the early 1980s through an attitudinal change on the part of the political leader (De Long 2003). South Korea and Taiwan used selective subsidization instead of trade liberalization to generate growth. Singapore used expanding public investment in the economy through tax incentives rather than making foreign investment attractive. The third lesson is that the institutional innovations used by one country are unlikely to work in another country, which implies that attempts to copy the successful policies of another country often fail. For instance, China's two-track strategy was successful but it failed when it was transplanted to Russia because of institutional differences between these two countries. Accordingly, policy reforms should be based on sound economic principles that take into account only local capabilities, conditions, and opportunities. The fourth lesson is that sustained growth requires extensive institutional reforms over time to maintain productive dynamism and resilience to external shocks and to prevent a collapse of growth. It is not surprising to find that only a few East Asian countries have managed to steadily converge to the standard of living of advanced countries.

More sophisticated institutions guide the exchange of goods, services, property, and assets when the exchange expands beyond a small community to city, to country, to region, and internationally. When exchanges take place in a small community, there is no need for sophisticated institutions since the transactions are informal, based on personal knowledge, and not a one-time exchange. Exchanges take place between people who have common knowledge of each other and the products through repetitive dealings, and exchanges are guided by a uniform ideology, along with established customs and traditions. A primary factor that can ensure convergence with the living standards of advanced countries is the acquisition of high-quality institutions. The institution-building strategy for achieving sustainable growth is a cumulative process according to economic historians who view economic history as a study of how to reduce transaction costs (North 1987, 1990) in the economy. Such a focus converts history to the study of the evolution of institutions that have guided human activities based on the carrot-and-stick approach to induce/force socially responsible transactions. In the global trade environment the role of good international institutions and enforcement of the rule of the law are extremely important for businesses to succeed.

Government Failure Approach

In practical terms, several government-imposed failures can negatively influence the investment climate in a country. These failures relate to either the existence of a government high wage environment that can cause distorted market functioning, or high inflation, or/and boom-and-bust business cycles in the economy. These create uncertainty, excessive labor regulations, and other arbitrary regulations that raise the cost of doing business. Excessive licensing requirements that cause delays and corruption contribute to the exploitation of politically less-connected people. Similarly, excessive labor market regulation across Indian states is thought to have contributed to the low labor productivity of workers as a form of government-imposed failure.

India's present minority government of Manmohan Singh is addressing infrastructure market reforms successfully by using public-private partner-ship-type funding arrangements. Labor markets reform is progressing with "stealth reforms" but even this approach is facing vigorous opposition from the coalition partners. But there is quiet determination to keep moving forward with reforms. One way to obtain knowledge about core government-imposed imperfections is to conduct a focused enterprise survey and other related techniques. Once imperfections are identified and verified from a focus group study, the government can select a suitable policy at the margin. A good account of the nature of constraints imposed by government-imposed imperfections and how to deal with them is available from Shleifer and Vishny (1998).

Market Failure Approach

This approach to stimulating growth spurts in the economy is based on three types of arguments. One argument relies on the coordination failure induced by the presence of scale economies. The big-push theory of development, articulated by Rosenstein-Rodan (1943), was the first attempt to model this approach. In an environment where scale economies are important, the economy can become stuck in a low-level steady state. This economic environment provides justification for the government to play a proactive role in coordinating investment in both modern and traditional industries (see Murphy, Shleifer, and Vishny 1989). Another argument is that in the presence of the nonpecuniary learning imperfections inherent in low-income environments, the main issues involve how to adopt an existing technology or how to innovate and create a new technology. This type of learning usually involves some external social benefits. Such imperfections justify a proactive government role that invests in the economy to stimulate growth.

Experience has shown that a second-best type of policy intervention is most effective. This approach, used by East Asian countries in the form of incentives contingent on good performance, has worked quite well. Hausmann and Rodrik (2002) evaluated their type of carrot-and-stick strategy and found that it did work. Overall, the policy used in this approach is unconventional in the sense that its success depends on the presence of favorable circumstances in the country. Moreover, the use of standard criteria is hardly a guarantee that success will be realized, as the experience of Latin American countries has confirmed. The danger of such experiences is that they make a virtue out of institutional heterodox policies. China's success in using two-track policy reforms and India's success with gradual policy reforms are cases in point. The best known case of successful growth is Hong Kong where special preconditions, such as its entrepôt role in trade, strong institutions imparted by Britain, and capital flight from China, played important roles.

The availability of two approaches for stimulating growth can be helpful in framing policy discussions and providing a focus for setting short-term priorities. First and foremost, it is important to understand that the most effective leverage for growth stimulation is a good understanding of local circumstances. Another important point is that there is some merit for consulting businesses to learn where the most effective margins for change reside. This task can be challenging in situations where learning spillovers are involved and coordination failures are blocking take-off, thus making survey results less reliable. One way to address this challenge is to make sure that survey questions are carefully crafted to elicit relevant responses from the businesses. The big-push approach involves many challenges as compared with the government-failure approach. One of the lessons learned from past historical experience is that creative interventions can be very effective in the market-failure approach, even when the "investment climate" is poor. However, the reform program used in this approach can cause confrontations between political leaders and the entrepreneurial class. Second, the success of this approach depends upon having a reasonably competent and uncorrupted government because it requires micromanagement of the economy. Third, although the reform-policy framework of the Washington Consensus program calls for honest behavior on the part of politicians, it is important to understand that even these policies are corruptible when a country's underlying environment permits or supports corruption. It is possible, in principle, to assign rank order to policies but this would require a fully specified structural model of the country instead of the reduced models that are normally used for this purpose.

An Institution-Building Strategy

The goal of this growth strategy is to acquire high-quality institutions so that growth can be sustained over the medium and long terms. In its broadest definition, institutions are formal and informal under the prevailing rules of the economic game in society, according to Douglass North (1990), who approaches economic history as the study of how successful societies have been in reducing transaction costs relating to exchange over time. Institutions provide the carrots (incentives) and sticks (punishments) that direct and guide all forms of activities, including economic activity. A brief account of the role informal institutions will be provided for completeness, but our primary focus for the following discussion is formal institutions. There are two reasons for this type of focus: (1) the relative importance of formal institutions tends to increase as the scope of the market exchange increases; and (2) the use of formal institutions has an advantage over the use of informal institutions because they have lower marginal costs, even though they have high up-front fixed costs (Dixit 2004, ch.3). The larger the markets the more impersonal and complex the transactions between parties, and their knowledge about themselves and about the products and services being exchanged decreases. Formal

institutions can fill these gaps by designing and providing rules and regulations for exchange in such situations, which can often be a single occurrence.
One also needs sophisticated and formal institutions where intertemporal
exchanges are involved and where individuals have to save and invest to accumulate physical and human capital. A downside of such an institutional
building process is that a third party with coercive power is needed to set
standards and monitor the rules. The rise of the state with its unequal means of
coercive power provides an opportunity for interest groups to take advantage
of the state, regardless of efficiency benefits. That is, rules will sometimes
be devised and enforced on behalf of the politically advantaged, even though
such rules do not lower the costs of transactions in the aggregate. Another
reason good institutions may not emerge occurs when the reduction of costs
is not a benefit vital to the survival of the political leader or the oligarchy
supporting the leader. The challenge is that specialization and the division
of labor that goes with growth can produce a divergence in perceptions of
reality and in views of fairness and justice in institutional arrangements.
The conflict arising from this may increase transaction costs. Therefore, the
institution-building strategy is, at best, viewed as a cumulative process that
is seldom smooth.

   This brings us to the question of what kinds of institutions are needed
for growth and why they are needed. The institutions of property rights and
contract enforcement are jointly needed to perform the important function of
creating markets. Property rights eliminate free-rider problems inherent in the
organization of communal ownership. In addition, such rights provide greater
freedom of choice to the citizens of a country by allowing them to accumulate
assets as a store of wealth. Markets for land, residential homes, materials,
and equipment would not exist without well-defined private ownership. In the
absence of these markets, the sale and transfer of these assets would be much
more difficult and costly. These rights provide incentives for improvements,
innovations, and investments in goods and services. A patent on intellectual
property or an idea is another form of property right that gives an author or
the composer of a creative work the exclusive rights to how his/her book or
symphony can be used. These require international agreements on a common
set of rules and regulations. A number of subtle issues involved in reaching a
consensus on the establishment of such rights have made agreement difficult
to reach at the World Trade Organization (WTO). Moreover, despite signing
the WTO agreement, many developing countries do not enforce the rules
with much vigor. This shows how difficult and time-consuming it can be to
create such institutions. The courts, another market-enabling institution for
enforcing contracts between people and businesses, implement the rule of
law in the economy.

One of the lessons learned from the history of advanced countries is that markets are not self-regulating. Markets usually require prudent regulation to minimize abuses of market power, establish product and safety standards, and deal with problems of internalizing externalities and asymmetry of information. These functions are performed by market-regulatory institutions that use a variety of mechanisms to deal with these abuses and market failures. Markets also need fiscal and monetary tools to deal with the problems of unemployment, business cycles, and inflation that are an integral part of the destructive process of competitive market economies. These market-stabilizing functions are performed by monetary and fiscal institutions and institutions of prudential supervision and management. In addition, there is no guarantee that market outcomes will always be equitable for the majority. This calls for market-legitimizing institutions such as democracy (through periodic elections), social protection, and social insurance. It also means that social policies suited to local preferences have both economic and political advantages.

The economic history of today's rich countries can be interpreted as an evolutionary learning process on making capitalism not only more productive but also socially responsible. This learning is embedded in the creation of institutions that are maintained by the government. Good institutions are defined as those that allow emerging countries to sustain growth spurts generated in the short run over the medium and long runs, and to have the chance to achieve convergence with the standard of living of today's rich countries.

The Economic Role of Institutions

Institutions matter because they provide appropriate incentives, impose constraints on the behavior of economic agents, and align individual rational behavior with the desired societal behavior. They provide the carrots and sticks to individuals in society for investing to build physical capital by saving a portion of their current income and to build human capital by accumulating knowledge and skills through education and apprenticeship programs. They encourage entrepreneurs to take risks, and firms to seek creative ways to cut production costs through improving productivity, and designing and implementing business policies, procedures, and strategies to find cooperative and workable business solutions in a given economic environment.

Romer (1998) views growth-enhancing institutions as "meta-ideas" because they tend to be both *non-rival* and *nonexcludable* just as the sciences are. The British invention of patents and copyrights in the seventeenth century and the invention of agricultural extension service in the nineteenth century by North Americans are two examples of meta-ideas. A common explanation for persistent poverty in many developing countries is that they lack objects in the form of resources or capital goods. Countries like Japan, Singapore, and Korea had a little of both but something additional must have been involved relating to their growth miracle.

A key message of the endogenous growth theory is the notion that it is "ideas" not "objects" that poor countries lack. The invention of the transistor by Bell Labs did not yield commercial value until many applied ideas were developed by private firms, which improved the basic science and found ways to reduce the cost of a transistor by a factor of 1 million. Economic growth occurs when people make use of resources (objects) and rearrange them in ways that are more valuable. One of the lessons of human history is that economic growth springs from producing improved quality products using fewer resources rather than from producing more goods with more resources. A useful metaphor was developed by Romer (1998) likening production in an economy to the creation of new recipes in a kitchen. He has argued that growth springs from using better recipes with fewer negative side effects per unit of value of the raw materials rather than from producing more food using more raw materials.

Social Capital and Informal Institutions

One broad definition of social capital includes not only social relationships but also the norms and values associated with them (see Putnam 1995). Thus, social capital is an asset rooted in relationships such as trust and trustworthiness. Trust can generate a joint effort, and a trustworthy individual is more likely to gain the support of others in achieving his/her goals, even when formal relationships do not exist. But trust generally emerges out of networks as a consequence of ongoing relationships. Shared norms and values or shared ideologies can facilitate common understanding and help to foster proper conduct in a social system, thus serving as a valuable resource. Shared values or ideologies capture the essence of the public good aspect of social capital (e.g., see Coleman 1990, 315).

The structural or location dimension of social relations is also important because it provides individuals with an advantage in getting the job done, access to information, and accessing specific resources. The concept of social capital is thus believed to be important at both the individual and the societal levels. It is also important because it prompts individuals and society to behave in ways motivated by other than pure greed and hence it has a public good characteristic. Social capital can thus be regarded as a form of informal institution because it helps to reduce the transaction costs of economic exchange. For instance, social norms, visions, and values that are collectively held by a society can serve as a social capital, which benefits the society. Thus, trust can serve as a governance mechanism in an embedded relationship within a firm, public corporation, or political organization. Collectively held values can serve as a public good in a society, even in the absence of a specific link in that society. It is therefore not surprising that social capital has been conceptually analyzed and used operationally at several levels of economic units, such as firms, corporations, societies, and regions.

Trust is believed to have played an important role in the development and growth of the information technology (IT) industry in India. Trust between Indian engineers and American managers formed as part of their ongoing business relationship in Silicon Valley, where Indian engineers worked in various IT firms on H-1 visas during the information technology boom. Upon returning home, the Indian engineers secured orders from firms in the United States.

Informal institutions such as norms and common goals, and values (see Coase 1998 and Nee 1998) such as social capital, are important for another reason. New institutional economists study the relationship between formal and informal institutions because it serves as a mechanism for reducing the cost of exchange. A lack of close coupling of informal and formal institutions often raises the cost of exchange in a society, while close coupling reduces the cost. The development of institutions, however, is neither easy nor smooth in a society. In some situations the formal institutions needed for growth may not develop. One reason for this is that the creation and development of institutions require a third party with coercive power over individuals, such as the government.

Khanna and Palepu (2004) argue that one of the benefits of family business group firms is that they can substitute for the failures of both "the invisible hands of the markets" and some of the "grabbing hands of the government." A short list of these failures would include the shortcomings of the capital and labor markets in the former category, and the shortcomings of both the regulatory system and contract enforcement because of long delays in the latter category. While this is one benefit of family business groups, hidden costs are also associated with this structure. Under certain circumstances this form can facilitate creation of the problem of entrenchment (Morck, Wolfenzon, and Yeung 2004).

There is ample evidence that the quality and form of formal institutions vary across countries and hence governance matters. One World Bank study empirically evaluated the impact of good-quality governance on economic growth and found that high-quality governance has a significant positive effect on growth rates. A recent study by Hall and Jones (1997) also found strong support for the hypothesis that differences in the levels of economic success across countries are driven mainly by the quality of institutions and policies that frame the economic environment in which to produce and make transactions.

High-quality institutions in, for example, the United States, Japan, Canada, and Europe have all managed to accumulate similar levels of wealth and a high standard of living for their citizens. While a different form of capitalism prevails in each of these examples, in all cases it conforms to the high-level economic principles that were listed earlier. This is good news for the emerging market countries since they need not copy either the legal codes or the forms of institutions in the advanced countries. However, it raises a question concerning whether a "copycat" strategy or "experimentation" strategy is better for acquiring good institutions given the high costs of building them. The former strategy can backfire given the context specificity of the various forms.

Summary and Concluding Remarks

In this chapter we provided a broad-based framework for assessing the past and future growth prospects of India's economy. Based on the metric of this framework, readers will perhaps conclude, as the author has, that the past high growth performance was not a miracle in the sense that it can be easily explained by the known determinants of high growth in all countries. India's high growth performance since the 1980s is a direct result of purposive investments for building human capital, accumulation of capitals, creating institutional capabilities to support functioning of markets, and creating supportive conditions for achieving the "demographic transition." The past high levels of savings in the country and some development loans have helped to finance these investments. Some less tangible factors such as the culture and mores of the country have played a supporting role by influencing the growth rate. A belief in the principles of democracy, formal education, secularism, and diversity, notwithstanding occasional difficulties holding on to these values due to human frailties have played an important role in growth surges in India. The surge in the growth rate was realized when the excessive burden of over-regulation of the private sector was reduced and incentives for investing in the economy to business firms were provided using gradual-reforms strategy.

The long-standing traditions of family business groups belonging to certain ethnic and sectarian groups go back centuries, and new modern businesses often belonging to the same family groups have contributed to growth prospects. These business groups utilize the "trust mechanism" to serve as a substitute for perceived or real weaknesses in the existing political and financial institutions. In recent years, the attitude toward and perception of the migration of skilled citizens, trade (regional and multinational trade), and reforms have changed from concern to celebration in India. The country no longer thinks of skills migration, trade, and institutional reforms as threats but as opportunities. This change in attitude places India on the cusp of great achievement.

A number of observers have stressed that the approach of India to realizing high growth rates is driven by bottom-up activities of the entrepreneurs and business firms. The country has already produced dozens of world-class firms such as Infosys, Ranbaxy, and Reliance. During the last four years, several Indian companies received the much-coveted Deming Prize for managerial innovation. The country has a well-developed private sector as reflected in the fact that at one end of the scale it has large business houses like The Tata Group, a conglomerate that manufactures automobiles and steel as well as software and consulting systems. At the other end of the scale, the country has hundreds of small-to-medium size firms. Several of these firms are growing at a very rapid pace posting gains of 10 to 25 percent a year. Indian success in the IT industry is well documented but the performance of other industries has improved considerably. For instance, in the auto parts industry, the revenue more than doubled in one year, from $4 billion to above $10 billion. Another dimension of bottom-up activity of the Indian economy is that the middle class has been a very important contributor to the demand side of the growth process. Personal consumption of the country makes up 67 percent of its GDP. The country has a sturdy "rule of law" and a well-run financial system to finance consumer durable goods and homes. Indian artists and designers now speak of extending their influence overseas. Movie stars of Bollywood speak of building their audience globally from their home base of half a billion fans in the country, as reported in a major story in *Newsweek*, March 6, 2006, titled, "India Rising." Poverty rates have improved and will continue to improve over time.

In my view, future growth prospects are excellent to achieve an average growth rate of 8 percent per year for several decades into the future, provided the current balance between reality and idealism in policymaking is maintained. According to the much-quoted global economic forecast by the investment firm Goldman Sachs, India's gross domestic product is poised to grow at 7 to 8 percent per annum into the new century. In the view of Montek Singh Ahluwalia, director of the Independent Evaluation Office of the International Monetary Fund, it is feasible to add 2 percent to India's current growth rate over the next two decades. According to Huang and Khanna (2003), the use of a microeconomics development strategy instead of a foreign direct investment development strategy is well suited for high growth rate success for India by the year 2020. In their view, India is well positioned to catch up with China and could surpass it. Finally, according to a recently released blue-sky study by the Center of Indian Industries and McKinsey, India's manufacturing exports are poised to reach US$ 300 billion by 2015. This amounts to a surge of 650 percent in manufacturing exports in various skill-based industries such as specialized automotive parts, electrical and electronic parts, chemicals and pharmaceuticals products, and so forth.

Notes

The author acknowledges support for this research from a grant partly financed by Wilfrid Laurier University (WLU) operating funds and partly by the Social Sciences and Humanities Research Council of Canada General Research Grant awarded to WLU. Rahul Raj, Anjum Siddiqui, and Yash Sharad read an earlier version of this chapter and provided feedback. Zhang Yang and Mainul Islam Chowdhury provided research support.

1. Japan's growth miracle was aided by a national consensus on structural and economic development among those who ruled in the name of Emperor Meiji, and Taiwan's growth miracle benefited from the favorable initial condition of equal distribution of land. It is difficult to imagine how a country can emulate either of these situations.

2. India's national income grew at the rate of 1 percent during the period 1900–1947. The performance of the Indian economy during the first fifty years of the past century was far superior to the last fifty years by all measures, as argued by Basu (2004, 16–18).

3. The explanatory variables in the growth regression included the share of investment in GDP, the population growth rate, and the log of output per worker in 1960. The coefficients of these variables demonstrate the natural interpretations of Solow's theoretical predictions. This regression explains 40 percent of the variation in 1960–92 growth rates of eighty-five countries. One conclusion of this study is that the policy reforms of the Rajiv Gandhi government increased the steady-state value of growth by 54 percent. Another conclusion is that India's growth failures in the first generation after independence were absolute, not relative (De Long 2003, 187–94).

4. Participation in trade may boost a country's economic growth rate for several reasons; first, the firms get access to an enlarged knowledge pool as compared to the position of autarky. Second, the trade helps in acquiring new technological knowledge through contacts between importers and exporters. Third, trade expands the customer base and bolsters home country firms' incentive to undertake more industrial research.

5. Country Group V, comprising the countries of Asia and Africa, entered demographic transition in the late 1990s, implying that this group will reach low fertility and high growth equilibrium as countries in Groups I–IV did earlier. (For details see, Model III; and Lucas (2002, 121, Figure 5.4, 174, Figure 5.9).

6. Openness to trade and institutions are only partially endogenous. Based on a more careful analysis it was found that the quality of institutions is the key to growth sustainability, geography is not destiny, and acquisition of good institutions requires experimentation.

References

Acemoglu, Daron; Phillippe Aghion; and Fabrizio Zilibotti. 2002. "Distance to Frontier, Selection, and Economic Growth." NBER Working Paper no. 9066.

Acemoglu, Daron; Simon Johnson; and James A. Robinson. 2001. "The Colonial Origins of Comparative Development: An Empirical Investigation." *American Economic Review* 91, no. 5: 1369–1401.

Aghion, Phillippe, and Peter Howitt. 1992. "A Model of Growth Through Creative Destruction." *Econometrica,* 60, no. 2 (March): 323–51.

Basu, Kausik. 2004. *India's Emerging Economy: Performance and Prospects.* London: MIT Press.

Caballero, Ricardo, and Adam B. Jaffe. 1993. "How High" are the Giants" Shoulders: An Empirical Assessment of Knowledge Spillovers and Creative Destruction in Model of Economic Growth."*NBER Macroeconomics Annual*, 8:8 15–73.

Chandler, Alfred. 1977. *The Visible Hand: The Managerial Revolution in American Business*. Cambridge: Belknap Press.

Coase, Ronald. 1998. "The New Institutional Economics." *American Economic Review* 88 (May): 72–74.

Coleman, J.S. 1990. *Foundations of Social Theory*. Cambridge, MA: Harvard University Press.

De Long, Brad. 2003. "India Since Independence: An Analytic Growth Narrative." In *In Search of Prosperity: Analytic Narratives of Economic Growth*, ed. Dani Rodrik, 184–204. Princeton, NJ: Princeton University Press.

Dixit, Avinash. 2004. *Lawlessness and Economics: Alternative Modes of Economic Governance*. Princeton, NJ: Princeton University Press.

Grossman, Gene M., and Elhanan Helpman. 1991. *Innovation and Growth in a Global Economy*. Cambridge: MIT Press.

Hall, Robert E., and Charles I. Jones. 1997. "Levels of Economic Activity Across Countries." *American Economic Review* 87, no. 2: 178–83.

Hausmann, Ricardo, and Dani Rodrik. 2002. "Economic Development as Self-Discovery." NBER Discussion Paper no. S8952.

Hirschman, Albert O. 1958. *The Strategy of Economic Development*. New Haven, CT: Yale University Press.

Huang, Yasheng, and Tarun Khanna. 2003. "Can India Overtake China?" *Foreign Policy* 37: (July/August): 74–81.

Jacobs, Jane. 1969. *The Economy of Cities*. New York: Random House.

Khanna, Tarun, and Krishna Palepu. 2004. "The Evolution of Concentrate Ownership in India." NBER Working Paper no. 10613, July.

Lucas, Robert E. Jr. 2002. *Lectures on Economic Growth*. Cambridge, MA: Harvard University Press.

Morck, Randell; Daniel Wolfenzon; and Bernard Yeung. 2004. "Corporate Governance, Economic Entrenchment, and Growth." NBER Working Paper no. 10692 (August).

Murphy, Kevin M.; Andrei Shleifer; and Robert W. Vishny. 1989. "Industrialisation and the Big Push." *Journal of Political Economy* 97, no. 5: 1003–26.

Nee, Victor. 1998. "Norms, Network in Economics and Organizational Performance." *American Economic Review* 88 (May): 85–89.

Nelson, Richard R. 1984. *Technology Policies: A Five Nations Comparison*. American Enterprise Institute: Washington, D.C.

North, Douglass C. 1987. "Institutions, Transactions Costs and Economic Growth." *Economic Inquiry* 25: 419–28.

———. 1990. *Institutions, Institutional Change, and Economic Performance*. New York: Cambridge University Press.

Olsen, Mancur Jr. 1982. *The Rise and Decline of Nations*. New Haven, CT: Yale University Press.

Parente, Stephen L., and Edward C. Prescott. 1994. "Barriers to Technology Adoption and Development." *Journal of Political Economy*, 102: 298–321.

Putnam, R.D. 1995. "Bowling Alone: America Declining Social Capital." *Journal of Democracy* 6: 65–78.

Rodrik, Dani. 2004. "Growth Strategies." Working draft, John F. Kennedy School of Government, August.

———, ed. 2003. *In Search of Prosperity: An Analytical Narratives of Economic Growth.* Princeton, NJ: Princeton University Press.

Romer, Paul M. 1986. "Increasing Returns and Long-Run Growth." *Journal of Political Economy* 94: 1002–37.

———. 1998. "Economic Growth." *Fortune Encyclopaedia of Economics*, ed. David R. Henderson, 183–89. New York: Warner Books.

Rosenstein-Rodan, Paul. 1943. "Problems of Industrialization of Eastern and Southeastern Europe." *Economic Journal* 53: 210–11.

Shleifer, Andrei, and Robert W. Vishny. 1998. *The Grabbing Hand: Government Pathologies and Their Cures.* Cambridge, MA: Harvard University Press.

Solow, Robert. 1956. "A Contribution to the Theory of Economic Growth." *Quarterly Journal of Economics* 70: 65–94.

Stiglitz, J.E. 1988. "Economic Organization, Information, and Development." In *Handbook of Development Economics*, Vol. 1, ed. H.B. Chenery and T.N. Srinivasan, 93–160. Amsterdam: North-Holland.

Yergin, Daniel, and Joseph Stanislaw. 2002. Commanding Heights: The Battle Between Government and the Marketplace That Is Remaking the Modern World. New York: Simon and Schuster.

4

Twin Deficits in South Asian Economies

Observations and Empirical Evidence

Ahmed M. Khalid

The South Asian countries have experienced uneven development since independence. Economic mismanagement has been the root cause of the problems faced by the economies of the South Asian region. Based on major economic indicators, in the 1960s, the South Asian economies performed better than many countries in the Southeast and East Asian region. However, by the 1990s, the Southeast and East Asian economies had outperformed the South Asian region and their growth pattern is believed to be sustainable. On the other hand, a fair assessment of the South Asian region reveals a long period of stagnation. The economic mismanagement of the regional economies resulted in market distortions, inefficiencies, misallocation of resources, and higher income inequality. These internal sector inefficiencies were visible in the system of revenue collection, heavy reliance on the public sector, and oversized governments. The result was a high and persistent budget deficit. A lack of well-developed money and capital markets, a centrally controlled central bank, and a system of directed credit extension through the banking system further exacerbated the problem and gave rise to other issues such as high inflation, low foreign reserves, unstable currency, and a current account deficit. The simultaneous occurrence of deficits in both the budget and current accounts is known as the problem of "twin deficits."

A positive relationship between budget deficits (BD) and current account deficits (CAD) is well documented in the literature.[1] A simple definition of BD and CAD suggests that the budget deficit is the difference between total tax revenues and total government expenditures while the current account deficit is the difference between the revenues and costs of trade plus net transfers to the country. The historical data presented in later sections of this chapter support the presence of both of these deficits in the sample countries. Given the economic mismanagement stated above, one would conjecture that the two deficits are related, which is a testable hypothesis and the main focus of this chapter. We not only test a causal relationship between the two deficits but also investigate the direction of causality, if any. First, however, it is imperative to briefly discuss the economic progress made by these regional economies since independence as well as the historical trend of internal and external accounts.

Twin Deficits: Theoretical Perspective and Empirical Evidence

The emergence of record current account and federal budget deficits in many developed and developing countries as well as in emerging economies focused the attention of researchers on analyzing the problem known as the "twin deficits." Many analysts suspect that these two deficits are closely, and perhaps even causally, related. Indeed, national income accounting identities guarantee that a budget deficit must create either an excess of private savings over investments or an excess of imports over exports. Standard economic reasoning suggests that a shift to larger government deficits entails a decline in government savings and an increase in borrowing, which decreases the domestic supply of funds available to finance new investments. This in turn leads to an inflow of funds from overseas via an appreciation of real interest rates. An offsetting adjustment is then required to establish international account balance. In short, many economists postulate that a budget deficit may well produce a current account deficit.

The link between the two deficits implicitly depends on a dynamically stable savings–investment relationship. A counterargument suggesting no apparent relationship between the two deficits questions such a dynamically stable relationship between savings and investment. An unstable investment and savings relationship might serve to mitigate high correspondence between the two deficits. This leads to the argument that the current account deficit was largely caused by the economy's decline in competitiveness, inability to maintain the national savings–investment balance, and a lack of domestic savings.

The conventional accounting relationship using national income accounting identities may be used to analyze the relationship between a fiscal deficit and the current account deficit. Equation (1) below indicates how domestic output (Y) is divided between private consumption (Cp), private investment (Ip), government expenditure for consumption and investment purchases (G), exports and imports of goods and services (X and M, respectively), and the interest paid on the country's net ownership of foreign assets (r^F).

$$Y = Cp + Ip + G + X - M + r^F \qquad (1)$$

One can rewrite this identity by defining fiscal/budget deficit (BD) as the sum of government expenditure less tax revenue (T), and the current account deficit of the balance of payments (CAD), together with private savings (Sp) as follows:

$$BD = G - T \qquad (2)$$

$$CAD = -(X - M + r^F) \qquad (3)$$

$$Sp = Y - T - Cp \qquad (4)$$

Using the above equations, a direct relationship between the two deficits can be specified as:

$$BD = CAD + (Ip - Sp) \qquad (5)$$

Identity (5) states that the government budget deficit (surplus) is equal to the current account deficit (surplus) plus the excess of investment over private savings. Suppose that the government fixes spending (G), and cuts taxes (T), thereby creating a deficit. Identity (5) indicates that, as a result, either the current account surplus ($X - M + r^F$) must decline or the excess of investment over savings ($Ip - Sp$) must decline, or both.

Having established a relationship between the two deficits using national income identities, we now move to the empirical evidence regarding the validity of such a relationship. The existence of large and highly sophisticated capital markets in the developed countries can provide a substantial portion of funds to finance both public and private domestic needs, and hence, the configuration of private investment and savings may absorb the effect of fiscal policy without transmitting it to the external balance. However, the developing countries lack deep domestic capital markets that necessitate huge external financing for their large fiscal deficits. In addition, many developing countries are debtors whose economic growth is largely dependent on foreign capital inflows and lending. Debts incurred by these nations imply that a large part of their income is spent on debt servicing and interest payments, which leads to a possible deterioration in the current account balance. This continuous increase in national debt can eventually lead to a rise in the budget deficit.

Empirical analyses on this important issue have failed to provide any consensus. Some research has demonstrated that there is no systematic association between the current account deficit and the budget deficit (Miller and Russek 1989; Dewald and Ulan 1990; Enders and Lee 1990; Alse and Bahmani-Oskooee 1992; Rahman and Mishra 1992; Rosensweig and Tallman 1993; McNelis and Siddiqui 1994). On the other hand, some found these variables to be cointegrated (Laney 1986; Abell 1990; Jeon and Lee 1991). Biswas, Tribedy, and Saunders (1992) found a bidirectional causal relationship between actual budget deficits and net exports for the United States using annual data over the period 1950–88. Khalid and Teo (1999) found mixed results using samples of developed and developing countries with more evidence of a causal relationship between the two deficits in developing countries than in developed ones. Leachman and Francis (2002) and Hatemi-J and Shukur (2002) reported mixed evidence using varying sample periods for the U.S. economy. One objective of this chapter is to perform econometric testing using data from six South Asian countries to verify whether there is a causal relationship between the two deficits. However, it is important to examine more closely the twin deficits issue in the South Asian perspective before moving to empirical analysis.

Twin Deficits: The South Asian Experience

Internal and External Balances in South Asia

Although the South Asian economies have slightly different economic models and political structure, they experienced a long period of economic stagnation or slow growth since independence. This economic stagnation gave rise to many macroeconomic imbalances including rising budget deficits and current account deficits, which is the focus of this chapter. It is, therefore, imperative to present a brief historical overview of internal and external balances in the six regions. Such an overview may also help to determine the root cause of the twin deficits problem and to identify any association between them. The discussion in this section is also supported by statistics provided in Table 4.1.[2] We begin the discussion with Bangladesh.

Bangladesh

Bangladesh is burdened by a persistent budget deficit. Expenditure control on planned expenditures is so weak that five-year budgets have exceeded the budget by a margin of some 6 to 8 percent of budget allocation. Discipline in accounting and auditing appears to be lacking. A structural reason for the deficit is also high subsidies to the two remaining sectors, the large agricultural and small cottage industry sectors, which receive subsidies for assistance in price support and controls. Deficits as percent of GDP in the 1990s peaked to a high of (-)6.8 in 1991. Increased debt servicing is one main reason for

Table 4.1

Selected Economic Indicators (1961–2002)

Indicators	1961–1970	1971–1980	1981–1990	1991–1995	1996–2000	2000	2001	2002
Bangladesh								
GDP growth (%)	—	4.15	4.01	4.39	5.21	5.95	5.27	4.80
Per capita GDP (US$)	—	—	164	281	329	331	324	—
Gross domestic savings/GDP	—	—	3.21	13.8	15.3	22.1	20.08	23.6
Fixed capital Formation/GDP	—	—	11.22	17.93	21.51	23.02	23.09	23.16
Fiscal balance/GDP	—	—	-6.8	-5.3	-3.7	-6.2	-6.1	-4.4
Trade balance/GDP	—	—	-9.42	-4.51	-4.37	-3.64	-4.51	—
Current account Balance/GDP	—	—	-3.28	0.07	-0.95	-0.67	-1.18	0.4
Bhutan								
GDP rowth (%)	—	—	7.56	5.69	6.24	5.13	6.6	7.7
Per capita GDP (US$)	—	—	156	147	207	231	—	—

(continued)

Table 4.1 (continued)

Indicators	1961–1970	1971–1980	1981–1990	1991–1995	1996–2000	2000	2001	2002
Gross domestic savings/GDP	—	—	14.2	34.7	28.9	23.4	24.0	24.5
Fixed capital Formation/GDP	—	—	36.65	42.42	41.43	43.54	48.0	48.0
Fiscal balance/GDP	—	—	—	-0.17	-0.86	-3.52	-11.8	-6.8
Trade balance/GDP	—	—	-25.4	-11.58	—	—	—	—
Current account Balance/GDP	—	—	-36.95	-1.68	-7.62	6.10	0.2	-1.7
India								
GDP growth (%)	4.11	3.06	4.72	6.71	5.73	4.20	5.49	4.4
Per capita GDP (US$)	97.82	167.70	314.56	348.37	441.20	467.23	478.20	—
Gross domestic savings/GDP	—	22.3	21.9	23.1	24.1	23.4	24.0	24.5
Fixed capital Formation/GDP	14.8	16.98	20.78	27.0	21.9	21.9	21.7	23.9
Fiscal balance/GDP	-4.15	-4.29	-7.43	-6.68	-5.14	-5.17	-4.70	-7.4
Trade balance/GDP	—	—	-2.26	-1.70	-2.42	-2.60	-2.6	—
Current ccount Balance/GDP	—	—	-1.77	-1.46	-1.10	-0.90	0.3	0.6
Debt/GDP	—	—	47.89	59.83	51.43	55.30	57.31	—

Nepal								
GDP growth (%)	224	2.11	4.11	5.10	4.96	6.23	4.81	-0.6
Per capita GDP (US$)	70	107	164	190	221	233	232	—
Gross domestic Savings/GDP	—	—	10.4	10.9	15.6	18.8	19.0	17.4
Fixed capital Formation/GDP	—	—	17.82	20.68	20.87	19.32	19.02	19.66
Fiscal balance/GDP	-0.42	-2.16	-6.53	-5.67	-4.02	-3.28	-4.51	-3.91
Trade balance/GDP	—	—	-12.43	-16.22	-20.21	-15.25	-13.98	—
Current account Balance/GDP	—	—	-5.21	-7.61	-5.53	-5.60	-6.20	-7.0
Debt/GDP	—	—	—	66.54	64.27	64.57	63.77	54.66
Pakistan								
GDP growth (%)	3.35	4.81	6.19	4.85	3.07	4.26	2.72	4.41
Per capita GDP (US$)	138.86	180.18	327.06	404.85	438.82	426.64	380.54	439
Gross domestic Savings/GDP	—	13.81	13.83	14.81	13.29	14.4	14.6	13.6
Fixed capital Formation/GDP	15.37	15.38	16.96	18.07	15.41	14.37	14.29	12.33

(continued)

100

Table 4.1 *(continued)*

Indicators	1961–1970	1971–1980	1981–1990	1991–1995	1996–2000	2000	2001	2002
Fiscal balance/GDP	-5.17	-7.41	-6.74	-7.67	-6.91	-5.47	-4.71	-4.62
Trade balance/GDP	—	-8.06	-9.31	-5.15	-3.73	-2.4	-2.3	-0.5
Current account Balance/GDP	—	-5.35	-2.91	-4.49	-3.17	-0.14	3.41	4.5
Debt/GDP	33.91	61.96	64.15	—	—	90.00	—	—
Sri Lanka								
GDP growth (%)	8.83	4.39	4.65	5.55	5.07	6.58	-1.45	3.53
Per capita GDP (US$)	153	241	382	607	816	844	820	—
Gross domestic savings/GDP	—	—	14.6	13.9	17.8	17.4	15.3	15.8
Fixed capital Formation/GDP	15.17	17.53	24.91	24.71	25.74	28.04	22.03	22.47
Fiscal balance/GDP	-6.32	-8.63	-10.14	-7.61	-7.34	-9.46	-9.87	-9.0
Trade balance/GDP	—	—	-9.34	-8.06	-4.90	-6.39	-3.53	—
Current account Balance/GDP	—	—	-6.43	-5.46	-3.79	-6.39	-1.69	-2.5
Debt/GDP	—	—	87.25	96.03	92.19	96.90	—	—

Source: Asian Development Outlook, 2003; Ariff and Khalid (2005).

the high budget deficit, which requires more than 10 percent of the income generated through exports of goods and services.

The persistent budget deficits have been financed by domestic issues of the government and agency bonds (and international loans). Unlike the rapidly developing countries, government expenditures have doubled over the past twelve years in this country. Expenditures used to be well under 10 percent, until 1980, while in 2002 it was greater than 14 percent of GDP.

Foreign debt has ballooned over the years. With improvements in reserves and also in foreign exchange earnings from exports and remittances from nationals working in foreign countries, the debt servicing ratio has come down to 13 percent. This augurs well, but further improvements are needed to bring debt servicing to levels below 5 percent in the long run. In this case, the sale of public firms could provide the resources. Further improvements in exports are expected, which will also help. The trade and current account balances continue to exhibit instability.

Bhutan

Bhutan has a record of modest budget deficits mainly due to its attempt to cover its current expenditures with domestic revenues and to finance capital expenditures with grants and soft loans, which are heavily dependent on assistance from India. Although current revenues have been in excess of current expenditures since 1996, the insufficient inflow of grants and assistance to cover developmental expenditures has led to an overall budget deficit since then. Bhutan experienced huge and fluctuating deficits in trade and current accounts with its main trading partner, India, during most of the 1980s and early 1990s. The current account deficit widened from 12 percent of GDP in 1998 to 25.8 percent of GDP in 1999 (Asian Development Bank 2000a).

India

Because of overextended financing by the government to provide capital and to offset the losses incurred by public enterprises, there has been a persistent loss of control in managing government finances in India. This has been exacerbated by the absence of any meaningful tax reforms. The tax reforms implemented as of 1994 have produced some favorable results, but real reform came only in 1998. Revenues are always far short of expenses. Part of this shortfall is offset by the official development assistance from the developed countries while the rest has to be offset by domestic or foreign borrowing. India's consistent 3 percent savings to investment gap has been filled by foreign loans (e.g., in 1996, this was 4.4 percent of GDP). Foreign loans stand at 24 percent of GDP, a level much better than that found in many developed and developing countries. India has also resorted to public sector borrowing, which has led to the ballooning of domestic debt to about 20 percent of GDP. In addition, the country also has international debts for loans taken under multilateral lending for development.

The external sector also enjoyed some far-reaching reforms in the 1990s. As a result of these reforms and with the removal of all restrictions for currency convertibility on producers in March 1993, the external sector experienced a substantial improvement. Later, in July 1994, the currency became fully convertible satisfying Article 8 of the International Monetary Fund (IMF). While capital accounts were liberalized, there are still controls on capital accounts of the nonexporting domestic firms (*Economic Times* 2004).

Nepal

During the 1980s, gross domestic savings (as a percentage of GDP) in Nepal registered on average a mere 11 percent, with a slight improvement to 12 percent in the first half of the 1990s. Gross domestic investment (as a percentage of GDP) averaged about 19 percent during the 1980s and rose to about 21 percent in the first half of the 1990s. By 2002, the two indicators were around 17 percent and 20 percent, respectively. This imbalance leaves a large resource gap ranging from 8 percent in the 1980s to about 11 percent in 1996. The first three years of this decade witnessed huge deficits in the fiscal sector with a peak of 11.8 percent (of GDP) in 2001 (World Bank 2003). With insufficiently developed (or mobilized) domestic resources, most of these fiscal deficits are financed through foreign financing. As a result, debt servicing increased from 18 percent in the 1980s to 38 percent in the 1990s. At the same time, Nepal's export performance is not promising and has resulted in large trade deficits (recorded at 14 percent of GDP in 2001). The current account has also shown a similar picture with a deficit of around 6 percent over the past ten years (Asian Development Bank 2000b). Part of the reason for this trend of high imbalances is sociopolitical factors, which are discussed elsewhere in this chapter.

Pakistan

Pakistan faced severe economic and financial difficulties during the 1990s. The very high indebtedness that arose from pursuing a twin policy of subsidies to some sectors and high defense spending brought only negative results: debt soared and inefficiency persisted. Severe fiscal and external imbalances and a very high debt-service ratio worked jointly to create a vicious circle where the absence of an efficient revenue collection mechanism left no choice but to borrow from domestic and external sources to meet mounting government spending. Despite the assurances and securities provided, investor confidence did not improve given the continued political instability.

In the external sector, the country faced three basic problems: (1) declining remittances from nationals working abroad; (2) reduced demand for exports; and (3) a huge allocation of funds for debt servicing. Foreign debt in 1999 stood at US$29.0 billion, which was 44.5 percent of GDP. Although efforts were made to accelerate exports, this sector remained sluggish and continued to worsen with a decline of 2.7 percent in 1997 (Government of Pakistan).

Fiscal balances showed a major improvement since 1991–96, when they reached a peak budget deficit of 7.7 percent of GDP, to 4.6 percent of GDP in 2002. Part of this was attributed to pressure from the IMF and the World Bank under their adjustment programs. The fiscal sector received a reform package aimed at raising money. A lack of fiscal discipline emerged as a serious management problem. The government also implemented supply-side policies with the objective of reducing tax rates while broadening the tax base, and policies were devised to reduce expenses. One priority was to reduce expenses in the services sector operated under federal or provincial governments. Policies were formulated and implemented as per the IMF requirement to gradually curtail worsening fiscal deficits: to get to 4 percent of GDP from around 7 percent. Due to political instability, some of these policies were unable to achieve the objectives envisaged earlier.

The external account showed significant improvement with the trade deficit moving from a high of 12.6 percent of GDP in 1984 to 0.5 percent of GDP in 2002. Similarly, the current account balance moved from a deficit in 2000 to a surplus in 2001. The 2003 figures showed further improvement in the current account balance to GDP ratio, from 4.8 percent in fiscal year 2002 to 5.9 percent in fiscal year 2003. This was mainly due to a record increase in exports of US$11.1 billion and a further record of US$4.2 billion in inward remittances. These statistics are consistent with the twin deficit hypothesis in which a decline in both the fiscal and the current account deficits is averted over time by reforms.

High indebtedness remained a major bottleneck for economic growth. Total external debt has increased from US$15 billion in 1991 to US$26 billion by 2001. Debt servicing consumed around 21 percent of export earnings in 2001. This amount would be more than enough to fund the budget necessary for educational improvements to provide the population with the applied skills that are badly needed for Pakistan's potential industrialization. The total debt (i.e., domestic and foreign) is 95.1 percent of GDP (and about 600 percent of total revenues) with almost 66 percent of the total revenues used for debt servicing. The country registered a record high level of external debt of Rs1.787 trillion (around US$30 billion) in May 2003 (*Dawn* 2003). Total magnitude amounts to about US$55 billion, of which US$30.0 billion is external debt.

Sri Lanka

Since independence and up to the end of the 1980s, spending on public sector development was the main area of government concern. It was only recently that the private sector was encouraged to become involved in these activities to help relieve some of the burden on public sector spending. Relatively large government spending amounted to an average 30 percent of GDP over the past ten years with an average annual increase of about 18 percent. Compared with the large share of public expenditure in GDP during the 1970s, total revenues accounted for only 20 percent, which further declined to 19 percent in 1996. The economic reform package of 1977 introduced some measures to improve the taxation structure. At the time, the government introduced a goods and services tax (GST), a diesel and luxury tax on vehicles, and a turnover tax on imports.

In the external sector, total trade as a percentage of GDP increased to 68 percent in 1996 as compared with 35 percent in 1977. The major policy changes in the external sector were the unification of the exchange rate and the adoption of a managed float system in 1977, opening up of the current account, changes in the tariff structure, quantitative restrictions, and export licensing requirements.

One important issue in external sector policy is mounting external debt, which accounted for 34 percent of GDP in 1978 but rose to 57 percent in 1988, later moderating to 49 percent of GDP in 1996. The debt-service ratio as a percentage of GDP accounts for 10.3 percent.

The Historical Trend of Twin Deficits in South Asia

Figures 4.1a–4.1f show the historical trend of the two deficits in six South Asian countries. In Figure 4.1a, the data for Bangladesh show an association between the two deficits until the mid-1980s. However, there does not seem to be any apparent relationship between the two deficits from 1986 onward. The graphs in Figure 4.1b for Bhutan also negate any correlation between the two deficits where CAD is subject to large variations. Figure 4.1c, however, depicts a different picture for India where the two series seem to be closely related. Thus econometric testing is necessary to determine whether this relationship is statistically significant, and, if so, the direction of such causality. Figure 4.1d for Nepal shows a similar pattern where the two deficits move together for most of the period with the exception of a few years in the 1990s. Figure 4.1e for Pakistan and 4.1f for Sri Lanka provide a clear picture that the two

Figure 4.1a   **Budget Deficits and Current Account Deficits in Bangladesh**
(1976–2002)

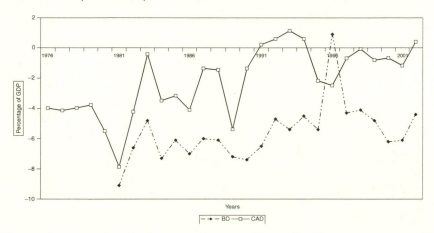

Figure 4.1b.   **Budget Deficits and Current Account Deficits in Bhutan**
(1981–2002)

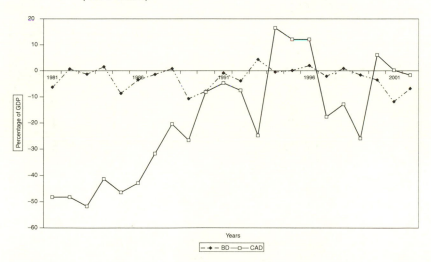

deficits are closely related during the sample period under study. In summary, these figures suggest that there may be evidence to support twin deficits for India, Nepal, Pakistan, and Sri Lanka. However, our hypothesis is that no such relationship exists for Bangladesh and Bhutan. We now turn to an empirical estimation of our model to verify these hypotheses.

Figure 4.1c.   **Budget Deficits and Current Account Deficits in India**
(1961–2002)

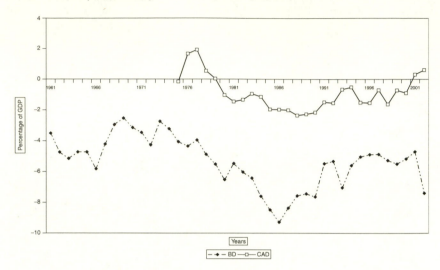

Figure 4.1d.   **Budget Deficits and Current Account Deficits in Nepal**
(1961–2002)

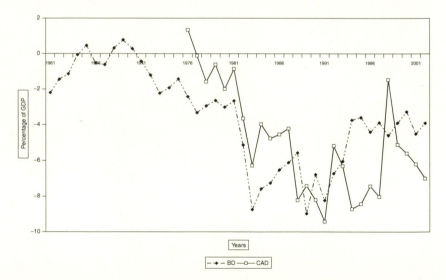

Twin Deficits in South Asian Economies: Econometric Analysis

In view of the proposition postulated in the previous section, the objective
of this section is to examine the validity of the twin deficit hypothesis using

Figure 4.1e.   **Budget Deficits and Current Account Deficits in Pakistan**
(1961–2002)

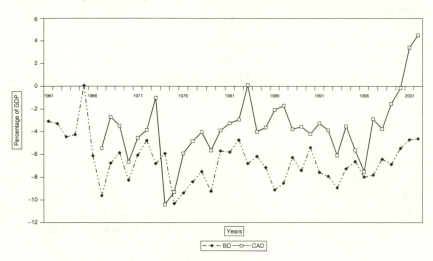

Figure 4.1f.   **Budget Deficits and Current Account Deficits in Sri Lanka**
(1961–2002)

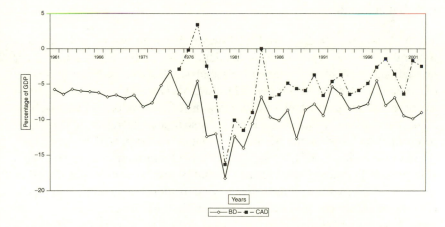

time series data for our sample of six South Asian countries. In this exercise we not only examine the empirical validity of the twin deficits hypothesis for our sample of South Asian countries but also determine the direction of causality. The findings of this empirical analysis will help to formulate appropriate policies for some countries facing the tremendous problem of budget and current account deficits. These empirical tests will also provide cross-country comparisons regarding the presence of any long-run relationship between the two deficits.

Methodology and Data

The standard methodology used in the empirical analysis is well known and may not require an elaborate explanation. First, we use augmented Dickey-Fuller (ADF) and Phillip-Perron (PP) testing to identify the order of integration in the series. The Johansen and Juselius (1990) maximum likelihood method is then used to identify the number of cointegrating vectors. The next step is to form an error correction model (ECM) to see the short-run dynamics and the long-run relationship simultaneously. Granger causality tests are then applied in both single equation and vector autoregressive (VAR) to identify the causal relationship and its direction between the two deficits for the sample countries.

We examine the long-term relationship between the current account deficit and budget deficit in six South Asian countries. Data for this analysis are annual, ranging from 1960 to 2004 (or as specified in Table 4.1). Because the variables are scaled relative to GNP, we use CAD to denote the ratio of current account deficit to GDP and BD to denote the ratio of budget deficit to GDP. The data are taken from the IMF-IFS-CDROM.

Empirical Results

The first step in testing a causal relationship between two or more series is to test the time series properties of the data. First, we test the stationarity (or nonstationarity) of the series used in this analysis. Table 4.2 provides the results of the unit root test for both series (BD and CAD) for all six sample countries. These results suggest that all series are first-difference stationary based on both ADF statistics and PP statistics.[3] Table 4.2 also reports the results of lag-length determination based on the Aikake information criterion (AIC).

Since the series are I(1), we need to test whether they are cointegrated. This is important in determining whether causality tests should be performed in levels or first difference. If the series have unit roots but are not cointegrated then the causality test will be performed in first difference. However, if the series have unit roots and are cointegrated, then we will perform the causality tests in levels or will develop an error-correction model to determine the presence and direction of a causal relationship between the two series. We use Johansen's likelihood ratio test method to test for cointegration. The results are reported in Table 4.3. These results suggest that the two series (BD and CAD) are not cointegrated for Bangladesh, Bhutan, and Pakistan. The series show a long-term relationship (are cointegrated) for India and Sri Lanka, because the

Table 4.2

Unit Root Test Results (first difference)

Country	Period	Specification	Lag-length	DF/ADF	PP
Budget deficit (% of GDP)					
Bangladesh	1981–2002	Constant, Trend	$K = 1$	–4.35**	–7.72*
Bhutan	1981–2002	No constant; no trend	$K = 1$	–4.15*	–2.98*
India	1975–2002	Constant; no trend	$K = 1$	–3.80*	–5.61*
Nepal	1976–2002	Constant; no trend	$K = 1$	–3.26**	–5.78*
Pakistan	1967–2002	Constant; no trend	$K = 1$	–5.46*	–8.48*
Sri Lanka	1975–2002	Constant; no trend	$K = 4$	–6.02*	–8.36*
Current account deficit (% of GDP)					
Bangladesh	1981–2002	Constant, trend	$K = 1$	–5.51*	–5.26*
Bhutan	1981–2002	Constant, trend	$K = 1$	–4.54*	–6.43*
India	1975–2002	No constant; no trend	$K = 2$	–2.42**	–5.55*
Nepal	1976–2002	Constant; trend	$K = 3$	–5.41*	–7.48*
Pakistan	1967–2002	Constant; trend	$K = 1$	–5.85*	–2.87
Sri Lanka	1975–2002	Constant; no trend	$K = 1$	–4.33*	–6.24*

Note: The asterisks * and ** represent rejection of the null hypothesis of nonstationarity time series at the 1 percent and 5 percent significance levels, respectively.

null of no cointegration cannot be rejected at the 5 percent level. The results are lag-length sensitive for Nepal. If a single lag is used, the data do not support any cointegration among the two series. However, there is evidence of cointegration if a lag length of 3 is used. Based on these results, further tests of Granger causality for Bangladesh, Bhutan, and Pakistan are performed using data in first difference, while tests for India and Sri Lanka are based on levels. We use both level and first-difference data for Nepal. We also use an ECM for India, Nepal, and Sri Lanka to test for Granger causality.

Table 4.3

Johansen Cointegration Test (variables: DB/GDP, CAD/GDP)

Eigenvalue	Likelihood ratio	Critical values 5%	1%	Hypothesized no. of cointegration equations
Bangladesh				
0.535 (*k* = 1)	21.54	25.32	30.45	None
0.268	6.241	12.25	16.26	At most 1
Bhutan				
0.224 (*k* = 1)	8.357	12.53	16.31	None
0.152	3.287	3.84	6.51	At most 1
India				
0.482 (*k* = 1)	18.684**	15.41	20.04	None
0.085	2.230	3.76	6.65	At most 1
0.428 (*k* = 2)	18.722**	15.41	20.04	None
0.178	4.176**	3.76	6.65	At most 1
Nepal				
0.205 (*k* = 1)	8.758	15.41	20.04	None
0.114	3.018	3.76	6.65	At most 1
0.783 (*k* = 3)	15.931**	15.41	20.04	None
0.448	6.628**	3.76	6.65	At most 1
Pakistan				
0.308 (*k* = 1)	15.371	15.41	20.04	None
0.081	2.865	3.76	6.65	At most 1
Sri Lanka				
0.443 (*k* = 1)	19.434**	15.41	20.04	None
0.150	4.219**	3.76	6.65	At most 1
0.492 (*k* = 4)	19.620**	15.41	20.04	None
0.161	4.039**	3.76	6.65	At most 1

Note: The asterisks * and ** denote the 1 percent and 5 percent significance levels, respectively.

The first set of causality results is summarized in Table 4.4. These results do not support any causal relationship between BD and CAD for Bangladesh and Bhutan. Assuming a single lag length for Nepal when the series are not cointegrated, also suggests no evidence of any causal relationship between BD and CAD. However, the results suggest that in Pakistan budget deficits are

Table 4.4

Tests of Granger Causality

Country	Level/first difference	Unidirectional causality BD → CAD	Reverse causality CAD → BD	Bidirectional causality BD ↔ CAD
Bangladesh	First diff	0.06904	0.09113	—
Bhutan	First diff	0.05798	0.42169	—
India (k = 1)	Level	4.04715*	0.10361	BD → CAD
India (k = 2)	Level	6.00559*	0.08063	BD → CAD
Nepal (k = 1)	First diff	0.04653	1.77412	—
Nepal (k = 4)	Level	0.25912	0.82924	—
Pakistan	First diff	0.09871	8.89789*	CAD → BD
Sri Lanka (k = 3)	Level	1.80285	3.95910*	CAD → BD
Sri Lanka (k = 3)	Level	1.94225	2.45370***	CAD → BD

Note: The asterisks *, **, and *** represent statistical significance of F-test statistics at the 1 percent, 5 percent, and 10 percent levels, respectively.

caused by current account deficits. This makes sense, given Pakistan's history of very high debt service ratio, which consumes most of the revenues generated domestically and leaves just a small amount to meet public expenditure. A similar pattern emerges for Sri Lanka where BD is caused by high CAD, irrespective of the lag length. On the contrary, the results in Table 4.3 suggest that in India, it is CAD that influences BD. Again this result for India is valid when two different lag lengths are used. We find no evidence of bidirectional causality in our sample countries. We also perform Granger causality test using VARs, and the results are reported in Table 4.5. These results support the same evidence reported above.

These results clearly suggest that BD and CAD in the South Asian region are either independent or unidirectional (either CAD to BD or BD to CAD). The conventional wisdom explaining the relationship between the twin deficits is definitely not compatible with the evidence that we have obtained. This is not unexpected because, as we pointed out earlier, the conventional theory ignores many other macro policies that may also influence the value of domestic currency, its competitiveness, and hence, the current account balance. Clearly, the contemporary view of the twin deficits connection is more compatible with the results we have obtained and it better illustrates the complex interdependencies that link the current account and budget deficits to each

Table 4.5

Tests of Granger Causality (in VARs)

Bangladesh

Effect → Cause (↓)	D(BD)	D(CAD)
D(BD)	—	0.17
D(CAD)	0.39	—

Bhutan

Effect → Cause (↓)	D(BD)	D(CAD)
D(BD)	—	0.19
D(CAD)	0.52	—

India

Effect → Cause (↓)	BD	CAD
BD	—	8.96**
CAD	1.08	—

Nepal

Effect → Cause (↓)	BD	CAD
BD	—	0.30
CAD	5.06*	—

Pakistan

Effect → Cause (↓)	BD	CAD
BD	—	0.62
CAD	12.27***	—

Sri Lanka

Effect → Cause (↓)	BD	CAD
BD	—	4.71**
CAD	10.07	—

Note: The asterisks *, **, and *** represent rejection of Granger noncausality at the 10 percent, 5 percent, and 1 percent levels, respectively.

other, to other macroeconomic variables, and to structural conditions.

These results are not surprising given the lack of sophisticated domestic capital markets and low savings in most of these developing countries, which necessitates foreign financing for the largest proportion of their fiscal deficits. Private sources of funds in normal times in these developing countries could provide financing for both public and domestic needs, and at the same time the country could even be a net lender abroad. In addition, most developing countries are debt-ridden and future servicing of debts and interest payments may lead to an impending deterioration of the current account balance.

Concluding Remarks

This chapter has empirically examined the twin deficits argument that rising fiscal deficits were the primary cause of the recent surge in current account deficits in many countries. Using a sample of six South Asian countries, the chapter analyzed the issue of twin deficits in a comprehensive manner. Besides some empirical estimation of the twin deficits hypothesis, the chapter also discussed at length the historical economic performance of these six economies. It is interesting to note that many of the six economies showed a reasonable economic growth pattern in the 1960s but were unable to maintain it in later years. As a result of macroeconomic mismanagement, the whole region has been unable to achieve what South Asia has done in only a couple of decades. One major cost of this low growth (or no growth) is rising imbalances in the internal and external account, namely, budget deficits and current account deficits. The chapter analyzed the issue of twin deficits both theoretically and empirically in the South Asian context.

Specifically, econometric testing was performed to analyze a long-run equilibrium relationship between the two deficits. The empirical results of this study show that such a relationship exists in four of the six regional economies. When compared with other empirical research for developed countries, these results suggest that a high correspondence between the two deficits in the long run is more likely to occur in the developing countries than in the developed ones. These results may be justified in view of the lack of a deep and sophisticated domestic capital market to finance the fiscal deficit in developing countries. Therefore, the countries studied here have to rely more on external financing leading to an inevitable rise in the external balance deficit. In addition, future servicing of debts may exacerbate the deteriorating current account deficit.

The results of Granger causality testing suggest that a predominant direction of causality may run from the current account deficit to the budget deficit, unlike what most standard analyses would assume. This is true for Nepal,

Pakistan, and Sri Lanka. Perhaps, the opposite is possible when a deteriorating current account deficit leads to a slower growth of national income and hence, an increased budget deficit.

Many economists have argued that the way to reduce chronic current account deficits is to raise national saving by reducing the budget deficit and increasing the rate of private saving. However, the unidirectional causal relation running from the current account deficit to the budget deficit suggests that one simply cannot rely only on curtailing the federal budget deficit in an attempt to trim the current account deficit. Thus, the federal budget cannot be treated as a fully controlled policy variable. Although discretionary fiscal policy has important macroeconomic implications, one cannot ignore the budgetary implications of exogenous changes in foreign trade variables. The trade balance, which results from exogenous factors, affects the budget balance. We believe that a real solution to the problem of fiscal deficits and current account imbalances lies with a coherent package consisting of both fiscal and monetary policies. Policy measures focusing on improved productivity, exchange rate, and monetary policy will complement a policy of budget cuts.

Notes

1. Some of this literature is briefly discussed in the following section of this chapter.

2. We restrict our discussion here to the issue of twin deficits and do not elaborate on the overall economic performance of these economies over the past five decades. More country-specific details may be found in Ariff and Khalid (2000).

3. While we tested in both levels and first differences, only first-difference results are reported here.

References

Abell, John D. 1990., "Twin Deficits during the 1980s: An Empirical Investigation." *Journal of Macroeconomics* 12, no. 1: 81–96.

Alse, J., and M. Bahmani-Oskooee. 1992. "Are the Twin Deficits Really Related? A Comment." *Contemporary Policy Issues* 10, no. 1: 108–11.

Ariff, M., and Ahmed M. Khalid. 2000. *Liberalization, Growth and the Asian Financial Crisis: Lessons for Developing and Transitional Economies in Asia*. London: Edward Elgar.

———. 2005. *Liberalization and in Asia: 21st Century Challenges*. London: Edward Elgar.

Asian Development Bank. 2000a. Country Assistance Plan: Bhutan (2001–2003). Manila.

———. 2000b. Country Assistance Plan: Nepal (2001–2003). Manila.

Biwas, B.; G. Tribedy; and P. Saunders. 1992. "Further Analysis of the Twin Deficits." *Contemporary Policy Issues* 10, no. 1: 104–8.

Dawn. 2003. Dawn Internet Edition, Pakistan, www.dawn.com.

Dewald, William G., and Michael Ulan. 1990. "The Twin Deficits Illusion." *Cato Journal* 9, no. 3: 689–707.

Economic Times. 2004. "India's Not the Only Nation with Huge Budget Deficits." *Economic Times* Online Edition, January 26, http://economictimes.indiatimes.com.

Enders, Walter, and Bong Soo Lee. 1990. "Current Account and Budget Deficits: Twins or Distant Cousins?" *Review of Economics and Statistics* 72, no. 3: 373–81.

Engle R.F., and C.W.J. Granger. 1987. "Cointegration and Error Correction: Representation, Estimation and Testing." *Econometrica* 55: 251–76.

Government of Pakistan, Ministry of Finance. Internet reports, www.finance.gov.pk.

Hatemi-J, Abdulnasser, and Ghazi Shukur. 2002. "Multivariate-based Causality Tests of Twin Deficits in the US." *Journal of Applied Statistics* 29, no. 6: 817–24.

International Monetary Fund. International Financial Statistics. IMF-IFS-CDROM.

Jeon, Bang Nam, and Daniel Y. Lee. 1991. "The Twin Deficits in the Government Budget and the Trade Deficit." In *Pennsylvania Economic Association: Proceedings of the Sixth Annual Meeting*, ed. Stanley G. Long. Johnstown, PA: University of Pittsburgh.

Johansen, S., and K. Juselius. 1990. "Maximum Likelihood Estimation and Inference on Cointegration: With Application to the Demand for Money." *Oxford Bulletin of Economics and Statistics* 52: 169–210.

Khalid, Ahmed M., and Teo Wee Guan. 1999. "Causality Tests of Budget and Current Account Deficits: Cross-Country Comparisons." *Empirical Economics* 24, no. 3 (August): 389–402.

Laney, Leroy O. 1986. "Twin Deficits in the 1980s. What Are the Linkages?" *Business Economics* 21, no. 2: 40–45.

Leachman, Lori L., and Bill Francis. 2002. "Twin Deficits: Apparition or Reality." *Applied Economics* 34: 1121–32.

McNelis, Paul D., and A. Siddiqui. 1994. "Debt and Deficit Dynamics in New Zealand: Did Financial Liberalization Matter?" *International Economic Journal* 8, no. 3: 71–87.

Miller, Stephen M., and Frank S. Russek. 1989. "Are the Twin Deficits Really Related?" *Contemporary Policy Issues* 7, no. 4: 112–13.

Perron, P. 1992. "Trend, Unit Root and Structural Change: A Multi-Country Study with Historical Data." *Proceedings of the American Statistical Association, Business and Economic Statistics Section*, 144–49.

Rahman, Matiur, and Banamber Mishra. 1992. "Cointegration of US Budget and Current Account Deficits: Twins or Strangers?" *Journal of Economics and Finance* 16, no. 2: 119–27.

Rosensweig, Jeffrey A., and Ellis W. Tallman. 1993. "Fiscal Policy and Trade Adjustment: Are the Deficits Really Twins?" *Economic Inquiry* 31, no. 4: 580–94.

World Bank. 2003. *Financing Accountability in Nepal: A Country Assessment*. World Bank Country Study, Washington, DC.

5

Emergence, Severity, and Contours of the Fiscal Deficit in India and South Asia

Raghbendra Jha

Why Does the Fiscal Deficit Matter?

An excess of government expenditure over government revenue is termed the fiscal deficit.[1] This chapter concerns the way this deficit has evolved in the South Asian economies and what implications the deficit and its financing have for these economies.

Recall from the simple national income identity that:

$$Y = C + I + G + X - M - T$$

where Y, C, I, G, X, M, and T are, respectively, national income, consumption, investment, government expenditure, exports, imports, and public revenue. The fiscal deficit, then, is:

$$G - T = (Y - C) - I - (X - M) = (S - I) - (X - M)$$

where S is savings. Thus, any fiscal deficit has to be financed by either an excess of domestic savings over domestic investment or an excess of imports over exports (foreign savings) or both. This simple equation makes clear that fiscal deficits have a cost: they either lower the domestic resources for investment or impact the trade balance or both. If either of these is "excessive," there are costs for the domestic economy in terms of lower economic growth or external stability. This point can be illustrated with some data for India: over the period 1970–71 to 1999–2000, the coefficient of correlation between the fiscal deficit and the current account deficit for India was as high as 0.71, indicating the spillover of the fiscal deficit to the external sector. Further, as

Saggar (2003) shows, there is also substantial financing of India's fiscal deficit by domestic savings.

A high fiscal deficit impinges on the economy in several ways. It alters the allocation of resources between the private and public sectors. Within the public sector it may favor some forms of spending over others, again distorting market forces. In particular, in developing countries, public expenditures on wasteful subsidies for food, fertilizers, petroleum, and the like start taking up higher proportions of state expenditure as the fiscal deficit rises. This process also builds up expectations of future government expenditure patterns. A high fiscal deficit leads to higher interest rates, thus crowding out private investment. The increased debt service expenses lead to distortions in the distribution of income. Higher debt service charges reduce the amount of public investment (as well as private investment if public and private investment are complementary) that can take place, and hence lower potential economic growth. This detracts from efforts to raise living standards and lower poverty.

Both theory and evidence suggest that persistently large fiscal deficits pose real threats to economic stability and growth. Budget deficits, from the national income identity, detract from domestic savings and reduce the resources available for investment and growth, assuming that foreign savings are either not plentiful or not reliable in view of crises (most recently since the late 1990s), or both. Further, if there is substantial debt overhang, the government's ability to conduct countercyclical public expenditure policy is compromised. During an expansion, tax revenues go up and so can public expenditure, whereas during a recession tax revenues go down and, with large debt servicing charges, little is left for public expenditures, even essential ones. Thus, fiscal policy ceases to be stabilizing. Furthermore, to the extent that the deficit is financed through monetization, monetary policy becomes dependent upon budgetary policy and has less stabilization potential. Excessive budget deficits could lead to a combination of inflation, exchange rate crises, external debt crises, and high real interest rates, the latter particularly dependent on the extent of accumulated debt. The link between inflation and the fiscal deficit is straightforward in theory. When faced with a high deficit and limited resources to finance it, a government may often resort to monetization, printing money to cover the deficit. Thus monetary policy gets linked to fiscal policy and the independence of both is compromised. Further, the higher monetization leads to higher inflation (Catão and Terrones 2001). Since the inflation tax is a particularly regressive tax, this provides a further reason to curb the fiscal deficit. Furthermore, once a default situation occurs, most likely on external debt, it becomes even more difficult to establish credibility in capital markets and borrowing must occur on increasingly difficult terms (Reinhart, Rogoff, and Savastano 2003). This imposes another burden on the economy.

A further important question to address here is the impact of the fiscal deficit on the rate of growth. In the neoclassical model of economic growth in the tradition of Solow, over the long run, the level of income can be raised or lowered by fiscal changes, relative to some initial fiscal policy stance; but in the long run, income growth will return to its initial rate. However, since the mid-1980s new endogenous growth models have proposed a number of channels through which fiscal policy could have "permanent" growth effects. This raises the possibility that fiscal policy could have enduring effects on both growth rates and levels of income. Gemmell (2004) reviews the applicability of this analysis to developing countries and finds some tentative evidence that fiscal deficits may affect growth in such countries. Although Gemmell qualifies this evidence sufficiently, he does suggest that there are likely to be significant gains from fiscal adjustments such as consistently ensuring that an intertemporal budget constraint is satisfied. More important, however, is ensuring that such adjustment of the fiscal deficit takes place within a cogent program of tax and expenditure reform.

This chapter examines the contours of the fiscal deficit situation in South Asia, and, in particular, in the most significant country in the region—India.

The Fiscal Deficit: What Does It Measure?

The fiscal deficit is defined as the excess of government expenditure over government revenue. While it is an easy enough accounting concept to articulate, its conceptual foundation as an economic entity is not above controversy. A review of some of these difficulties can be found in Tanzi (1993).

One problem is that the conventional measure of the deficit fails to recognize the fact that different tax and expenditure categories have different effects on aggregate demand. For example, an excess of expenditure on the infrastructure creates productive capacity and will have a different impact than an excess of expenditure due to consumption subsidies.

A second problem arises because tax revenues are related to expenditures. The level of public expenditures determines national income, which then determines tax revenue, at least in part. Hence, there are important problems of mutual impact. Keeping this in mind, the notion of a *full employment budget surplus* was defined and used during the Kennedy and Johnson presidencies in the United States—a period of full employment. The idea was to define the deficit or surplus with reference to the employment of an important scarce factor—labor, in the case of the United States. In the context of developing countries in South Asia, such a notion would be suspect since the binding constraint on output in their cases is not the supply of labor, and a more relevant constraint would be the availability of credit in terms of hard currencies. Finally

Tanzi mentions difficulties arising from variations in sources of financing the deficit. In developing countries several sources of financing have been used: central bank financing, commercial bank financing, domestic sale of government bonds to cover the deficit, and foreign financing. Each of these has different macroeconomic consequences. Central bank financing raises the monetary base and the money supply, thereby blurring the distinction between monetary and fiscal policies and thus reducing overall policy effectiveness (Jha 2003a). Foreign financing will raise the cost of servicing external debt whereas domestic bond issues will raise interest rates. An additional difficulty is that some sources of finance are available only under particular circumstances. For example, a country with a thin bond market can hardly afford to issue government bonds to cover the fiscal deficit and may have to rely on central bank financing or some such measure. A country with large external debt would, in all probability, be able to finance its deficit externally only by borrowing short term at high rates of interest. This would make it difficult to finance the external debt and may put pressure on the currency (Jha 2004). In developed countries bond markets are much better developed and deficits are largely financed by floating bonds that domestic residents as well as foreigners can buy.

Another notion that has been much discussed in the literature is that of a cyclically adjusted fiscal deficit. This approach notes that during a cyclical downturn, tax revenues are likely to fall and public expenditures rise because of automatic stabilizers, such as welfare and unemployment benefits. The reverse is likely to happen during a cyclical upturn.[2] An appropriate measure of the fiscal health of an economy would, therefore, adjust for these cyclical swings. The resulting measure of the deficit has been referred to as a cyclically adjusted fiscal deficit.

Similarly, some authors call for an inflation-adjusted measure of the deficit since inflation affects the real values of government assets and liabilities asymmetrically. However, Buiter (1985, 1993) has argued that even cyclically adjusted and inflation-adjusted measures of the deficit are only imprecise indicators of the true deficit. He argues that capital gains and losses on government assets and liabilities are not included in the conventional flow of funds accounts. Examples of these would include changes in relative prices, such as mineral prices, and changes in the real value of nominal debt during an episode of inflation.[3]

In many developing countries—particularly those in which public investment has played a significant role in the economy, like the South Asian countries—a distinction is made between revenue or current deficit and capital deficit. The former is the deficit on expenses of a recurrent nature after netting out investment expenditure. The latter is the deficit on account of public activities in building up national assets. Surely, if a country is running a large and growing deficit on such current transactions it is a reason for worry. However, the distinction between capital and current expenditures can often be an artificial one. It would be meaningful only if it were clear that all capital expenditures were productive in nature. Although capital expenditures are associated with capacity-building activity, it might be that some such expenditures are wasteful in nature. Sometimes the project in question may not have been evaluated carefully, it may involve capital-intensive equipment or be unduly import intensive, or it may be in some other way inappropriate for the economy.

Another problem with measuring deficits is that of accounting for arrears. This becomes particularly relevant in the case of repayment of foreign debt. If, for example, the interest payment on the foreign debt is rescheduled, should we say that the deficit has gone down? Similarly, if the government delays some payments, often the public wage bill, while continuing to take in all its revenues, does fiscal deficit go down? These questions become particularly relevant during a period of high inflation when delaying payments denominated in nominal terms can have significant impact on the real value of such payments.

A further problem arises when the fiscal deficit reported is only that of the central government. In countries with different levels of government this is an inappropriate indicator of the deficit. Even if the deficits of state and lower levels of government are included, there may be other government agencies that are running a deficit, which does not get reflected in the measured fiscal deficit. Examples include the deficits of central banks, the deficits of local (particularly municipal) governments in India and the so-called oil pool deficit in India where excesses of payments for petroleum imports over what is collected from consumers are recorded. The oil pool deficit, for example, can become large during a period of rises in the international prices of petroleum products and difficulties in raising the domestic prices of such products.[4] In the Indian case, for example, part of the burden of this adjustment has been shifted to the future by issuing "oil bonds." Such transactions do not get reflected in the fiscal deficit. In addition, the so-called contingent liabilities of the government become important when, for example, financial institutions have to be bailed out. The recent bailing out of the Unit Trust of India by the government of India is a case in point. All this then tends to make the fiscal deficit a not entirely satisfactory measure of the excess of government expenditure over revenues.

The difficulties in measuring and interpreting the deficit notwithstanding, it is useful to understand whether the underlying fiscal stance is sustainable. The literature on this issue is growing rapidly. In the next section I heuristically discuss the extant notion of internal debt sustainability and apply it to select South Asian countries for which continuous data are available.[5]

Sustainability of the Domestic Fiscal Debt

Rapid accumulation of domestic debt can lead to severe macroeconomic problems, and can impede control of the fiscal deficit itself. Servicing of the central government debt is one of the largest items in the government of India's budget. In fact, this magnitude outstrips major items of expenditure such as defense. This section develops the simple analytics of sustainability for the domestic as well as the external deficit and applies it to a spectrum of developing countries. For a review of alternative approaches to the sustainability of the fiscal deficit see Cuddington (1997), Chalk and Hemming (2000), de Haan and Zelhorst (1990), Easterly and Schmidt-Hebbel (1993), Hakkio and Rush (1991), Issler and Lima (2000), Sargent (1999), and Trehan and Walsh (1991).

The most straightforward way to assess the sustainability of a public debt situation is to start from the governmental intertemporal budget constraint. This is written in nominal terms as:

$$G_t - T_t + r_t B_{t-1} = B_t - B_{t-1} \qquad (1)$$

where G_t is the value of government expenditures (purchases of goods and services plus transfer payments), B_t is the government debt at the end of period t, T_t is the government's tax revenue, and r_t is the one-period rate of interest payable on the government debt. Equation (1) states that in the absence of money finance, the government budget deficit must be financed by new debt creation.[6] Hence, expressing equation (1) in terms of ratios to gross GDP yields:

$$b_t = (g_t + \tau_t) + (1+r)b_{t-1} \qquad (1')$$

where the lowercase letters denote the ratio of the corresponding uppercase variables to nominal GDP: $b_t = B_t / P_t Y_t$; $g_t = G_t / P_t Y_t$; and $\tau_t = T_t / P_t Y_t$; with P and Y being the price level and real GDP, respectively; $(g_t - \tau_t)$ is the primary deficit—the deficit without interest payments—expressed as a percentage of GDP. Equation (1') can then be written as:

$$b_t = (1+r_t)(1+\pi_t + \eta_t)^{-1} b_{t-1} + (g_t - \tau_t) \qquad (2)$$

where $\pi_t = (P_t - P_{t-1})/P_{t-1}$ is the rate of inflation and $\eta_t = (Y_t - Y_{t-1})/Y_{t-1}$ is the rate of growth of real GDP. In the derivation of equation (2) we have used the relation that:

$$P_t Y_t = (1+\pi_t)(1+\eta_t)P_{t-1}Y_{t-1} \approx (1+\pi_t + \eta_t)P_{t-1}Y_{t-1}$$

The sustainability of the fiscal deficit is thus intimately related to the primary deficit. Sustainability is essentially an intertemporal question over a long, strictly speaking infinite, horizon. Every temporary deficit can be sustainable so long as it is matched by an adequate future surplus. So if the primary deficit keeps growing, the fiscal deficit will not be sustainable. Another way to interpret the sustainability condition is that, in the long run, revenue and expenditure have a one-to-one relation with each other. If this is the case then, naturally, the public debt will reach a finite limit and will be sustainable. This is the intuition behind the tests for sustainability developed in Jha (2004).

The Fiscal Deficit Experience in South Asia

One problem in comparing the fiscal deficit figures across South Asia—at least in the near term—is the wide variation in data collection and dissemination standards across the region. For instance, among the South Asian countries only India participates in the International Monetary Fund's (IMF) Special Data Dissemination Standard. Among the Southeast Asian countries, Indonesia and Thailand subscribe to this standard, as a sequel to the currency crises in these countries. Bangladesh, Nepal, and Sri Lanka subscribe to the less demanding General Data Dissemination Standard (GDDS) whereas Pakistan does not. Among the Southeast Asian countries only Cambodia subscribes to the GDDS. The analysis reported in this chapter is therefore subject to this caveat about data quality.

Jha (2004) tests for the sustainability of the fiscal deficit and current account deficit in a number of developing countries. The intuition for this test is that if the primary deficit does not grow without limit or, equivalently, there is a one-to-one relation between revenue and expenditure in the long run, then any current deficit can be matched by surpluses sometime in the future. Application of this test for the South Asian countries yields interesting results, which are reported in Table 5.1.

The analysis with respect to the other South Asian countries could not be done because of a lack of comparable data over a long enough time period. It appears that all the South Asian countries—except for Sri Lanka—have problems of fiscal sustainability. Even in the case of Sri Lanka, the public debt has grown enormously over the past five years and it would appear that the country will violate the sustainability condition unless remedial measures are taken soon. Thus, unsustainable fiscal deficits appear to be the rule rather than the exception in South Asia and corrective action is urgently needed.

Table 5.2 provides some comparative data on the fiscal deficit situation in South Asian countries and contrasts it to select developing (Indonesia and

Table 5.1

Sustainability of Fiscal Deficit in Selected South Asian Countries

Country	Period	Sustainability restriction satisfied
India	1952–1998	No
Nepal	1960–1996	No
Pakistan	1955–1999	No
Sri Lanka	1952–1998	Yes

South Africa) and developed countries (Australia, Singapore, United Kingdom, and United States). However, since the Indian case is discussed in some detail later, data on India are not included in this table.

Fiscal deficits have been consistently high in Bangladesh, Pakistan, and Sri Lanka. Nepal had high fiscal deficits in the 1980s, and Bhutan has had very few episodes of high deficits, indeed, running a surplus in some years.[7] The South Asian experience can be contrasted to a developing country with low fiscal deficits such as Indonesia and one with a high fiscal deficit such as South Africa.[8] Australia, the United Kingdom, and the United States have had relatively lower fiscal deficits. Singapore has run up budget surpluses quite consistently.

The Fiscal Deficit Situation in India

We now address in some detail the fiscal deficit situation in India. Table 5.3 provides some data on central and state-level deficits.

Starting with 1970–71, India's fiscal deficit was well within manageable limits. Even the 1971 war and the 1973 oil price shocks did not take the combined fiscal deficit figure to very high levels. An important reason for this was that bond markets were captive with controlled interest rates and considerable reliance was placed on monetary financing of the deficit. Following the second oil price shock, in 1979, however, the deficit started climbing, even with controlled interest rates. The economic crisis of the late 1980s and early 1990s saw this figure rise to double-digit levels. Partly in response to the adjustment required as a condition of the structural adjustment loans taken from the IMF, the fiscal deficit began to drop. As will be indicated in Table 5.5, this adjustment involved reductions in development expenditure whereas current expenditure proved inflexible. Another part of this adjustment has centered on reductions in transfers to state governments, as a result of which public investment in important areas such as agriculture has stagnated, agriculture being largely

Table 5.2

Fiscal Deficit as Percentage of GDP

	Australia	Bangladesh	Bhutan	Indonesia	Nepal	Pakistan	Singapore	South Africa	Sri Lanka	United Kingdom	United States
1972	0.32		—	-2.29	-1.21	—	1.25	-4.03	—	-2.71	-1.59
1973	-0.88		—	-2.11	-2.23	-6.81	-0.11	-2.45	-5.22	-3.41	-1.24
1974	-0.43		—	-1.49	-1.93	-5.92	1.55	-4.69	-3.23	-4.58	-0.31
1975	-3.70		—	-3.51	-1.43	-10.31	0.88	-5.26	-6.41	-7.39	-3.46
1976	-4.56		—	-4.24	-2.43	-9.39	0.21	-6.58	-8.34	-5.80	-4.31
1977	-2.96		—	-1.97	-3.33	-8.40	0.99	-6.01	-4.59	-3.39	-2.65
1978	-3.32		—	-3.01	-2.95	-7.51	0.79	-5.23	-12.40	-5.25	-2.66
1979	-2.78		—	-2.16	-2.65	-9.23	2.16	-3.94	-12.03	-5.65	-1.44
1980	-1.63		—	-2.27	-3.02	-5.70	2.06	-2.29	-18.27	-4.66	-2.79
1981	-0.74		—	-1.98	-2.67	-5.80	0.71	-3.84	-12.37	-4.79	-2.57
1982	-0.36		0.65	-1.80	-5.13	-4.74	3.26	-3.70	-14.03	-3.44	-3.89
1983	-2.57		-1.25	-2.31	-8.75	-6.80	1.76	-5.01	-10.56	-4.42	-5.88
1984	-3.95		1.46	1.32	-7.58	-6.18	4.13	-4.56	-6.82	-3.17	-4.63
1985	-3.04		-8.31	-0.93	-7.25	-7.16	2.09	-3.92	-9.66	-2.89	-5.12
1986	-2.35		-3.27	-3.14	-6.53	-9.12	1.40	-5.26	-10.14	-2.39	-4.83

Year											
1987	-1.02		—	-0.77	-6.11	-8.52	-2.59	-6.88	-8.68	-1.02	-3.17
1988	0.73		0.68	-2.80	-5.57	-6.28	6.63	-5.18	-12.70	0.97	-3.10
1989	1.81		-11.32	-1.79	-8.98	-7.40	9.77	-0.23	-8.65	0.97	-2.66
1990	2.06		-8.33	0.36	-6.78	-5.40	10.52	-4.15	-7.82	0.64	-3.80
1991	0.49		-0.90	0.38	-8.24	-7.55	8.56	-4.21	-9.45	-1.21	-4.60
1992	-2.34		-4.17	-0.37	-6.73	-7.88	12.22	-9.35	-5.39	-4.80	-4.65
1993	-3.38		4.61	0.59	-6.04	-8.87	15.17	-9.83	-6.42	-7.26	-3.87
1994	-3.03	4.5	-0.57	0.89	-3.75	-7.21	15.83	-6.06	-8.54	-5.88	-2.90
1995	-2.45	5.3	0.08	2.13	-3.60	-6.57	14.33	-5.31	-8.27	-5.45	-2.13
1996	-0.95	4.5	2.20	1.11	-4.41	-7.83	10.34	-4.84	-7.80	-3.63	-1.49
1997	0.39	4.3	-2.30	-0.60	-3.89	-7.89	11.84	-3.06	-4.52	-2.00	-0.27
1998	2.85	4.1	—	-2.72	-4.60	-6.23	3.37	-2.56	-8.01	0.57	0.82
1999	1.46	4.8	—	—	-3.93	—	—	—	-6.85	0.03	1.34
2000	—	6.2	—	—	-3.73	—	—	—	—	—	—
2001		6.0									
2002		5.4									

Source: Ministry of Finance, Bangladesh, and Bangladesh Bureau of Statistics, and the World Bank (for Bangladesh), and International Monetary Fund, Government Finance Statistics for other countries.

Notes: A minus sign (−) indicates a deficit. Data for Bangladesh refer to financial year.

Table 5.3

India: Fiscal Deficit Total Internal Liabilities (center plus states; as % of GDP)

	Central government fiscal deficit	State government fiscal deficit	Central plus state government fiscal deficit
1970–71	3.26	2.1	5.36
1971–72	3.73	2.3	5.03
1972–73	4.96	2.7	7.66
1973–74	2.79	2.4	5.19
1974–75	3.14	1.7	4.84
1975–76	3.85	1.4	5.25
1976–77	4.48	1.8	6.28
1977–78	3.83	2.1	5.93
1978–79	5.48	2.5	7.98
1979–80	6.42	2.5	6.92
1980–81	6.10	2.7	8.8
1981–82	5.42	2.5	7.92
1982–83	6.97	2.8	9.17
1983–84	6.28	3.1	9.38
1984–85	7.53	3.5	8.03
1985–86	8.33	2.9	11.23
1986–87	8.99	3.2	12.19
1987–88	8.12	3.4	11.52
1988–89	7.81	2.9	10.71
1989–90	7.80	3.4	11.20
1990–91	8.33	3.5	11.83
1991–92	5.89	3.1	8.99
1992–93	5.69	3.0	8.69
1993–94	7.43	2.5	9.93
1994–95	5.99	2.9	8.89
1995–96	5.38	2.8	8.18
1996–97	5.23	2.7	7.93
1997–98	5.84	2.9	8.74
1998–99	6.51	4.3	10.81
1999–2000	5.41	4.7	10.11
2000–01	5.65	4.3	9.95
2001–02	6.14	4.2	10.34
2002–03	5.88	4.7	10.58

Source: Reserve Bank of India.

Table 5.4

Indian Tax–GDP Ratios: 1970–1971 to 2001–2002 (percentages)

	Total tax revenue (center plus states)			Central taxes		
	Direct	Indirect	Total	Direct	Indirect	Total
1	2	3	4	5	6	7
1970–71	2.21	8.19	10.40	1.90	5.12	7.02
1975–76	2.99	10.43	13.43	2.65	6.49	9.14
1980–81	2.27	11.53	13.80	2.08	7.08	9.17
1985–86	2.25	13.32	15.56	2.02	8.29	10.31
1990–91	2.16	13.27	15.43	1.94	8.19	10.12
1991–92	2.55	13.25	15.80	2.35	7.96	10.31
1992–93	2.59	12.66	15.26	2.42	7.55	9.97
1993–94	2.53	11.67	14.19	2.36	6.45	8.82
1994–95	2.85	11.75	14.60	2.66	6.45	9.11
1995–96	3.01	11.74	14.75	2.83	6.54	9.36
1996–97	3.00	11.69	14.69	2.84	6.64	9.48
1997–98	2.82	11.17	13.99	2.67	5.97	8.65
1998–99	2.82	10.56	13.38	2.68	5.58	8.26
1999–2000	3.15	11.59	14.75	3.00	6.42	9.42
2000–2001						
(R.E.)	n.a.	n.a.	15.32	3.57	5.93	9.50
2001–2 (B.E.)	n.a.	n.a.	16.21	3.72	6.17	9.89

Source: Government of India, Indian Public Finance 2001–2.

Note: The ratios to GDP of the previous years have undergone changes as new series GDP (base: 1993–94).

a state subject under the Indian constitution. As Figure 5.1 reveals, the share of the central government in the fiscal deficit has always been well in excess of 50 percent. The share of the central government in total deficit peaked at over 90 percent in 1979–80 and 1985–86 but has been on a downward trend since about 1994–95. This is consistent with more financial powers being transferred to states as part of the economic reforms program begun in 1991 (Jha 2003b) as well as the adoption of the recommendations of the Fifth Pay Commission for government employees, which sharply increased the salaries of government officials.

Table 5.4 reports results on tax revenue in India for select years and Table 5.5—results on public expenditure. Some important patterns emerge from these tables. The share of indirect taxes in both state and central revenues is consistently high, although the share of direct taxes has been on the rise in

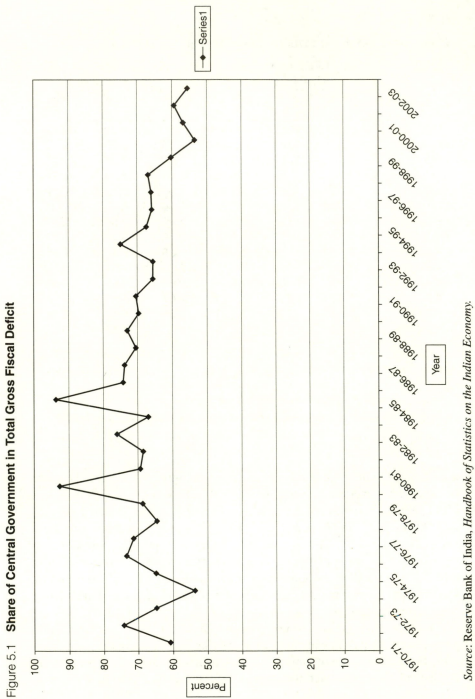

128

Figure 5.1 **Share of Central Government in Total Gross Fiscal Deficit**

Source: Reserve Bank of India, *Handbook of Statistics on the Indian Economy.*

Table 5.5

India: Combined Expenditure of Central and State Governments
(as % of GDP)

	1994–1995	1995–1996	1996–1997	1997–1998	1998–1999	1999–2000
Development expenditure (including loans and advances)	12.8	11.8	11.6	11.8	12.3	12.11
Nondevelopmental expenditure	12.8	13	12.3	12.8	13.8	13.9
Total expenditure of which	25.6	24.8	23.9	24.6	26.1	26
Expenditure on education, family welfare, health, water supply, and sanitation	4	3.9	3.9	4	4.5	4.5
Agriculture and allied services	2	1.8	1.7	1.7	1.9	1.9
Defense	2.3	2.3	2.2	2.3	2.3	2.4

Source: Government of India, Indian Public Finance 2001–2.

recent times with respect to central taxes. Between 1994–95 and 1999–2000 the share of developmental expenditure has been on the decline while nondevelopmental expenditure has registered a mild rise. The share of public expenditure in GDP has registered a rise, principally because of nondevelopment expenditure—particularly debt servicing. Also worth noting is the fact that expenditure shares of important categories such as health, education, water and sanitation, agriculture, and defense have tended to stagnate.

The Constitution of India has delimited the tax and expenditure powers of central and state governments. Hence, the dynamics of the accumulation of fiscal deficits at the central and state levels are different. It is also relevant that since the expenditure of state governments is partly financed by grants from the central government, fiscal adjustment in the states and the center are linked insofar as one way the center can reduce its fiscal deficit is to lower transfers to state governments.

Toward More Sustainable Fiscal Deficits in South Asia

Given that the fiscal situation in most South Asian countries is unsustainable, urgent steps to redress the situation need to be taken. Any policy to reduce the fiscal deficit by cutting expenditure and increasing taxes has a significant impact on the economy; it is therefore imperative that a program of deficit reduction be cast within an overall policy of expenditure and tax reforms. This requires actions on several fronts simultaneously.[9] First, an effort has to be made to raise tax and nontax revenues of the government in an efficient and transparent manner. Table 5.6 reveals that government revenues in South Asian countries (except Sri Lanka) are well below levels attained in developed countries (with the exception of the United States) and even below those attained by South Africa. However, the state in South Asian countries faces more severe challenges of development. It stands to reason, then, that it needs more resources with which to work.

The experience of some other developing countries has shown that it is possible to proceed along the lines suggested by tax reform theory and to obtain a degree of success (Chelliah Committee 1991). This theory calls for a mix of personal income taxes and indirect taxes based on final consumption and not intermediate use. Exemptions are granted with respect to basic necessities such as food, and additional excise taxes are placed on products (such as cigarettes) and processes (polluting industries) that cause significant external diseconomies. A value-added tax (VAT) often suits this purpose but it has to be planned for carefully. The VAT requires considerable sophistication in accounting and accounting procedures as well as mass education about the tax, and South Asian countries need to work toward these ends before adopting the VAT. In the case of federal countries such as India, the VAT will have to be a harmonized state and central tax.

The share of personal taxes in total tax revenue should rise. As Tables 5.7 and 5.8 indicate, tax revenues in South Asian countries are realized in disproportionately large amounts from indirect as opposed to direct taxes compared with developed countries and even countries such as Indonesia and South Africa. Commodity taxes are distortionary and often regressive since rich and poor pay taxes at the same rate. Tax reform theory (Jha 1998) advocates that income taxes be only mildly progressive, involve few exemptions, and cover all sources of income. Mild progression of the income tax ensures that disincentive effects on work are minimized. Expanding the tax base to include all incomes ensures that tax evasion is reduced, since income from a "taxable" source cannot be concealed as income from a "nontaxable" source. An effort should also be made to index tax liabilities to the rate of inflation so that "bracket creep" does not increase real tax burdens when real, before-tax incomes have remained unchanged. In the case of all South Asian countries, a lowering of income tax rates and broadening of the tax base by plugging loopholes and eliminating exemptions are called for.

It is also warranted that the share of corporate taxes in total revenue falls. An important consideration is the ability of the tax structure to attract new capital

Table 5.6

Total Revenue and Grants (as % of GDP)

	Australia	Bhutan	India	Indonesia	Nepal	Pakistan	South Africa	Sri Lanka	United Kingdom	United States
1972	22.30	—	—	12.60	7.55	—	20.53	—	33.16	18.17
1973	21.01	—	—	13.17	7.85	13.07	20.66	20.21	31.31	18.60
1974	22.07	—	10.42	16.38	7.61	14.23	20.90	19.41	35.24	19.35
1975	23.49	—	12.00	17.23	7.71	13.16	22.05	19.09	35.74	18.77
1976	23.84	—	12.40	18.15	8.32	14.41	21.77	18.94	35.38	17.93
1977	24.28	—	12.15	18.22	9.74	14.38	22.17	18.61	34.54	18.81
1978	24.52	—	12.69	17.47	10.08	14.89	22.47	27.91	32.87	18.78
1979	23.45	—	12.93	19.93	10.46	15.57	21.88	25.86	32.70	19.51
1980	23.90	—	12.17	21.40	11.22	17.05	22.99	24.15	35.59	19.99
1981	24.94	—	12.50	23.24	11.84	17.24	21.97	20.58	36.64	20.91
1982	25.22	31.36	12.86	19.34	11.70	16.33	23.11	19.74	38.92	20.42
1983	25.65	36.17	12.45	19.22	11.45	16.45	22.90	22.03	37.59	18.99
1984	24.96	36.30	13.01	20.35	10.63	17.39	23.92	24.30	37.55	18.68
1985	26.46	38.89	13.96	20.05	10.24	16.75	26.15	24.36	37.85	19.12
1986	26.89	37.38	14.51	18.51	10.19	18.31	25.30	22.84	36.82	18.72
1987	27.68	—	14.58	18.52	11.06	17.87	24.79	23.80	35.87	19.55
1988	27.10	37.92	14.23	15.35	11.98	18.54	25.77	21.78	35.84	19.19
1989	26.11	38.97	14.95	15.52	10.33	19.64	29.32	23.97	35.19	19.36
1990	25.85	31.37	13.62	17.93	10.25	19.98	27.11	23.20	36.53	18.92
1991	25.46	33.37	14.62	16.44	10.45	17.75	26.88	22.65	37.49	19.57

(continued)

132

Table 5.6 *(continued)*

	Australia	Bhutan	India	Indonesia	Nepal	Pakistan	South Africa	Sri Lanka	United Kingdom	United States
1992	23.73	33.62	14.36	17.21	9.80	18.50	25.60	22.12	36.26	18.58
1993	22.98	42.54	11.89	16.42	10.56	18.10	26.91	21.32	34.35	18.87
1994	23.24	39.79	12.81	17.35	10.67	17.73	26.34	20.43	35.10	19.15
1995	24.06	39.53	12.69	16.97	12.38	17.37	25.11	21.76	35.74	19.70
1996	24.61	41.43	12.70	16.23	12.64	17.33	25.37	20.05	36.08	19.88
1997	25.20	35.56	12.37	16.12	12.60	15.98	25.96	19.36	36.00	20.49
1998	24.74	—	12.11	16.28	12.27	15.71	26.93	17.90	37.45	20.90
1999	25.48	—	—	—	11.53	—	—	18.25	36.84	20.85
2000	—	—	—	—	—	—	—	—	—	—

Source: International Monetary Fund, Government Finance Statistics.

Note: Some South Asian countries are excluded because of unavailability of data.

Table 5.7

Taxes on Income, Profits, and Capital Gains (as % of GDP)

	Australia	Bhutan	India	Indonesia	Nepal	Pakistan	South Africa	Sri Lanka	UK	United States
1972	12.94	—	—	5.65	0.21	—	11.15	—	13.05	10.77
1977	15.33	—	2.43	12.28	0.77	1.77	12.50	2.57	14.48	10.72
1982	15.94	1.20	2.26	14.87	0.61	2.57	12.08	2.95	14.78	10.75
1987	16.72	—	1.99	8.81	0.70	—	12.73	2.50	13.95	10.24
1992	15.52	1.39	2.48	9.27	0.59	2.33	13.32	2.58	13.15	9.27
1997	16.93	3.76	2.53	9.19	1.41	3.37	13.65	2.42	13.30	11.25
1998	16.61	—	2.80	9.97	1.52	3.56	14.28	2.01	14.55	11.78
1999	—	—	—	—	1.70	—	—	2.54	14.49	11.64
2000	—	—	—	—	1.81	—	—	—	—	—

Source: International Monetary Fund, Government Finance Statistics.

Note: Some South Asian countries are excluded because of unavailability of data.

Table 5.8

Taxes on Goods and Services (as % of GDP)

	Australia	Bhutan	India	Indonesia	Nepal	Pakistan	South Africa	Sri Lanka	UK	United States
1972	4.85	—	—	2.84	1.38	—	4.37	—	8.97	1.30
1977	4.70	—	4.83	2.41	2.52	4.84	4.73	5.97	8.45	0.88
1982	5.55	3.38	4.73	2.00	3.28	5.18	6.42	6.37	10.79	1.12
1987	6.16	—	5.16	3.36	3.34	—	8.00	7.96	10.31	0.69
1992	4.79	3.77	4.63	4.45	3.35	5.44	8.20	9.44	11.07	0.72
1997	5.17	2.44	3.35	4.50	3.90	4.61	8.61	9.87	11.63	0.69
1998	5.01	—	3.19	3.97	3.82	4.20	8.96	9.01	11.59	0.65
1999	—	—	—	—	3.53	—	—	9.22	11.32	0.75
2000	—	—	—	—	3.71	—	—	--	—	—

Source: International Monetary Fund, Government Finance Statistics.

Note: Some South Asian countries are excluded because of unavailability of data.

and to prevent capital flight. A stable macroeconomic environment with low inflation, well-functioning capital markets, relatively stable exchange rates, and manageable government debt is very important in this regard. The tax/expenditure policies should work toward the creation of such an environment.

Table 5.9

Taxes on International Trade (as % of GDP)

	Australia	Bhutan	India	Indonesia	Nepal	Pakistan	South Africa	Sri Lanka	UK	United States
1972	1.15	—	—	2.19	1.91	—	0.94	—	0.55	0.30
1977	1.46	—	1.96	1.84	2.23	4.38	1.77	6.59	0.11	0.28
1982	1.32	0.04	3.00	0.91	2.66	4.88	1.13	5.21	0.07	0.28
1987	1.24	—	4.11	1.53	2.36	—	0.94	6.60	0.01	0.33
1992	0.84	0.18	3.37	0.90	2.25	5.10	0.60	5.09	—	0.29
1997	0.62	0.37	2.65	0.44	2.96	3.58	0.68	3.00	—	0.22
1998	0.63	—	2.42	0.71	2.83	2.70	0.69	2.77	—	0.23
1999	—	—	—	—	2.80	—	—	2.50	—	0.22
2000	—	—	—	—	2.92	—	—	—	—	—

Source: International Monetary Fund, Government Finance Statistics.

Since corporate profits are taxed anyway in the hands of shareholders, the justification for corporate taxes lies only in there being taxes on monopoly profits or income of foreigners. Hence corporate taxes should be moderate.

Furthermore, as Table 5.9 indicates, there is considerably more emphasis on distortionary taxation of international trade in South Asian countries as compared with developed countries. Such taxes cause considerable distortions in resource allocation and deny these countries the full advantages of freer trade. Reduction in import taxes can lead to improved prospects for economic growth and, ultimately, yield higher revenues since lower rates of taxes would be levied on a much expanded tax base.

Another important issue is that of tax assignment—particularly in federal countries. Typically, mobile tax bases are taxed by the central government. This includes corporate profits, incomes, and goods. State governments are not able to implement income tax properly, let alone build equity into it. However, in order to partially finance their expenditures, state governments can levy some commodity taxes provided these are well harmonized with central taxes so that distortionary impacts are minimized. Incentives need to be built into the system to raise the efficiency of tax collection by state governments. (See Jha et al. 1999b for a review of some options.)

In addition to tax reform, there is considerable scope for expenditure reform in South Asian countries. The level of public expenditure in South Asian countries, except for Sri Lanka, is low by the standards of the developed countries (Table 5.10). It is the composition and targeting of this expenditure that have been a problem. In the case of India, for instance, it has already been pointed

Table 5.10

Public Expenditure (as % of GDP)

	Australia	Bhutan	India	Indonesia	Nepal	Pakistan	Singapore	South Africa	Sri Lanka	United Kingdom	United States
1972	20.23	—	—	14.05	8.48	—	15.79	20.90	—	32.34	19.63
1977	25.58	—	11.95	18.59	13.13	16.40	19.96	24.16	22.97	36.78	20.98
1982	24.96	30.71	13.71	20.48	16.85	17.08	20.66	25.23	34.03	41.07	23.67
1987	28.50	—	17.92	19.47	17.40	22.33	34.00	30.44	31.71	37.11	22.65
1992	26.58	36.08	16.85	17.74	16.81	24.30	19.05	34.97	26.94	43.01	23.21
1997	26.19	35.36	15.21	15.98	16.78	22.78	16.97	29.40	25.69	38.07	20.73
1998	24.54	—	14.95	17.82	17.28	21.19	19.64	29.83	24.93	36.85	20.06
1999	24.83	—	—	—	16.12	—	—	—	24.07	36.40	19.50
2000	—	—	—	—	16.49	—	—	—	—	—	—

Source: International Monetary Fund, Government Finance Statistics.

out that a significant portion of the fiscal adjustment comes from a reduction in capital expenditures, since current expenditures—particularly various consumption subsidies—have been hard to cut. There is also considerable evidence to suggest that many of these subsidies are poorly targeted and do not benefit the intended groups—the poor. (See, for instance, Ministry of Finance, Government of India 1997, and Jha et al. 1999a.) Thus, there is a stronger case for an *expenditure switch* than for an *expenditure reduction*—a switch away from wasteful current expenditure to capital expenditure that lays the groundwork for further economic growth—particularly in key areas such as agriculture. Consumption subsidies should be lowered and, more important, better targeted toward the poor. While recommending increased capital expenditures by the government, we should insist upon a high degree of productivity of such expenditures, with the element of waste cut drastically. This requires substantial innovation in accounting and regulatory structures, not to mention governance. When nonmerit subsidies are reduced and an effective program of privatization is put in place, the released revenues can be used to retire some of the public debt and ease pressure on interest rates. Where the public sector is bound to be present, say in industries with natural monopoly characteristics, an appropriate pricing policy should be pursued. For example, efficiency would require that cross-subsidization in industries producing joint products gradually be eliminated (Jha 1998, ch. 17). This would involve, for example, the elimination of the subsidy on postcards by other classes of mail. Administered price mechanisms have often been associated with inefficiency (Jha and Sahni 1993) and should be dismantled. As far as possible, the pricing mechanism should not be used as a mechanism for redistribution. The deleterious effects on resource allocation are far more serious than the alleged benefits of such generalized tampering with the working of the price mechanism. It is widely accepted now that redistribution is best effected through the direct tax structure and targeted social services.

Conclusions

This chapter has examined the underpinnings of the fiscal crisis in South Asia—particularly in India. Our analysis has revealed that the fiscal deficit situation in most of these countries is precarious and unsustainable, and needs urgent redressing. The high levels of fiscal deficit are already exacting a toll on these economies and, unless corrective action is taken soon, more serious consequences may follow. This chapter also outlined the broad contours of a tax and expenditure reform program that would both lower the fiscal deficit and improve the allocation of resources and hence growth prospects in these economies. Whether these or similar policies are adopted in time depends, of course, on the political economy requirements of these reforms.

Notes

1. Some have also called this the budgetary deficit. This includes debt servicing of existing public debt. If we take out interest payment on the public debt the resulting notion of deficit is often called the primary deficit.

2. However, in developing countries, such as those in South Asia, there are hardly any automatic stabilizers in place and fiscal policy is procyclical.

3. Recent arguments along the lines suggested by Buiter include those by Easterly (1999) who argues that fiscal adjustment can be illusionary. In particular, this is the case when such adjustment lowers the public debt but leaves unchanged the net worth of the government. In other words, governments may find ways of maintaining their consumption even when they are actually involved in a process of reducing public debt.

4. On February 28, 2001, India's oil pool deficit alone stood at 0.5 percent of GDP (*Economic Times*, March 1, 2001).

5. For further discussion of internal and external debt sustainability in the specific context of developing countries see Jha (2004), Jha (2003b), and Jha and Sharma (2004).

6. For the case of simplicity of exposition, I exclude foreign financing of the deficit.

7. The Bhutanese case is special since India finances more than 60 percent of the budgetary expenditure of the Bhutanese government.

8. Thus, Indonesia's crisis of the late 1990s was not the result of high fiscal deficits but of imbalances in the external accounts and exchange rate policy with feedback to the banking sector.

9. For a review of taxation policy in developing countries see Heady (2004).

References

Buiter, W. 1985. "A Guide to Public Sector Debts and Deficits." *Economic Policy* 1, no. 1: 13–79.

———. 1993. "Measurement of the Public Sector Deficit and Its Implications for Policy Evaluation and Design." In *How to Measure the Fiscal Deficit*, ed. M. Blejer and A. Cheasty, 297–344. Washington, DC: International Monetary Fund.

Catão, L., and M. Terrones. 2001. "Fiscal Deficits and Inflation: A New Look at the Emerging Market Evidence." IMF Working Paper WP/01/74.

Chalk, N., and N. Hemming. 2000. "Assessing Fiscal Sustainability in Theory and Practice." IMF Working Paper, WP/00/81.

Chelliah Committee. 1991. *Report of the Chelliah Committee on Tax Reforms*. New Delhi: Ministry of Finance, Government of India.

Cuddington, J. 1997. "Analyzing the Sustainability of Fiscal Deficits in Developing Countries." Policy Research Working Paper Series 1784. Washington, DC: World Bank.

de Haan, J., and D. Zelhorst. 1990. "The Impact of Government Deficits on Money Growth in Developing Countries." *Journal of International Money and Finance* 9, no. 3: 455–69.

Easterly, W. 1999. "When Is Fiscal Adjustment an Illusion?" *Economic Policy* 28, no. 1: 57–86.

Easterly, W., and K. Schmidt-Hebbel. 1993. "Fiscal Deficits and Macroeconomic Performance in Developing Countries." *World Bank Research Observer* 8, no. 2: 211–37.

Gemmell, N. 2006. "Fiscal Policy in a Growth Framework." In *Fiscal Policy for Development: Poverty, Reconstruction and Growth,* ed. Tony Addison and Alan Roe. Houndmills, UK and New York: Palgrave Macmillan.

Hakkio, G., and M. Rush. 1991. "Is the Budget Deficit 'Too Large'?" *Economic Inquiry* 29, no. 3: 429–45.

Heady, C. 2006. "Taxation Policy in Low-Income Countries." In *Fiscal Policy for Development: Poverty, Reconstruction and Growth,* ed. Tony Addison and Alan Roe. Houndmills, UK and New York: Palgrave Macmillan.

Issler, J., and L. Lima. 2000. "Public Debt Sustainability and Endogenous Seignora in Brazil: Time Series Evidence from 1947–1992." *Journal of Development Economics* 62, no. 1: 131–47.

Jha, R. 1998. *Modern Public Economics.* London and New York: Routledge.

———. 2003a. *Macroeconomics for Developing Countries.* 2d ed. London and New York: Routledge.

———, ed. 2003b. *Indian Economic Reforms.* Houndmills, UK and New York: Palgrave Macmillan.

———. 2006. "The Macroeconomics of Fiscal Policy in Developing Countries." In *Fiscal Policy for Development: Poverty, Reconstruction and Growth*, ed. Tony Addison and Alan Roe. Houndmills, UK and New York: Palgrave Macmillan.

Jha, R., and B.S. Sahni. 1993. *Industrial Efficiency: An Indian Perspective.* New Delhi: Wiley Eastern.

Jha, R., and Sharma, A. 2004. "Structural Breaks, Unit Roots and Cointegration: A Further Test of the Sustainability of the Indian Fiscal Deficit." *Public Finance Review* 32, no. 2: 196–219.

Jha, R.; M. Mohanty; S. Chatterjee; and P. Chitkara. 1999b. "Tax Efficiency in Selected Indian States." *Empirical Economics* 24, no. 3: 641–54.

Jha, R.; K.V.B. Murthy; H.K. Nagarajan; and A. Seth. 1999a. "Real Consumption Levels and the Public Distribution System in India." *Economic and Political Weekly* 34, no. 15: 919–27.

Ministry of Finance, Government of India. 1997. "Government Subsidies in India." Discussion Paper, Department of Economic Affairs, New Delhi.

Reinhart, C.; K. Rogoff; and M. Savastano. 2003. "Debt Intolerance." Brookings Papers on Economic Activity, no. 1.

Saggar, M. 2003. "A Perspective on Saving, Investment and Macroeconomic Policies in India in the 1990s." In *Indian Economic Reforms*, ed. Raghbendra Jha. Basingstoke, Hampshire, UK: Palgrave Macmillan.

Sargent, T. 1999. "A Primer on Monetary and Fiscal Policy." *Journal of Banking and Finance* 23, no. 8: 1463–82.

Tanzi, V. 1993. "Fiscal Deficit Measurement: Basic Issues." In *How to Measure the Fiscal Deficit*, ed. M. Blejer and A.Cheasty, 13–21. Washington, DC: International Monetary Fund.

Trehan, B., and C. Walsh. 1991. "Testing Intertemporal Budget Constraints: Theory and Applications to the US Federal Budget and Current Account Deficits." *Journal of Money, Credit and Banking* 23, no. 2: 206–23.

6

Foreign Public Capital and Economic Growth of Developing Countries

A Selected Survey

Abdul Waheed

A major economic policy objective in most of the developing countries is fostering economic growth, which usually requires good quality and higher quantity of investment. In turn, more resources for investment require higher levels of both domestic and foreign savings. While the impact of domestic savings on economic growth is unambiguous, there is controversy at the theoretical and empirical levels over the effect of foreign capital (or foreign savings) on both economic growth and domestic savings. A detailed study of macroeconomic effects of foreign capital can help in settling the controversy. This chapter should be seen in this context.

Foreign capital is a broad concept, but here we refer only to the type of foreign capital that is basically official development finance. The literature survey in this chapter does not include the history and politics of foreign capital or private development finance.[1]

Theoretical Literature on the Effects of Foreign Capital

Context and Origins

The subject of economic growth has been and continues to be a controversial area within the study of economics. No general theory of economic growth can prescribe policy at all stages of economic development or for all types of economic systems. The early economists, such as Smith, Ricardo, Marshall, Lewis, and Schumpeter, paid little or no attention either to foreign capital as a particular form of international transfer or to additional resources as a crucial factor in promoting economic growth and development. For example, Adam Smith believed that unhampered trade and competitive enterprise provided the conditions for maximum growth. For David Ricardo, capital accumulation was the key to growth, but that accumulation was motivated by the rate of profit. Alfred Marshall set forth a number of fundamental determinants and factors influencing growth. These are willingness and ability to save, improved transport, external economies, increasing returns, and the existence of extensive markets. Arthur Lewis systematically differentiated between physical and human capital, and underlined the importance of the latter in promoting economic growth of developing countries. For Joseph Schumpeter, the fundamental determinant of growth was neither savings nor capital but the entrepreneur or innovator (for more details, see Mikesell 1968, 27–30). Thus, all of these economists gave little importance to the idea that growth is limited by the supply of foreign capital.

Conventional foreign capital theories have their origin in Keynesian economics, and it is the challenge that John Maynard Keynes (1883–1946) made to the key assumptions of neoclassical theory that led him to recommend a particular form of state intervention. This provides the basis for arguing that the first foreign capital theories were influenced by contemporary Keynesian analysis (Riddell 1987, 87). However, Keynes's own theory was not one of dynamic growth. It was left to Harrod and Domar to extend the basic ideas of Keynesian analysis.

The Harrod-Domar Model

The two independent, yet similar, models of Sir Roy Harrod (1939) and Evsey Domar (1946) extended the basic ideas of Keynesian analysis. Like the classical economists, they assigned a central role to capital formation for promoting economic growth. It was, in particular, their introduction of the concept of incremental capital–output ratio and the assumption that it remained fixed over a specific time period that enabled them to form a long-term dynamic model.

The Harrod-Domar (H-D) model uses a mathematical equation to show a direct relationship between savings and the rate of economic growth, and an indirect relationship between the capital–output ratio and economic growth. The H-D model, which attempts to integrate Keynesian analysis with elements of economic growth, assumes that economic growth is a direct result of capital accumulation in the form of savings. Development economists have used the H-D model to calculate a *financing gap* that needed to be filled for an economy to develop. They argue that the binding constraint on production is insufficient physical capital. This view was consistent with the general perspective on development at the time and the notion of developing countries as labor surplus economies. Therefore, with the help of foreign capital, an economy can grow at a rate faster than that permitted by its domestic capital alone. This foreign capital that supplements domestic capital may come from private capital inflows from overseas or public capital inflows.

The attraction of the H-D model to policy analysts and planners is obvious. It relates directly to what they are interested in predicting, namely, investment requirements. It also avoids the difficulties of measuring capital stock. The popularity of the H-D model is confirmed by its adoption by many international organizations. The World Bank Revised Minimum Standard Model (RMSM, known as RimSim) still uses the H-D model for growth projection and financing requirements. The International Monetary Fund (IMF) also projects investment requirements as the "target growth rate times the ICOR" (incremental capital–output ratio) (for more details, see Easterly 1997).

Despite the practicality, popularity, and simplicity of the H-D model, it carries certain strong assumptions that must be borne in mind, particularly with respect to the less developed countries (LDCs). First, agricultural output must be realized. Second, management should be very competent in ensuring the judicious combination and utilization of all inputs. Third, credit must be channeled to support productive activities. Fourth, transfer of foreign resources is expected to lead to the transfer of technology and/or resource mobilization (see Dordunoo 2002, 3). The failure of these conditions can result in a negative ICOR, which does not make sense. A negative and highly volatile ICOR reflects noninvestment influences that affect output in a development process. Despite its strong assumptions, the Harrod-Domar model provides the simplest possible framework within which the relationships among the aggregate macroeconomic variables can be examined.

Rostow's Approach

W.W. Rostow was one of the first to make explicit reference to contemporary Keynesian theory and to incorporate these ideas into the economic purpose of foreign capital assistance. In many ways Rostow can be seen as a bridge between the politics and economics of foreign capital, as his economic reasoning was clearly positioned within a specific political ideology.

Writing in the mid-1950s, Rostow (1956) mentioned five stages of economic growth, the most important among them being the process of "take-off" into "self-sustaining growth." Relying on the Harrod-Domar model, for take-off to occur, Rostow defined three necessary conditions. First, there has to be a significant increase in the rate of net investment, say 5 percent to 10 percent. Second, one or more of the manufacturing sectors of the economy

has to exhibit a high rate of growth. Third, there needs to be an institutionally favorable environment (see Rostow 1956, 32). Thus, Rostow assigned a
crucial role to the investment rate for accelerating the process of economic
growth and achieving take-off.

While Rostow's stage theory gained wide appeal, it also attracted much
criticism during the 1960s. The criticisms concerned the tautological nature
of stage definition (one cannot distinguish between the end of one and the
beginning of another), a lack of empirical testing by Rostow, contradictory
quantitative evidence, and the assumption that poor countries are in the
traditional stage. However, whatever political message Rostow intended to
convey, he certainly also provided an economic explanation for the role of
foreign capital in accelerating the pace of economic development.

Rosenstein-Rodan's Approach

The arguments by Harrod-Domar and Rostow were succinctly stated by
Rosenstein-Rodan (1961) in his exposition of the savings gap approach to
foreign capital. He argued that foreign capital assistance is required to fill a
savings gap, and, ultimately, to make a transition to self-sustaining growth.
This transition is achieved if the marginal propensity to save exceeds the
average saving rate, so that the latter rises with income. Eventually domestic savings will be sufficient to finance the desired growth rate without
foreign public capital assistance, while private foreign capital imports may
continue.

While Rosenstein-Rodan provides an explanation for the role of foreign
capital assistance in the development process, he is equally anxious to point
out that major constraints inhibit the successful injection of foreign capital
assistance in accelerating the pace of economic development in developing
countries. Indeed, if these inhibiting factors predominate, his theoretical
perspective would lead to a rejection of the view that more foreign capital
will mean more development.

One problem with Rosenstein-Rodan's savings gap approach is that it
failed to take into account specific foreign exchange requirements for both
current production and capital formation in developing countries. The multiple
requirements of foreign capital—to provide additional savings and also to
finance intermediate and investment imports—were highlighted in the two-
gap theory proposed by Chenery and his collaborators.

The Gap Models

One of the most comprehensive theoretical justifications for foreign capital,
developed by Chenery and Strout (1966) and clearly following in the footsteps

of its predecessors, is the two-gap model. It is Keynesian, in the sense that it incorporates the mechanics of the Harrod-Domar model; it is neoclassical in its assumption that countries tend to be self-regulatory; it is Rostovian, because it incorporates conditions for take-off; and it is Rodanian in the sense that it considers the savings gap.

The Chenery and Strout theory is characterized by two different kinds of gaps in domestic resources that can be filled by foreign capital. In the first, called investment-limited growth, skills and savings are in short supply. In the second, trade-limited growth, foreign exchange is in short supply because export earnings are lower than import needs. These authors suggest that foreign capital can help to bridge each of these gaps until the self-sustaining stage is achieved.

The two-gap model also started a debate that highlighted the importance of each gap. Fei and Paauw (1965) emphasized the savings gap and highlighted the concept of "self-help." McKinnon (1964) analyzed the nature of the savings limit, the trade limit, and (briefly) the skilled limit on growth, but gave primary emphasis to trade limitation. He believed that foreign capital could have a large favorable impact on the growth rate, even where the absolute amount of capital flow is small, when the foreign capital is used to remove bottlenecks by providing strategic goods and services not produced in the developing economy.

The two-gap theory has been subject to a number of general criticisms. Two criticisms were made by Bruton (1969, 444–45). The first, from a neoclassical perspective, maintains that the trade limit is unlikely to occur in a well-managed economy and it is the saving problem, not the trade problem that the economy basically faces. The second criticism was that the inflow of external resources can be directed to consumer durable industries. As a result of it, the country has new activities the product of which cannot be exported. This will lead to an increase in domestic consumption, thereby affecting negatively the direct one-to-one relationship between capital inflow and increase in domestic savings level. White (1992, 176) also criticized the two-gap theory. First, the underlying Harrod-Domar model was considered a simplistic representation of the growth process in that many other factors besides capital accumulation can affect growth. Second, it does not incorporate any mechanisms by which foreign capital may not be matched by one-to-one increases in investment, government development expenditure, or foreign exchange.

While the development of the two-gap theory is an important contribution to the literature on economic development, more recently, there has been increasing interest in the three-gap model. This introduced fiscal constraint (by distinguishing public savings from private savings) as a third gap limiting the growth prospects of highly indebted developing economies (Bacha 1990; Solimano 1990; Taylor 1990).

In developing countries, the government often faces a deficit in its budget. The expectation is that taxes should cover a large share of public spending. However, there are many constraints on the level of taxation: political, structural, administrative, and purely social. Experience indicates that it is very difficult to significantly raise the tax level of developing countries. Developing countries can also try to tap domestic savings through the sale of bonds in the domestic market. This possibility, however, is also limited in these countries (for more details, see Tanzi and Blejer 1988). Public spending can be financed through monetary expansion, which tends to have an inflationary impact. These factors motivate governments toward foreign public borrowing and the existence of a third gap in developing countries.

The Dutch Disease Mechanism

Foreign capital inflow may have negative macroeconomic effects on external competitiveness and economic growth through the "Dutch disease" mechanism. Van Wijnbergen (1986) describes the Dutch disease mechanism, whereby foreign capital assistance is associated with real exchange rate appreciation. In his model, the relative price of traded to nontraded goods is the real exchange rate, and the increase in the relative price of nontraded goods is real exchange rate appreciation. According to Van Wijnbergen, some part of foreign capital assistance will be spent on nontraded goods, which will increase their relative price, placing upward pressure on the real exchange rate. The impact of these price changes will be to reallocate resources toward the nontraded goods sectors.

White (1992, 216) highlighted a number of disadvantages that may occur in the long term because of foreign capital flows. First, when foreign resource flows cease, the real exchange rate will depreciate, the availability of foreign exchange decreases, and the investment in tradable goods becomes more desirable. The imperfect nature of capital markets in developing countries results in a suboptimal level of investment in traded goods. Second, the reduced output caused by foreign capital inflow undermines future increases in productivity. Third, since it is commonly assumed that technical progress is faster in the traded goods sectors than in the nontraded goods sectors, the productive shift to nontraded goods will reduce the rate of technical progress and, therefore, the growth rate of the economy.

Foreign Capital and Domestic Savings

Of the wide variety of issues raised in the foreign capital debate, the one that has received much attention in the technical literature is the relationship between foreign capital and savings in recipient countries; that is, whether foreign capital supplements or substitutes domestic savings.

According to the Harrod-Domar model, the growth rate of output is equal to the savings rate s divided by the incremental capital output ratio k: $g = s/k$, where g is the growth rate of output. The dual-gap analysis argued that foreign capital acts to supplement domestic savings and hence raises the growth rate to $(s + f)/k$, where f is foreign capital inflow. This increase in growth rate raises incomes and, since it is believed that the marginal propensity to save is greater than the average propensity to save in LDCs, the savings rate increases and the higher growth rate becomes self-sustaining. Thus, according to this view, inflows of foreign capital would have the effect of raising the savings rate in subsequent periods.

Although there was no shortage of scholars expressing skepticism about the role of foreign capital in promoting economic growth and savings, this had little impact upon conventional thinking until the publication of two papers by Griffin (1970) and Griffin and Enos (1970), in which they challenged the benefits of foreign capital but cast their arguments in the Harrod-Domar framework. According to Griffin and Enos, foreign capital inflows, rather than supplementing domestic savings, act as a substitute for them. This mechanism operates in both public and private sectors. Faced with inflows of foreign capital, recipient governments may reduce their tax collection effort and change the composition of their consumption. Similarly, the availability of low-interest loans may reduce incentives to save in the private sector.

Having accepted that foreign capital causes the domestic savings rate to decline, Griffin continues by arguing that at least some of the foreign capital (say, α) will be spent on consumption rather than investment, and that the incremental capital–output ratio will rise with foreign capital, given the donor's bias toward prestige capital-intensive projects that were not necessarily the most productive from the recipient's viewpoint. Thus, the original Harrod-Domar model of $g = s/k$ was modified to:

$$g = [s* + (1-a)f]/k*$$

where $s*$ is the post-aid saving rate, α is the proportion of foreign capital spent on consumption or nonproductive expenditure, and $k*$ is the post-aid incremental capital–output ratio. Thus, foreign capital reduces growth and domestic savings.

Colman and Nixson (1978, 115) claimed that Griffin's argument contains a "basic algebraic flaw," insofar as while consumption is modeled as a function of income plus foreign capital, savings is modeled as a function of income alone. They countered that, like consumption; savings should also be made a function of income plus foreign capital. If this is done, the negative relationship between foreign capital and savings disappears.[2] According to White (1992, 178) there is no economic model in Griffin's analysis but only an accounting identity. The absence of an economic model is a serious criticism of Griffin's approach. Further, in Griffin's analysis, foreign capital is treated as untied income, yet tying of foreign assistance to investment has no effect on domestic savings.

Fungibility of Foreign Capital

As stated earlier, it is generally believed that foreign capital will increase growth in the recipient country. Much of the traditional argument has been based on the two-gap theory: if the binding constraint is foreign exchange, then additional capital inflows will raise import capacity, import-constrained investment, and thereby economic growth.

This simple view has been challenged on various grounds. One reason is fungibility of foreign capital inflows. Foreign capital is said to be fungible if its inflow, primarily intended to raise investment and imports, does not lead to an increase in these variables by the value of the inflow. It may lead to higher government consumption or to lower taxes, which will affect the national savings level and thus offset some of the positive effects on investment and growth. Foreign capital inflows can also reduce exports through appreciation of the real exchange rate (the Dutch disease mechanism), meaning that import capacity may not increase by the full amount of resource inflow.

Pack and Pack (1990, 188) provided a theoretical explanation of the fungibility issue. According to them, the governments of LDCs have indifference curves between two goods or sectors and a budget line whose height is determined by its own revenue plus that available from abroad and whose slope reflects the relative cost of two activities. The magnitude of fungibility depends on the shape of the indifference map. If indifference curves are homothetic, part of the categorical assistance will be spent on the objectives desired by the donor, part will be spent on other publicly provided goods or employed to reduce taxes. If the indifference curves are nonhomothetic, considerable substitution may occur, with expenditures on the category targeted by the foreign assistance conceivably declining.

Theoretical Literature on Debt Issues

Debt Cycle Model

The behavior of gross capital inflow varies in different stages, which may be called the debt cycle, and which is closely linked with the course of economic development. Avramovic and colleagues (1964, 53–54) explained the three stages of the debt cycle.

First Stage: In the first stage of the development process, as investment increases, savings, starting from a low level, are inadequate to finance domestic investment requirements. A country has to borrow not only to finance part of the investment, but also to meet amortization charges and to pay interest on the debt that is accumulated in this process. The external indebtedness increases rapidly; since interest on debt incurred previously is paid out of new borrowing, which also carries interest, the familiar law of compound interest operates in all its force.

Second Stage: In the second stage, the savings would still not be sufficient to meet the entire additional burden of interest and amortization payments on accumulated debt. As the second stage proceeds, an increasing part of the interest cost is paid out of domestic savings. No net repayment takes place yet; but as borrowing to pay interest become smaller and smaller, external indebtedness rises at a pace which is continuously diminishing. At the very end of the second stage, borrowing is undertaken only for rolling over and refinancing operations, that is, to cover amortization. Debt has reached its highest peak and ceases to grow.

Third Stage: In this stage domestic savings are sufficient to finance all domestic investment, and in addition they are enough to pay for the entire cost of accumulated debt. The law of compound interest now works in reverse and outstanding external debt diminishes rapidly. The country now pays back all the cost that was postponed in earlier periods. The debt cycle has been completed; the foreign capital has helped the country to enter the continuously rising upward curve of economic growth.

A later study (see World Bank 1985, 47) further elaborated that in a debt cycle a country passes through five stages.

- *Stage I. Young debtor:* characterized by a trade deficit, net outflow of interest payments, net inflow of capital, and rising debt.
- *Stage II. Mature debtor:* characterized by a decreasing trade deficit, beginning of a surplus, net outflow of interest payments, decreasing net inflow of capital, and debt rising at a diminishing rate.
- *Stage III. Debt reducer:* characterized by a rising trade surplus, diminishing net outflow of interest payment, net outflow of capital, and a falling net foreign debt.
- *Stage IV. Young creditor:* characterized by a decreasing trade surplus and then deficit, net outflow of interest payments and then inflow, outflow of capital at a decreasing rate and net accumulation of foreign assets.
- *Stage V. Mature creditor:* characterized by trade deficit, net inflow of interest payments; diminishing net flows of capital, and slow-growing or constant net foreign assets position.

For a country to become a net creditor, three conditions must be fulfilled: first, that the savings gap can in due course be reversed; second, that the foreign exchange gap can be reversed; and third, that the funds are invested in projects that yield a rate of return in excess of the interest rate on the debt. The debt servicing problem arises when one or more of these conditions is not fulfilled.

Debt Overhang Theory

One situation that attracted considerable attention is the possibility that an increase in the level of debt, beyond a certain point, strictly reduces the re-payments creditors can expect to receive. Such a situation has been called a "debt overhang." According to Krugman (1988, 255) "a country has a debt overhang problem when the expected present value of potential future resource transfer is less than its debt." The concept is further explored in a number of other papers including Claessens and Diwan (1989), Geiger (1990), and Sachs (1990).

Sachs (1990) argued that external debt overhang is a major cause of stunted economic growth in heavily indebted countries, and that there is an urgent need for debt reduction and an international debt relief facility. The rationale for this debt relief is twofold: (1) the required debt service payments for some countries are so large that prospects for a return to a growth path are dim; and (2) the existence of a large debt overhang inhibits private investment and government adoption of adjustment programs. The genesis of the deliberating effect of external public debt on economic growth lies in the argument that high governmental debt service payments require high tax rates, which in turn discourage capital formation and repatriation of flight capital.

Claessens and Diwan (1989) recognized two types of debt overhang—weak debt overhang and strong debt overhang. In cases of weak debt overhang, new loans and precommitments on investment can be sufficient to restore credit-worthiness and achieve a higher growth rate. On the other hand, in cases of strong debt overhang, debt relief is also needed to restore high growth.

According to Geiger (1990, 186), some of the ways that excessive debt burden appears to affect economic development are: (a) large debt service requirements divert foreign exchange and capital from internal investment to debt service; (b) the inability of the country to service the debt will eventu-ally cause difficulties in borrowing for new projects; (c) the accumulation of debt reduces the country's efficiency, and makes it difficult for the country to adjust efficaciously to major shocks; and (d) because of the increased pressure to obtain more foreign exchange to service the debt, the indebted nation restricts imports, thus reducing the trade. If it is argued that external trade improves factor productivity (because of economies of scale), increases incentives for technological innovation, increases competition, and promotes a better use of resources and the transmission of these effects throughout the economy, then it can be rationalized that the excessive debt burden reduces technological growth.

The debt overhang problem can be represented by the debt Laffer curve (see Pattillo, Poirson, and Ricci 2002, 33), which posits that larger debt stock tends to be associated with lower probabilities of debt repayment. On the upward sloping or "right side" of the curve, increases in the face value are associated with increases in expected repayment, while increases in debt reduce expected debt repayment on the downward sloping or "wrong side" of the curve.

Thus, debt relief through debt service or debt stock reduction becomes a rational choice for both creditors and debtors when a debtor is said to be on the "wrong side" of the debt Laffer curve. It is in the interest of the creditors to reduce the level of debt through voluntary debt forgiveness. This results in increased investment and growth in a debtor country and subsequently increases debt service payments to the creditors.

Conclusion

The survey of the best-known theoretical perspectives shows that to date no single theory or perspective has emerged demonstrating anything close to a consensus regarding the macroeconomic effects of foreign capital. In order to reach a consensus and to extend the base of theoretical literature, the following directions for further research are proposed:

- It is a cause of great concern that little attention has been paid in the theoretical literature to the social and institutional impact of foreign capital inflows. There is a need for more theoretical work in this area.
- The impact of foreign public capital inflows on the private sector needs much explanation on the theoretical front. It is an important area of theoretical research given the current trend of privatization, denationalization, and liberalization.
- The theoretical explanation of the debt servicing problem should go beyond the indicator approach. There is a need for a complete theory on the debt accumulation process and the debt servicing problem.

In conclusion, it can be said that surveys are meant to be read rather than summarized, and it becomes more difficult when we are dealing with controversial theoretical issues. This chapter has attempted to give a sampling of theoretical approaches from the existing literature and to explain what are believed to be the most important developments.[3] Sometimes, these explanations may turn out to be oversimplified; in other cases they may be overabbreviated. To obtain a greater understanding of the existing theories, the original work should be consulted. Nevertheless, it is hoped that this description of theoretical developments will help and encourage empirical studies in this area.

Notes

The author thanks Mitsuo Ezaki for encouragement and helpful comments. Thanks are also due to Anjum Siddiqui for many helpful and incisive comments.

1. For a detailed historical review of foreign capital inflows, see Hughes (1979) and Fishlow (1988). For a discussion of the politics of foreign capital assistance, see Hussein (1988).

2. For an algebraic explanation of this argument, see Colman and Nixson 1978, p. 126.

3. For a detailed survey of empirical studies on the macroeconomic effects of foreign capital, see Waheed (2004).

References

Avramovic, D., et al. 1964. *Economic Growth and External Debt.* Baltimore: Johns Hopkins University Press.

Bacha, E.L. 1990. "A Three-Gap Model of Foreign Transfers and the GDP Growth Rate in Developing Countries." *Journal of Development Economics* 32, no. 2: 279–96.

Bruton, H.J. 1969. "The Two-Gap Approach to Aid and Development: Comment." *American Economic Review* 59, no. 3: 439–46.

Cassen, R., et al. 1986. *Does Aid Work?* Oxford: Clarendon Press.

Chenery, H.B., and A.M. Strout. 1966. "Foreign Assistance and Economic Development." *American Economic Review* 56, no. 4: 679–733.

Claessens, S., and I. Diwan. 1989. "Conditionality and Debt Relief." Working Paper Series no. 213. World Bank.

Colman, D., and F. Nixson. 1978. *Economics of Change in Less Developed Countries.* Oxford: Philip Alan.

Domar, E. 1946. "Capital Expansion, Rate of Growth and Employment." *Econometrica* 14, no. 2: 137–47.

Dordunoo, C.K. 2002. "Ghana: Aggregate Supply Growth Models and Policy Implications." Paper presented at the Seventh Annual Conference on Econometric Modeling for Africa. Kruger National Park, South Africa, July 2–4.

Easterly, W. 1997. "The Ghost of Financing Gap: How the Harrod-Domar Growth Model Still Haunts Development Economics." Policy Research Working Paper no. 1807. World Bank, Washington, DC.

Fei, J.C.H., and D.S. Paauw. 1965. "Foreign Assistance and Self-Help: A Reappraisal of Development Finance." *Review of Economics and Statistics* 47, no. 3: 251–67.

Fishlow, A. 1988. "External Borrowing and Debt Management." In *The Open Economy: Tools for Policy Makers in Developing Countries,* ed. R. Dornbusch et al., 187–222. New York: Oxford University Press.

Geiger, L.T. 1990. "Debt and Economic Development in Latin America." *Journal of Developing Areas* 24, no. 2: 181–94.

Griffin, K. 1970. "Foreign Capital, Domestic Savings and Economic Development." *Bulletin of the Oxford University Institute of Economics and Statistics* 32, no. 2: 99–112.

Griffin, K.B., and J.L. Enos. 1970. "Foreign Assistance; Objectives and Consequences." *Economic Development and Cultural Change* 18, no. 3: 313–27.

Harrod, Sir Roy E. 1939. "An Essay in Dynamic Theory." *Economic Journal* 49, no. 193: 14–33.

Hughes, H. 1979. "Debt and Development: The Role of Foreign Capital in Economic Growth." *World Development* 7, no. 2: 95–112.

Hussein, M.A. 1988. "Is Foreign Aid an Obstruction to Democracy and Development in the Third World?" *Pakistan Development Review* 27, no. 4: 529–34.

Krugman, P. 1988. "Financing vs. Forgiving a Debt Overhang." *Journal of Development Economics* 29, no. 3: 253–68.

McKinnon, R.I. 1964. "Foreign Exchange Constraints in Economic Development and Efficient Aid Allocation." *Economic Journal* 74, no. 294: 388–409.

Mikesell, R.F. 1968. *The Economics of Foreign Aid.* London: Weidenfeld and Nicolson.

Pack, H., and J.R. Pack. 1990. "Is Foreign Aid Fungible? The Case of Indonesia." *Economic Journal* 100, no. 339: 188–94.

Pattilo, C.; H. Poirson; and L. Ricci. 2002. "External Debt and Growth." *Finance and Development* 39, no. 2: 32–35.

Riddell, R. 1987. *Foreign Aid Reconsidered.* Baltimore, MD: Johns Hopkins University Press.

Rosenstein-Rodan, P.N. 1961. "International Aid for Undeveloped Countries." *Review of Economics and Statistics* 43, no. 2: 107–38.

Rostow, W.W. 1956. "The Take-Off into Self-Sustained Growth." *Economic Journal* 66, no. 261: 25–48.

Sachs, J.D. 1990. "A Strategy for Efficient Debt Reduction." *Journal of Economic Perspective* 4, no. 1: 19–29.

Solimano, A. 1990. "Macroeconomic Constraints for Medium Term Growth and Distribution: A Model for Chile." Working Paper Series no. 400. World Bank.

Tanzi, V., and M.I. Blejer. 1988. "Public Debt and Fiscal Policy in Developing Countries." In *The Economics of Public Debt*, ed. J.A. Kenneth and M.J. Boskin, 230–63. London: Macmillan.

Taylor, L. 1990. "Foreign Resource Flows and Developing Country Growth: A Three-Gap Approach." In *Problems of Developing Countries in the 1990s*, ed. F.D. McCarthy, 55–90. World Bank Discussion Paper 97. Washington, DC.

Van Wijnbergen, S. 1986. "Macroeconomic Aspects of the Effectiveness of Foreign Aid: The Two-Gap Model, Home Goods Disequilibrium and Real Exchange Rate Misalignment." *Journal of International Economics* 21, nos. 1/2: 123–36.

Waheed, A. 2004. "Foreign Capital Inflows and Economic Growth of Developing Countries: A Critical Survey of Empirical Studies." *Journal of Economic Cooperation among Islamic Countries* 25, no. 1: 1–36.

White, H. 1992. "The Macroeconomic Impact of Development Aid: A Critical Survey." *Journal of Development Studies* 28, no. 2: 163–240.

World Bank. 1985. *World Development Report, 1985.* Washington, DC.

7

Foreign Investment and Economic Growth

A Case Study of India

Sajid Anwar and Parikshit K. Basu

The 1990s were globally a period of high foreign investment triggered by improvements in communication technology and greater recognition of the benefits of foreign investment. Improvement in communications technology allowed firms to develop increasingly effective strategies resulting in an efficient use of available capital. The change in attitudes of governments resulted in a reduction of direct and indirect obstacles to foreign investment. In order to attract foreign investment, governments of some Asian economies increased incentives to foreign investors. Privatization and deregulation resulted in further increases in foreign investment. Thomsen (1999), Czinkota, Ronkainen, and Moffett (2005) and Hill (2005) have argued that worldwide increases in foreign investment can also be attributed to globalization. Foreign investment has become an integral part of corporate strategies in recent years. The growth of foreign investment has considerably increased due to the fact that competing firms follow each other into the new market.[1]

Prior to the financial crisis of 1997–98, Asia had been attracting a significant proportion of foreign investment in developing countries for many years.[2] There was a sharp decline in foreign investment in Asia in 1998. China emerged as a popular destination for foreign investment in the early 1990s. By 1993, China was the second largest recipient of foreign investment in the world. Although there is an increase in foreign investment in India, in overall terms, the level of foreign investment as compared to that in China is insignificant (see Figure 7.1).

The importance of foreign direct investment (FDI) to China's economy is significant. For example, multinational enterprises doing business in China

152

Figure 7.1   **Foreign Investment in Millions of U.S. Dollars**

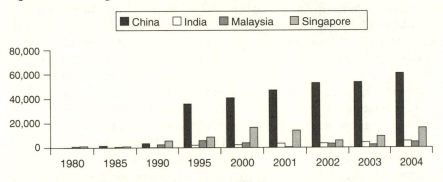

Source: UNCTAD *Handbook of Statistics* 2005.

contributed $27 billion through corporate tax in 2000 (UNCTAD 2001), which represents 18 percent of China's entire corporate tax revenue in 2000. The attractiveness of China as a destination for FDI inflows is attributed to its huge domestic market; the increased purchasing power of local consumers; political pragmatism in liberalizing China's regulatory framework and membership in the World Trade Organization (WTO).

Since its independence from the United Kingdom, India has largely pursued inward-looking import substitution policies. These policies resulted in moderate growth that relied mainly on growth in domestic demand. The end of the Cold War resulted in a strategic shift in India's external trade and investment policies. Foreign investors find India to be an attractive destination because of a large domestic market, political stability, a well-developed and respected legal system, and the availability of a highly skilled workforce. The recent Asian financial crisis shows that foreign investment alone cannot guarantee economic growth. After all, the primary concern of foreign investors is their profit. Excessive foreign investment can in fact be bad for a country. It is therefore important at the government level that each proposal for foreign investment is properly evaluated in terms of its potential costs and benefits before approval.

The aim of this chapter is to examine the costs and benefits of foreign investment with particular reference to India during 1991–92 and 2001–2, the first decade after economic reform measures were introduced. It is very crucial to steer the economy in the initial years of reform. In 1991, foreign investment in India was negligible. At the same time, lack of capital was very prominent and was affecting economic growth adversely. Thus attracting foreign investment was one of the priority areas at that point of time.

Among the South Asian economies, India is the largest recipient of FDI, and it is emerging as one of the major economic powers in the region, rivaling China. Since the introduction of major economic and financial reforms just over a decade ago, India has started receiving foreign investments in increasing volume. In fact, since the collapse of the Soviet Union, a number of countries have taken steps to liberalize their trade and foreign investment policies. However, India maintains its unique position for several reasons. It was never closed to the outside world in the way that the former socialist bloc countries were. With the second largest population in the world, India followed a very controlled industrial policy where licensing had created public and private sector monopolies in a number of areas. A liberal democratic setup and a fairly independent judiciary made the country very attractive to potential foreign investors in the Western world. However, very tight government control kept foreign investors away. The tight government control hindered economic growth. As compared with some Southeast Asian economies (e.g., Malaysia and Singapore), the Indian economy registered insignificant growth. It is widely believed that the phenomenal growth experienced by some Southeast Asian economies during the past two decades was partly fueled by massive foreign investment. At the same time, the Indian economy was struggling due to inefficiencies. Corruption was another serious concern that could be attributed to state control. Recognition of inefficiencies and changes in the external climate effectively forced India to liberalize its trade and industrial policy in 1991, which led to an inflow of foreign investment. Foreign investment appears to have helped India to maintain a real economic growth rate of over 5 percent annually in recent years. An examination of the Indian experience should be useful to economic policymakers in the neighboring countries.

Foreign Direct Investment and the Developing Countries

Economic growth is closely related to the free market system. Under a free market system, the government provides only those goods and services that cannot be efficiently produced by the private sector. This includes public goods such as production infrastructure, national defense, and legal protection. During the 1960s and 1970s, development policy analysts believed that less developed countries could improve their economic well-being either through export promotion or though import substitution. In fact, in the post–World War II period, the South American economies generally followed import substitution policies and the East and Southeast Asian nations (particularly from the 1960s) followed the broad export orientation approach (Glick and Moreno 1997). However, within Asia, from the very beginning, only Hong Kong and Singapore relied heavily on free trade policies. Others such as Taiwan, Korea, and even Japan followed market-friendly interventionist policies that consisted of a mix of export promotion and selective import barriers. Between 1965 and the mid-1990s, the real GDP of some Asian countries (Korea, Hong Kong, Singapore, and Korea) grew at an annual average rate of 9 percent, more than twice that of the South American economies (Glick and Moreno 1997). Both exports and imports grew twice as fast in East Asia as in South America. Openness and a steady inflow of foreign investment played major roles in this process.

Foreign investment has been a key factor driving export-led growth in East and Southeast Asia. South Asian countries are now attempting to emulate the same approach. Foreign investment can be divided into two broad categories, foreign direct investment and foreign portfolio investment (FPI). FDI is usually defined as a holding of 10 percent or more of ordinary shares or voting stock in an enterprise (Appleyard, Field, and Cobb 2006). This implies that as compared with FPI, FDI involves ownership and control. In other words, FDI occurs when an investor based in one country (i.e., the home country) acquires an asset in another country (i.e., the host country) with the intent to manage that asset. FDI is essentially investment by a foreign investor aiming to obtain a lasting interest in an enterprise. Multinational corporations (MNCs) are the most common conduits for FDI. FDI enables multinationals to expand in global markets. It is well known that MNCs use FDI to avoid trade barriers, reduce exchange risk, secure low-cost inputs, or tailor products more closely to local markets.

FDI can be divided into two categories: horizontal foreign direct investment and vertical foreign direct investment (Hill 2005). Horizontal FDI is investment in the same industry abroad that the firm operates in at home. Horizontal FDI is a strategy to increase market share in a global economy, and is a more attractive option when there are high export costs, government intervention, and the threat to intellectual property and loss of control through licensing. Vertical FDI takes two forms: backward and forward. Backward vertical FDI is investment in an industry abroad that provides inputs for a firm's domestic production processes, whereas forward vertical FDI is investment in an industry abroad that sells the outputs of a firm's domestic production processes (Hill 2005).

Foreign investment enables firms to look beyond the constraints of their domestic markets to combine investment, trade, and collaborative arrangements to expand internationally. The location decision of FDI is based on a number of factors such as market opportunities and the quality and price of the available resources. The ultimate long-term goal remains profit that is based on competitiveness. Factors that create a conducive and accommodating environment for FDI inflow include stable macroeconomic conditions; a high quality infrastructure; liberal trade and investment policies; a fast-growing market; and a relatively cheap but skilled and disciplined labor force. Countries seeking significant FDI attempt to lure MNCs through favorable policies such as tax breaks, debt financing, favorable labor policies, and liberalization of foreign investment regimes. Factors that hinder FDI include an unstable political situation; uncooperative government officials (e.g., excessive red tape); unsupportive attitudes of local players; ambiguous host government policies (e.g., inadequacy of regulatory regimes and/or lack of transparency in corporate governance); unsupportive feelings of local people (e.g., antiglobalization sentiment); inadequate supporting industries; and infrastructure problems (e.g., weakened commercial infrastructure).[3]

Potential benefits of FDI to the host country arise from the fact that FDI represents a form of economic integration. Economic integration has the potential to generate higher levels of material well-being for citizens of the host country. Countries differ in their endowments of natural resources and factors of production. These differences, together with differences in economic policies, give rise to differences in the cost of production. Economic integration allows countries to direct resources, both real and financial, toward those activities in which they possess a comparative cost advantage. The resulting specialization increases efficiency in production. Economic integration widens markets and, in doing so, increases the competitive pressure that accompanies larger numbers of buyers and sellers. Small countries appear to be more prone to anticompetitive practices because of the small size of their domestic markets. Opening such markets to competition from imports and the entry of MNCs can counter local monopoly power, thereby forcing all firms to operate more efficiently. FDI can act as a vehicle through which technical competencies, managerial styles, and best working practices can be transferred to local firms (Czinkota and Kotabe, 1998).

Inflows of FDI can also increase the amount of capital in the host country, unless the MNCs borrow capital from the domestic market. Generally, an increase in the supply of capital is likely to raise labor productivity and hence the wage rate. FDI can strengthen the capability of developing countries such as India to reach international markets through its international links. This is particularly true as far as the Indian information technology industry is concerned. Competitive pressure created by FDI can also force the local firms to increase spending on research and development.

The relatively stable flows of FDI during the Asian financial turmoil highlight the advantages of FDI as a form of external finance.[4] The continuity of FDI inflow into the crisis-hit economies partly reduced the financial fluctuations and helped stabilize the economies of Malaysia, South Korea, and Thailand.[5]

FDI may not be beneficial to developing countries if, for example, an MNC or its affiliate shows little interest in developing local assets at their optimal rate, or deliberately slows their rate of development to suit their own designs. In other words, foreign firms are just out for what they can get. MNCs can shift profits from their activities in one country into another to avoid taxes. This can occur through the manipulation of "transfer pricing."[6] Profits earned in the host country would be artificially low, therefore attracting low tax liability.

As far as FDI in developing countries is concerned, MNCs often move the high valued-added activities and high-paying jobs from the host country to the headquarters. The higher the value added in a value-added activity, the higher its contribution to GDP and therefore to per capita GDP. High value-added activities also attract skilled workers, while the presence of high-paying jobs keeps skilled people in a country (Harper 2001). MNCs care less about industrial pollution than local firms do. In some cases, FDI allows MNCs to avoid compliance with public policies through shifting its operations to another country. There is also concern regarding the MNCs' vulnerability to foreign government pressure and its effect on host country national interests. Some have argued that the benefits of increased economic growth have been lopsided.

Developed countries remain the prime destination, accounting for more than three-quarters of global inflows. For example, almost 50 percent of U.S. FDI takes place in Europe and vice versa (Appleyard and Field 2001). The United Nations Conference on Trade and Development (UNCTAD 2001) highlights the rapid expansion of FDI flows and the resulting international production in the world; the report also points to the uneven distribution of FDI. For example, the world's top thirty host countries account for 95 percent of total world inflows and 90 percent of (FDI) stocks. The top thirty home countries account for around 90 percent of outward FDI flows and stocks, mainly industrialized economies. The headquarters of almost ninety out of the largest hundred MNCs are located in Europe, Japan, or the United States. The developing countries appear to be at risk of becoming more marginalized in a fast-globalizing world economy. Developing countries lacking in a skilled labor force, high-quality production infrastructure, and export facilities, and without prosperous domestic consumers are unlikely to attract significant FDI.

Increasing FDI in China demonstrates that MNCs have been forced to rely on developing countries as a source of labor. Increases in wages resulting from FDI in developing countries are likely to create a situation where a significant proportion of the goods produced by the MNCs are sold to the local population. It has been argued that the relocation of production units to lower-wage economies is likely to boost long-term economic growth in the host countries. FDI increases the degree of dependence between the developed and the developing countries, which facilitates technology transfer. The recent push for worldwide free trade and the rapid pace of globalization are likely to increase foreign investment in developing countries.[7]

Foreign Direct Investment in India

With a population of more than 1 billion, India is now widely regarded as one of the major emerging economic powers in Asia. As its political and judicial systems conform to the norms of the developed Western world, India has the potential to become a major recipient of foreign investment in Asia if supportive policies are adopted by the government. From independence in 1947 to the first half of the 1980s, India relied heavily on inward-looking economic policies developed though a central planning mechanism. The focus of the economic policies and planning was on self-reliance. Consequently, foreign involvement was actively discouraged in most areas (Dutta 1998). The official policy was to welcome foreign investment on a selective basis in areas considered to be advantageous to the Indian economy.

The end of the Cold War witnessed a significant shift in government policies with respect to foreign investment. A broad range of reforms was formally initiated in 1991. These reforms resulted in an industrial policy that was aimed at freeing Indian industry from excessive government control. The government policy shift facilitated, among other results, the inflow of significant foreign investments. It was felt that foreign investment would facilitate not only technology transfer but marketing expertise, and the introduction of modern managerial techniques that would boost India's exports (Datar and Basu 2003). In other words, foreign investment was favored not only because of its direct benefits but also for its potential indirect benefits to export industries. Foreign investment policies have been further liberalized since 1991, which could explain a rapid rise in FDI in recent years. India is also likely to join the Association of Southeast Asian Nations (ASEAN) in the near future, which will promote freer trade with the member countries.

Gradual liberalization has resulted in a situation where, at present, except for a few areas, the process of foreign investment approval has been significantly simplified. Parties interested in investing in India are required to inform the Reserve Bank of India within thirty days of bringing in their investments. Foreign investors can set up 100 percent subsidiaries in, among others, manufacturing activities in special economic zones, in most areas of telecommunications and oil refining, and in nonbanking financial companies. Even the defense sector is now open to private sector participation with FDI permitted up to 26 percent (Government of India 2003a).

As a result of progressively liberalized policies, annual inflows of foreign investments in India, both in terms of FDI and portfolio investment, have steadily increased over the years. From a meager amount of $97 million in 1990–91, FDI inflows rose to more than $6 billion in 2001–2 (see Table 7.1). Direct equity participation by foreign companies consistently accounted for a significant proportion of FDI inflow.

Figure 7.2 presents annual growth rates of FDI inflows in India during the postreform period. Phenomenal growth is evident during the initial years, as it started from a very low base. The rate started declining in 1996–97 with the onset of the Asian financial crisis. Most of the Southeast Asian economies

Table 7.1

Foreign Investment in India (US$ millions)

	1990–1991	1995–1996	1999–2000	2000–2001	2001–2002
Foreign direct investment	97	2,144	2,155	4,029	6,131
• Equity	—	2,144	2,155	2,400	4,095
• Reinvested earnings	—	—	—	1,350	1,646
• Other capital	—	—	—	279	390
Portfolio investment	6	2,748	3,026	2,760	2,021
Total foreign investments	103	4,892	5,181	6,789	8,152
Foreign direct investment as % of total foreign investments	94.2	43.8	41.6	59.3	75.2

Source: Reserve Bank of India, *RBI Bulletin*, September 2003, table 46.

Figure 7.2   **Annual Growth in FDI Inflows in India 1991–2002** (%)

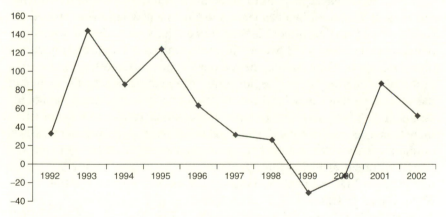

Source: Reserve Bank of India, *RBI Bulletin*, September 2003, table no. 46.

experienced severe economic crisis during 1997–98 and FDI inflows were adversely affected. Although India was not directly affected by the Asian financial crisis, it could not escape the indirect adverse effects. FDI inflow to India declined during 1998–2000. The situation improved thereafter and India was able to attract an all-time high level of FDI in 2001–2. However, global

Figure 7.3   **India's Inflow of FDI as % of China's Inflow of FDI, 1995–2004**

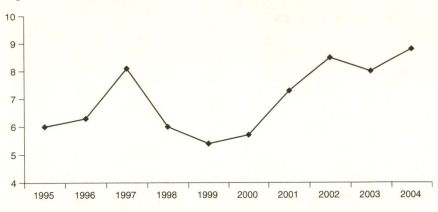

Source: UNCTAD *Handbook of Statistics* (2005).

economic uncertainties arising due to the events of September 11, 2001, in the United States have contributed to increased uncertainty and volatility in FDI flows to India.

India's performance in terms of attracting FDI is often compared with that of China. India gained independence and China a new regime at around the same time and have taken steps to further liberalize their trade and investment policies in recent years.[8] However, the two countries are quite dissimilar in a number of ways. For example, the political, economic, and judicial systems in the two countries are still significantly different. Based on the available data, it is clear that China has been more successful in attracting foreign investment than India has. China started its economic reform process in 1978, more than a decade before India initiated major reforms. As indicated earlier, during the early 1990s, China became a major recipient of FDI. India is the largest recipient of FDI among the South Asian nations. Figure 7.3 shows that the total FDI received by India represents only a small fraction of the FDI received by China.

In 1998, India received approximately 2.7 percent of worldwide FDI. During the same period, China and Malaysia received 12.7 percent and 16.5 percent, respectively, of worldwide FDI (Forbes 2002, 134). In 2001, China's share of global inflow of FDI was 6.4 percent versus less than 0.5 percent for India (UNCTAD 2001). Excluding Japan, China received 43 percent of FDI in Asia in 1996 and 46 percent in 2002 (Government of India 2003a). During the same period, India's share increased from 2.7 percent to 3.3 percent.

Although as per the official statistics, China attracts much bigger amounts of FDI annually; the difference could be explained by different definitions of FDI adopted by the two countries (Bajpai and Dasgupta 2004; Luce 2002). China includes all 12 elements of FDI as per IMF definition, whereas India includes only one of the elements (equity capital).

The reforms undertaken by the Indian government in 1991 have resulted in an increase in the economic growth rate as well as in the inflow of FDI. In 1950–74, the average annual growth rate of the Indian economy (in terms of real GDP) was 1.5 percent as compared with 4.2 percent for China, 2.6 percent for Malaysia, 3.6 percent for Thailand, and 2.8 percent for the Philippines (Krueger and Chinoy 2002, 11). In the 1980s and 1990s, the average annual real GDP growth rate in India jumped to about 5.6 percent (Government of India 2003a, Table 1.2).[9] Per capita GDP also increased at a rate of more than 4 percent per annum during the 1990s (ibid.).

Although the pace of overall reforms slowed down in India in the second half of the 1990s due to a change in governments at the national level and in some of the states, FDI inflows continued at a satisfactory pace.[10] The inflow of FDI has a significant positive impact on the growth of employment and productivity in the private sector. In 1980–90, annual employment growth in the private sector was about 0.4 percent. This annual growth rate increased to about 3 percent in the subsequent decade (1991–98). At the same time, employment growth in the public sector remained more or less stable during the entire period (1.25 percent and 1.62 percent, respectively, in the two periods mentioned above).[11] Foreign investment in general and FDI in particular flowed predominantly to the private sector units in India. Using a crude measure of labor productivity (real wages per worker), demonstrates that the private sector has improved its position since FDI flows started, whereas the public sector's position has remained unchanged. Using the same Annual Survey of Industries data, it is estimated that the real wage in the private sector has grown at an annual rate of 4.75 percent during 1991–98 as against 2.3 percent during 1979–90. Growth in the public sector real wage rate remained unchanged at about 3.8 percent in both periods.

Economic reforms and the inflow of foreign investment have helped the export sector in India. During 1991–92 to 2001–2, India's total exports expanded at an average annual rate of 8.8 percent, from US$18.145 billion to US$43.827 billion. During the same period, imports increased at an annual rate of 7.9 percent (from US$24.073 billion to US$51.413 billion) (*Reserve Bank of India Bulletin*, September 2003, table 41). Despite an increase in exports, India has consistently registered trade and current account deficits but the situation is improving. Export growth certainly looks promising. During the 1980s the average annual growth rate was 6.1 percent, which represents an improvement over the 1970s when the growth rate was 6.8 percent (Krueger and Chinoy 2002, 13). However, India's share of world exports remained insignificant at around 0.5 percent over the past three decades (ibid.).

Ideally one of the major benefits of FDI for a recipient country should be access to new and more efficient technology. But in the case of India, FDI has not so far resulted in technology transfer. It has been observed that the types of technology transferred by foreign investors, at least in the initial years, was mainly intermediate and standardized. To date, China's experience appears to be very similar to that of India. Major providers of FDI in China (e.g., Hong Kong and Taiwan) are known for low and standardized levels of technology, not for sophisticated types (Coughlin and Segev 2000). Thus, as a result of increasing FDI, technology gaps between India/China and the developed Western economies have not yet been narrowed significantly.

Major Sources of Foreign Direct Investment

The United States accounts for more than one-fifth of FDI proposals approved in India so far (see Table 7.2). U.S. investors have consistently maintained their share in recent years. In addition, nonresident Indians contribute another 3.7 percent of FDI, of which U.S. residents may constitute a significant proportion. It is surprising to note that Mauritius is the second largest source of FDI in India. In fact, during certain years (e.g., 2000) it has been the largest source country. Mauritius's population includes a large number of native Indians. In addition, certain tax benefits may have encouraged investors to source their funds back to India through Mauritius.[12] Among the Asian nations, Japan and Korea account for a significant proportion of FDI in India. Malaysia and Singapore also figure prominently on the list. Specific euro issues have become a major source of FDI in recent years. However, as can been seen from Table 7.2, euro issues are highly volatile.

Sectoral Trends

In the early years, manufacturing, service, and the food and dairy industries figured prominently among FDI recipients in India. Subsequently, the engineering industries' share increased at a much faster pace than the others. Engineering industries are now the major recipient of FDI in India (see Table 7.3). Within the engineering sector, power and oil refineries and telecommunications are most popular among the foreign investors. India is now attracting a rising proportion of foreign investment from global growth industries. More than 40 percent of the world's 500 largest companies now carry out some of their back office processing in India (Luce 2002).

Table 7.2

Major Sources of Foreign Direct Investment in India: Proposals Approved (millions of rupees)

	2000	2001	2002	2003[a]	Total (1991–2003)[a]	% of total from all sources
United States	41,950	49,215	20,511	4,047	577,568	20.2
Mauritius	72,340	28,925	18,466	2,847	344,562	12.0
United Kingdom	4,112	49,942	18,043	816	232,682	8.1
Japan	8,275	7,353	7,408	748	114,861	4.0
Korea	411	668	290	470	98,740	3.4
Germany	5,938	4,139	2,531	977	92,617	3.2
Netherlands	45	36,936	5,524	640	90,098	3.1
Australia	617	844	773	73	67,859	2.4
France	2,021	6,798	6,229	257	65,659	2.3
Malaysia	159	1,058	3,726	57	60,606	2.1
Singapore	3,232	3,799	3,722	1,254	53,604	1.9
Other countries						16.7
NRI[b]	16,186	6,080	3,604	2,236	107,264	3.7
Euro issue[c]	198,025	59,350	817	158	484,710	16.9
All sources	370,394	268,747	111,398	17,436	2,865,556	100.0

Source: Secretariat for Industrial Assistance (SIA), Government of India, http://dipp.gov.in/.
[a]Figures for 2003 includes proposals approved only until May 31, 2003.
[b]Represents proposals only.
[c]Represents proposals for Global Depository Receipts (GDR) and Foreign Currency Convertible Bonds (FCCBs).

Table 7.3

Breakdown of Approved Foreign Direct Investment (FDI) Proposals, by Sector (August 1991 to May 2003)

	No. of financial proposals approved	Amount of FDI approved (million rupees)	% of total approval
Engineering	8,267	2,046,521	71.44
• Metallurgical	382	154,878	5.41
• Fuels (power and oil refinery)	669	776,240	27.10
• Electrical equipment	4,055	283,707	9.90
• Telecommunications	752	563,894	19.68
• Transport	992	212,367	7.41
• Other engineering	1,417	55,435	1.94
Chemicals and fertilizers	1,011	133,328	4.65
Drugs and pharmaceuticals	293	31,920	1.11
Textiles	617	34,949	1.22
Paper and pulp	131	35,465	1.24
Food processing	741	94,862	3.31
Consultancy	755	26,743	0.93
Service sector*	1,025	185,877	6.49
Hotel and tourism	454	49,841	1.74
Trading	674	27,314	0.95
Miscellaneous	2,604	197,786	6.92
Total	16,572	2,864,606	100.00

Source: Secretariat for Industrial Assistance (SIA), Government of India, http://dipp.gov.in/.
* Includes financial, nonfinancial, banking, insurance, and hospital and diagnostic centers.

As engineering industries are the predominant recipient of FDI in India, it would be interesting to review their performances in terms of productivity and export growth in the postreform period. However, due to a lack of appropriate data and the lagged nature of available micro-level data, it is very difficult to conduct meaningful research on industry/sector performance in India. Kumari (2003) observed that "foreign equity participation and imported intermediate inputs had a significant positive relationship with export growth in the pre-reform period.[13] In the post-reform period, the export growth of companies having even indigenous intermediate inputs increased" (p. 178). Kumari further observed that domestic companies with little or no foreign investments also performed well in terms of export growth. Apparently, small and medium-size engineering companies moved more to the international market in the postreform period with foreign technology and not necessarily with foreign financial investments.

Regional Distribution of Foreign Direct Investment

India is a federation of twenty-nine states and six union territories. The problems faced by the states and territories include income inequality, lack of resources (and proper distribution channels), rising population, and poverty. Four states from the southern and western parts of the country and the national capital (Delhi) account for more than half (52.5 percent) of total FDI approvals so far. These are the richer and higher growth states as well. Not surprisingly, the leading industrial state of Maharashtra (with Mumbai as its capital) leads the list. These states attract large amounts of IT- and manufacturing-related investments.

According to the annual report of the Ministry of Commerce and Industry (quoted in Tutakne, Gupta, and Pradeep 2003, 204), the choice of location by a foreign investor in any particular state depends on the market size, availability of skilled manpower, and other incentives provided by the state governments. Although states like Maharashtra, Gujarat, and Andhra Pradesh are the major recipients of FDI (see Table 7.4), their experience with reforms is varied. Tutakne, Gupta, and Pradeep (2003) found that reform had a direct positive and significant impact on private and foreign investments only in Andhra Pradesh.

The performance of the major FDI recipient states in terms of annual growth of gross state domestic product varies. In 1991–99, Gujarat and Maharashtra achieved significantly higher growth, 8.2 percent and 8.0 percent, respectively, as compared with other states and the national average of 6.5 percent (Ahluwalia 2002, 93). The growth performance of the other major recipients such as Tamil Nadu and Karnataka was not as impressive (6.0 percent and 5.9 percent, respectively), although higher than the national average. Ahluwalia (2002) believes that the rate of investment (domestic and foreign investment together) is one of the most important factors explaining differences in growth. However, lack of appropriate data makes it difficult to establish a significant statistical relationship in this regard in the Indian context.

Table 7.4

Breakdown of Approved Foreign Direct Investment (FDI) Proposals, by State (August 1991–May 2003)

	Number of proposals approved	Amount of FDI approved (millions of rupees)	FDI share (%)
Maharashtra	3,198	497,465	17.37
Delhi	2,085	342,105	11.94
Tamil Nadu	1,807	239,251	8.35
Karnataka	1,760	237,494	8.29
Gujarat	605	187,010	6.53
Andhra Pradesh	876	133,010	4.64
Madhya Pradesh	165	92,711	3.24
West Bengal	446	90,256	3.15
Orissa	89	82,293	2.87
Uttar Pradesh	504	48,584	1.70
Haryana	526	36,590	1.28
Rajasthan	232	30,066	1.05
Other states	3,431	757,794	26.45
Total	16,572	2,864,606	100.00

Source: Secretariat for Industrial Assistance (SIA), Government of India, http://dipp.gov.in/.

Bhide and Shand (2003) paint a similar picture. They classify the Indian states into high-, medium-, and low-growth categories. The four high-growth states (Maharashtra, Karnataka, Tamil Nadu, and Gujarat, all belonging to the western and southern parts of India) are consistent in achieving higher growth rates (in total and per capita GDP) in the pre- and postreform periods and in attracting foreign investments.

Along with economic growth, the overall reform process has increased interregional disparity in India. Ahluwalia (2002, 93) estimated the Gini coefficient of interstate inequality in India. His work shows that the estimated Gini coefficient rose from 0.152 in 1980–81 to 0.175 in 1989–90 and then jumped to 0.233 in 1998–99.

Thus, based on the available evidence, richer states received a higher proportion of FDI and achieved higher growth, which has led to a widening gap between the rich and the relatively poorer states.

Determinants of Foreign Direct Investment in India

The increasing pace of globalization and the resultant growth of flexible accumulation processes allow the transnational and multinational corporations to search for cheaper sources of production centers across the national boundaries. The recipient economies, particularly the developing countries, vie with each other to offer the most favorable investment climate (Basu 2002). The Southeast Asian experience shows that there is a positive correlation between a favorable investment climate and the level of FDI inflows.

The major determinants of FDI inflow to India are the nature of the domestic market and its trade and domestic policies. Chakraborty and Basu (2002) identified a two-way link between FDI and economic growth in India using a structural cointegration model. Their research supports the view that GDP growth in India has made a significant contribution to FDI growth rather than the other way around. They also observed that trade liberalization policy in India in recent years has a short-run impact on FDI flow, and FDI in India is, to a certain extent, labor replacing.

Using regression analysis, Venkataramany (2003) attempted to identify the determinant of FDI in India at three levels—total, target industry level, and source country level. His results indicate that a strong positive relationship exists between FDI and changes in GDP and term deposit interest rates at all three levels. A similarly strong negative relationship exists with respect to changes in inflation and commercial interest rates. No significant relationship is found with respect to changes in exports in particular.

Concluding Remarks

FDI can take numerous forms and is expanding due to fewer trade restrictions and an improved regulatory framework that encourages international trade and investment. FDI has been a feature of the world economy for many years in one form or another. Increase in the pace of globalization over the past decade can be attributed to the relatively more recent phenomenon of backward and forward vertical FDI. A strategic shift in government policies toward foreign trade and investment during the 1980s resulted in a rapid rise in FDI in India. Political stability along with a well-developed legal system, the availability of a highly skilled labor force, and a large domestic market make India an ideal place for foreign investment. In theory, foreign investments can facilitate economic growth, exports, and technology transfer. During the postreform period, India's economic growth situation has improved along with the flow of FDI. Increased exports can also be partly attributed to increased FDI. However, it is difficult to measure the exact contribution of

FDI inflow to economic growth in general and export growth in particular. A range of factors has contributed to improved economic and export performance. In this sense, inflow of FDI may be considered as both cause and effect of various changes that have taken place in the Indian economy since 1991. Increasing flows of foreign investment have contributed toward higher growth (at least partially), and higher growth prospects have attracted more foreign investment. In terms of technology transfer, India resembles most of the other developing countries and does not seem to have achieved significant success. It is unlikely for the benefits of technology transfer to the Indian economy to be broad and universal. With the advent of new technology and globalization, acquisition and production processes have changed significantly. Multinational and transnational corporations now control production bases in developing countries. While new and sophisticated technologies remain under the control of MNCs, only low and standardized technologies are transferred to the developing countries through FDI.

The benefits of increasing foreign investment and of the economic reform process in general have not been distributed evenly among regions or among individuals in India. The regional income distribution appears to have become more skewed in the postreform period. Richer and relatively more industrialized regions extract the maximum benefits out of foreign investment and related facilities. Foreign investment is usually concentrated in large cities with well-developed infrastructures. This has also contributed to uneven regional growth and the resultant mass migration from relatively less developed regions to the developing regions.

This situation echoes the global problem: with the increasing pace of financial globalization, foreign capital started flowing in larger proportions to developing countries. At the same time, income distribution appears to have worsened globally. The problem is far worse in the case of most developing countries. The supporters of globalization claim that this is only a temporary phenomenon and that a more balanced development will result in the long run. But it is hard to quantify how long this will take, and the process that may lead to an equitable distribution of income is not very clear. In the meantime, the increasing inequality of income distribution is creating major socioeconomic and political problems in most developing countries, including India.

Needless to say, excessive dependence on foreign capital for economic development could be disastrous in the long run. Lessons need to be learned from the recent experience of Southeast Asian economies. Although India at present is not heavily reliant on foreign investment, it is important that all foreign investment proposals be carefully scrutinized. In reality, foreign capital is desirable only in high growth areas. Accordingly, the use of FDI needs to be monitored carefully to avoid any potential crises in the future. India still does not have a strong financial system with sufficient prudential regulations. The recent Asian financial crisis has shown that the misuse and misappropriation of foreign investments can be one of the major sources of economic and financial crisis.

After the initial decade, FDI inflow in India was found to be more stable than it was in the past. In line with subdued economic activities all over the world in the post-September 11 (2001) period, FDI inflows in India were low during 2002–3 and 2003–4. They picked up significantly again in 2004–5 (GOI 2006). In general, the inflows maintained their upward trend. During 2002–3 and 2004–5, annual average FDI inflows were about US$5 billion as against US$4.1 billion for the previous three years. As of January 2006, cumulative FDI inflows in India amounted to US$37.7 billion. Significant growth of portfolio foreign investments has been a feature of foreign investments scenarios in recent years (RBI online).

Origins of FDI for India have not changed much in the post-2001 period. The USA and Mauritius continued to be the dominant sources for approvals and actual inflows. In recent years, higher FDI inflows were observed in manufacturing industries such as electrical equipment and transportation. Additional FDI inflows during 2004–5 primarily moved toward India's fast-growing IT sector. As of January 2006, the highest proportion (16.2 percent) of total FDI inflows went to the electrical equipments sector, which includes computer software and electronics (GOI 2006a).

China and India are the two major recipients of foreign investments in recent years. Although China still occupied the top position in FDI Confidence Index, India steadily climbed to the second position in December 2005 from third position in 2004 and sixth in 2003 (Global Business Policy Council 2005). The gap between China and India is closing fast. If a uniform definition is applied, FDI inflows in both countries could be very similar.

In overall terms, the impact of FDI inflow in India can be described as mixed at best. While it is certainly a welcome feature for the capital-starved economy, one must be conscious about its undesirable impact. The total impact of the entire reform process (of which FDI is a part) is yet to be realized. While decision making may involve value judgments, it is imperative that decision making involving foreign investment proposals be based on merit. India's pace of economic growth is steadier now than the first decade of economic reform. "India appears to have permanently broken out of its leisurely 'Hindu rate of growth' . . . and its performance is beginning to approach the East Asian level" (Huang 2006). India's relationship now with Western economies including the United States is one of its best in many years. Many world-class companies are emerging from India now.

All these should be instrumental in attracting more foreign investment to India in years to come.

Notes

1. See Ball (2004), Gastanaga, Nugent, and Pashamova (1998), Hill (2003), and Czinkota, Ronkainen, and Moffett (2005) for a review of the relevant literature.

2. Foreign investment in some Asian economies has grown at an impressive rate since the late 1980s. This growth can be attributed mostly to Japanese investment, triggered by the appreciation of the yen, which encouraged Japanese manufacturers to move offshore. The share of Japanese manufacturing investment in economies such as Malaysia, Indonesia, the Philippines, and Thailand has grown from as low as 8 percent in the late 1980s to as high as 18 percent in the early 1990s. Although Japanese foreign investment in Asia has not regained its peak, it maintained a 16–17 percent share until 1999 (see ASEAN Investment Report 1999).

3. Political instability is one of the major factors affecting the flow of FDI in South Asian countries such as Bangladesh, Nepal, Pakistan, and Sri Lanka. In the case of Pakistan, conflict with India, internal unrest, and the lack of a strong and credible judiciary provide further disincentives for serious foreign investors.

4. FDI is a more reliable form of finance for countries than portfolio investment or short-term lending. FDI flows to individual countries are normally less volatile than other international capital flows, they change direction less frequently and the range of fluctuation around their mean is smaller (Lipsey 2001).

5. See UNCTAD (2002). The continued inflow of FDI demonstrates the long-term commitment of some MNCs.

6. Transfer pricing refers to notional prices at which goods and services are exchanged between different national subsidiaries of a foreign firm (see Mansfield 2003).

7. See Cantwell (1995), Czinkota and Kotabe (1998), Czinkota and Ronkainen (2001), Kim and Singal (2000), Krugman and Venables (1995), O'Rourke and Williamson (1999), and Wong and Adams (2002) for a discussion of related issues.

8. India gained its independence from British colonial rule in 1947, whereas the present regime took control of China in 1949. The Chinese government started its reform process in 1978–79 and India formally introduced its reforms in 1991. The reform process in India unofficially started in the late 1980s.

9. In 1980–85, 1986–90, 1991–95 and 1996–2001, the growth rates improved consistently to 5.5 percent, 5.8 percent, 5 percent, and 6.6 percent, respectively. The growth rate in 1991–95 was relatively lower due to poor performance in 1991–92, when growth was only 1.1 percent.

10. There have been two important political changes in India since the mid-1990s. Rightist and more nationalist political parties have gained power, which appears to have slowed down the process of opening up the economy. At the same time, coalition governments (in some cases consisting of a very large number of heterogeneous political parties with conflicting interests) have become quite common in recent years. This development has slowed down the process of any active policy initiatives in almost all areas.

11. Growth rates are estimated using the Annual Survey of Industries (ASI), Government of India data for various years, available from the EPW Research Foundation (Mumbai, India, 2002).

12. The same situation applies to FDI in China to a certain extent. It is widely believed that a significant proportion of FDI in China from Hong Kong consists of Chinese funds sourced through Hong Kong.

13. She used regression models with panel data covering forty-four engineering companies for the years 1985–86 to 1994–95.

References

Ahluwalia, M. 2002. "State-level Performance under Economic Reforms in India." In *Economic Policy Reforms and the Indian Economy*, ed. Anne O. Krueger, 91–125. Chicago: University of Chicago Press.

Appleyard, D.; A. Field; and S. Cobb. 2006. *International Economics*. 5th ed. Boston: McGraw-Hill/Irwin.

Bajpai, N., and N. Dasgupta. 2004. "FDI to China and India: The Definitional Differences" *Business Line, The Hindu*, May 15. Available at www.thehindubusinessline.com/2004/05/15/stories/2004051500081000.htm (accessed May 2006).

Ball, D. 2004. *International Business*. New York: McGraw-Hill.

Basu, P.K. 2002. "Financial Globalization and National Economic Sustainability." *Global Economy Quarterly* 3, no. 2: 265–81.

Bhide, S., and R. Shand. 2003. "Growth in India's State Economies before and with Reforms: Shares and Determinants." In *Indian Economic Reforms*, ed. Raghbendra Jha, 275–94. London: Palgrave Macmillan.

Cantwell, J. 1995. "The Globalization of Technology: What Remains of the Product Cycle Model?" *Cambridge Journal of Economics* 19: 155–74.

Chakraborty, C., and P. Basu. 2002. "Foreign Direct Investment and Growth in India: A Cointegration Approach." *Applied Economics* 34, no. 9 (June 15): 1061–73.

Coughlin, C., and E. Segev. 2000. "Foreign Direct Investment in China: A Spatial Econometric Study." *World Economy* 23, no. 1: 1–23.

Czinkota, M., and M. Kotabe. 1998. *Trends in International Business*. Orlando, FL: Harcourt.

Czinkota, M., and I. Ronkainen. 2001. "Globalization: An Introduction and Assessment of Realities and Strategies." In *Best Practices in International Business*, ed. Czinkota and Ronkainen, 1–7. Orlando, FL: Harcourt.

Czinkota, M.R.; I.A. Ronkainen; and M.H. Moffett. 2005. *International Business*. 7th and 6th eds. Boston: Dryden Press.

Datar, M., and P.K. Basu. 2003. "Financial Sector Reforms in India: An Institutional Economics Perspective." Paper presented at the annual conference of the Indian Economic Association, Kolhapur, India, December.

Dutta, D. 1998. "Fifty Years of Economic Development in India: Rhetoric and Reality." In *Fifty Years of Indian Development: India in Retrospective, Future Directions and Investment Outlook*, ed. P.K. Basu, N.D. Karunaratne, and C.A. Tisdell, 5–22. Brisbane: University of Queensland Press.

Forbes, Naushad. 2002. "Doing Business in India: What Has Liberalization Changed?" In *Economic Policy Reforms and the Indian Economy*, ed. Anne O. Krueger, 129–67. Chicago: University of Chicago Press.

Gastanaga, V.M.; J.B. Nugent; and B. Pashamova. 1998. "Host Country Reforms and FDI Inflows: How Much Difference Do They Make?" *World Development* 26, no. 7: 1299–314.

Government of India. 2006a. *FDI Statistics*. New Delhi:Ministry of Commerce and Industry. Available at http://dipp.gov.in/ (accessed May 2006).

———. 2006b. *Economic Survey 2005–6*. New Delhi:Ministry of Finance. Available at http://indiabudget.nic.in/es2005–06/esmain.htm (accessed May 2006).

———. 2002. *Economic Survey 2001–2*. New Delhi: Ministry of Finance.

———. 2003a. *Economic Survey 2002–3*. New Delhi: Ministry of Finance.

———. 2003b. *Manual on Foreign Direct Investment in India- Policy and Procedures*. Secretariat for Industrial Assistance, New Delhi: Ministry of Commerce and Industry.

Glick, R., and R. Moreno. 1997. "The East Asian Miracle: Growth Because of Government Intervention and Protection or in Spite of It?" *Business Economics 32:20–26*.

Global Business Policy Council. 2005. *Foreign Direct Investment Confidence Index Vol. 8*. GBPC. Available at www.atkearney.com/main.taf?p=5,3,1,138 (accessed May 2006).

Hill, C. 2005. *International Business*. 5th ed. Boston: McGraw-Hill/Irwin.

Huang, Y. 2006. "What China Can Learn from India." *Economist's View*. Available at http://economistsview.typepad.com/economistsview/2006/01/what_china_can_.html (accessed May 2006).

Kim, E.H., and V. Singal. 2000. "The Fear of Globalizing Markets." *Emerging Market Review* 1: 183–98.

Krueger, A., and S. Chinoy. 2002. "The Indian Economy in the Global Context." In *Economic Policy Reforms and the Indian Economy*, ed. A.O. Krueger, 9–45. Chicago: University of Chicago Press.

Krugman, P., and A.J. Venables. 1995. "Globalization and the Inequality of Nations." *Quarterly Journal of Economics* 110, no. 4: 857–80.

Kumari, A. 2003. "Technology, Productivity and Export Growth of Engineering Industry in India." In *Indian Economic Reforms*, ed. Raghbendra Jha, 167–85. London: Palgrave Macmillan.

Lipsey, R. 2001. "Foreign Direct Investors in Three Crisis." NBER Working Paper no. 8084, National Bureau of Economic Research, Cambridge, MA.

Luce, E. 2002. "India Stirs: The Country Is Experiencing a Sharp Increase in Foreign Direct Investment." *Financial Times*, August 29. Available at http://meaindia.nic.in/iimedia/2002/10/iimv01.htm#edward (accessed October 2003).

Mansfield, R. 2003. *Managerial Economics*. 9th ed. Boston: McGraw-Hill.

O'Rourke, K., and J. Williamson. 1999. *Globalization and History*. Cambridge, MA: MIT Press.

Reserve Bank of India Online. Available at www.rbi.org.in (accessed May 2006).

Thomsen, S. 1999. "Southeast Asia: The Role of Foreign Direct Investment Policies in Development." Working Papers on International Investment. Organization for Economic Cooperation and Development, Paris.

Tutakne, S.; S. Gupta; and A. Pradeep. 2003. "Public and Private Investment Expenditure and Its Linkages with FDI: A Case Study of India." In *Indian Economic Reforms*, ed. Raghbendra Jha, 186–205. London: Palgrave Macmillan.

United Nations Conference on Trade and Development (UNCTAD). 2001. *Handbook of Statistics*. Available at http://stats.unctad.org/fdi/eng (accessed October 2003).

United Nations Conference on Trade and Development (UNCTAD). 2005. *Handbook of Statistics*. Available at http://stats.unctad.org/fdi (accessed May 2006).

———. 2002. *Handbook of Statistics*. Available at http://stats.unctad.org/fdi/eng.

Venkataramany, S. 2003. "Determinants of Foreign Direct Investment in India: An Empirical Analysis of Source Countries and Target Industries." Ashland, OH: Ashland University. Available at http://blake.montclair.edu/~cibconf/conference/DATA/Theme2/India.pdf (accessed May 2006).

Wong, Y.C., and C. Adams. 2002. "Trends in Global and Regional Foreign Direct Investment Flows." Paper presented at the conference on Foreign Direct Investment Opportunities and Challenges for Cambodia, Laos, and Vietnam, jointly organized by the International Monetary Fund and the State Bank of Vietnam, Hanoi, Vietnam, August 16–17.

8

Human Capital Investment and Development in South Asia

Anjum Siddiqui

It is a tautology that education substantially improves one's productive capacity, thus enhancing economic "well-being." Whether the economic growth of nations is caused by higher (tertiary) education or mass attainment in primary education is a subject on which opinions differ in terms of magnitude of effects. Nevertheless, empirical findings show that education at the primary and secondary levels has a multitude of positive development effects. It improves labor productivity, reduces fertility, and improves health and nutrition. Moreover, improvement in female literacy is especially conducive to educational attainment by children and reduced population growth rates. These commonsense and well-known development benefits of education have, however, been traditionally ignored by South Asian governments in choosing their spending priorities.

The developing economies of South Asia, saddled with high budgetary and current account deficits, have not adequately funded investment in education, which has remained a low priority. As a consequence, South Asia ranks very poorly on all human development indicators, demonstrating low literacy, poor enrollment rates, high dropout rates from primary schools, and inadequate facilities for high quality education in science and technology.

Following the development of neoclassical growth theories, and subsequent findings confirming the models' inadequacy concerning economic growth through higher saving rates and consequently higher capital-labor ratios, human capital has emerged as an important determinant of economic growth. Numerous empirical studies across regions confirm the predictions of the theoretical models through strong positive correlations between various proxies of human capital and economic growth. The growth experience of the newly industrialized countries (NICs) also confirms the theoretical predictions. In NICs where the education sector has responded to the skills requirements of the productive sector, rapid growth has been experienced over the past three decades.

The Neoclassical Growth Theory

Building on the Harrod-Domar growth model, Solow's (1956) seminal article provided the foundations of modern growth theory. In a two-factor economy consisting of labor and capital with constant returns to scale properties of the aggregate production function, the model predicts a constant steady-state growth rate of per capita income, equal to the growth rate of technology. Here "steady state" is defined as the state where there is no tendency for the growth rates to change (also known as the "balanced growth path").

In this simplified model, Solow assumes that the savings, capital depreciation, and population growth rates are constant. With a growing population, capital stock must increase to keep the per capita capital at the same or higher level. Also, depreciation of capital requires replacement investment. New capital is added only when savings can offset the negative effects on capital labor ratios of depreciation and population growth. Otherwise, per capita capital stock declines. When the economy is on the balanced growth path, savings exactly offset the reduction in the capital output ratio, due to population growth and depreciation. This means that at the balanced growth path there will be no growth in per capita capital, thus output per capita will also remain constant. The only factor that may change the output per capita is the exogenous technological growth rate. With better technology, output per capita may increase, without having to change per capita capital. Another conclusion of the neoclassical models is that with easy transfer of technology, poorer countries will grow at faster rates than richer countries and all economies will eventually converge to the same steady state.

The key assumptions that lead to convergence of output toward the steady state or balanced growth path level are diminishing marginal product of per capita capital and constant returns to scale. Diminishing marginal product implies that as the level of input (capital) increases, the increment in the output will be relatively less than the increase in input; constant returns to scale implies that if all factors of production (in this case, capital and labor) are doubled, then production will also double.

Endogenous Growth Theories Incorporating Human Capital

Though elegantly presented, neoclassical models of economic growth have not been able to explain some of the key facts regarding the performance of various economies. Contrary to theoretical predictions, economic convergence of rich and poor countries was not achieved, and indeed, the disparity has increased in a number of cases. A need was felt to address the weakness of the Solow model manifested in the assumption of exogenous technology. Consequently, endogenous growth models were developed that generated technology and economic growth through accumulation in human capital.

This breakthrough in development thinking is credited to Paul Romer (1986, 1990), who also argued that the assumption of constant returns to scale may not correctly reflect the existing production process. Romer introduced the important idea that knowledge is a part of capital in the broader sense, and may have spillover effects in the aggregate, which makes the production process acquire an increasing return to scale property. The central idea is that the incorporation of knowledge as a part of capital allows the potential for a perpetually growing economy, without its having to come to a standstill (in growth rate of output per capita), as predicted by the neoclassical models. The growth rate is thus endogenized.[1]

Lucas (1988) followed the idea of Uzawa (1965), where there are different technologies producing physical and human capital, taking into account the opportunity cost of accumulating knowledge. If there is nonnegative gross investment in both types of capital (physical and human), the growth rate of income will be influenced by the deviation from steady state level of the ratio of physical capital to human capital. The production of both consumption goods and physical capital requires human capital as an input. Therefore, the allocation of human capital becomes a decision variable in the production of consumption goods and investment goods (physical capital). Lucas emphasizes that if the returns from education, the process that produces human capital, are low vis-à-vis the productive sector, there will be a negative effect on the economy's long-run growth rate.

Glomm and Ravikumar (1992) extend the theoretical framework of Lucas and Romer to examine the effects of government-sponsored programs versus private programs for investment in human capital, using an overlapping generations model, with heterogeneous individuals. They predict a reduction in income inequality with public education, but higher per capita earnings through private education. Laitner's (1993) model shows that human capital induces faster economic growth as compared with what would have taken place with Solow's exogenous technological progress. In another study, Laitner (2000) analyzes the effects of higher attainment levels in education. His model predicts diverging growth in earnings in favor of high education groups due to inherent variability in ability.

Human Capital and Economic Growth: The Evidence

Numerous empirical studies have been done to measure the contribution of human capital to economic growth. However, it is widely believed that private returns to human capital are not able to explain the social returns due to externalities. Siansei and Van Reenen (2003) provide an extensive survey of the literature on the empirics of "returns to education" at a macro level.

Barro (1991) used the Summers-Heston data set to examine the growth rate of ninety-eight countries for the period 1960–85 and used "gross enrollment" in schools as a proxy variable for human capital.[2] Barro used OLS regressions to estimate the relationship between per capita GDP growth and the dependent variables. He found that per capita growth in 1960–85 was positively related to the initial level (1960 in his study) of human capital, proxied by enrollment ratios at the primary and secondary levels. Barro also found that the partial correlation of GDP growth and human capital was 0.73.

Murphy, Shleifer, and Vishny (1991) also used the Summers-Heston data set and found that countries with a higher proportion of engineering college enrollment grow faster than countries with a higher enrollment in law. The authors used engineering enrollment as a proxy for human capital generation in the productive sector and law enrollment as a proxy for the rent-seeking sector.

Mankiw, Romer, and Weil (1992) used the same data set in an attempt to estimate a Solow-type growth model augmented by human capital. Their findings suggest that the average ratio of real investment to GDP and the average percentage of the working age population in secondary school (taken as a proxy for human capital) explain over 70 percent of the variation in real GDP growth after controlling for the rates of population growth, exogenous technological progress, and depreciation. They also found evidence of conditional convergence of economic growth rates across countries.

Levine and Renelt (1992) also employed the Summers-Heston data set. Using secondary school enrollment rate as a proxy for human capital, they found a strong positive relationship between growth rate and the educational proxy.

Barro and Lee (1994) analyzed sources of economic growth using seemingly unrelated regressions on the Barro-Lee data set for 119 countries,[3] and found that each additional year of secondary schooling completed by males and females increases the economic growth rate by 1.4 percent and 0.9 percent, respectively.

Jorgensen and Fraumeni (1992) attempted to measure the impact of investment in education on productivity growth in the United States and found that 83 percent of the economic growth can be attributed to educational investment in the post–World War II period. Englander and Gurney (1994) found the secondary school enrollment rate to be robustly correlated with productivity increases in member countries of the Organization for Economic Cooperation and Development (OECD). Islam (1995) used the panel data approach to measure convergence among economies and found that when average schooling of the population over age twenty-five is taken as a proxy for human capital, the convergence is smaller and the coefficient of human capital variable is negatively signed. However, Hall and Jones (1999) found that physical and human capital account for a small percentage of per capita income growth. They also found that social infrastructure is strongly associated with per capita output.

Endogeneity in Estimated Models

While various empirical studies reveal a strong positive relationship between educational attainment and economic growth, contradictory evidence has been found on the direction of causality between these variables. It is quite plausible that higher human capital leads to more output, which in turn generates higher human capital. Essentially, human capital is a productive process, which requires input. For example, in the OECD countries, financing per student at the tertiary level is approximately $5,000 per annum versus a meager $40 in the least developed countries. This is possible because OECD countries have per capita GDP greater than $20,000 per annum as compared with less than $500 for most of the least developed countries.

Econometric analysis, particularly Barro-style growth accounting analysis, using one or more proxies for human capital will have the observed problem of endogeneity, which would yield statistically significant but biased regression coefficients. On the basis of such results it would not be possible to conclude that educational attainment affects per capita output growth. While this problem can be overcome by using instrumental variables, it is often difficult to find such variables in macro data. The main attribute of an instrumental variable is that it should be highly correlated with the variable that it proxies; however, it should not be correlated with the variable that it is trying to explain, and such a variable is hard to find.

Human Development in South Asian Countries

Economic growth does not capture the overall development and well-being of people in a country, but despite this shortcoming, in the empirical literature GDP growth is a commonly used variable in regressions of cross-country comparisons. Similarly, proxies for human capital, such as educational attainment at the primary, secondary, and tertiary levels, do not fully reflect the overall quality and accumulation of human capital, but in the absence of better measures and proxies for educational attainment, these variables are commonly used.

Human Development Index

To improve upon the economic welfare measure, the United Nations Development Programme (UNDP) has constructed a Human Development Index (HDI), which covers the key development aspects, for example, knowledge, longevity, and general well-being. More specifically, the HDI index is a simple average of the life expectancy index, education index, and GDP index. The education index measures a country's achievement in both literacy and enrollment in primary, secondary and tertiary levels. The education index is a weighted average of the literacy and enrollment indices. All South Asian countries fall within the group of middle human development economies, except Pakistan, which falls in the group of low human development economies, according to the *Human Development Report 2004* (see Table 8.1). Sri Lanka leads these economies in terms of human development, with an HDI rank of 96 among all 175 UN member countries for which the index was calculated. India, Bangladesh, Nepal, and Pakistan have ranks of 127, 138, 140, and 142, respectively. The Human Development Index values for the South Asian countries are: Sri Lanka (0.74), India (0.59), Bangladesh (0.50), Nepal (0.50), and Pakistan (0.49). Notably, the East Asian economies have 0.74 and the high-income OECD countries have 0.91 as the average HDI value for countries in the respective regions. In terms of regional comparison, South Asian countries lag behind East Asian and Pacific countries, Arab states, and the Latin American and Caribbean countries, in all criteria of human development.

Next, we take a closer look at the indicators of educational attainment, that is, literacy, gross enrollment ratios, and tertiary education, and we also examine the level of government expenditure in various countries.

Literacy

Nearly 98 percent of the world's illiterate population lives in developing countries. Half of these people live in South Asia. Literacy is defined by UNESCO as the ability to read a newspaper or write a simple paragraph in any language that is spoken in a country. The (2002) adult literacy rate in South Asia (57.6 percent) has slipped behind sub-Saharan Africa (63.2 percent) as well as that of the Arab states (63.3 percent), and since 1970 literacy has increased at only half the rate of those regions. As of 2000, every second illiterate person in the world lives in India, which also has one of the

Table 8.1

Monitoring Human Development

Human Development Index rank*		Education index	GDP index	Human development index (HDI) value 2002
84	Maldives	0.91	0.65	0.752
96	Sri Lanka	0.83	0.6	0.74
127	India	0.59	0.55	0.595
134	Bhutan	0.48	0.5	0.536
138	Bangladesh	0.45	0.47	0.509
140	Nepal	0.5	0.44	0.504
142	Pakistan	0.4	0.49	0.497
Least developed countries		0.49	0.42	0.446
Arab states		0.61	0.65	0.651
East Asia and the Pacific		0.83	0.64	0.74
Latin America and the Caribbean		0.86	0.72	0.777
South Asia		0.57	0.55	0.584
Sub-Saharan Africa		0.56	0.48	0.465
OECD		0.94	0.92	0.911
High human development		0.95	0.92	0.915
Medium human development		0.75	0.63	0.695
Low human development		0.5	0.41	0.438
World		0.76	0.73	0.729

Source: United Nations Development Programme, *Human Development Report 2004*.
*Ranking in a sample of 175 countries.

highest female–male literacy gaps in the world surpassed by only five countries: Bhutan, Syria, Togo, Malawi, and Mozambique. The state of Rajasthan in India alone has a population as large as all these countries combined, and no country in the world has a higher female–male literacy gap than Rajasthan, where the literacy rate for women is a mere 5 percent—an appalling statistic in inequality of opportunity.

Within South Asia, Nepal presents the worst literacy statistics. It has the lowest female literacy rate in the world at 13 percent and the fourth lowest adult literacy rate in the world at 28 percent. However, Sri Lanka is one of the success stories in South Asia. The total adult literacy rate in Sri Lanka is 92 percent, with a 94 percent literacy rate for men and an 87 percent literacy rate for women. Gender inequality in education is a primary feature of most South Asian countries except Sri Lanka, and this phenomenon often stems from societal conventions and religion, primarily due to conservatism and ignorance.

Table 8.2

Literacy

Countries	Adult literacy rate[a] (% ages 15 and above)		Youth literacy rate[a] (% ages 15–24)	
	1990	2002	1990	2002
Maldives	94.8	97.2	98.1	99.2
Sri Lanka	88.7	92.1	95.1	97
India	49.3	61.3[b]	64.3	—
Bhutan	—	—	—	—
Bangladesh	34.2	41.1	42	49.7
Nepal	30.4	44	46.6	62.7
Pakistan	35.4	41.5[b,c]	47.4	53.9[b,c]
All developing countries	67.3	76.7	85.5	88.1
Least developed countries	43	52.5	54.9	64.3
Arab states	50.8	63.3	68.4	81.2
East Asia and the Pacific	79.8	90.3	95.1	98
Latin America and the Caribbean	85	88.6	92.7	94.8
South Asia	47	57.6	—	—
Sub-Saharan Africa	50.8	63.2	66.8	76.8

Source: United Nations Development Programme, *Human Development Report*, 2004.
[a]Due to differences in methodology and timeliness of data, comparisons across countries should be made with caution.
[b]Census data.
[c]Data refer to a year between 1995 and 1999.

Table 8.2 shows that from 1990 to 2002, there was much improvement in various South Asian countries in lowering illiteracy among the adult (ages fifteen and older) and the youth (ages fifteen to twenty-four). However, the youth illiteracy rates in South Asian countries are behind even those found in Sub-Saharan Africa. Notably, Sri Lanka is an exception where youth illiteracy is only 3 percent.

Gross Enrollment Ratios

Gross enrollment ratios (Table 8.3) are primary indicators of a country's educational access. The ratio is the estimated proportion of the relevant age group enrolled at different levels of education, primary, secondary, or tertiary. In India, one-third of all children ages six to fourteen do not attend school.

Table 8.3

Enrollment

Countries	Children reaching grade five (%)	Net primary enrollment ratio (%)[a] 1990–1991		Net secondary enrollment ratio (%)[a,b] 1990–1991		Tertiary students in science, math, and engineering (% of all tertiary students) 1994–1997[c]
Maldives	-	87	96	—	31	—
Sri Lanka	=	90	105	—	—	29
India	59	—	83	—	—	25
Bhutan	91	—	—	—	—	—
Bangladesh	65	71	87	19	44	—
Nepal	78	85	70	—	—	14
Pakistan	=	35	—	—	—	—

Source: United Nations Development Programme, *Human Development Report, 2004.*

[a]The net enrollment ratio is the ratio of enrolled children of official age for the education level indicated to the total population of that age. Net enrollment ratios exceeding 100 percent reflect discrepancies between these two data sets. Data on net enrollment ratios refer to the 2001–2 school year, and data on children reaching grade five to the 2000–2001 school year, unless otherwise specified. Data for some countries may refer to national or UNESCO Institute for Statistics estimates. For details, see www.uis.unesco.org/. Because data are from different sources, comparisons across countries should be made with caution.

[b]Enrollment ratios are based on the new International Standard Classification of Education, adopted in 1997 (UNESCO, International Standard Classification of Education 1997 [http://portal.unesco.org/uis/TEMPLATE/pdf/isced/ISCED_A.pdf]; accessed March 2003), and so may not be strictly comparable with those for earlier years.

[c]Data refer to the most recent year available during the period specified.

This is equal to 23 million boys and 36 million girls, which is almost double the entire population of Canada.

There has been a significant increase in the primary enrollment ratio within the South Asian region, with Pakistan lagging behind its neighbors. Over the ten-year period 1990–91 to 2001–2, the primary enrollment ratio in Bangladesh improved from 71 percent to 87 percent. Though informal observation of societal structure may give a very different impression, the statistics show strong achievement. In Sri Lanka the primary enrollment ratio has historically been very high and continues at that level. India and Nepal have recorded ratios of 83 percent and 70 percent for 2001–2. In Nepal's case the ratio has shown a decline since 1990–91 when it was 85 percent. Bangladesh has shown a very good improvement in both primary and secondary school enrollment ratios.

According to the *Human Development Report 2004*, overall the region has achieved a 98 percent gross primary enrollment ratio in 2000 as compared with 77 percent in 1990. This places South Asia on a par with most other more developed regions. However, South Asia lags far behind other regions in secondary and tertiary levels of education. The region had an average of 48 percent and 10 percent secondary and tertiary enrollment ratios, respectively, in 2000; whereas East Asia, the Pacific, and Latin America, and the Caribbean had 58 percent and 14 percent secondary enrollment ratios, and 86 percent and 21 percent tertiary enrollment ratios in 2000. The high-income countries have over 100 percent in secondary and 62 percent enrollment in tertiary levels.

As an interesting caveat regarding enrollment, the media claim that approximately 1.7 million children attend religious schools (*madrassas*) in Pakistan. This claim, if true, would indicate that current estimates of primary school enrollment in Pakistan are biased in a downward direction. Using published survey data and also data from a census of schooling choice, Andrabi et al. (2005) conclude that these claims are highly exaggerated, both in absolute and in percentage terms, and that madrassas account for less than 1 percent of all enrollment in the country. Moreover, madrassas do not form part of the decision making of the average or even the majority of Pakistani households in terms of where to send their children to school. A detailed census and household survey on schooling is required to settle this issue.

Tertiary Education

Table 8.3 provides some available statistics over the period 1994–97 on enrollment in tertiary education. Both Sri Lanka and India are ahead of the pack in South Asia. It is apparent that at the tertiary level, gender parity is highly skewed toward the male population. Also, at the tertiary level only 14–29 percent of the students are enrolled in science, math, and engineering. The major tertiary education centers in South Asia are largely in India, where 25 percent of the tertiary education students are enrolled in science and related subjects, according to the *Human Development Report 2004*. The report also states that at the tertiary level, the region is led by India, which has a 10 percent enrollment ratio with a very large population base. The other countries within the region have less than 7 percent in tertiary enrollment. China also has a 7 percent enrollment ratio; East Asia is slightly better at 14 percent; however, enrollment ratios in South Korea are high at 78 percent, followed by Malaysia at 28 percent.

Government Expenditure on Education

Interestingly, as a percentage of gross domestic product, public expenditure on education in South Asia is among the highest in the world. While it is correct, this fact can be very misleading (see Table 8.4). Unfortunately, given low per capita GDP, this expenditure may not be sufficient to ensure improved enrollment ratios, particularly at the secondary and tertiary levels. Bangladesh, India, Nepal, and Pakistan spent 15.8 percent, 12.7 percent, 13.9 percent, and 7.8 percent, respectively, of total government expenditure on education in 1999–2001. High-income countries also spent a similar amount of 12 percent of annual government expenditure on education in 2000. However, as high-income countries have per capita GDP that is almost fifty times higher than most South Asian countries, the above expenditure level can only mean that investment per capita in education in the South Asian countries is very low and not conducive to spurring economic growth and technological development. This is confirmed by South Asia's current annual expenditure on education, which is only 1.9 percent of GNP. In contrast, military spending in the region is 3.8 percent of GNP, and as high as 7 percent in Pakistan, which has 50 percent more soldiers than teachers.

Determinants of Schooling

As we have seen above, at the micro level an individual decision maker is confronted with the choice of investing time in education or in earning a living. This constitutes the demand for schooling in a society. As almost 50 percent of the population in South Asia earns subsistence wages, families in extreme poverty often compromise on school enrollment. Thus, the level of family income has a major influence on the decision to enroll in primary schools and on whether to continue education up to the secondary and tertiary levels. For example, in Bangladesh 60 percent of the poor adolescents complete first grade, but only 36 percent complete fifth grade. It is tempting to say that these children are all needed by their families to earn income. However poverty is not the only factor. The poor quality of public schools, teacher absenteeism, and lack of community support for schools are strong factors explaining the high dropout rates.

Other than the opportunity cost of education, factors that may influence demand for enrollment and educational attainment include parental education, number of siblings, gender of children, societal conventions, and religion. In addition, a high level of maternal education translates into better resources for the family, which can be utilized for children's education. Poor health of

Table 8.4

Public Expenditure on Education

Countries	Public expenditure on education (% of GDP)		Public expenditure on education (% of total government expenditure)	
	1990[a,b]	1999–2001[a, c]	1990[a,b]	1999–2001[a, c]
Maldives	4.0	—	10.0	—
Sri Lanka	2.6	1.3	8.1	—
India	3.9	4.1	12.2	12.7
Bhutan	—	5.2	—	12.9
Bangladesh	1.5	2.3	10.3	15.8
Nepal	2.0	3.4	8.5	13.9
Pakistan	2.6	1.8[d]	7.4	7.8[d]

Source: United Nations Development Programme, *Human Development Report, 2004*.

Notes: As a result of limitations in the data and methodological changes, comparisons of education expenditure across countries and over time must be made with caution.

[a]Data refer to total public expenditure on education, including current and capital expenditure.

[b]Data may not be comparable between countries as a result of differences in methods of data collection.

[c]Data refer to the most recent year available during the period specified.

[d]Data refer to a UNESCO Institute for Statistics estimate where no national estimate is available.

parents or children may also be a deterrent to attending school. The lack of financial resources for a doctor's care and medication prolongs absenteeism in schools and increases dropout rates.

On the supply side of education, proper infrastructure is necessary for there to be any increase in the number of schools. Broadly, infrastructure includes availability of quality teachers, accessibility to schools, and affordability of educational materials, among other things. In South Asia, other than the public sector, many nongovernmental organizations (NGOs) are also actively involved in the provision of education and thus they provide some cushion with regard to infrastructure. However, the current status is far from adequate.

Various studies have been done to assess the determinants of schooling in different developing countries, including South Asia. Dreze and Kingdon (2001) found that in India, parental education and motivation, dependency ratio, work opportunities, village development, midday meals, and infrastructure quality have a statistically significant relationship with educational attainment. They find midday meals to be a particularly effective way of inducing more children to the schools in rural India. Pal (2003) examined the determinants of schooling in India among boys and girls and found that parental preferences and opportunity cost of domestic work are primary factors influencing gender inequality in education. Duraisamy (2000) found that parental education and family income are the main factors influencing children's education. In parental education, maternal education has been observed to be more important in increasing enrollment and thereby reducing the possibility of child labor. Ramachandran et al. (2003) found that sex, caste, occupational status, and village location have a significant relationship with enrollment. Jayachandran (2002) found that school accessibility as well as parental education have a positive impact, while poverty and household size have a negative effect on enrollment of children in India. In addition, schooling and the rate of women's labor force participation are positively related. Siddiqui and Iram (2006) also found that in Pakistan a host of socioeconomic factors including a set of poverty-related variables such as income and child characteristics (age and number of siblings) had a significant effect on school progression from primary through secondary to postsecondary levels.

The *World Development Report 2004* corroborates the findings of the general literature on education and schooling and lists some common deterrents to educational attainment in the developing and least developed countries. These are:

1. Unaffordable access—although in South Asia we see large improvements in enrollment, the completion of primary school remains very low. The low completion rate of fifth grade is seen mainly among the poorest 50 percent.
2. Dysfunctional schools—it has been found that many schools in rural South Asia do not function properly, with teachers engaged in other earning activities. Proper monetary incentives are required on a sustainable basis to create a more conducive environment for adequate teaching resources.
3. Low client responsiveness—although primary education in public schools is free, local community support for these institutions is weak. In the villages social support for the schools is important for proper functioning.
4. Low technical quality of the instructors—language, teaching skills, and subject knowledge are poor and centered on archaic methods of rote learning and assessment.
5. Stagnant productivity—tests of reading, writing, and numeric skills show very little improvement.

The *World Development Report 2004* emphasizes that in order to modernize the education system, basic structural modifications are required in terms of accountability of administrators and teachers, and participation of communities.

Evaluating the Programs of the Educational Sector

The World Bank has been active in assisting various countries of the region to achieve the Millennium Development Goals. This assistance is aimed toward fighting the menaces of mass poverty, illiteracy, and poor health that are observed in South Asian countries. The bank has provided technical and financial resources for various education-related projects.

According to the World Bank's own internal assessment, education projects in the early 1990s and before either lacked analysis or had poor quality analysis; and of the projects approved in 1998, more than 40 percent had proposed inadequate measures for evaluation (O'Rourke 1999). Despite the World Bank's stated desire to assist in social and economic development, the monitoring and implementation of projects have been weak.

Below we analyze some of these selected projects in India, Pakistan, and Bangladesh, the three largest countries of South Asia and where enrollment and literacy lag behind similar countries in the rest of the world.

Bangladesh

In Bangladesh, as part of the exercise to evaluate the educational assistance program, a test of basic skills in reading, writing, and mathematics was administered to over 5,000 people age eleven or older, living in rural areas. The results were mixed and not very encouraging: 29 percent of the sample was not able to pass the test in any area of competency in terms of minimum requirements of achievement. Women fared the worst: less than 20 percent of adult females achieved minimum skills in the administered literacy areas. The study concluded that even the majority of those who had completed primary school education could not attain the minimum requirements. A useful finding was that those who were still enrolled in school tended to perform better than those who had dropped out (Greaney, Khandker, and Alam 1998). The situation has not changed much in the early 2000s as there has been no fundamental reform in the education sector. South Asian governments are more interested in obtaining lines of credit from the World Bank than in addressing the issues on ground. For example, when the World Bank disbursed a $300 million Banking Sector Reform Loan in 2001 to Pakistan, the much needed foreign exchange was readily accepted by the country but the promised banking sector efficiencies were not achieved.

However, in 2004 Bangladesh received a new grant of $51 million toward its Millennium Development Goal of "Education for All." This grant is targeted toward putting back into school the 3 million children of ages six to ten who are not currently attending school. If the program succeeds, these children will be put back into nonformal schools (as opposed to the government's formal primary school system). The nonformal school system provides three years of schooling, it is community based, and managed through assistance from NGOs. The nonformal schools (or Learning Centers as they are called) cater to children from the poorest segments of society, who do not have access to primary education. About 8–10 percent of students, or about 1.7 million, attend nonformal schools in Bangladesh. The project has a fair chance of succeeding given the strategy of providing education allowances for eligible students and grants for nonformal Learning Centers where the students enroll. Incentives definitely work in South Asia as they reduce the opportunity cost of education. Dreze and Kingdon (2001) had earlier found that the provision of midday meals was an effective way to induce more enrollments in rural India.

On the positive side, Bangladesh, despite being one of the poorest countries in the world, has been making progress toward achieving the Millennium Development Goals. Nearly 18 million children are enrolled in government-approved primary schools. Net enrollment rates have risen from 64 percent to 80 percent over the decade 1991–2000.

Pakistan

Pakistan's education sector statistics tell an appalling tale: It is one of twelve countries in the world that spends less than 2 percent of its GNP on education; an average boy receives only five years of schooling while girls are even worse off with just two and a half years in school; and only one-third of primary school goers ages five to nine complete fifth grade. The World Bank has been active in Pakistan over the past decade in funding social and economic programs through its poverty alleviation assistance.

Since 9/11, the United States has stated that "combating terror and the conditions that breed terror in the frontline states of Afghanistan and Pakistan" are crucial to U.S. foreign policy. The Intelligence Reform and Terrorism Prevention Act endorses U.S. support "to improve and expand access to education for all (Pakistani) citizens." The United States has its own vested interest in supporting education programs, and defines "education reform" as the spread of the secular education system and the institution of a moderate curriculum in religious schools across Pakistan (Kronstadt 2004). The U.S. Agency for International Development reports that U.S. funding for education was $24 million and is expected to triple to $67 million in 2005. Given Pakistan's poor state of human development, this is a meager amount. Moreover, the Pakistani government's commitment to education cannot be taken too seriously, in that for every dollar spent on education, it spends $16 on defense. The government has also not been able to send back to school those children who are actively engaged as child labor in textiles, carpet weaving, and agriculture.

However, the government of Pakistan claims that its education efforts have met with success. Primary school dropout rates have been reduced by about half, from 60 percent in 1991 to 30 percent in 2000. The veracity of these claims is hard to quantify as Pakistan is among the countries with the poorest availability of national statistics in South Asia. The World Bank has previously assisted the government in its Social Action Program (SAP), which was targeted toward social development including health and education. The program failed to achieve its objectives. Enrollment rates have declined in Pakistan over the past decade and gender inequality in literacy persists.

The government's "Education Sector Reform Strategic Plan (2001–6)" cites the causes of educational malaise in terms of the poor quality of teachers and a lack of supply of schools (Government of Pakiston 2002–3). Nowhere does it acknowledge its own lack of adequate funding as one of the primary causes of low literacy and enrollment ratios in Pakistan. It merely states that there is a "failure of the system" to deliver quality education in Pakistan. In this report the government sidesteps the real educational issues and blames the village *mullahs* (Muslim priests) and mosque schools for low literacy in Pakistan. These schools and mullahs are also found in large numbers in Bangladesh, but that country has managed to show positive improvement in education indicators such as overall literacy and enrollment rates and reduction in gender disparity. Notwithstanding the conservatism and obduracy of religious schools, any reference to religious schools is largely a nonissue in the debate on why Pakistan has one of the lowest enrollment rates and one of the highest gender disparities in educational access. Poverty and income disparity also cannot be used as "the cause" of low education attainment. Sri Lanka is not a developed country, but the determination of its government to improve its human development indicators defies the "logic" that poorer countries cannot educate their population. Pakistan, Bangladesh, India, and Nepal should take a page out of Sri Lanka's success in educating the masses.

Perhaps we should look at the government spending priorities to assess the true causes of poor achievement in education. The government of Pakistan's own estimate is that the education sector requires annual funding of Rs. 55.5 billion, for which federal financing is Rs. 30.24 billion and the deficit is Rs. 29 billion. Of the Rs. 30 billion in government spending on education, 90 percent goes into salaries, which leaves a meager educational outlay of Rs. 3 million (see the Education Sector Reforms, Government of Pakistan 2002–3). The shortfall is to be funded by the World Bank and other multilateral organizations. There is a classic moral hazard problem here. The World Bank's ready supply of shortfall money will not provide any incentive to the government to increase its own contribution toward education. The bank should fundamentally change its assistance strategy by giving matching grants toward education through setting minimum expenditure targets, just as it sets for budget deficits and in the form of other conditions for providing country assistance.

The World Bank must insist on implementation, and it is in this way that it can play an effective role in affecting educational outcomes in Pakistan. The bank cannot merely remain a passive player, supplying credit on demand. Moreover, the Ministry of Education has to be audited by the World Bank to supply correct facts and figures on educational achievement and its ghost schools; the latter exist only on paper, and, by some estimates, were paid Rs. 1.4 billion in annual salaries, and yet no legal action has been taken.

In the light of repeated failures by successive governments to deliver on their promises of social programs, there is general skepticism in trusting the forecasts with respect to Millennium Development Goals. Disturbing statistics from Karachi, Pakistan's most prosperous city, add to the dismay. A survey conducted by a local NGO in collaboration with the Sindh Education Department revealed that only about 27.5 percent of the school-age children in the city are enrolled in schools ("Pakistan" 2003). According to figures of the United Nations Children's Fund, a nationwide sample of children in fifth grade revealed that only 33 percent could read with comprehension, while a mere 17 percent were able to write a simple letter. It stands to reason that governance and implementation issues are factors determining the success of the education sector reform plan so elegantly formulated by the Ministry of Education. The World Bank has its work cut out.

Finally, based on the continued lack of funding for education, it seems highly unlikely that Pakistan will achieve the Millennium Development Goals of ensuring that all boys and girls complete primary school, and that gender disparities in primary and secondary education are eliminated, preferably by 2005, and at all levels by 2015.

India

The World Bank has been active in India on a number of projects, although India opened its doors to educational funding in the late 1980s. Since 1980, the World Bank has invested $2 billion in various projects, approving six basic education projects and four vocational and technical education and training projects.

India has taken a step forward in seeking World Bank assistance for technical education, which has not been the case in Pakistan and Bangladesh. A similar technical focus greatly assisted South Korea and Malaysia in training a large skilled manufacturing workforce. The primary education projects in India cannot yet be fully evaluated as they are under implementation, although, on the positive side, government officials are showing commitment to these projects.

In 1991–2000 enrollments in the Utter Pradesh basic education project increased by 67 percent at the primary level and 74 percent at the lower secondary level, and the gross enrollment ratio increased from 66 percent to 107 percent against a target level of 78 percent (Abadzi 2002). Girls' enrollment increased by 97 percent and their attendance was around 77–87 percent. However, as has been the problem throughout South Asia, learning outcomes when tested were not impressive, demonstrating minimal improvement in baseline to mid-term learning comparisons.

These achievement statistics should be independently verified by NGOs and private researchers. Furthermore, funding for projects at various levels should be audited by independent auditors both during and after project completion. The bank should also ascertain what proportion of the project funds went toward salaries and buildings and what proportion was utilized for students and their learning materials. An analysis of the funds going toward salaries shows that in Pakistan, 90 percent or more of educational funds are dispensed as salary, leaving little if any funding for learning and education. Independent audits by credible auditors are essential in South Asia to prevent pilferage of funds, as South Asian countries like Pakistan and Bangladesh rank very high in terms of corruption. If the World Bank does not take concrete steps toward such audits, its otherwise good intentions and projects will suffer from the same underachievement as has been the experience from the 1950s to the early 1990s.

The World Bank's Operations Evaluations Department also found that the availability of teachers with respect to the Uttar Pradesh Project was difficult. This is not unusual and is a general rural problem widely encountered in all countries of South Asia. Without an adequate incentive structure, the problem will continue unabated as has been the case over the past six decades. Perhaps, the World Bank should set up model schools in various districts and use that experience to the benefit of other schools in the country of assistance.

The World Bank and the government of India claim that 100,000 teachers were trained in the Uttar Pradesh Project, which is indeed a mammoth undertaking, but by their own account, productivity gains as measured through students' learning outcomes are far from desired levels. Once again, we emphasize that there is great mistrust of the literacy and enrollment statistics churned out by the bureaucratic machinery in South Asia (Kingdon and Dreze 1998), and that all such government claims should be verified by third parties selected through a transparent process. The World Bank report also states that primary school enrollment statistics provided by the government could be inflated by as much as 20 percent (Abadzi 2002).

In India, the World Bank will also have to find ways to prevent the teachers from pushing out low-caste children from classrooms and assigning them menial tasks culturally associated with their caste (*Statesman*, January 26, 2000). Some such discrimination is still going on in World Bank–financed schools. It is amazing that this practice is going on in Kerala, which is widely reputed to be a more literate province of India and counted as a success story in literacy.

Conclusion

Education is widely accepted as a factor facilitating sustainable improvement in any country's overall living standards, attitudes, productivity, health, and nutrition. This chapter highlighted the role of human capital as an engine of sustainable growth and found that human capital commonly proxied by enrollment ratios in primary and secondary educational levels has a positive statistical relationship with income growth.

The chapter also found that both supply- and demand-side factors have a crucial role in determining the quantity and quality of education that will be attained in the developing economies of South Asia. Governments have a crucial role to play in the provision of the supply of education. This includes basic infrastructure through school buildings as well as quality and quantity of teachers in all areas of their respective countries. The demand for education can also be influenced by the government insofar as a crucial variable in such demand is parental education and family health, including the health of eligible school-going children. Thus, education, health, and economic growth are intimately interrelated.

Excluding Sri Lanka, which is the success story of South Asia, the record of all governments in the region with respect to human development indicators is poor. Only recently, have governments seemed to be waking up from years of neglect, and we have observed a flurry of World Bank projects and government education programs to improve literacy and other human development indicators. There is concern that literacy rates are being overstated,[4] and not being measured in a relevant way (in terms of its relationship to growth and development), and that the low completion rate of fifth grade and gender inequality has not been arrested. Better measures of education and literacy have become necessary. It is most relevant to carry out research to determine which measure of literacy is most related to sustainable economic growth. Finally, the World Bank can only do so much; the achievement of Millennium

Development Goals will be possible only with a large increase in education spending per capita by the respective South Asian governments.

Notes

1. Arrow (1962), Becker (1962), and Uzawa (1965) pursued theoretical modeling on the effects of human capital. Using the idea of "learning by doing" of Arrow, Romer (1986) incorporated the possible spillover effect of capital (broadly including human skills) and has shown that given the possible increasing returns, a competitive equilibrium generates lower growth rates vis-à-vis a social planner-dictated efficient equilibrium. The reason is that individuals do not take into account the social return and optimize on the basis of private returns to capital. Thus, government subsidies in the capital sector would increase growth rates.

2. Summers-Heston Penn World Tables are available through the National Bureau of Economic Research (NBER) Web site www.nber.org.

3. The Barro-Lee data set can be accessed through the NBER Web site www.nber.org.

4. Mentioned in "India: Policies to Reduce Poverty and Accelerate Sustainable Development," World Bank Report no. 19471, January 31, 2000. However, the Elementary Education Bureau has defended the accuracy of the Indian data on literacy and enrollment.

References

Abadzi, H. 2002. "India: Education Sector Development in the 1990s." World Bank, Operations Evaluation Department. Working Paper.

Andrabi, Tahir; Das Jishnu; Khwaja Asim Ijaz; and Tristan Zajonc. 2005. "Religious School Enrollment in Pakistan: A Look at the Data." World Bank Policy Research Working Paper Series no. WPS 3521.

Arrow, K.J. 1962. "The Economic Implications of Learning by Doing." *Review of Economic Studies* 29, no. 3. (June): 155–73.

Barro, R.J. 1991. "Economic Growth in a Cross Section of Countries." *Quarterly Journal of Economics* 106, no. 2:. 407–43.

Barro, R.J., and J. Lee. 1994. "Sources of Economic Growth." *Carnegie Rochester Conference Series on Public Policy*, no. 40: 1–46.

Becker, G.S. 1962. "Investment in Human Capital: A Theoretical Analysis." Part 2: Investment in Human Beings. *Journal of Political Economy* 70, no. 5: 9–49.

Dreze, J., and G.G. Kingdon. 2001. "School Participation in Rural India." *Review of Development Economics* 5, no. 1: pp 1–24.

Duraisamy, M. 2000. "Child Schooling and Child Work in India." *Econometric Society World Congress 2000 Contributed Papers 083.*

Englander, A.S., and A. Gurney. 1994. "Medium Term Determinants of OECD Productivity." *OECD Economic Studies* 22: 49–109.

Glomm, G., and B. Ravikumar. 1992. "Public versus Private Investment in Human Capital: Endogenous Growth and Income Inequality." *Journal of Political Economy* 100, no. 4: 818–34.

Government of Pakistan. 2002–3. Ministry of Education, "ESR and the Interim Poverty Reduction Strategy Paper (I-PRSP)."

Greaney, V.; R.S. Khandker; and M. Alam. 1998. "Bangladesh: Assessing Basic Skills."

(March). Available at www.worldbank.org/education/economicsed/tools/training/evalBangladesh.htm.

Hall, R.E., and C.I. Jones. 1999. "Why Do Some Countries Produce So Much More Output Per Worker Than Others?" *Quarterly Journal of Economics* 114, no. 1: 83–116.

Islam N. 1995. "Growth Empirics: A Panel Data Approach." *Quarterly Journal of Economics* 110: 1127–70.

Jayachandran, U. 2002. "Socioeconomic Determinants of School Attendance in India." Working Paper no. 103 (June), Center for Development Economics, India.

Jorgenson, D.W., and B.M. Fraumeni. 1992. "Investment in Education and U.S. Economic Growth." *Scandinavian Journal of Economics* 94: S51–70.

Kronstadt, Alan K. 2004. "Education Reform in Pakistan." Congressional Research Service Report, December 23.

Laitner, J. 1993. "Long-Run Growth and Human Capital." *Canadian Journal of Economics* 26, no. 4: 796–814.

———. 2000. "Earnings within Education Groups and Overall Productivity Growth." *Journal of Political Economy* 108, no. 4: 807–32.

Levine, R., and D. Renelt. 1992. "A Sensitivity Analysis of Cross-Country Growth Regressions." *American Economic Review* 82, no. 4: 942–63.

Lucas, R.E. 1988. "On the Mechanics of Economic Development." *Journal of Monetary Economics* 22: 3–42.

Mankiw, N.G.; D. Romer; and D.N. Weil. 1992. "A Contribution to the Empirics of Economic Growth." *Quarterly Journal of Economics* 107, no. 2: 407–37.

Murphy, K.M.; A. Shleifer; and R.W. Vishny. 1991. "The Allocation of Talent: Implications for Growth." *Quarterly Journal of Economics* 106, no. 2: 503–30.

O'Rourke, M. 1999. "Evaluating the Development Impact of Education Projects: Introduction." World Bank, June 16. Available at www.worldbank.org/education/economicsed/tools/training/eval/intro.html.

"Pakistan: Number of School-Going Children on the Decline [REPORT]." 2003. *ACR Weekly Newsletter* 2, no. 26 (June 25). Available at http://acr.hrschool.org/mainfile.php/0133/.

Pal, S. 2003. "How Much of the Gender Difference in Child School Enrolment Can Be Explained? Evidence from Rural India." HEW 0309004, Economics Working Paper Archive at WUSTL.

Ramachandran, V.K.; M. Swaminathan; and V. Rawal. 2003. "Barriers to Expansion of Mass Literacy and Primary Schooling in West Bengal: Study Based on Primary Data from Selected Villages." Trivendrum Working Papers 345, Centre for Development Studies, Trivendrum, India.

Romer, P.M. 1986. "Increasing Returns and Long-Run Growth." *Journal of Political Economy* 94, no. 5: 1002–37.

———. 1990. "Endogenous Technological Change." Part 2: The Problem of Development: A Conference of the Institute for the Study of Free Enterprise Systems. *Journal of Political Economy* 98, no. 5: S71–S102.

Siansei, B., and J. Van Reenen. 2003. "The Returns to Education: Macroeconomics." *Journal of Economic Surveys* 17, no. 2: 157–244.

Solow R.M. 1956. "A Contribution to the Theory of Economic Growth." *Quarterly Journal of Economics* 70, no. 1: 65–94.

United Nations Development Programme (UNDP). 2004. *Human Development Report 2004*.

Uzawa, H. 1965. "Optimum Technical Change in an Aggregative Model of Economic Growth." *International Economic Review* 6, no. 1 (January): 18–31.

World Bank. 2004. *World Development Report 2004*.

9

Poverty in Pakistan and South Asia

Concept, Measurement, and Analysis

Umer Khalid

In the current era of globalization, the debate on poverty has assumed far greater importance in light of the widening gap in per capita income between the developed and developing countries. This has led to increased efforts at the international level to alleviate poverty and improve the economic welfare of the poorer regions of the world. These include the adoption of the "Millennium Development Goals" by the General Assembly of the United Nations in 2000,[1] and a greater emphasis on poverty reduction in the lending programs of the multilateral aid agencies such as the World Bank and the International Monetary Fund (IMF). According to the *World Development Report 2000–2001*, almost half of the world's population—2.8 billion out of 6 billion—live on less than $2 a day, while one-fifth—1.2 billion—live on less than $1 a day, with 44 percent of them living in South Asia. While South Asia accounts for 44 percent of the world's poor, its share in the global population amounts to half of that, 22 percent. What is poverty and how is it measured? Has poverty increased in South Asia as a result of globalization marked by the adoption of more open and liberal trade regimes by the economies of the region? Have the World Bank/IMF-sponsored structural adjustment programs helped in alleviating or increasing poverty in the region? These are some of the questions I will attempt to answer in this chapter. While examining poverty in the South Asian region, the analysis in this chapter has a special focus on Pakistan.

What Is Poverty?

There are many different definitions and concepts of poverty. Poverty is said to exist when one or more people fail to attain a level of well-being (usually material) deemed to constitute a reasonable minimum by the standards of a society (Ravallion 1992).

In this chapter, we employ the typical definition of poverty, which takes into consideration whether individuals or households have enough resources or abilities to meet their basic needs. This aspect is based on individuals' level of income, consumption, education, and other attributes, with some defined threshold below which they are considered as being poor in that aspect. Poverty is the deprivation of essential assets and opportunities to which every human being is entitled. Thus, poverty can also be considered from a nonmonetary perspective. Monetary poverty is not the exclusive paradigm for poverty measurement and nonmonetary dimensions of poverty are useful in assessing poverty components.

Poverty is also associated with insufficient outcomes with respect to health, nutrition, and literacy, with deficient social relations, insecurity, low self-confidence, and powerlessness.

Measuring Poverty

Having defined poverty, we come next to the question, how is poverty measured? A poverty measure is a summary statistic on the economic welfare of the poor in a society. There is no universally accepted single measure of poverty. The most important purpose of a poverty measure is to enable poverty comparisons. These are required for an overall assessment of a country's progress in alleviating poverty or for the evaluation of specific policies or projects. Poverty comparisons are also made over time to assess overall performance from the point of view of the poor.

The following three measures of poverty are generally employed in poverty literature analysis:

1. *Headcount index.* This is by far the most widely used measure of poverty. The headcount index simply measures the proportion of population that is counted as poor. The great virtues of this index are that it is simple to construct and easy to understand. However, the measure has two major weaknesses: it does not take into account the intensity of poverty; it does not indicate *how poor* the poor are, and hence does not change if people below the poverty threshold (poverty line) become poorer.

2. *Poverty gap index.* A moderately popular measure of poverty is the poverty gap index, which adds up the extent to which individuals fall below a defined threshold, the poverty line. It is a measure of the depth of poverty. It calculates the mean distance below the poverty line as a proportion of the poverty line, where the mean is taken over the whole population, counting the nonpoor as having zero poverty gap.

3. *Poverty severity index.* Also called the Foster Greer Thorbecke (FGT) index, the poverty severity index is the average value of the square of depth

of poverty for each individual. Thus, the poorest people contribute relatively more to the index. While this measure has clear advantages for some purposes, such as comparing policies aimed at reaching the poorest, it is not easy to interpret. For poverty comparisons, however, the key point is that a ranking of dates, places, or policies in terms of FGT should reflect well their ranking in terms of the severity of poverty. What makes the measure useful is not the precise numbers it obtains, but its ability to order distributions in a better way than the alternatives.

The computation of the above poverty indicators requires estimates of individual economic welfare and the poverty line. There are a number of different approaches to measuring welfare. Typically, poverty comparisons in developing countries put a high weight on nutritional attainments, consistent with the behavior of poor people in a specific society. A comprehensive measure of consumption (for example, total expenditure on all goods and services consumed, including nonmarket goods, such as consumption of a farmer's own product) has been more popular than using current income in the development literature. This is due in part to the fact that incomes are harder to measure accurately. The following methods can be used to measure individual standards of living.

a. *Consumption per equivalent male adult.* Since households differ in size and composition, a simple comparison of aggregate household consumption can be misleading about the welfare of individual members of the household. Therefore, for any given household, an equivalence scale is used to approximate the number of single adults, based on observed consumption behavior. There are a number of value judgments embedded in this practice; for example, differences in needs are reflected in differences in consumption. Adult females and children are assigned a male equivalence of less than one since they typically consume less; however, that may not mean that they have lower "needs" but rather have less power within the household.

b. *Undernutrition.* This is a distinct concept, although closely associated with poverty. Undernutrition can be viewed as a specific type of poverty, namely, food energy poverty. There are a number of arguments for and against using this as a measure of well-being. A practical advantage is that this measure does not have to be adjusted for inflation and would not be constrained by any inadequacy of price data. However, nutrition is not the only aspect that matters to the well-being of people, including the poor. Thus, poverty comparisons based solely on nutrition may be limited and deceptive.

The next step in the computation of a poverty measure requires the definition of a poverty line. The poverty line defines the level of consumption needed for a household (or individual) to escape from poverty. It is a measure that separates the poor from the nonpoor, where the poor are those whose income (or consumption) falls below the poverty line. Poverty lines are generally drawn in absolute and/or in relative terms.

An absolute poverty line measures the number of people living below a certain income threshold or the number of households unable to afford certain basic goods and services. A relative poverty line, on the other hand, measures the extent to which a household's financial resources fall below an average income threshold for the economy. Although living standards and real incomes have grown because of higher employment and sustained economic growth over recent years, the gains in income and wealth have been unevenly distributed across the population.

Both of these measures are useful in their own right, but for a comparison over time, the absolute measure is more appropriate for developing countries like Pakistan because it shows the extent to which deprivation of the poor is alleviated. The relative measure, on the other hand, shows the position of an individual relative to others and it is not possible to compare poverty levels over time or across regions and countries.

Extent of Poverty in Pakistan

A review of the existing work on poverty shows a large number of attempts to estimate the incidence of poverty in Pakistan over the past two decades. Most of these studies are concerned with estimating the percentage of the population or households that lies below a well-defined, well-estimated poverty line. These studies have used data from the Household Income and Expenditure Surveys (HIES) conducted by the Federal Bureau of Statistics of the Government of Pakistan in different years to estimate poverty rates. The estimates are sensitive to the choice of poverty line and the methods employed to estimate poverty. Therefore, it is difficult to evaluate underlying trends of poverty in a consistent manner. The work on measurement of poverty includes Malik (1992), Anwar (1996), Amjad and Kemal (1997), Arif, Nazli, and Haq (2002), the Federal Bureau of Statistics (FBS 2001), and the World Bank (1995, 2002). Table 9.1 summarizes the emergent trends in poverty according to these studies.

According to Jafri (1999), poverty decreased between 1987–88 and 1990–91 while Malik (1992), Anwar (1996), and Amjad and Kemal (1997) found an increase in poverty during the same period. Likewise, Jafri (1999) also estimated that poverty increased in urban areas but declined in rural areas

Table 9.1

Headcount Measure for Pakistan: 1987–1988 to 1998–1999

Years	Malik (1992) 2,550 calories	Anwar (1996) 2,550 calories	Amjad and Kemal (1997)	Jafri (1999)	Qureshi and Arif (2001)	Arif, Nazli, and Haq (2002)	World Bank (2002)	FBS (2001) 2,550 calories
1987–1988	13.0	13.81	17.32	29.2	—	—	37.4	—
1990–1991	—	17.26	22.10	26.1	—	—	34.0	—
1992–1993	—	—	22.40	26.8	—	—	25.7	26.6
1993–1994	—	—	—	28.7	—	27.4	28.6	29.3
1996–1997	—	—	—	—	—	29.6	24.0	26.3
1998–1999	—	—	—	—	35.2	35.2	32.6	32.2

Source: Anwar and Qureshi (2002).

between 1990–91 and 1992–93. On the other hand, the World Bank (2002) showed a decline in poverty in both urban and rural areas of the country during the same period. More recently, Arif and colleagues (2000) reported an increase in poverty between 1993–94 and 1996–97, whereas the FBS (2001) and World Bank (2002) estimated a decline in poverty during the same period. These poverty estimates are not only sensitive to the choice of poverty lines and the use of different types of household data sets but also result from the type of adjustment made for the household size in determining differences in subsistence needs per capita.

However, a major disagreement emerged regarding the extent of poverty in the late 1980s when the World Bank (1995), using the basic needs approach, estimated 37 percent of the population as lying below the poverty line in 1987–88, whereas Malik (1992), Anwar (1996), and Amjad and Kemal (1997), using a poverty line based on minimum calorie need, estimated poverty incidence in the range of 13 to 17 percent.

The World Bank (2002) report shows national and regional poverty trends during the 1990s and concludes that poverty in Pakistan was as high at the end of the 1990s as at the beginning of the 1990s. The level of poverty estimated in the report at the end of the 1990s seems consistent with the results of the other studies. However, the main conclusion drawn in the report, that poverty rates stagnated during the 1990s, is contrary to the findings of many other studies on poverty trends in Pakistan (Table 9.1). On the basis of these studies one can conclude that poverty almost doubled from 17 percent in 1990–91 to 32 percent in 1998–99.

Since a large number of people strive to live at the subsistence level in Pakistan, it is appropriate to discuss only those studies that focus on poor nutrition as a poverty criterion, where the poverty line is defined at 2,550 calories minimum nutritional requirement, augmented by a modest allowance for nonfood needs. This approach defines an individual as poor if income or expenditure is insufficient to obtain the minimum necessities for the maintenance of physical efficiency such as food, clothing, housing, and so forth.[2] Amjad and Kemal (1997) and Qureshi and Arif (1999) estimated a consistent time series of poverty incidence using poverty lines based on the above definition (Table 9.2). We observe that poverty declined consistently from over 46 percent in 1969–70 to around 17 percent by 1987–88, but started rising afterward, nearly doubling to 32.6 percent by the end of the 1990s.

Steps Taken by the Government to Alleviate Poverty

The development challenges for Pakistan include achieving high and sustained broad-based economic growth, particularly in rural areas; reducing poverty; providing essential social and economic services and infrastructure to the poor;

Table 9.2

Poverty Trends in Pakistan (headcount ratios)

Years	Overall Pakistan	Rural	Urban
1963–1964	40.24	38.94	44.53
1966–1977	44.50	45.62	40.96
1969–1970	46.50	49.11	38.76
1979	30.68	32.51	25.94
1984–1985	24.47	25.87	21.17
1987–1988	17.32	18.32	14.99
1990–1991	22.11	23.59	18.64
1992–1993	22.40	23.35	15.50
1996–1997	31.00	32.00	27.00
1998–1999	32.60	34.80	25.90

Sources: Amjad and Kemal (1997); Qureshi and Arif (1999).

creating job opportunities; and improving governance. In November 2000, the government adopted a strategy to reduce poverty and restore economic stability. The strategy was articulated in the Interim Poverty Reduction Strategy Paper (IPRSP), which provided an integrated focus on a diverse set of factors that impact poverty and other development outcomes. The IPRSP was developed into a full Poverty Reduction Strategy Paper (PRSP) in December 2003, to serve as a blueprint for the government's poverty reduction strategy (Government of Pakistan 2003). The poverty reduction strategy of the PRSP is built upon the following four pillars:

1. accelerating economic growth while maintaining macroeconomic stability;
2. improving governance and devolution;
3. investing in human capital; and
4. targeting the poor and the vulnerable.

1. The first pillar of the PRSP emphasizes accelerated and sustained economic growth that requires a macroeconomic framework that can ensure continuity in macroeconomic stability, assure high levels of public spending to support key elements of poverty reduction strategy, and stimulate and further expand private investment. This pillar's policy and structural elements are: macroeconomic framework, monetary and fiscal policy; financial sector reform; capital market development; trade liberalization and export growth; investment policy reform and privatization; streamlining of the regulatory framework; improvement of the environment for small and medium-size

enterprises (SMEs); the provision of supportive infrastructure; rural development strategy; and housing finance.

2. Governance is critically important in economic growth and the development of human capital. In Pakistan, addressing the governance component of the poverty reduction strategy has required major transformation of governance structures and systems, as well as of political and organizational culture, especially at the local grassroots level. The main elements of the second pillar include devolution; fiscal decentralization; access to justice; police reforms; civil service reform; pay and pension reform; capacity building; anticorruption strategy; procurement reform; freedom of information; fiscal and financial transparency; and the strengthening of statistics.

3. A weak social profile is detrimental to growth, as human development is essential for attracting investment and generating capacity for sustainable growth. As most social development indicators for Pakistan compare poorly with those of other developing countries at similar levels of per capita income, the structural elements of the third pillar of the PRSP include improvements in education and health delivery; drinking water and sanitation; youth development; and strengthening of the commission for human development.

4. As part of the fourth pillar, the government is making targeted interventions to address poverty and generate income and employment through public works (Khushal Pakistan Program, Tameer-e-Pakistan Program, Tameer-e-Punjab, Tameer-e-Sarhad Programs); Drought Emergency Relief Assistance and micro-credit to improve life in the rural areas; and facilitation of SME development. The policy of targeted interventions will continue as one of the fundamental pillars of the growth and poverty reduction strategy.

Impact of IMF/World Bank Structural Adjustment Programs on Poverty in Pakistan

In the late 1980s, stabilization measures as well as liberalization reforms were implemented within the framework of the IMF/World Bank to change the structure of the economy so as to improve the balance of current account and budget deficit. The main components of short-term stabilization measures were tight monetary and fiscal policies coupled with wage and employment restraint and exchange rate policies; longer-term liberalization measures included reduced tariff rates and the removal of nontariff barriers, the removal of price controls, and the removal of exchange rate distortions through devaluation of domestic currency.

As part of the IMF conditions, the lowering of tariffs reduced protections for domestic industry, while the persistent depreciation of exchange rates and liberalization of domestic interest rates increased the domestic cost of production for industrial goods. As a result, investment declined persistently from 18.8 percent in 1995–96 to 17.7 percent in 1996–97, to 17.1 percent in 1997–98, and to 14.8 percent in 1998–99. Consequently, the GDP growth rate declined substantially, from an average of 6.1 percent in the 1980s to 4.6 percent in the 1990s.

Stabilization measures succeeded in sharply reducing the current account deficit as well as the budget deficit, bringing it down to 6 percent of GDP in 1993–94. However, the stabilization achieved was short-lived as the reform process lost momentum due to major slippages in the reform process in the form of increased tax exemptions and concessions leading to the implementation of further stabilization measures.

Revenue from custom duties declined sharply from 5.9 percent of GDP in 1989–90 to 2.2 percent of GDP in 1999–2000, resulting in an increased reliance on revenue through domestic taxes such as general sales tax (Anwar 2002). As a result, the revenue from sales tax increased from 1.8 percent of GDP in 1989–90 to 3.4 percent of GDP in 1999–2000, but the increase was not sufficient to compensate for the loss of revenue from trade taxes over the period. Although the government resorted to raising domestic tax rates to offset losses of revenue due to tariff reductions, the increased tax rates on a shrinking tax base led to further shrinkage in the tax base due to tax evasion, which resulted in a stagnant tax–GDP ratio.

The stagnant tax–GDP ratio resulted in decreased development expenditure on reducing the budget deficit. As a result, development expenditure declined steadily from 6.4 percent of GDP in 1990–91 to 3.2 percent of GDP in 1999–2000. This cut in development expenditure not only has affected the growth rate of GDP adversely but also resulted in reduced employment opportunities for the poor, and it has worsened the quality and quantity of service provided to the poor through the social and economic infrastructure.

As seen in the previous section, the evidence suggests overall increasing trends in absolute poverty between 1963–64 and 1971–72 in Pakistan. Amjad and Kemal (1997), Anwar (1996), the World Bank (1995, 2002), and Qureshi and Arif (1999) analyzed poverty trends during the period of structural adjustment and liberalization. The stabilization measures sought excessive reductions in aggregate demand through expenditure-reducing policies such as wage restraint, employment freezes, reduced development expenditure, subsidy cuts, and cuts in expenditure on social services, mainly education and health. On the other hand, liberalization policies sought to remove structural rigidities and distortion in the incentive system to enhance the growth rate of GDP. Average growth rates fell, inflation accelerated, and unemployment rose following the implementation of the stabilization and liberalization reforms. All of these reforms—including privatization, wage and employment restraints in the public sector, cuts in subsidies, cuts in development expenditure, increases in sales taxes and utility charges, frequent devaluation together with declining remittances—seem to have reduced the real income of the vulnerable groups of the population and to have increased poverty substantially in the 1990s (Anwar 2002).

Poverty Trends in Other South Asian Countries

India

The evaluation of poverty trends in India has been made more complex by certain changes in the methodology of the main official consumer expenditure surveys, the National Sample Surveys, forming the basis for poverty estimates in India. These have made the recent survey data noncomparable with earlier rounds of the same survey.[3] Deaton and Dreze (2002) present a new set of poverty estimates for India and Indian states for 1987–88, 1993–94, and 1999–2000, which makes the headcount ratios for all three time periods comparable. These poverty estimates, along with the headcount rate obtained from the official methodology, are given in Table 9.3.

A comparison of both official estimates and adjusted estimates shows that much lower poverty trends are observed in both rural and urban India using the adjusted poverty estimates. Thus, the picture that emerges from the revised estimates is that of a persistent and sustained decline in poverty in India during the reference period. There has, however, been a divergence in poverty reduction across the different states of India. Poorer northern states have lagged behind the other major states in lowering poverty over the past two decades. One possible explanation could be the fact that regional economic growth has been slower in the north due to a weaker investment climate in these lagging states.

Table 9.3

Poverty Trends in India (headcount ratios)

	Official methodology		Adjusted estimates	
	Rural	Urban	Rural	Urban
1987–1988	39.4	39.1	39.0	22.5
1993–1994	37.1	32.9	33.0	17.8
1999–2000	26.8	24.1	26.3	12.0

Source: Deaton and Dreze (2002).

Table 9.4

Poverty Trends in Bangladesh (headcount ratios)

Years	Overall Bangladesh	Rural	Urban
1988–1989	57.1	59.2	43.9
1991–1992	58.8	61.2	44.9
1995–1997	53.1	56.7	35.0
1997	46.0	46.8	43.4
1998–1999	44.7	44.9	43.3

Source: Mahbub ul-Haq Human Development Centre (2001).

Economic growth has been a leading determinant of poverty reduction experienced by India (ibid.). Additional evidence on the key role of growth is provided by cross-country studies on the relationship between growth and poverty reduction (Ravallion 2001). Thus, policies that enhance overall economic growth are the key to improving the incomes of poor people in developing countries like India.

Bangladesh

The incidence of poverty in Bangladesh declined from 57 percent in 1988–89 to 45 percent in 1999. Table 9.4 summarizes trends in the headcount ratio in Bangladesh. Between 1988–89 and 1995–96, urban poverty declined at a faster rate than rural poverty.

Rural poverty is seen to decline over the years, reaching 45 percent by 1998–99, while urban poverty rises in later years of the 1990s. There is a common perception that the presence of micro-credit delivery systems in Bangladesh has helped provide a cushion for poor households in case of shocks like crop failures, floods, and other natural disasters (Mahbub ul-Haq Human Development Centre 2003).

Sri Lanka

The official poverty estimates for Sri Lanka show fluctuations and no downward trend in the incidence of poverty, according to the headcount ratio (Table 9.5). There is a substantial difference across the regions: poverty incidence is the highest in the estate sector at 45 percent and lowest in urban areas at 25 percent (Mahbub ul-Haq Human Development Centre 2003).

Table 9.5

Poverty Trends in Sri Lanka (headcount ratios)

	1990–1991	1995–1996	1996–1997
Lower poverty line	20	25	19
Higher poverty line	33	39	31

Source: Mahbub ul-Haq Human Development Centre (2001).

Table 9.6

People Living on Less Than $1 a Day

Region	1987	1998	Change
East Asia and Pacific	417.5	278.3	−139.2
Europe and Central Asia	1.1	24.0	22.9
Latin America and the Caribbean	63.7	78.2	14.5
Middle East and North Africa	9.3	5.5	−3.8
South Asia	474.4	522.0	47.6
Sub-Saharan Africa	217.2	290.9	73.7

Source: World Bank (2000).

Poverty in South Asia: A Comparison with Other Regions

South Asia is home to nearly 22 percent of the world's population, but its share in world poverty is highest among all regions. In 1987, 40.1 percent of the world's poorest people, subsisting on less than $1 a day, lived in South Asia (Figure 9.1a). In comparison, the incidence of poverty in East Asia and the Pacific was just over 35 percent, in sub-Saharan Africa, 18.4 percent, and in Latin America and the Caribbean, 5.4 percent. During the decade of the 1990s, poverty increased further in the region (Figure 9.1b). reaching 43.5 percent by 1998. A substantial decline in poverty is observed for East Asia and the Pacific, where the incidence of poverty fell by twelve percentage points.

In terms of the absolute number of people living in poverty, we see that more than 474 million people in South Asia were poor in 1987 (Table 9.6). This number had increased to 522 million by 1998, an increase of around 48 million over a period of eleven years. Sub-Saharan Africa saw the highest increase, 73.7 million, in the number of people living in absolute poverty. On the other hand, in East Asia and the Pacific, the number of people living in absolute poverty declined by over 139 million.

Figure 9.1   **Distribution of Population Living on Less Than $1 a Day, 1987 and 1988**

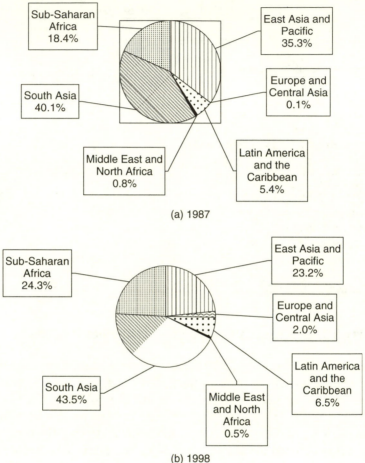

(a) 1987

(b) 1998

Conclusion

This chapter has examined poverty trends in the South Asian countries, with a detailed analysis of Pakistan. Poverty is seen to encompass both monetary and nonmonetary dimensions, although money metric measures are generally employed in any analysis of poverty. In Pakistan, we observed an increased incidence of poverty in the decade of the 1990s—the period coinciding with the opening up of the economy to increased trade and capital flows, and the implementation of structural adjustment programs under the auspices of the

IMF and World Bank. The reforms undertaken as part of these programs seem to have reduced the real income of the vulnerable groups of the population, thereby leading to higher levels of poverty during this period. In neighboring India, on the other hand, a persistent decline in poverty is seen over the same period. In other countries of the region, mixed trends of poverty incidence are observed.

A comparison of South Asia with other regions of the world reveals that the proportion of the world's poor living in South Asia has actually increased between 1987 and 1998. This leads us to conclude that globalization, as manifested by the increasing integration of South Asian economies into the global economy, has brought about increased poverty levels in South Asia relative to other regions of the world. However, this conclusion needs to be qualified as this increase in poverty is also associated with a rise in corruption and the mismanagement of scarce national resources.

Notes

1. The first of the Millennium Development Goals aims to "reduce by half, between 1990 and 2015, the proportion of people whose income is less than $1 a day."

2. For definition and derivation of poverty lines, see Malik (1988) and Anwar (1998).

3. The basic change was in terms of the reference period for a range of consumption items, from 30 days to 7 days and from 30 days to 365 days.

References

Amjad, Rashid, and A.R. Kemal. 1997. "Macro-Economic Policies and Their Impact on Poverty Alleviation in Pakistan." *Pakistan Development Review* 36, no. 1: 39–68.

Anwar, Talat. 1996. "Structural Adjustment and Poverty: The Case of Pakistan." *Pakistan Development Review* 35, no. 4: 911–26.

———. 1998. "Absolute Poverty in Pakistan: Evidence and Alleviating Strategy." Pakistan Academy for Rural Development, Peshawar. *Journal of Rural Development and Administration* 2.

———. 2002. "Impact of Globalization and Liberalization on Growth, Employment and Poverty: A Case Study of Pakistan." United Nations University/World Institute for Development Economic Research, Helsinki, Finland. Discussion Paper no. 2002/17.

Anwar, Talat, and Sarfraz Qureshi. 2002. "Trends in Absolute Poverty in Pakistan 1990–91 and 2001." *Pakistan Development Review* 41, no. 4.

Arif, G.M.; H. Nazli; and R. Haq. 2002. "Rural Non-agriculture Employment and Poverty in Pakistan." *Pakistan Development Review* 39, no. 4: 1089–110.

Deaton, Angus, and Jean Dreze. 2002. "Poverty and Inequality in India: A Re-Examination." *Economic and Political Weekly*, September 7.

Federal Bureau of Statistics (FBS). 2001. *Poverty in Pakistan*. Statistics Division, Islamabad.

Government of Pakistan. 2003. *Accelerating Economic Growth and Reducing Poverty: The Road Ahead*. Poverty Reduction Strategy Paper Secretariat, Islamabad.

Mahbub ul-Haq Human Development Centre. 2001. *Human Development in South Asia 2001: Globalization and Human Development.* Karachi: Oxford University Press.

——. 2003. *Human Development in South Asia 2003: The Employment Challenge.* Karachi: Oxford University Press.

Malik, Mohammad H. 1988. "Existing Evidence on Poverty." *Pakistan Development Review* 27, no. 4.

Malik, Sohail J. 1992. "Rural Poverty in Pakistan: Some Recent Evidence." *Pakistan Development Review* 31, no. 4.

Qureshi, Sarfraz, and G.M. Arif. 1999. *Profile of Poverty in Pakistan 1998–99.* Pakistan Institute of Development Economics, Islamabad. MIMAP Technical Paper Series no. 5.

Ravallion, Martin. 1992. *Poverty Comparison: A Guide to Concepts and Methods.* Living Standards Measurement Study Working Paper 88. Washington, DC.

——. 2001. "Growth, Inequality and Poverty: Looking Beyond Averages." *World Development* 29, no. 11: 1803–16.

World Bank. 1995. *Pakistan Poverty Assessment.* Washington, DC.

——. 2000. *World Development Report 2000/2001: Attacking Poverty.* Washington, DC.

——. 2002. *Poverty in Pakistan: Vulnerabilities, Social Gaps and Rural Dynamics.* Washington, DC.

Part III

Globalization, Trade, and Development

10

South Asia's Trade and Commercial Relations with Canada

Ann Weston

Importance of Trade in the South Asian Economies

The South Asian economies have generally become more open in the past decade, as measured by the share of exports and imports of goods and services in their gross domestic product (GDP); an exception is Pakistan, where the ratio fell slightly, from 39 percent to 38 percent between 1990 and 2002, but even so it remained more open than Bangladesh or India, where the ratios increased from 20 percent to 33 percent and 16 percent to 31 percent, respectively, over the same time period (Table 10.1).

Governments in the region are now committed to liberalizing their trade regimes, as part of an increasing outward economic orientation. Bangladesh, India, the Maldives, Pakistan, and Sri Lanka were founding members of the World Trade Organization (WTO), and Nepal became a member in 2003, while Bhutan is in the early stage of accession and Afghanistan has not yet applied. An excellent source of information about trade policies in WTO members is the trade policy reviews produced by the WTO: there are now reports for Bangladesh (2000), India (2002a), the Maldives (2003), Pakistan (2002b), and Sri Lanka (2004).

In the course of liberalization, a particular concern for most governments has been how to ensure that the changes in trade policies and practices lead to an expansion of trade, growth, employment, and poverty reduction—conversely to ensure that trade does not exacerbate unemployment and poverty. This has been an issue particularly as regards trade in agricultural products, with major agricultural exporters such as Canada and the United States putting pressure on larger economies such as India to reduce their tariffs and other rules protecting their markets from foreign produce, as discussed further below. Governments have other concerns too, ranging from the need to manage trade deficits, to food security, and to industrial development.

Table 10.1

Importance of Trade: Imports (M) **and Exports** (X) **as a Share of GDP** (%)

	M/G DP 1990	M/GDP 2002	X/GDP 1990	X/GDP 2002	M + X / GDP 1990	M + X / GDP 2002
Afghanistan						
Bangladesh	14	19	6	14	20	33
Bhutan					0	0
India	9	16	7	15	16	31
Maldives	64	67	24	88	88	155
Nepal	22	29	11	16	33	45
Pakistan	23	19	16	19	39	38
Sri Lanka	38	43	29	36	67	79

Source: United Nations Development Programme, *Human Development Report 2004*, table 15, 194.

Volume, Composition, and Direction of South Asian Trade

South Asia's share of world trade in merchandise over the past decade has remained less than 2 percent—despite the increase in outward orientation—as other countries ave also expanded their trade. The region's share of world exports increased from 1.2 percent to 1.4 percent in the decade to 2002,[1] while its share of world imports grew from 1.4 percent to 1.6 percent. India is by far the largest trader, followed by Pakistan, Bangladesh, and then Sri Lanka (Table 10.2). A notable development is the fact that since 1997 Bangladesh has overtaken Sri Lanka in terms of exports; its exports grew by 190 percent, the highest relative increase of all South Asian countries.

Exports of services are also important to consider. India earned $23.5 billion from its commercial services exports, or roughly half (48 percent) as much as its other exports in 2002, although for the other countries they are less significant. With an annual growth rate of 19 percent from 1995 to 2002, India rose to the rank of the tenth largest world exporter of services—well above its twenty-first place in terms of exports of goods.[2] Its foreign exchange earnings from service sector exports have helped to offset the trade deficit in goods (following an increase in the volume of imports). Also important have been the large flows of private transfers or remittances (which in 2003 amounted to US$18.9 billion).

While commodity exports are still important to the region—and governments are concerned about declining world prices for commodities such as cotton,

Table 10.2

South Asian Merchandise Trade with the World (millions of dollars)

	1992	1993	1994	1995	1996	1997	1998	1999	2000	2001	2002
Exports											
Afghanistan	131	106	168	156	173	201	209	167	186	113	101
Bangladesh	2,098	2,545	2,934	3,733	4,009	4,840	5,141	5,458	6,399	6,085	6,093
Bhutan	66	65	66	103	100	118	108	116	116	116	—
India	19,628	21,572	25,022	30,630	33,105	35,008	33,437	35,667	42,379	43,347	49251
Maldives	40	35	46	50	59	73	74	64	76	76	90
Nepal	369	384	362	345	385	406	474	602	804	737	568
Pakistan	7,351	6,720	7,400	8,029	9,365	8,758	8,514	8,491	9,028	9,238	9,913
Sri Lanka	2,455	2,859	3,208	3,798	4,095	4,639	4,809	4,594	5,430	4,816	4,699
S. Asia	32,138	34,286	39,206	46,844	51,291	54,043	52,766	55,159	64,418	64,528	70,715
World excluding European Union intra-exports a	2,721,000	2,836,000	3,250,000	3,828,000	4,032,000	4,254,000	4,085,000	4,280,000	4,999,000	4,758,000	4,946,000
% share of world	1.2%	1.2%	1.2%	1.2%	1.3%	1.3%	1.3%	1.3%	1.3%	1.4%	1.4%

(continued)

Table 10.2 (continued)

	1992	1993	1994	1995	1996	1997	1998	1999	2000	2001	2002
Imports											
Afghanistan	411	419	375	368	500	436	373	411	550	551	950
Bangladesh	3,732	3,994	4,602	6,502	6,621	6,898	6,974	7,694	8,360	8,350	7,914
Bhutan	125	90	92	112	128	137	134	182	180	180	—
India	23,579	22,788	26,843	34,707	37,942	41,432,	42,980	46,979	51,523	50,392	56,595
Maldives	189	191	222	268	302	349	354	402	389	395	392
Nepal	776	890	1,155	1,333	1,398	1,693	1,246	1,422	1,573	1,473	1,419
Pakistan	9,423	9,545	8,931	11,515	12,189	11,650	9,330	10,297	11,293	10,191	11,233
Sri Lanka	3,500	4,005	4,767	5,306	5,442	5,864	5,905	5,961	7,177	5,973	6,104
S. Asia	41,735	41,922	46,987	60,111	64,522	68,459	67,296	73,348	81,045	77,505	84,607
World excluding European Union intra-imports a	2,835,000	2,931,000	3,348,000	3,941,000	4,172,000	4,398,000	4,248,000	4,470,000	5,247,000	5,015,000	5,179,000
% share of world	1.5%	1.4%	1.4%	1.5%	1.5%	1.6%	1.6%	1.6%	1.5%	1.5%	1.6%

Source: World Trade Organization data online, accessed October 13, 2004.

rice, and tea, especially as the price of imported commodities such as oil have risen—more than two-thirds of exports are now manufactured products for Bangladesh, India, Pakistan, Sri Lanka, and Nepal. In many cases this reflects the growth of the textiles and clothing industry, following the restraints under the Multifiber Arrangement (MFA) imposed on garment exports from other countries in East and Southeast Asia. As a result, these countries were particularly concerned about the impact that the ending of the MFA in 2005 would have on their economies (see below). A large number of people, and especially young women, are now employed in the garment industry.

By far the largest export markets for most countries have been the European Union (EU) and the United States, with each accounting for about a quarter of the total South Asian exports. Intra–South Asian trade is still relatively underdeveloped—with less than 5 percent of total trade, which is much lower than any other regional grouping—although it has grown gradually over the past decade. For Nepal, it is much more important (about 30 percent), given the country's close dependence on the Indian market for both exports and imports. A new development in recent years has been trade with other countries in Asia, notably China.

Evolution of South Asian Trade Policies and Priorities

The past decade has seen a major shift in South Asian trade policies. Many of these changes reflected domestic realization of economic gains to be made from a more outward orientation, and the expectation that such policies would help to attract private foreign investment. The conclusion of the Uruguay Round of multilateral trade negotiations and the creation of the World Trade Organization in 1994 accelerated and consolidated the process of change. In the case of Nepal, its accession to the WTO in 2003 involved a number of obligations, despite its status as a less developed country (LDC). Bhutan submitted a Memorandum on the Foreign Trade Regime in 2003 and its Working Party has met twice. Afghanistan established a Working Party in 2004, but it has yet to meet and a Memorandum has not been submitted.

Just one indicator of liberalization has been the cut in tariff rates in all countries. In Sri Lanka, for instance, the average applied tariff in 2001 was 8.2 percent on all goods (19 percent on agricultural products and 6.7 percent on other goods) (see Table 10.3). This compares with an average in 1995 of 20 percent. In Pakistan the average tariff fell from 56 percent in 1993/94 to 17.1 percent in 2003. With the exception of Sri Lanka, most South Asian tariff levels still remain considerably higher than those in other Asian countries (for instance in Indonesia and Malaysia, overall simple applied average tariffs were 6.0 percent and 7.5 percent, respectively in 2001).[3] One of the constraints in bringing tariffs lower may be that they still account for a significant share

Table 10.3

Tariffs in South Asia

	Year		Average	Agriculture	Nonagriculture
Bangladesh	2003	Bound	163.8	188.5	35.7
		Actual	19.5	21.7	19.2
India	2002	Bound	49.8	114.5	34.3
		Actual	29.0	36.9	27.7
Nepal	2002	Actual	13.6	13.4	13.7
Pakistan	2003	Bound	52.4	97.1	35.3
		Actual	17.1	20.4	16.6
Sri Lanka	2001	Bound	29.8	49.7	19.3
		Actual	8.2	19.0	6.7

Source: World Trade Organization Web site, Country Profiles.

of total tax revenue—as much as 25.5 percent in India in 1999–2001, 31.2 percent in Nepal (2000–2002), 13.9 percent in Pakistan (2000–2002), and 19.2 percent in Sri Lanka (1995–97).[4] In many countries the tariff schedule remains complex, with multiple tariff levels, which typically increase with the degree of value-added, thereby giving higher effective protection rates to domestic processing industries.

Another issue for their trading partners has been the discrepancy between applied tariffs and the levels that South Asian countries have bound in the WTO. Bangladesh has the highest bound tariffs in the region at 188.5 percent on agricultural goods and 35.7 percent on other goods (Table 10.3). Sri Lanka took advantage of the flexibility implied in the difference between its actual and bound tariffs to raise its applied tariffs in its 2003 budget in order to raise government revenues. And in 2000, when India removed most of its import quotas (the exceptions being for security or quarantine reasons) it increased tariff levels on a temporary basis to offset some of the immediate impact on domestic producers. But governments are under pressure in the WTO to bring their tariff bindings closer to actual rates.

Besides tariff cuts, South Asian governments have reduced a number of other barriers to trade. For instance, in Sri Lanka, there are no import quotas or quantitative restrictions, though several items (mostly chemical products, transport equipment, and agricultural products) are still subject to import licensing on economic as well as security, health, and environmental grounds (WTO 2004: 38–39). Imports of certain plants and animals are banned (such as genetically modified food products). Pakistan has removed its import restrictions on balance of payments grounds, though it has retained some prohibitions and restrictions on a few items. It still has a large number of state enterprises involved in trade—making the government the largest importer according to the WTO (2002b, 52). And government procurement is still used to support local industry (with price preferences of up to 25 percent for domestic suppliers).

The region remains one of the most protected—whether in terms of tariffs or other types of policies restraining imports. And India in particular is under pressure in the WTO Doha Round of negotiations to make further liberalization measures, in a wide range of areas, in return for whatever concessions it may be seeking. India has begun to use antidumping duties on imports to protect domestic producers, with as many as 210 measures in force in June 2003, and another eight cases of safeguards (in October 2003). But in most of the other South Asian countries, the requisite antidumping or countervailing duties or safeguards legislation is not in place or else it has not been used in recent years.

Liberalization has also been applied to exports, largely with the removal of duties and export prohibitions designed originally to promote the processing of commodities before export. There are still some controls—for instance, in Sri Lanka, there are a number of licenses and cesses on exports such as coconut and tea intended to control quality and raise revenue for research and product development. In Pakistan, preshipment registration is required of sensitive exports such as cotton and rice. Governments also offer incentives for exports in the form of rebates on import duties, export processing zones, and various forms of financial assistance.

The challenge for governments in the region is to improve and secure access for their exports, particularly to the EU and U.S. markets. South Asia is one of the few developing country regions without any special bilateral or regional preferential trade arrangements in either the EU or the U.S. markets. LDCs, such as Afghanistan, Bangladesh, Nepal, and the Maldives, have been granted special access to the EU market under the EU's "Everything But Arms" initiative. But India, Pakistan, and Sri Lanka are treated like China or other Asian exporters to the EU—they are eligible for some unilateral tariff cuts under the Generalized System of Preferences but nothing more. East and Southeast Asia are included in the Asia-Pacific Economic Cooperation grouping, which aims to promote trade through various types of cooperation within the Asia-Pacific region. Some East/Southeast Asian countries are in bilateral free trade discussions with the United States. Latin America, for its part, is involved in the Free Trade Area of the Americas (FTAA) discussions with the United States and Canada, while some seventy countries in the Africa, Caribbean, and Pacific regions benefit from privileged access to the EU under the Cotonou Convention and are negotiating successor Economic Partnership Agreements with the EU. Many African countries also benefit from the U.S. African Growth and Opportunities Act under which the United States grants duty-free treatment on various exports, including clothing, meeting certain rules of origin. But the United States has offered no such privilege to Bangladesh or any other Asian LDC, because they are considered too competitive. So, the South Asian strategy has been to rely on the WTO to negotiate improvements in access to the EU and U.S. markets. (These are discussed further in the next section.)

Efforts to promote subregional trade have been complicated by concern about disparities in competitiveness as well as political differences between India and Pakistan (e.g., over Kashmir). Nonetheless steps have been taken including the signing of the South Asian Association for Regional Cooperation (SAARC) in 1985 and the creation of a SAARC secretariat in Nepal, which has organized several technical meetings and studies to advance thinking about measures to promote regional economic relationships including trade within region. Governments discussed first a South Asian Preferential Trade Agreement (from 1995) and then a South Asia Free Trade Agreement (SAFTA), with 2001 being set as the initial target date, but this proved unrealistic. With the political and military tensions between India and Pakistan, there was no SAARC summit from 1999 to 2002. A more realistic timetable was proposed in 1999 by a group of eminent persons who recommended that SAFTA be set up by 2008 (2010 for LDCs) and that this be followed by the creation of a customs union by 2015, with an eventual economic union by 2020.[5]

Tariffs have been cut on about 1,700 HS6 digit items—covering about 40 percent of Pakistan's exports within the region, followed by Nepal (35 percent), India (30 percent), Bhutan (17 percent), and Sri Lanka (12 percent).[6] Frustrated with this slow pace, some countries have decided to pursue bilateral agreements with each other, as in the case of Sri Lanka and India, Sri Lanka and Pakistan, and Bangladesh and India.

Most of the gains from a free trade agreement (FTA) are expected to go to India, reflecting in part its more diversified export structure[7] while the other countries will either gain or lose marginally—according to some estimates, the benefits to South Asia of unilateral or multilateral trade liberalization or FTAs with the United States or EU would be greater. Some analysts have argued that South Asia should consider following the approach of the Association of Southeast Asian Nations (ASEAN), which have cut tariffs on their imports from all sources rather than limiting them to intraregional trade.[8]

At the same time, various South Asian countries have individually pursued closer links with countries outside the region. For instance, Pakistan has a preferential trade agreement with Iran and Turkey under the Economic Cooperation Organization, though it is limited to a 10 percent tariff margin for a specific list of products and a number of measures such as simplified visa procedures for business people in order to facilitate trade. In 2003, India signed an agreement with Mercosur (Southern Cone Common Market), leading to a free trade agreement for certain goods and services. The aim is to gradually expand the coverage of the agreement and to include measures to promote investment, technology and other forms of economic cooperation. According to some estimates, this initiative could lead bilateral trade to grow from the present level of US$1.3–1.6 billion to US$13 billion.[9] And India has indicated its interest in joining the ASEAN free trade agreement, which seeks to bring tariffs below 5 percent by 2010 on a comprehensive list of products.

Engagement in the World Trade Organization

The WTO is an important venue for the South Asian countries to promote their trade interests. India and Bangladesh have assumed particular leadership roles, while Pakistan, Sri Lanka, and Nepal have also been quite active members. Among the areas that they have pursued, which will be considered here in further detail, are: the ending of quotas on textiles and clothing trade, other nonagricultural market access issues, services exports (mode 4 and outsourcing), agricultural subsidies, and governance of the multilateral trading system, including special and differential treatment for LDCs and other developing countries.

Textiles and Clothing

Textiles and clothing (T&C) exports are important for all South Asian countries—with the sector accounting for as much as a third of manufacturing output in Bangladesh and Nepal, a quarter in Pakistan and Sri Lanka, and an eighth in India, and typically for higher shares of manufacturing employment.[10] So the ending in January 2005 of the Multifiber Arrangement (MFA), which has governed world T&C trade, is of particular interest. India, Bangladesh, and Pakistan are among the world's top fifteen exporters, jointly accounting for 6 percent of world exports in 2003, while India and Pakistan account for 7.2 percent of world exports of textiles.[11] The key issue is how producers in all South Asian countries will compete when there are no longer any quotas restricting exports especially from major suppliers like China and India to the U.S., EU, and Canadian markets. Most studies identify China as the leading beneficiary—with the World Bank suggesting that China's share of world exports will rise to 50 percent by 2010 from the present level of 20 percent—and there is already widespread evidence of quota elimination being followed by surges in imports from China and cuts from other suppliers.[12] Another key beneficiary, according to some estimates, is India, with half of its Uruguay Round gains attributed to the end of the MFA. Less competitive suppliers may be somewhat protected by preferential tariff schemes and other measures that may increasingly be used to restrict more competitive suppliers such as antidumping duties, special safeguards (against China), and product and labor standards.

In response to concerns about large potential losses in employment and export earnings, governments in the smaller exporting countries have considered a variety of options, such as improving access to textiles at world prices through duty remission schemes as well as improving customs procedures and transport infrastructure. Bangladesh, Sri Lanka, and Nepal have also joined another ten or so countries to ask WTO members to consider various ways to compensate them for any negative impacts they may experience. For Bangladesh and Nepal, one strategy has been to seek duty-free access for LDCs, which would give them a 10–15 percent tariff margin over China—while this has been agreed in the EU and Canada, albeit subject to certain rules of origin, the United States has limited its support to LDCs in Africa.

Nonagricultural Market Access

South Asian governments have been quite involved in the discussions in the WTO Doha Development Agenda on nonagricultural market access, pressing developed countries to reduce tariff peaks and escalating tariffs on certain labor-intensive products as well as restraining the use of antidumping and countervailing duties, arbitrary sanitary and phytosanitary measures and other product standards, and other controls supposedly introduced for security reasons. Such measures have affected a range of exports from the region.

At the same time, South Asian governments have been resisting pressure to drastically reduce their own tariffs. In September 2003, at the WTO ministerial meeting in Cancún, Mexico, they joined with others in rejecting the formula proposed in the draft text that would have led to many developing countries making much larger absolute cuts (i.e., in percentage points) than developed countries. According to some estimates, the more ambitious tariff cut proposals, while bringing greater long-term gains in exports and welfare, could lead to major adjustment challenges. This would be the case particularly in South Asia, with India facing some of the largest projected increases in imports and losses of tariff revenues among all countries.[13] Instead, India proposed a linear approach, with lower reductions being required of developing countries (e.g., 33.3 percent compared to 50 percent for developed countries). At the end of July 2004, however, WTO members agreed to move ahead with a nonlinear approach, combined with the complete removal or harmonization of tariffs in particular sectors, with the exact formula still to be negotiated.[14] Both developed and developing countries may decide to go further in some product categories and to exclude other more sensitive ones, as the cuts will be considered for each product line in turn. The principle of special and differential treatment has been reaffirmed, which should allow developing countries to make fewer and/or slower cuts in their tariffs. But they are still under pressure to make significant changes in return for improved market access. Exceptions will be made for LDCs like Bangladesh and Nepal; they will be expected to increase their tariff bindings rather than make any cuts. But there has been no time-bound commitment to grant them duty-free access to all developed country markets; instead this remains an optional policy.

Services

Another key objective for South Asia in the ongoing WTO negotiations is to secure improved access for their service exports. Two areas in particular are important—securing the existing market for them to export services under "Mode 1," which involves cross-border trade, and increasing opportunities for nationals to supply services in foreign markets under "Mode 4," which involves the movement of the service providers themselves into foreign markets. Exports of outsourced services such as software development, data processing, and other backroom office services (including call centers) have expanded in India in particular. These are at risk following moves in the United States and United Kingdom, among others, to consider limits on outsourcing, for instance, through public procurement conditions, and in response India is anxious to secure its market access by pressing for commitments in the WTO on unrestricted market access and unqualified national treatment under Mode 1.

In terms of Mode 4, past WTO commitments have focused on business people and professionals, though with less than twenty countries offering unrestricted market access or national treatment. While South Asia has service providers in these categories, another objective has been to expand the coverage of less-skilled services such as construction. This would help to expand the region's receipts of remittances, which in 2002 amounted to more than US$16 billion—equivalent to as much as 47 percent of export earnings in Bangladesh, 36 percent in Pakistan, 27 percent in Sri Lanka, and 17 percent in India.[15]

In return, South Asia, and especially India, is facing pressure to liberalize its services sector. There has been some opening of their markets, notably telecommunications (and this in turn has contributed to the expansion of software exports), as well as transportation and finance/insurance. But further concessions, including lowering limits on private foreign investment in these sectors (under Mode 3, i.e., relating to commercial presence) will likely be required in return for the commitments being sought from developed countries under Mode 4.

Agriculture

World trade in agriculture has been seriously distorted by a wide range of export subsidies and domestic support measures, particularly in developed countries, amounting to some US$350 billion every year, the equivalent of 60 percent of the value of world agricultural trade. These subsidies have caused the EU and the United States, in particular, to dump produce on world markets, depressing world prices and thus affecting the livelihoods of many farmers and farmworkers in developing countries. In the case of cotton, for instance, it is estimated that subsidies were largely responsible for the 66 percent fall in prices from 1995 to 2001. In the Uruguay Round, it was agreed that these distortions should be capped and gradually reduced, along with cuts in tariffs. But disagreements over the pace and end goal of liberalization have continued to plague WTO negotiations. In Cancún, proposals from the United States and the EU appeared likely to prolong subsidies for some time, while expecting developing countries to open their markets to subsidized agricultural produce, and this contributed to the collapse of the WTO ministerial meeting.[16] With agriculture continuing to play a key role in employment and income, even if its share of exports has declined over the years, this is an important area for South Asia. Products that have been particularly affected include cotton, rice, sugar, and wheat. Estimates for India, for instance, suggest that agricultural exports would increase by 40 percent (or US$2.7 billion) if all agricultural distortions were removed (i.e., tariff peaks, escalating tariffs, and other types of trade barriers as well as subsidies).[17]

In order to press their case for more cuts on developed country subsidies and agricultural tariffs, while maintaining some protection for domestic producers of special products, India and Pakistan joined with several other large developing countries (including Brazil, Egypt, and China) to form the so-called Group of Twenty-one. The group's initial membership accounted for 51 percent of the world's population, 63 percent of farmers, 20 percent of agricultural production, 26 percent of agricultural exports, 17 percent of agricultural imports, and 17 percent of world exports. Among the proposals that they and other countries advanced for special and differential treatment were: lower reduction commitments for tariffs and domestic support such as de minimis payments, longer implementation periods, special safeguard mechanisms, special products (with additional flexibilities or exemptions according to their food security, livelihood security, and rural development needs), preferential access to developed country markets, and special provisions for LDCs.[18]

Negotiations following Cancún, in which India played an active part along with Brazil, the United States, the EU, and Australia, contributed to the agreement with other WTO members in July 2004 on how to move forward. Key elements for South Asian developing countries were: developed countries' agreement to eliminate all export subsidies including export credits or guarantees, specific cuts in domestic support, and a tiered formula for tariff cuts, which was more likely than the previous blended formula to improve access to their markets. There were also clearer references to special and differential treatment than in the past, such as an exemption of developing country domestic support for subsistence and resource-poor farmers, special consideration for developing country state trading enterprises seeking to ensure food security, and less tariff quota expansion commitments. Several details remain to be spelled out, however, such as the end date by which export subsidies are to be eliminated and the levels of tariff cuts. And some observers were concerned that the cuts in domestic support from bound levels would have little impact on actual U.S. support in the short term, while allowing developed countries flexibility for certain sensitive products could limit improvements in market access.[19]

Governance of the Multilateral Trading System

More generally, the WTO provides an important venue for South Asian countries to promote—and protect—their trade interests. Besides their active participation in WTO negotiations, the countries that are members have been able to use the WTO in several other ways. One has been the resolution of trade disputes with other countries. India has been the most active (as shown in Table 10.4) both in bringing cases in support of its exporting interests (notably textile and clothing, steel) and in defending its domestic policies (such as its import restrictions of autos on balance of payments grounds) against complaints by other countries. In some of these cases it has been joined by both developing and developed countries. Only one case involved two countries within South Asia—Bangladesh brought a case to the WTO against India's use of antidumping duties on its battery exports.

Bangladesh has been particularly active in leading the LDC group to secure consideration within the WTO of their special needs, in terms of access to developed country markets, their own obligations, and technical assistance, among others. As already mentioned, a number of key developed countries, with the major exception of the United States, have introduced duty-free, quota-free regimes for imports from LDCs, though in some cases these are subject to restrictive rules of origin, and in no case have the commitments been bound in the WTO. Securing similar access to the United States is a key objective for Bangladesh, in part to offset the increased competition from China following the end of the MFA, as well as the preferred status granted to countries such as Mexico with which the United States now has free trade agreements.

Table 10.4

World Trade Organization Disputes Involving South Asia (total cases: 36)

Brought by	Against	Numbers	Issue/product
India	United States	6	Coats, shirts, shrimp, steel Dumping act, textiles and clothing rules of origin
India	European Communities (EC)	5	Bedlinen, fabric, rice, steel Tariff preferences for other developing countries
India	Argentina	1	Medicines
India	Brazil	1	Jute
India	Poland	1	Cars
India	South Africa	1	ADD on medicines
India	Turkey	1	Textiles and clothing
EC	India	8	Cars, commodity exports, import restrictions, patents, custom duties
United States	India	3	Import restrictions, patents, car trade and investment
Australia	India	1	Import restrictions
Bangladesh	India	1	Batteries
Canada	India	1	Import restrictions
New Zealand	India	1	Import restrictions
Switzerland	India	1	Import restrictions
Pakistan	United States	1	Cotton yarn
United States	Pakistan	1	Patents
EC	Pakistan	1	Exports of hides and skins
Bangladesh	United States	1	Textiles and clothing rules of origin

Source: Derived from World Trade Organization Web site.

Canada's Trade Relations with South Asia

Canada and South Asia are small trading partners—South Asia accounted for 0.5 percent of Canada's imports and 0.2 percent of its exports on average in the decade to 2004. India is by far the largest source of Canada's merchandise imports from South Asia (66 percent) and destination for exports (60 percent). Growth in Canadian imports from Bangladesh, particularly in 2003, has made it the second largest supplier (16 percent) followed by Pakistan (13 percent); in contrast, Pakistan remains the second largest export market (25 percent) followed by Bangladesh (10 percent). (Details are given in Tables 10.5 and 10.6.)

Table 10.5

Canadian Exports to South Asia (1994–2003, million Canadian dollars)

	1994	1995	1996	1997	1998	1999	2000	2001	2002	2003
Afghanistan	0.17	6.53	0.45	5.24	0.08	0.80	0.16	0.17	1.88	8.92
Bangladesh	101.56	90.36	62.13	95.83	128.90	162.18	128.83	130.59	69.96	125.00
Bhutan	0.02	0.02	0.39	0.00	0.00	0.00	0.00	0.09	0.02	0.00
India	286.24	440.30	352.68	490.80	419.53	481.23	559.43	676.43	674.39	732.78
Maldives	4.42	0.37	20.69	9.46	7.99	12.62	4.46	7.43	3.81	2.62
Nepal	3.99	4.52	3.10	5.21	6.42	3.87	4.17	1.80	4.11	3.22
Pakistan	70.79	127.96	86.59	140.65	88.13	82.68	82.64	73.35	85.96	299.99
Sri Lanka	16.35	21.58	52.34	54.44	35.32	51.80	47.87	30.48	20.20	46.13
Total South Asia	483.55	691.64	578.38	801.63	686.35	795.19	827.55	920.34	860.34	1,218.68
Total (all countries)	225,679.00	262,267.00	275,819.00	298,072.00	318,444.00	355,420.00	413,215.00	404,085.00	396,379.00	380,659.00
South Asia share of total (%)	0.2	0.3	0.2	0.3	0.2	0.2	0.2	0.2	0.2	0.3

Source: Industry Canada, Strategis data online, accessed May 15, 2004.

Table 10.6

Canadian Imports from South Asia (1994–2003, million Canadian dollars)

	1994	1995	1996	1997	1998	1999	2000	2001	2002	2003	2003/ 1994
Afghanistan	0.35	0.42	0.22	0.82	0.50	0.42	0.58	0.42	0.36	0.62	177%
Bangladesh	74.17	100.92	87.97	121.00	140.24	148.62	178.22	189.83	164.55	350.43	472%
Bhutan	0.00	0.00	0.01	0.06	0.00	0.00	0.01	0.00	0.01	0.01	3004%
India	458.75	541.38	603.60	743.19	898.58	1,017.76	1,231.89	1,154.70	1,326.27	1,423.27	310%
Maldives	0.24	0.04	0.18	0.20	3.44	4.61	8.15	14.56	2.78	7.43	3137%
Nepal	4.85	4.98	4.35	5.45	3.57	6.59	10.35	9.44	8.83	9.85	203%
Pakistan	198.63	204.33	165.39	206.08	229.55	247.86	273.01	275.31	289.30	275.24	139%
Sri Lanka	67.66	76.40	71.46	83.29	97.11	92.48	137.27	119.15	111.12	103.13	152%
Total South Asia	804.66	928.47	933.19	1,160.10	1,372.99	1,518.34	1,839.48	1,763.43	1,903.22	2,169.98	270%
Total (all countries)											
South Asia share of total (%)	0.4	0.4	0.4	0.4	0.5	0.5	0.5	0.5	0.5	0.6	

Source: Industry Canada, Strategis data online, accessed May 15, 2004.

Canada's exports to the subcontinent are dominated by traditional products such as oilseeds, newsprint and woodpulp, potassium chloride, aircraft, wheat, electrical parts, lentils, and asbestos, while imports from South Asia are dominated by clothing and textile products, heterocyclic compounds, diamonds, shrimps/prawns, carpets, and rice.

A problem with these statistics is that they do not capture the growth in services trade. Typically, for every dollar of Canadian exports of goods, another dollar of services is exported. In India, Canada is interested in promoting sales of insurance and other financial services, mining, environmental, and educational services. On the import side, Canada likely purchases various types of office and information technology services from South Asia but the exact magnitude is not known.

Another trade-related issue concerns investment flows—again data are not good. In 2002 Canada reported a stock of C$144 million invested in India, up from C$84 million in 1991 (but no data are published for the other South Asian countries). There is also some South Asian investment in Canada, particularly in the software sector—for instance, Tata Group has a research and development subsidiary in Toronto, specializing in documentation software.

There have been various efforts to promote bilateral trade. Canada has granted imports from the region preferential tariffs under the General Preferential Tariff (GPT) offered to all developing countries since 1983. Despite a number of subsequent modifications, the impact of the GPT was weakened by a number of factors. First, it excluded a number of key South Asian exports, notably textiles, clothing, and footwear—not only did these products continue to pay above average tariffs, the volume of imports was restrained by quotas under the Multifiber Arrangement. Second, strict rules of origin required a minimum value added, which precluded some products from qualifying. Third, the tariff reduction was only partial. Fourth, in the meantime, Canada offered duty-free treatment on imports from other countries with whom it signed free trade agreements, notably the United States and Mexico (under the North American Free Trade Agreement, or NAFTA). Finally, some products also faced antidumping duties. In fact, the GPT was a misnomer—it was not generally applied to all products and it was not preferential relative to Canada's imports from its free trade partners.

Canadian import data show that the average tariff paid on imports from South Asia in 2003 was 9.3 percent, with imports from Bangladesh paying the highest (16.2 percent), followed by Sri Lanka (13.9 percent), the Maldives (13.7 percent), and Pakistan (12.7 percent). In contrast Indian imports paid only 7.4 percent, reflecting the more diversified nature of Indian exports, and in particular the lower share of textiles and clothing products in its trade with Canada.

The situation changed in 2003, with the introduction of the Least Developed Country Initiative (LDCI) (see Box 10.1). In effect this has created a hierarchy of suppliers in South Asia, with Afghanistan, Bangladesh, Bhutan, Maldives, and Nepal being LDCs. This is likely to alter the nature of the dialogue with South Asia—the LDCs will continue to press Canada to improve the LDCI, for example, to make it binding under the WTO and to simplify the rules of origin and related procedures to ensure that nearly all of their exports to Canada enter duty-free. In contrast, India, Pakistan, and Sri Lanka will be faced with requests for concessions in the form of cuts in their import tariffs and liberalization of other domestic regulations

---

Box 10.1

Canada's Least Developed Countries Initiative (LDCI)

In 2003, Canada removed all tariffs and quotas on all imports from the least developed countries—with the exception of dairy, poultry, and eggs (which remained under supply management in Canada). The scheme offers fairly generous rules of origin; it also covers all LDCs with the exception of Burma, which was excluded on political grounds. Some clothing manufacturers had urged the Canadian government not to include Bangladesh on the list of beneficiary countries, on the grounds that it was already competitive in the Canadian market. (In fact, Bangladesh's share of imports in 2002 was only 2.3 percent.) They had also sought strict rules of origin, which would limit the clothing entering Canada tariff- and quota-free to those items that used LDC-made cloth or contained a high amount of value-added in the exporting LDC. Such strict rules have often limited the value of preferential schemes for clothing, partly to limit the possibility that other countries will benefit, for example, by shipping their cloth, or semifinished items of clothing, to the LDC for a small amount of value to be added, in order then to gain tariff- or quota-free access. Major textile-producing countries like the United States allow for the use of their cloth to count against value added in the exporting country as a way to secure markets for their textile exports. Canada's production of textiles for use in clothing, however, is relatively small.

Trade data for 2003 suggest that the LDCI has benefited a number of LDCs. Bangladesh was able to more than double its share of Canadian clothing imports to 4.99 percent (an increase of some C$160 million), while total exports to Canada grew from C$164 million to C$351 million. In the case of Nepal, exports grew somewhat less, by 10 percent, from C$8.8 million to C$9.9 million. Canadian imports from all LDCs rose from C$627

(continued)

million to C$1078 million from 2002 to 2003, while the average tariff they paid fell from 5.36 percent to 0.86 percent (see Figure 10.1).

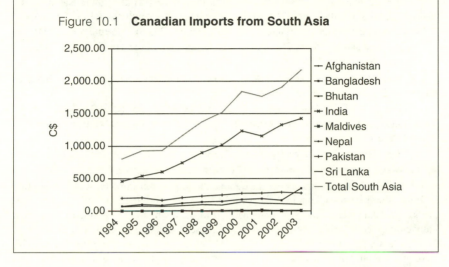

Figure 10.1   **Canadian Imports from South Asia**

constraining Canadian exports and investment in their economies, in return for any tariff cuts or other liberalization measures in Canada on exports of particular interest to them.

While Canadian trade priorities continue to focus on traditional markets such as the United States, and newer trading partners such as China and Mexico (now second and fourth), it has signaled particular interest in India as an emerging market, with growing purchasing power. Canada has called for India to: reduce tariffs on products such as canola oil and spirits, remove various other requirements facing agricultural exports, reconsider the use of trade remedy/safeguard action against various Canadian exports (newsprint, vitamin C, specialty steel, and edible oil), liberalize its telecommunications sector, and raise the ceiling on investment in sectors such as insurance and banking.[20] In Pakistan, there are similar concerns with regulations governing agricultural imports from Canada—whether the standards applied are more trade restrictive than necessary (such as rules governing bovine embryos or GMO biosafety guidelines)—as well as financing/leasing rules, which are said to affect the sales of Canadian aircraft and parts. But for the rest of South Asia, no issues have been raised.

Notes

1. These figures are shares of world trade less intra-EU trade.
2. WTO country profile, June 2004; again these figures exclude intra-EU trade.

3. World Bank, *World Development Indicators, 2004*.

4. WTO, country profiles.

5. Arvind Panagariya, "South Asia: Does Preferential Trade Liberalisation Make Sense?" and J. S. Bandara and W. Yu, "How Desirable Is the South Asian Free Trade Area? A Quantitative Economic Assessment," *World Economy* 26, no. 9 (September 2003).

6. Bandara and Yu, "How Desirable Is the South Asian Free Trade Area?" 1300.

7. Ibid., p. 1318.

8. Panagariya also argues for unilateral liberalization as preferable, and less likely to lead to trade diversion (Panagariya, "South Asia," 1290).

9. United Nations Conference on Trade and Development (UNCTAD), Forum on Regionalism and South-South Cooperation, "The Case of India and Mercosur," June 13, 2004, TD/L370, 2.

10. World Bank, *World Development Indicators, 2004*. The data are for 2001.

11. WTO, *International Trade Statistics 2004*, available online.

12. In Canada, for instance, after the quota on men's woven shirts (HS6205) was lifted in 1998, imports from China in 2001 were 237 percent more than in 1997, whereas imports from Bangladesh fell by 58 percent. And in 2002 when U.S. imports of quota-free baby clothes from China rose by 306 percent, those from Bangladesh fell by 16 percent. Nonetheless a report by the U.S. International Trade Commission suggests that Bangladesh will remain one of the major suppliers of clothing to the United States, along with India and Vietnam, although in a more concentrated range of products.

13. Santiago Fernandez de Córdoba, Sam Laird, and David Vanzetti, "Trick or Treat? Development Opportunities and Challenges in the WTO Negotiations on Industrial Tariffs," draft, May 2004.

14. WTO, Doha Work Programme. Decision Adopted by the General Council on August 1, 2004, WT/L/579.

15. World Bank, World Development Indicators, 2004, 241. According to OECD estimates, if OECD countries allowed temporary access to foreign service providers equal to 3 percent of their labor force, this would generate global gains of US$150 billion, or more than the entire estimated gains from completely liberalizing trade in goods (Mattoo and Stern 2003, 364).

16. As the Indian trade minister noted: "by allowing distortions to continue and in some cases to increase . . . we are compounding the distortions of the Uruguay Round . . . the heightened ambition on market access . . . provides S&D in favour of developed countries is utterly incomprehensible . . . how can we expect developing countries to reduce tariffs on a number of items to between 0 percent and 5 percent when the distortions against which such tariffs are supposed to compensate are sought to be enhanced?"

17. Anderson 2003 quoted in UNCTAD, "Trade Liberalisation and Poverty in India," draft, 2004, 29.

18. Sam Laird, Ralf Peters, and David Vanzetti, "Southern Discomfort: Agricultural Policies, Trade and Poverty," UNCTAD, mimeo, July 2004.

19. *Bridges Weekly Trade News Digest* 8, no. 27, August 3, 2004, www.icstd.org/weekly/04–08–03/story2.htm.

20. *Opening Doors to the World, Canada's International Market Access Priorities–2004*, 116, www.dfait-maeci.gc.ca/tan-nac/2004/pdf/cimap-en.pdf.

References

Mattoo, Aaditya, and Robert Stern, eds. 2003. *India and the WTO.* World Bank, Washington, DC: Oxford University Press.

World Trade Organization. 2000. *Trade Policy Review, Bangladesh.*

———. 2002a. *Trade Policy Review, India.*

———. 2002b. *Trade Policy Review, Pakistan.*

———. 2003. *Trade Policy Review, Maldives.*

———. 2004. *Trade Policy Review, Sri Lanka.*

11

Regional Economic Cooperation Under SAARC

Possibilities and Constraints

Dushni Weerakoon

As a region, South Asia was fairly late in embracing the concept of regional economic cooperation that gathered fresh momentum in the latter half of the 1980s. It took a decade after the initial establishment of the South Asian Association for Regional Cooperation (SAARC) in 1985 for South Asia to turn its attention to the promotion of trade through a regional agreement. Nevertheless, having accepted the concept of regional economic cooperation, SAARC was quick to set itself an ambitious agenda. The proposal to set up a South Asian Preferential Trade Agreement (SAPTA) was accepted and came into formal operation in December 1995. In 1996, SAARC member countries agreed in principle to go a step further and attempt to enact a South Asian Free Trade Agreement (SAFTA). The transition to SAFTA has been inordinately delayed with the postponement of successive summits between 1999 and 2002. As a result, the drafting of the Framework Agreement commenced only in 2002 with final agreement reached in January 2004. With outstanding negotiations finalized, SAFTA is to begin implementation in July 2006. Despite the apparent commitment to economic cooperation within a regional framework, South Asian countries have, in reality, exhibited a marked reluctance to open their markets to each other. Much of the failure can be attributed to the swings in political relations between India and Pakistan, a seemingly irreversible situation in which SAARC appears to have lost its relevance as a forum through which an economic agenda can be meaningfully realized.

The purpose of this chapter is to examine whether regional economic cooperation—constrained as it is by political factors—has a future in South Asia in the context of a rapidly changing global economic environment.

234

Free Trade in South Asia: The Empirical Evidence

South Asian countries that had fairly open economies in the immediate postindependence period in the 1940s had become some of the most highly protectionist in the world by the 1970s. Tariff, and even more important, nontariff barriers (NTBs) were extremely high, state interventions in economic activity had become pervasive, attitudes to foreign investments were negative, often hostile, and stringent exchange controls were in place. But this started to change in the late 1970s. In 1977, Sri Lanka initiated a process of policy liberalization, and was in turn followed by other countries in the 1980s. However, this was often a rather hesitant liberalization process, and was very uneven across countries. It was from the early 1990s, with the start of a major reform process in India that the region as a whole really started to liberalize. By the end of the decade, although important policy barriers to trade and foreign investment remained, enormous progress had been made in the direction of trade liberalization throughout the region. But it should be noted that even by the mid-1990s, in a global comparison of import protection rates, South Asia remained a highly protected region (Blackhurst, Enders, and François 1996).

In the area of trade policy, comprehensive tariff reforms were implemented, aimed at, among other things, progressive reductions in the level and dispersion of tariffs and quantitative restrictions. In July 1991, India began the process of dismantling its highly complex import licensing system, permitting the phase-out of all NTBs on tradables except those on consumer goods. In 1993, Pakistan took further measures to rationalize its tariff structure after the substantive attempts at trade policy reforms initiated in 1988. Similarly, Sri Lanka also embarked on further tariff cuts and simplification of the tariff structure in 1990 under its "second wave" of liberalization. In 1992, Bangladesh accelerated its tariff reform program initiated in 1986 with significant compression of customs duty rates. Thus, average customs duties in South Asia have been declining progressively since the 1980s (Figure 11.1).

Complementary developments in the global economy in the latter part of the 1980s and early 1990s also began to exert an influence on the South Asian region. The global economy witnessed an explosion of regional trade agreements (RTAs) from the latter half of the 1980s, prompted by the apparent faltering of negotiations under the framework of the Uruguay Round of multilateral trade negotiations. South Asia—although slow to take up the issue of regional economic cooperation—also began to take cognizance of developments in the global economy and hastened to implement its own regional trade agenda. The emergence of new RTAs in North America and Latin America and the expansion of existing ones in Europe and East Asia saw the

Figure 11.1   **Average Customs Duties and Percentage of Tariff Lines Subject to Quantitative Restrictions**

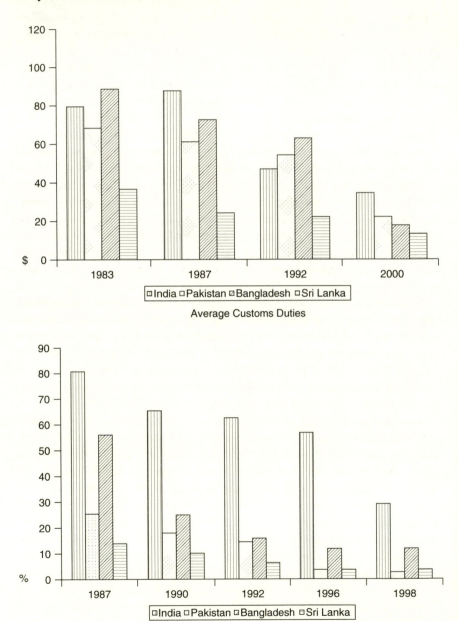

Average Customs Duties

Quantitative Restrictions

increasing marginalization of South Asia as a region in the global economy. For South Asian countries, in the absence of an entry point into one or more of these more dynamic regional bodies, the next best option appeared to be to cooperate among themselves in the hope that it would generate economic benefits in the medium to longer term.

Preferential trade agreements are judged in economic terms by their impact on trade flows and on the welfare of both the participants and the rest of the world. Arrangements that are "trade creating" will result in a greater volume of trade as compared with the situation before the arrangement. This comes about through enhanced efficiency in production and lowered prices. On the other hand, arrangements that are "trade diverting" will result in a lower volume of trade through raising the level of overall protection and distorting trade and investment patterns (see Viner 1950).

A number of empirical studies have looked at the prospects for regional integration in South Asia but the results remain mixed. A 1993 World Bank study concluded that most of the preconditions required for a successful trading arrangement were not present in South Asia (de Melo, Panagariya, and Rodrik 1993). These preconditions included: high prearrangement tariffs; a high level of trade in the region before the arrangement; the existence of complementary rather than competitive trade; and differences in economic structures in the countries concerned. The study found that only the first condition was met in the case of South Asia and it concluded that the region would be better off liberalizing trade unilaterally and joining an already established group. Studies by Srinivasan and Canonero (1993) and Srinivasan (1994) using the gravity model also suggest that South Asia is better off undertaking unilateral liberalization. However, they also find room for some potential gains from preferential liberalization and argue that smaller countries are likely to gain more than larger countries from regional integration.[1] The results of a study by Pigato et al. (1997) suggest that regional liberalization will generate significant welfare gains both for India and the rest of South Asia.[2] However, India's gains are estimated to be much higher under unilateral liberalization than under preferential liberalization. On the other hand, the benefits to the rest of South Asia from preferential liberalization are larger than that from unilateral liberalization. Besides the welfare gains suggested by the simulations, the case for encouraging an intensification of regional cooperation rests on broader considerations. First, the study suggests that it could complement efforts to open up to world competition and make the region a more attractive location for multinational companies and foreign capital. Second, and most important, it is considered a step toward better political relations and peace. It is argued that additional economic benefits from reduced military spending following a settlement of regional disputes could well be substantial.

Alternatively, others argue strongly that regional trade integration initiatives in South Asia will yield a net welfare loss and slowdown unilateral liberalization (Panagariya 1999).

While the empirical evidence has remained inconclusive, a notion that deeper regional trade integration can create spillovers that would strengthen ties between member countries has persisted in the minds of South Asian policymakers. This was bolstered by the belief that increased economic integration would carry with it the ability not only to secure new and larger markets for traditional products but also to enable the diversification of domestic economic structures. An integrated market was also viewed as a means of enhancing the ability to take advantage of global investment capital, and manufacturing, and services-related technological efficiencies.

The inability to derive firm conclusions on the economic impact of integration is not unique to South Asia. The debate on the costs and benefits of preferential trade initiatives—whether theoretically or empirically—remains largely unresolved, as does the question of whether a region-wide free trade agreement (FTA) will benefit small countries more or less than large countries. Theoretically, it can be argued that openness to trade will allow small economies to specialize in a few product sectors or services and to derive larger benefits by overcoming the limitations of scale economies due to the small size of their domestic markets.[3] On a priori grounds, some yardsticks have been set out whereby trade-creating and thus welfare-increasing circumstances are established to estimate potential gains from participating in a preferential trading arrangement (see Michaely 1996). These include:

- the higher the level of the pre-union tariff in the home country;
- the higher the tariff level of the partner country;
- the larger the volume of trade with the partner country;
- the smaller the volume of trade with the rest of the world;
- the closer the relative prices in trade with the partner country are to those prevailing in the rest of the world;
- the larger the economic size of the country's partners in the agreement (where economic size in this instance is represented by GDP and volume of trade);
- the more diversified the economic structure of the country's partners to the arrangement;
- the more the economic structure of the partner/s resembles the rest of the world outside the preferential agreement.

Applying these criteria, the highest levels of average customs duties at the present time are to be found in Bangladesh and to a lesser extent in India. Thus, Bangladesh would stand to gain from participation in preferential/free trade

Table 11.1

Volume of Trade (2004)

	Share of South Asian Association for Regional Cooperation trade in total trade of country	Share of trade with India in total trade of country
Bangladesh	11.2	10.1
India	3.0	—
Maldives	19.8	8.7
Nepal	41.7	41.2
Pakistan	3.3	2.0
Sri Lanka	15.1	13.3

Source: International Monetary Fund, *Direction of Trade Statistics Yearbook 2005*.

integration. By contrast, Sri Lanka has the lowest average tariff and its gains from the liberalization of tariffs would be much less. Under the criterion dealing with the pre-union volume of trade, it is a fact that the share of any single South Asian country in the trade of another is quite low (with the exception of Nepal whose total trade with India accounts for over 40 percent of its total world trade). Nevertheless, Sri Lanka, the Maldives, and Bangladesh also have a fairly high proportion of their total trade with India (Table 11.1). The Maldives in fact has a higher share (11 percent) of trade with Sri Lanka. For these countries, participation in an FTA would be relatively more beneficial as the proportion of their pre-union trade is much higher.

The larger the partner in a preferential trading arrangement, the higher the potential benefits for other participants. The size of the Indian market is overwhelmingly dominant as compared with any other country in the region. Therefore, according to the criteria on volume of trade and economic size in general, entering into an FTA in which India is participating should be beneficial for the medium-size and smaller economies of the region. In addition, under the criteria dealing with economic diversification and similarity of the partner's economic structure with the rest of the world, the smaller economies stand to gain. India is relatively economically diversified and is a significant producer and exporter of diversified manufactured items. This can serve the smaller countries in their attempt to both diversify their exports and at the same time obtain a variety of consumer and producer goods at the lowest prices possible. An agreement of a small economy with a large one can be economically promising and potentially beneficial to the small country. Outside of trade liberalization under the multilateral trading system of the World

Trade Organization (WTO), a potentially rewarding trade policy option for small and relatively lesser developed economies would be participation in as large (both in number and economic size of participants) and as liberal (from a market access point of view) a preferential trading arrangement as possible. Thus, potential benefits to the smaller economies of South Asia will be critically dependent on how liberal preferential trade will be in reality.

Although trade complementarities in South Asia are limited at present due to similar production structures, the potential for intra-South Asian cooperation in both trade and investment is not entirely absent.[4] There are important structural changes in intraregional trade that may be important indicators of future trends. Textiles and machinery and equipment have become increasingly more important in intraregional trade and a larger proportion of exports within the region are now manufactured products, while in the past, primary products were more important (Jayasuriya and Weerakoon 2001). This shift into manufactured product trade, associated with the higher level of industrialization of the region, opens up opportunities for scale economies and intra-industry trade to play an increasing role.

The Experience of Preferential Trade in South Asia

Although the acceleration of economic growth through regional cooperation was incorporated as an objective of the SAARC charter in 1985, it was not until the late 1980s that South Asian governments made an explicit commitment toward promoting an economic agenda. A Committee for Economic Cooperation was set up in 1991 to examine a proposal for a preferential trade agreement (PTA), the framework of which was finalized in 1993. The resultant South Asian Preferential Trade Agreement provides for the exchange of concessions between members on tariffs, para-tariffs, and nontariff barriers. Four basic modes of negotiations were provided, namely: (1) product-by-product; (2) across-the-board; (3) sectoral; and (4) direct trade measures.[5]

SAPTA came into formal operation with the ratification of the first round of negotiations on 226 product items in December 1995. A second round of negotiations on a further 1,900 product items was completed in 1996 and a third round, encompassing 2,500 product items was concluded in 1998. India has offered the largest number of concessions, followed by Bangladesh, Pakistan, and Nepal (Table 11.2).[6] India has also offered the highest margins on tariff concessions, but given that its most-favored-nation rates have tended to be higher than those of its partners, this is to be expected.

As the rounds of negotiations proceeded, some concessions were offered in the face of increasing criticism of the limited nature of tariff preferences granted. While the first and second rounds were conducted on the basis of a

Table 11.2

Number of Tariff Lines and Tariff Range Negotiated Under the South Asian Preferential Trade Agreement (SAPTA)

Country		Number of tariff lines	Tariff range[a]		
			SAPTA-1	SAPTA-2	SAPTA-3
Bangladesh	All	407	10	10	10
	Less developed countries (LDCs)	144	10	10	10–15
Bhutan	All	109	15	10–15	10
	LDCs	124	10–15	10–15	10–20
India	All	472	10–90	10–50	10–25
	LDCs	2082	50–100	50–100	50
Maldives	All	172	7.5	7.5–10	10
	LDCs	6	7.5	7.5–10	—
Nepal	All	328	7.5–10	7.5–10	5–10
	LDCs	163	10	15	10–15
Pakistan	All	262	10	10–15	10–20
	LDCs	229	15	15	30
Sri Lanka	All	155	10–20	10–20	10
	LDCs	44	15–25	60	10–75
SAARC[b]	All	1095	7.5–90	7.5–50	5–25
	LDCs	2762	7.5–100	7.5–100	5–25

Source: Compiled from the Consolidated National Schedule of Concessions of Member States.
[a]As percentage of most-favored-nation tariff rate.
[b]South Asian Association for Regional Cooperation.

product-by-product coverage, the third round included chapter-wise negotiations on a very limited basis. In 1998, the rules of origin requirements of 50 percent (40 percent for the less developed country [LDC] members of SAARC) were relaxed to 40 percent (and 30 percent for LDC members). In addition, each country was required to identify existing para-tariff and nontariff barriers prevailing on items on which concessions had been granted. Nevertheless, such concessions failed to address the larger problems associated with the SAPTA process. These have been well identified in the literature (Mukherji 2000b; Weerakoon 2001). The most limiting factor has been the actual trade coverage of preferential access granted. In fact, it has been estimated that on average only 8.4 percent of tariff lines in the case of imports from non-LDCs and 6.2 percent in the case of imports from the LDCs are covered by the tariff concessions in the three concluded by 1998 (World Bank 2003). In reality,

Table 11.3

Intracountry Trade of the South Asian Association for Regional Cooperation (SAARC)

	Intra-SAARC trade (US$ millions)	World trade of SAARC countries (US$ millions)	Share of intra-SAARC trade in world trade of SAARC countries (%)
1980	1,210	37,885	3.2
1985	1,054	44,041	2.4
1990	1,584	65,041	2.4
1995	4,228	104,159	4.1
2000	5,884	141,978	4.1
2004	11,342	232,155	4.8

Source: International Monetary Fund, *Direction of Trade Statistics*, various issues.

products imported under SAPTA concessions translated to only 15 percent of total imports between SAARC member countries (Mukherji 2000b).

As would be expected, SAPTA has therefore had little or no impact in changing the existing trade patterns in South Asia. Intra-SAARC trade, which accounted for less than 3 percent of trade in South Asia for much of the 1980s, increased gradually to over 4 percent in the first half of the 1990s, primarily on account of the increased trade flows associated with unilateral liberalization efforts across the region (Table 11.3). There has been no discernible increase with the implementation of SAPTA given the singularly ineffective mode of negotiations.

Nevertheless, there was a general feeling of optimism as the groundwork was being initiated to consider issues related to the transition to a free trade area. India took the lead under its "Gujaral Doctrine" to remove nontariff barriers on nearly 2,000 products for its South Asian neighbors ahead of its WTO commitments, and proposed that implementation of SAFTA should be brought forward to 2001 (from the proposed date of 2005) at the SAARC Heads of State Summit in 1998.[7] Unfortunately, political relations between India and Pakistan were to deteriorate with the election of the more right-wing Bharatiya Janata Party (BJP) government, and subsequent nuclear test explosions by both India and Pakistan in 1998. The incursion of Pakistan into Indian-held territory (Kargil) in 1999 and the resultant military standoff, and the change of leadership in Pakistan on the heels of a military coup were to further weaken relations between the two countries. As the deterioration in bilateral relations spilled over on to the SAARC process there was an inevitable toll on the SAARC economic agenda, prompting a change of direction that could well be argued to have made the SAPTA/SAFTA process of marginal interest to the region.

The change in direction was manifested in the form of bilateral trade agreements between SAARC countries. While India had already granted access to its market on a preferential bilateral basis to Bhutan and Nepal, the defining agreement was to come in the form of the Indo-Lanka Free Trade Agreement (ILFTA) signed in December 1998. Under the ILFTA, India agreed to remove tariffs on 1,351 products, immediately after the treaty came into force.[8] However, both countries agreed to maintain negative lists that would safeguard "sensitive" domestic industries whereby the FTA would not apply to items placed under such a list. India submitted a negative list of 429 items and agreed to phase out prevailing tariffs on the balance items over a span of three years: 50 percent reduction of Indian customs duties in the first year; 75 percent in the second year; and 100 percent in the third year.[9] Sri Lanka will, therefore, be able to have duty free access to the Indian market (excluding those items coming under the negative list) three years after the FTA becomes operative.

In return, Sri Lanka submitted a negative list consisting of 1,180 items and undertook to grant immediate duty-free access to India on 319 items. In addition, a 50 percent margin of preference was offered on a further 889 items, with the preferential reduction raised to 70, 90, and 100 percent over a three-year period. The duty on the balance items (excluding those that do not fall within Sri Lanka's negative list) are expected to be phased out over an eight-year period—35 percent of the existing duty level by the end of the first three of the eight years; 70 percent of the existing duty level by the end of the sixth year; and 100 percent removal of duties by the end of the eighth year. Thus, India will have duty-free access to the Sri Lankan market for her exports (excluding those items on the negative list) after eight years from the signing of the FTA.

The ILFTA is by no means a free trade agreement in the conventional definition, which assumes that tariffs will be eliminated with respect to "substantially all trade." Estimates of those items retained under negative lists suggest that items placed on Sri Lanka's negative list accounted for over 20 percent of India's total exports to Sri Lanka at the time the agreement came into force, and the Indian negative list accounted for over 13 percent of Sri Lanka's total exports to India (Table 11.4). Nonetheless, the agreement was certainly a step forward in comparison with market access granted under the SAPTA process.[10] This is clearly evident from the data in Table 11.5, which lists the number of concessions granted to Sri Lanka by India under SAPTA and the ILFTA applicable to goods actually traded between the two coun-

Table 11.4

Applicability of Free Trade Agreements to Indo–Sri Lanka Traded Commodities

	Sri Lanka's concessions		India's concessions	
	No.	%	No.	%
Negative	623	21.4	50	13.1
0%	3	0.1	68	17.9
50%	598	20.6	218	57.4
25%	—	—	44	11.6
Other	1,683	57.9	—	—
Total	2,907	100.0	380	100.0

Source: Compiled from Sri Lanka Customs Database.

tries. Under SAPTA concessions offered by India to non-LDC members (484 items), only 30 items were of actual trade interest to Sri Lanka. By contrast, the total number of traded goods on which immediate zero tariff reduction and 50 percent concessional reductions offered to Sri Lanka under the ILFTA amount to over 280 items.

While the idea of "fast-track" liberalization—allowing those countries willing to proceed at a quicker pace of liberalization the means to do so while others join the process at a slower pace—has been discussed for some time, the actual outcome has been that SAARC countries are increasingly engaging in bilateral agreements outside of the regional framework altogether. Pakistan in turn proposed an FTA with Sri Lanka, the Framework Agreement, which was signed in July 2002. The Pakistan–Sri Lanka FTA came into operation in June 2005 under which Pakistan maintained a negative list of 540 items while granting immediate duty free entry on 206 products and agreed to eliminate duties on other products over a three-year period. In return, Sri Lanka was permitted to maintain a negative list of 697 items while granting immediate duty free entry on 102 products and agreeing to phase out tariffs on a further 4527 items over five years. In addition, both India and Sri Lanka have indicated interest in extending FTAs to Bangladesh in the near future. Given the diversity of SAARC countries, bilateral FTAs are likely to differ significantly from one another in terms of coverage, rules and regulations, depth of tariff reductions, and so on. This will not only create serious problems for SAARC in managing its external trade relationship but also add to the cost of doing business, as investors and traders will have to deal with differences in scope and pace of tariff reduction and rules and regulations.

The fragmentation of the regional negotiations into bilateral deals holds serious implications for the transition to a free trade area. The SAFTA

Table 11.5

Concessions on Products Traded to Sri Lanka (SL) **by India Under the South Asian Preferential Trade Agreement** (SAPTA) **and the Indo-Lanka Free Trade Agreement** (ILFTA)

HS code chapters		Composition of SL exports to India	No. of concessions granted under SAPTA	No. of concessions granted under ILFTA*
01–05	Live animals, animal products	2.2		2
06–14	Vegetable products	38.8	6	20
15	Animal or vegetable fats and oils	7.3		3
16–24	Prepared foodstuffs	0.8	4	28
25–27	Mineral products	0.2	2	3
28–38	Chemical products	1.0	6	36
39–40	Plastics & rubber	11.3	4	10
41–43	Leather products	0.2		4
44–46	Wood products	0.1	3	7
47–49	Paper products	9.6	2	21
50–63	Textile articles	10.9		
64–67	Footwear	0.2	1	4
68–70	Stone, plaster, cement	1.0		11
71	Pearls	0.3		4
72–83	Base metal	14.0	1	37
84–85	Machinery and mechanical goods	1.7		58
86–89	Transport equipment	0.0	1	9
90–92	Optical, photographic equipment	0.1		10
93	Arms and ammunition	0.0		
94–96	Miscellaneous manufactured articles	0.2		19
97–99	Works of art	0.0		
Total		100.0	30	286

Source: Compiled from Sri Lanka Customs Database.
*Concessions on items offered immediate zero duty and 50 percent tariff reduction only.

agreement has permitted the exclusion of 20 percent of tariff lines (of a total of 5,224) under a "sensitive" list to be exempt from liberalization with no formal binding provision to prune the list over time. In practice, it has left the door open for the bulk of trade taking place within the region to fall within the sensitive lists of member countries. The SAFTA agreement is also to be implemented over a ten-year period during which time key bilateral FTAs—which are already more generous in scope and coverage—would be fully operational in the region.

The emergence of bilateral deals brings into question the rationale for continued engagement in the SAARC economic process for some of its members. Sri Lanka, for example, has little economic benefit to gain, having already assured itself of access to key partners in South Asia through bilateral deals. The only way that SAARC could have taken the initiative to regain its relevance as a forum to drive the economic integration process in South Asia is if the SAFTA treaty had gone beyond the current bilateral agreements in freeing trade between member states. The key question then is whether the political-economy relationships that govern negotiations would have permitted such a scenario to unfold.

The Political-Economy Relations in South Asia: Is There a Role for SAFTA?

The underlying political-economy relations that have governed SAARC were evident even at its inception. As succinctly outlined by Maass (1999), the initial negotiations on membership pointed to the pervasive influence of geopolitics in the region. In defining which set of countries constitutes "South Asia," the status of Afghanistan was to dominate the discussion. Prior to the Soviet invasion of Afghanistan in 1979, it was largely perceived as a part of the South Asian region given its strategic importance as a gateway to the Indian subcontinent from Central Asia. Following the Soviet invasion (and the Iranian Revolution), Afghanistan came to be regarded more as a part of Southwest Asia, while Pakistan came to the forefront as an anticommunist "frontline" state. According to Maass (1999), India was therefore anxious to include Afghanistan in SAARC as one means of diluting Pakistan's strategic importance. While the final decision was to exclude Afghanistan, it is nevertheless an indicator of the often combative political relations that were to govern the SAARC process.

Despite the almost immediate skepticism, SAARC was launched on the premise that traditional conflicts in South Asia had lost much of their edge and the region was increasingly subject to new sources of conflict, which could be contained more effectively through bilateral and multilateral modes of cooperation. The new conflicts were argued to originate from three sources: involvement in each other's domestic conflicts; transfer of arms and weapons to the region from outside; and the possibility of a nuclear arms race between India and Pakistan (Maass 1999). To some extent they were seen as persisting from the lack of conflict control mechanisms in the region, and, here, the emergence of SAARC as a formal regional forum was seen in a positive light. In addition, it was also maintained that the ethnic diaspora across India and its neighbors created a natural progression to build support for regionalism by backing the emergence of a common South Asian identity. However, it can be rightly argued that when ethnic groups draw support across national boundaries, the optimistic assumption that old conflicts have waned is not entirely true.

In reality, the influence of old sources of conflict was fairly obvious from the early SAARC process, as member countries decided to exclude "contentious bilateral issues" from the agenda. It was seen as a pragmatic answer to complex issues in South Asia given the host of bilateral problems that existed—primarily between Pakistan and India, but also between India and its smaller neighbors including Nepal, Bangladesh, and Sri Lanka. It could well be argued, however, that the region lost a vital opportunity to permit a role for SAARC as a mediator in regional conflicts. As a result, the ebb and flow of bilateral relations, particularly between India and Pakistan, have had an undue influence in dictating the course of SAARC's economic agenda.

It is not surprising that some political economists have drawn what seems to be an inevitable conclusion that the most likely scenario for South Asia is that it will remain locked in an unstable situation (Maass 1999). The argument put forward is that in light of the Indocentric nature of the region, any change will require India to adopt a more accommodating stance.[11] However, it is appropriately argued that India may regard accommodation as unnecessary given that it considers itself powerful enough to cope with any tension in the subcontinent, where such reluctance in turn will then serve to strengthen anti-Indian hawks in Pakistan. Moreover, given the economic predominance of India in the region, any meaningful effort toward regional trade integration will require active Indian participation. However, such an integration of economies that has India as the dominant member may be perceived as a threat to blur Pakistan's political and strategic identity and thus may never be fully acceptable. It is difficult, therefore, to oppose the view that South Asia may never benefit from a true spirit of regionalism.

In this political-economy backdrop, it is questionable whether South Asian countries will commit to regional free trade that will require considerably more commitment to open access to their markets than has been shown in the past. SAFTA will generate a sense of genuine interest only if it goes well beyond the current bilateral agreements. Not only will it have to offer more liberal terms, but the timing of its implementation is also likely to be critical.

As the SAFTA process goes through the motions, it also appears increasingly to be out of step with strategic trade policy alternatives that are cropping up in the face of a rapidly changing global economic environment. India and

Sri Lanka have begun negotiations to go further from the framework agreement of the ILFTA toward a broad Economic Partnership Agreement. This is intended to take economic cooperation beyond trade in goods alone to include moves to increase market access to each other on a preferential basis in areas of investment and services. In turn, both India and Sri Lanka have begun to seek similar agreements with Singapore, while bilateral FTAs are also being pursued with more advanced economies. Such bilateral deals are also being complemented through engagement in other regional blocs to strengthen links with more advanced Southeast Asian economies through the Bangkok Agreement and the BIMSTEC (Bay of Bengal Initiative for Multi-Sectoral Technical and Economic Cooperation) agreement. India and Pakistan have also gained observer status at the Association of Southeast Asian Nations in pursuit of their strategic trade policies with East Asian economies. These new developments not only are likely to shape trade policies but also are seen as means by which a country's broad reform agenda can be tied in to facilitate more market-oriented reforms. The mere fact of attempting to negotiate with more advanced economies can help to galvanize the domestic reform process, particularly as they begin to go beyond trade in goods and come to include trade in services and investment. These initiatives are supported by emerging new evidence that appears to suggest that unlike the trade diverting effects of preferential trade agreements, the so-called third wave of PTAs, which cover nontrade provisions—particularly those related to investment and services—offer more optimistic findings in terms of real economic gains (Adams et al. 2003).

BIMSTEC, free of the bilateral tensions that have habitually dogged the SAARC process, has moved rapidly to a possible implementation of a FTA in 2006 where the Framework Agreement has already made provisions for the inclusion of negotiations on services and investment from 2007. Five of the SAFTA members are represented in the grouping (excluding Pakistan), in addition to having separate bilateral FTAs with India. The net result of these alternative arrangements may eventually become something approximating free trade within the region except for Pakistan. Such an outcome, however, would not be in the interests of the South Asian region and would mean compromising many of the political and economic goals intended to be achieved through greater regional cooperation.

Conclusion

Although SAARC was slow to embrace the concept of economic cooperation, having done so, it moved swiftly thereafter to set itself an ambitious agenda. It could well be argued that the initial schedule of moving South Asia toward a free trade area within a span of five years or so was too ambitious. It also had the unfortunate effect of raising expectations and of irrevocably tying the perceived success or failure of SAARC firmly to achievements on the economic front. In retrospect, given the long history of political tension in the region, it appears that SAARC leaders were perhaps naive in their belief that political differences could be set aside to allow headway on the economic front. Progress on economic cooperation has long been viewed as one of the means of building confidence through binding of South Asian economic interests. But the experience of SAPTA negotiations indicates not only the lack of commitment of SAARC countries to open their markets to each other but also that economic cooperation is doomed to achieve little in the absence of political goodwill among member countries. The introduction of bilateral free trade agreements among SAARC countries is likely to lead to further fragmentation of a common South Asian goal toward regional integration.

The question then remains whether economic cooperation within the framework of a regional arrangement in South Asia has any future. The first step that has to be taken is to acknowledge the limitations of past performance. In turn, this should lead to a healthy debate on whether deeper economic integration is desired by all member countries. If SAARC countries are to go forward without a loss of credibility, mere rhetoric on commitment to freer regional trade will not suffice. It will have to be matched at the negotiating table by a willingness to commit to a clearly delineated agenda and an undertaking to insulate the economic agenda as far as possible from regional politics. Recent experience has not been promising and leaves little room for optimism. As the momentum in trade policy negotiations moves away from SAARC, the consequences for the organization itself could be grave. There would then be little political impetus to make it more effective, even in the future.

Notes

1. While the gravity model has a number of advantages in analyzing intraregional trade, particularly for preferential trade agreements, it also has many limitations. It does not take into consideration the possible impact of the terms of trade associated with trade creation. Hence, the simulated results based on a gravity model are generally biased upward. The estimates also give the results in a static framework and the extent of intraregional trade will possibly increase further if the estimation is carried out in a dynamic framework, incorporating the effects of factors such as terms of trade, scale economies, technology spillovers, investment flows, and so on.

2. The study employs the Global Trade Policy Analysis Project model, which takes into account the production structure of each region of the world, bilateral trade between regions, and major global trade distortions.

3. For example, it has been estimated that small economies will benefit by gains from trade under the proposed Free Trade Agreement of the Americas (see World Bank 1995).

4. See Mukherji (1998) for a study of trade and investment links between India and Nepal, and Mukherji (2000a) for a study of trade and investment linkages between India and Sri Lanka. See also Jayasuriya and Weerakoon (2001) for a more detailed assessment of a potential trade–investment nexus in South Asia.

5. "Product-by-product" means negotiating a HS (harmonized system) six-digit tariff line. "Across-the-board" means a uniform reduction applying to all products under negotiation. "Sectoral basis" means negotiations on tariff, para-tariff, and NTBs, as well as other trade promotion or cooperation measures for specified products or groups of products closely related in end use or in production. "Direct trade measures" means negotiations to promote trade through buyback arrangements, state trading operations, government procurement, and so forth.

6. The LDC member states within SAARC have also been offered a larger share of such concessions vis-à-vis the non-LDC states. Thus, some concessions have been offered only to LDC states. The LDC members of SAPTA have also been offered higher tariff preferences than the non-LDC members.

7. The "Gujaral Doctrine" by India was essentially based on the principle of offering concessions to its smaller neighbors on a nonreciprocal basis.

8. The products were to be named within sixty days of the signing of the agreement. However, the exchange of lists was delayed until March 2000 for various reasons, including some opposition by both Indian and Sri Lankan interest groups.

9. With the exception of concessions on textile items in Chapters 51–56, 58–60, and 63, where the margin of preference will be restricted to 25 percent.

10. The ILFTA also has more relaxed rules of origin requirements vis-à-vis SAPTA, allowing products having a domestic value addition of 35 percent to qualify for preferential market access. In addition, those Sri Lankan exports having a minimum 10 percent content of inputs originating from India will qualify for preferential market access under a reduced total domestic value addition of 25 percent.

11. India accounts for 74 percent of the region's total population, 76 percent of its gross national product, and 64 percent of its export trade.

12. The ILFTA becomes fully operational by 2008 while the proposed FTA between Pakistan and Sri Lanka is also set to follow a similar time frame for implementation.

References

Adams, R.; P. Dee; J. Gali; and G. McGuire. 2003. "The Trade and Investment Effects of Preferential Trading Arrangements: Old and New Evidence." Productivity Commission Staff Working Paper, Canberra, May. www.pc.gov.au/research/swp/teipta/index.html.
Blackhurst, R.; A. Enders; and J.F. François. 1996. "The Uruguay Round and Market Access: Opportunities and Challenges for Developing Countries." In *The Uruguay Round and the Developing Countries*, ed. W. Martin and L.A. Winters, 125–55. Cambridge: Cambridge University Press.
De Melo, J.; A. Panagariya; and D. Rodrik. 1993. *The New Regionalism: A Country Perspective*. Washington, DC: World Bank.
Jayasuriya, S., and D. Weerakoon. 2001. "Foreign Direct Investment and Economic Integration in the SAARC Region." In *Trade, Finance and Investment in South Asia*, ed. T.N. Srinivasan. New Delhi: Social Sciences Press.

Maass, C.D. 1999. "South Asia: Drawn Between Cooperation and Conflict." In *The Dynamics of South Asia: Regional Cooperation and SAARC*, ed. E. Gonsalves and N. Jetley, 40–62. New Delhi: Sage.

Michaely, M. 1996. "Trade-Preferential Agreements in Latin America." World Bank Policy Research Working Paper, Washington, DC. http://econ.worldbank.org/external/.

Mukherji, I.N. 1998. "India's Trade and Investment Linkages with Nepal: Some Reflections." *South Asian Survey* 5, no. 2: 183–97.

———. 2000a. "Indo-Sri Lanka Trade and Investment Linkages: With Special Reference to SAPTA and Free Trade Agreement." *South Asia Economic Journal* 1, no. 1: 53–78.

———. 2000b. "Charting a Free Trade Area in South Asia: Instruments and Modalities." Paper presented at the Second Conference of the South Asia Network of Economic Research Institutes (SANEI), August 26–29, Kathmandu. www.saneinetwork.net/research.

Panagariya, A. 1999. "Trade Liberalization in South Asia: Recent Liberalization and Future Agenda." *World Economy* 22, no. 3: 353–78.

Pigato, M.; C. Farah; K. Itakura; K. Jun; W. Martin; K. Murrell; and T.G. Srinivasan. 1997. *South Asia's Integration into the World Economy*. Washington, DC: World Bank.

Srinivasan, T.N. 1994. "Regional Trading Arrangements and Beyond: Exploring Some Options for South Asia: Theory, Empirics and Policy," Report no 142. Washington, DC: World Bank.

Srinivasan, T.N., and G. Canonero. 1993. "Liberalisation of Trade Among Neighbours: Two Illustrative Models and Simulations." South Asia Discussion Paper Series, Supplement II to IDP no. 142.

Viner, J. 1950. *The Customs Union Issue*. New York: Carnegie Endowment for International Peace.

Weerakoon, D. 2001. "Indo-Sri Lanka Free Trade Agreement: How Free Is It?" *Economic and Political Weekly* 36, no. 8: 629–30.

World Bank. 1995. "Small Economies: Trade Liberalization, Trade Preferences and Growth." Washington, DC: World Bank.

———. 2003. "Regional Integration and Development." Washington, DC: World Bank.

12

Repositioning SAFTA in the Regionalism Debate

Saman Kelegama and Ratnakar Adhikari

Trade liberalization can follow various tracks—unilateral, bilateral, regional, and multilateral. There is a growing consensus among a large segment of stakeholders that multilateral trade liberalization is the first best option, not least because of the reciprocity and multilateralization of concessions (so-called most-favored-nation principle), where each country has an equal chance of gaining from the trade liberalization initiatives of other countries. The progress of the World Trade Organization (WTO) over the past ten years clearly indicates that trade liberalization under the multilateral regime is at best uncertain and slow.

Neoclassical economists argue that unilateral trade liberalization is the best option for a country; however, the political economy of trade liberalization is such that reciprocity is a sine qua non in trade liberalization initiatives in most developing countries. Since unilateral trade liberalization is not a practical option and multilateral trade liberalization is slow and uncertain, many countries have opted for regional trade liberalization through the formation of regional trade arrangements (RTAs). In the existing literature, RTAs have been hotly debated and there are two schools of thought. The first, led by Larry Summers (former U.S. Treasury secretary and currently president of Harvard University), maintains that RTAs are building blocks toward multilateral trade liberalization. The second, led by Jagdish Bhagwati (professor of economics at Columbia University), argues that RTAs are stumbling blocks to multilateral trade liberalization. Other economists have chosen to remain neutral.

South Asia decided to embrace an RTA in 1995 when the South Asian Preferential Trade Agreement (SAPTA) of the South Asian Association for Regional Cooperation (SAARC) was signed in 1995. In early 2004, the agreement on establishing the South Asian Free Trade Area (SAFTA) was signed. Six member countries of SAFTA have already pledged their support to the

WTO. Bhutan, which is the only nonmember of the WTO in the group, has manifested its commitment to the multilateral trade architecture espoused by the WTO by initiating its accession process. Thus, the SAARC RTA (i.e., SAFTA) is a parallel initiative to the multilateral trade liberalization commitments of SAARC member countries.

Critics have pointed out that there is no rationale for an RTA in South Asia because there are limited complementarities in the region; major trading partners of the individual South Asian countries are located in the West, for example. The latest World Bank report on South Asia's trade argues that an RTA in South Asia will lead more to substantial trade diversion than trade creation and considers an RTA in the region as a stumbling block to multilateral trade liberalization (World Bank 2003). This argument needs reexamination, and for this purpose it is worthwhile first to revisit the theoretical debate on regionalism.

The Debate on RTAs

Arguments in Favor of RTAs as Building Blocks

According to Larry Summers, any "ism" (bilateralism, regionalism, or multilateralism) is good as long as its ultimate objective is trade liberalization. Supporters of this school of thought, prominently Bergsten, argue:

> Regional arrangements promote freer trade and multilateralism in at least two senses: that trade creation has generally exceeded trade diversion, and that the RTAs contribute to both internal and international dynamics that enhance rather than reduce the prospects for global liberalization. The internal dynamic is particularly important for developing countries: regional commitments, which can be negotiated much faster than global pacts, lock in domestic reforms against the risk that successive governments will try to reverse them. Internationally, the RTAs often pioneer new liberalization ideas that can subsequently be generalized in the multilateral system. Moreover, regional liberalization creates incentives for other regions and individual countries to follow suit and thus to "ratchet up" the global process. (Bergsten 1997, 3)

The proponents of regionalism assert that it often has important demonstration effects. Regional initiatives can accustom officials, governments, and nations to the liberalization process and thus increase the probability that they will subsequently move on to similar multilateral actions. "Learning by doing" applies to trade liberalization as well as to economic development itself, and can often be experienced both more easily and more extensively in the regional context with far fewer negotiating partners.

They further contend that it has had positive rather than negative political effects. Trade and broader economic integration have created a European Union in which another war between Germany and France is literally impossible. Argentina and Brazil have used the Southern Cone Common Market (Mercosur) to end their historic rivalry, which had taken on nuclear overtones in recent decades. Central goals of the Asia-Pacific Economic Cooperation (APEC) forum include anchoring the United States as a stabilizing force in Asia and forging institutional links between such previous antagonists as Japan, China, and the rest of East Asia (Bergsten 1997, 3). It is also hoped that the political rivalry between India and Pakistan will be laid to rest after the formation of SAFTA, leading to deeper economic integration in days to come.

However, the favorable impact of an RTA is subject to the proviso that RTAs are able to achieve a deeper degree of economic integration than the multilateral trading system. This is well within the realm of feasibility because RTAs usually entail neighboring, like-minded countries. A smaller forum (with homogeneous or semihomogeneous membership) makes it possible to establish the necessary centralized institutions or federalizing policymaking and enforcement institutions (Das 2001, 22).

A group of trade economists follows the logic that the expansion of RTAs could have positive effects on the global economy provided the emerging RTAs are "open" to trade from outside. One key benefit to the global economy comes from the impact of RTAs in stimulating domestic growth, which in turn increases the demand for extraregional exports.

Baldwin contributes a major analysis dealing with this issue. Focusing exclusively on the incentive of outsiders to seek entry, Baldwin identifies a "domino" effect, which may yield global free trade through RTA expansion. Using a variant of what have come to be known as models of economic geography, Baldwin shows that under the "domino" effect, more and more outside countries have an incentive to become insiders as an RTA expands. The countries are assumed to differ in such a way that the RTA is not equally attractive to them. Initially, it attracts one member who finds the entry worthwhile. The addition of this member enlarges the internal market and makes it more attractive to yet another outside country at the margin. Once this country joins, yet another country finds accession profitable, and so on, until the RTA becomes global (Baldwin 1997).

Baldwin (1997) further indicates that this domino theory is derived from the expansion of the European Union. He then goes on to explain American dominos. Indeed, faced with the possibility of exclusion due to United States–Mexico trade, when the trade talks were going on between the United States and Mexico, Canada requested the parties to trilateralize talks, which led to the birth of the North American Free Trade Agreement (NAFTA). Similarly, when other Latin American countries that were interested in joining NAFTA received only a lukewarm response from President George H.W. Bush, four of them decided to form Mercosur. The pressure for inclusion was so great that Bolivia and Chile joined Mercosur as associate members. After the announcement of the formation of the Free Trade Area of the Americas (FTAA), which covers the entire Western Hemisphere, virtually every country in the Americas is looking forward to joining it under certain conditions.[1]

Not many Asian dominos have fallen so far, primarily because the Association of Southeast Asian Nations (ASEAN), the largest RTA in Asia, has expanded its membership to only ten countries. However, the first-ever free trade agreement, which Japan entered into with Singapore and ASEAN plus three (China, Japan, and Korea) is likely to result in the falling of Asian dominos of tremendous significance.[2]

Closer to home, recently, Bhutan and Nepal joined an exclusive club of five countries, Bangladesh, India, Myanmar, Sri Lanka, and Thailand Economic Cooperation (BIMSTEC), now renamed the Bay of Bengal Initiative for Multi-Sectoral Technical and Economic Cooperation, because they believed that they could be marginalized if they did not join the club.

Sapir conducted a study on the issue of the domino effect in Europe, which further supports the evidence of the prevalence of domino effects. According to Sapir (2001, 386), "The empirical findings of the study support the hypothesis that 'domino effects' have played an important role in Europe. These effects may be partly responsible for the successive enlargement of the European Community from its original 6 to its present 15 members." The fact that the membership of the European Union has grown to twenty-five further supports this analysis.

However, one important condition for the application of domino theory is that the incumbent members be "open" to include new members. If they have incentives to create barriers to entry by the new country in the group, the domino theory does not work. Therefore, the concept of "open regionalism" was propounded. Bergsten, one of the pioneers of the concept, argues:

> The concept represents an effort to achieve the best of both worlds: the benefits of regional liberalization, which even the critics acknowledge, without jeopardizing the continued vitality of the multilateral system. Indeed, proponents of open regionalism (including the author) view it as a device through which regionalism can be employed to accelerate the progress toward global liberalization and rule-making. (1997, 4)

APEC was modeled on this concept based on the suggestions of the Eminent Persons Group, which was chaired by Bergsten himself. However, Bergsten's idea of open regionalism is contradictory and vague, as will be discussed later.

Arguments for RTAs as Stumbling Blocks

As early as 1992, Bhagwati, who professes to be a multilateralist and a critic of regionalism, posed the following question: "Is regionalism truly a building, rather than a stumbling, block toward multilateral free trade for all: in other words, will it fragment, or integrate, the world economy?" (1999, 7). Bhagwati calls "the revival of regionalism" "unfortunate." He emphasizes the need "to contain and shape it in ways that it becomes maximally useful and minimally damaging, and consonant with the objectives of arriving at multilateral free trade for all" (1998, 169), which is the goal of free trade in his conception.

Expanding on these arguments, Panagariya (1998) uses two different analyses, a formal model as well as informal arguments to prove that regionalism is a stumbling block to multilateral trading systems. He considers two formal models, by Levy (1997) and Krishna (1998). According to Levy's model, when voters in two different countries that are members of both an FTA and multilateral trading system were given a choice, they felt that the FTA could not make previously unfeasible multilateral liberalization feasible. Krishna uses a three-country, partial-equilibrium, oligopoly model in which trade policy is chosen to maximize national firms' profits. He shows that the more trade diverts the FTA between two countries in this setup, the greater the backing it receives and the more it reduces the incentive to eventually liberalize with the third country. With sufficiently large trade diversion, an initially feasible multilateral liberalization can be rendered unfeasible by the FTA option (Panagariya 1998).

Similarly, using a three-country, two-good general equilibrium model, Lipsey demonstrated that, after the union is formed, the gain in consumption due to the reduction in the prices of the imported good by a union member could more than outweigh the loss from switching imported goods from the low-cost outside country to the high-cost union partner (Baghwati, Krishna, and Panagariya 1999, xvii).

He then analyzes the informal arguments in the following sequence. First, it has been suggested by Summers (1991) and others that multilateral negotiations will move more rapidly if the number of negotiators is reduced to approximately three, via bloc formation. This argument gained some popularity at the time the Uruguay Round (UR) negotiations were stalled but it has lost force since the successful completion of the round. The argument is that due to the large number of members involved at the WTO and the associated "free rider problem," negotiations at the WTO are slow and difficult. If the world is first divided into a handful of blocs, multilateral negotiations will become easier.

Second, according to the second informal argument, RTAs may serve as a threat to force unwilling parties to negotiate in earnest at the multilateral level. As per this argument, the EU was dragging its feet too long for the UR to be concluded, but when President Bill Clinton called for the formation of a free trade agreement with APEC, the EU decided to conclude the negotiations during the UR. However, Bhagwati (1999) disagrees with this interpretation. He asserts that the UR could conclude only because the United States wisely decided to close the UR deal, taking the offer on the table rather than seeking more concessions.

Third, it is argued that due to their high visibility, RTAs can energize and unify protectionist lobbies, turning them into effective obstacles against multilateral liberalization. Finally, there is the related issue of attention diversion and scarce negotiating resources. If the president of the United States and his trade representative are preoccupied with cutting deals in Latin America, they will have less time and motivation for multilateral negotiations (Bhagwati, Krishna, and Panagariya 1999, 22–25). A World Bank study further elaborates this point by arguing that negotiating an RTA will absorb a huge portion of the policymaking skills of a developing country. Perhaps one of the opportunity costs of RTAs is that less negotiating and political capital are available for multilateral negotiations (World Bank 2000).

Das (2001) argues that growth in regionalism does not necessarily have to lead to a shortcut to free trade or a liberalized trading regime. It is difficult to claim that the target of free or liberalized trade is easier to reach in large regional agreements like the FTAA and APEC forum with memberships as large as thirty-five and twenty-one, respectively. These two and other large regional groupings contain economies as different in size, outlook, and level of development as any in the WTO (Das 2001).

Panagariya (1998) criticizes "open regionalism" by highlighting three critical limitations of such a concept. His arguments can be summarized in three major points. First, discrimination against nonmembers at any point in time remains in place by definition as long as the regionalism is of the General Agreement on Tariffs and Trade (GATT) Article XXIV variety.[3] Second, openness is not as innocuous as it sounds—the admission price can include several unpleasant "side payments" that are essentially unrelated to trade. Third, open membership does not necessarily translate into speedy membership.[4]

Further, Zissimos and Vines assert:

> If the benefits from membership of an exclusive club are derived partly by making outsiders worse off, then the club will not throw open its doors to all comers. Facilitating trade between bloc members has exactly this effect. The purchasing power of bloc currencies increases, whilst that of outsiders declines. Consequently, trade blocs do not have an incentive to allow all applicants to join, because some of the benefits of membership come from being able to purchase the products of outsiders more cheaply on world markets. So there is a limit to the expansion that can be expected from existing blocs, and free trade between all countries will not arise. (2000, p. ii)

Open membership also raises the issue of broadening versus deepening. Broadening the membership of any regional grouping inherently complicates the process of deepening its integration. Too many new members can make decision making more time consuming and cumbersome. APEC realized this and imposed a moratorium on expanding membership in early 1998 (Kelegama 2000a).

Srinivasan too is quite vocal in criticizing "open regionalism." He argues, "If regional liberalization is to be extended on the same time table 'in practice and in law' to non-member countries on an MFN basis, it would be multilateral and not regional. If that is the case, why should any group initiate it on a regional basis in the first place?" (1996, p. 19). He goes on to call "open regionalism" an oxymoron. The practical problems of this concept have been highlighted by the current status of the APEC and the Indian Ocean Rim Association for Regional Cooperation (IOR-ARC), where progress has been far from satisfactory (Kelegama 2000a, 2000b, 2002).

Contemporary Debate on Regionalism: Other Viewpoints

A comprehensive study done by the World Bank (2000) concerning the debate on regional integration, titled *Trade Blocs*, finds that regionalism is generally a building block to multilateral trade liberalization. It explains how the benefits of trade creation resulting from an RTA outweigh the costs of trade diversion.[5] The study looks at seven recent regional arrangements by modeling the effect on trade among the countries in the bloc and the rest of the world to see the impact of trade diversion. The study reveals that in four of the seven countries there was no significant trade diversion, but in three countries the problem of trade diversion was large enough to be visible. Hence diversion is neither so common as to be general, nor so unusual as to be dismissible (World Bank 2000).

Complementarity between regionalism and multilateralism is also stressed by Ethier (1998), who argues that "the new regionalism is in good part a direct result of the success of multilateral liberalisation, as well as being the means by which new countries trying to enter the multilateral system (and small countries already in it) compete among themselves for direct investment." He also suggests that regionalism—by internalizing an important externality—plays a key role in expanding and preserving the liberal trading order.

Commenting on the complementarity of regional liberalization on services with multilateral liberalization, Hoekman (1995) suggests that both conceptual considerations and the available data on trade and investment flows suggest that RTAs in the area of services should be easier to negotiate and be more far-reaching than a multilateral agreement. However, he admits that the two approaches are substitutes. Reviewing existing agreements, he concludes that sectors that are excluded from (included in) RTAs are also excluded from (included in) multilateral liberalization. This suggests "the GATS [General Agreement on Trade in Services] is likely to be seen as complementary to the regional arrangements by major service industries in OECD [Organization for Economic Cooperation and Development] countries" (cited in Laird 1999, 1187).

After analyzing all the arguments discussed above, it is clear that there is no need to be unnecessarily nervous about regionalism and its potential to derail multilateral trade liberalization. To conclude the debate on regionalism versus globalism, the following statement made by Baldwin is noteworthy:

> Does recent regionalism threaten the future of the world trading system? My guess is that because trade is already quite free in the major trading nations, few regional liberalisations are capable of creating important anti-liberalisation forces (the exceptions are likely to be South-South FTAs). For this reason, most regional deals will weaken the key opponents of free trade (import competitors) while simultaneously strengthening its key proponents (exporters). Regional integration will, therefore, foster multilateral liberalisation and vice versa, just as it has done for the past 40 years. If this is right, regional deals are not building blocks or stumbling blocks. Regionalism is half of the trade liberalisation "wheel" that has been rolling towards global free trade since 1958. (1997, 888)

The increase in intraregional trade between the regional partners shows that the benefits of trade creation outweigh the costs associated with trade diversion. Regional economic integration has served the useful purpose of creating a thread for multilateral trade liberalization on several counts. If that were not the case, the size and number of RTAs would not have grown by leaps and bounds as has happened, especially since the formation of the WTO. Indeed, RTAs are the favorite of countries worldwide—whether they are members of the WTO or not.[6]

South Asian Perspective on RTAs

The initial conditions for South Asia to embark on an RTA do not seem very attractive. Limited complementarities, low intraregional trade (4–5 percent), political turbulence, and so on, act as impediments to embarking on the promotion of intraregional trade. However, there are some valid reasons for engaging in an RTA. The case for economic cooperation under an RTA can be justified from six perspectives.

First, nearly 60 percent of global trade now takes place under RTAs, of which there are nearly 230 in operation,[7] so there are compelling reasons to be in an RTA insofar as countries that are not members can become increasingly marginalized in the competitive world. In such a context, one can also question the rationale of multilateral trade liberalization, identified as the first best option by economists led by Bhagwati. This theory is based on strong assumptions such as perfect competition, which no longer exists in a world with numerous RTAs. In an imperfect world, the so-called second best option may be the only option available, thus the case for an RTA is strong.

Second, a large amount of informal trade is taking place in the region, and if this is added to the formal trade, the overall intraregional trade will amount to nearly 8 percent in the SAARC. An additional argument is that despite intraregional trade estimated at 22 percent in ASEAN, if the reexports from Singapore are taken into account, ASEAN intraregional trade decreases to 12 percent. Thus, it is argued that there is not much difference between SAARC and ASEAN in intraregional trade, taking into account that preferential trading in ASEAN started twenty years before SAARC.

Third, RTAs are not necessarily formed to increase low intraregional trade to a higher level. In Europe intraregional trade was at 44 percent at the time of formation of the EC. The real objective here, according to the Cecchini Report, was to promote the economics of neighborhood and engage in industrial restructuring by exploiting economies of scale and specialization (Cecchini et al. 1988). In other words, to promote industrial restructuring through complementarities and synergies.

Fourth, the cost of noncooperation supports the case for an RTA. The Consumer Unity & Trust Society showed that consumers in Pakistan paid extra costs of US$36.3 million, US$48.9 million, and US $33.7 million over the calendar years 1992, 1993, and 1994, respectively, for their governments importing 82 to 83 percent of their tea import requirements from outside the region, such as the United Kingdom and Kenya (CUTS 1996). Although India is self-sufficient in sugar, it underproduced in 1992 and 1993 and had to import sugar. Though Pakistan had exportable surplus during that year, India chose to import sugar from outside the region, thus incurring additional costs of US$151 million in 1992 and US$215 million in 1993. Likewise, Pakistan is known to import steel from China at a price twice that of exports from India. RIS used the unit value method in a comparative static framework to work out the cost of noncooperation in the SAARC due to sourcing of imports from non-SAARC countries. They found the cost of noncooperation for Sri Lanka and Pakistan to be US$266 million and US$511 million, respectively (RIS 2004).

Fifth, the experience of the Indo Lanka Free Trade Agreement (ILFTA) highlights the benefits of an RTA. Despite fears expressed by many pessimists in Sri Lanka, the agreement led to a reduction in Sri Lanka's trade deficit with India from 11:1 in 1999 to 3.5:1 in 2004. The total trade turnover between the two countries which stood at Rs. 49.6 billion in 2002, increased to Rs. 176.4 billion in 2004 (US$1.8 billion). Exports from Sri Lanka that were Rs. 4.2 billion in 2000, swelled to Rs. 16.1 billion in 2002 and Rs. 39 billion in 2004. Similarly imports from India into Sri Lanka, also increased from Rs. 45.4 billion in 2002 to Rs. 79.8 billion in 2002, and Rs. 137.8 billion in 2004. Expressed in dollar terms, Sri Lankan exports jumped from US$38 million in 1998 to US$385 million in 2004—a hefty increase. Indian exports to Sri Lanka also shot up from US$539 million to US$1.35 billion during the same period. Sri Lanka has now emerged as India's number one business partner in South Asia, over taking much larger neighbors (Jayasekera, 2005).

What the Sri Lankan experience shows is that if the regulatory framework in an RTA is correctly designed to accommodate the disparity between the countries, then a small country can in fact gain from an RTA. In this case, the time frame of tariff phase-out and the rules of origin negative list were designed to accommodate the smallness of Sri Lanka's export and production capacity. Fortunately, special and differential treatment to the least developed countries of the region has also been a cornerstone of SAFTA (Adhikari, 2005).

Sixth, the argument that the South–South RTAs are not very effective in promoting intraregional trade may not make much sense if we look at South–South trade from the intraregional investment perspective. It has been empirically demonstrated that the transfer of resources and technology through South–South joint ventures is more appropriate and cost effective for the receiving country than similar transfers effected by transnational corporations based in industrial countries. For instance, technology transferred to joint ventures has been found to be appropriately scaled down to a smaller size, made more appropriate for factor endowments of developing countries, and adapted to local raw materials and market conditions (RIS 2004). These joint ventures can promote and supplement South–South trade. Joint ventures that have buyback arrangements with the home country can help in correcting the perennial trade imbalances that may emerge because of the limited export capabilities of host countries.

In ASEAN, Japanese investment-driven exchanges have contributed to stimulating intraregional trade among ASEAN countries. ASEAN also started with limited complementarities in the 1970s with intraregional trade at 6 percent, but by exploiting the investment–trade nexus, ASEAN managed to increase its intraregional trade to 22 percent as of 2004. In the Greater Mekong Region, infrastructure funded by the Asian Development Bank stimulated the supply side and contributed to increasing trade among member countries. These experiences whereby dormant complementarities are invigorated by investment have been well documented in the literature.

As in the EU, if industrial restructuring in the region based on economies of scale and specialization is promoted via a SAARC investment area, there may be much to be gained. For instance, after the EU was established, IBM closed down its individual plants in member countries and initiated specialization by producing PCs in the United Kingdom, main frames in Germany, telecom equipment in Italy, and so on. RIS (2004) argues that a SAARC investment area can facilitate the efficiency-seeking restructuring of industry in regions, thus enabling them to exploit economies of scale and specialization. In this event, Sri Lanka could emerge as the region's shipping hub and also the hub for rubber-based industries, Bangladesh could emerge as the hub for energy-based industries, Bhutan for forest-based industries, India for IT and textile industries, Maldives for fisheries industries, and so on.

While the arguments for an RTA exist in South Asia, the question is how to exploit this potential. For SAFTA to be a formidable FTA, it has to cover a large portion of trade that is currently taking place in South Asia. The SAARC Preferential Trade Agreement (SAPTA)—the precursor to SAFTA—was authorized under the WTO's "Enabling Clause,"[8] which allows developing countries to form RTAs within themselves. However, more serious RTAs are authorized under Article XXIV of the GATT, even if they can in theory be authorized under the Enabling Clause. Because RTAs can be welfare enhancing only if they result in more trade creation than trade diversion and act as building blocks to multilateral trade liberalization, the drafters of GATT included the requirement to "liberalize substantially all the trade" under this Article. This means only serious RTAs can fulfill the stringent criteria laid down by Article XXIV. Therefore, it can be argued that SAFTA needs to be notified under this Article so as to make it a formidable RTA (Kelegama and Adhikari 2002). These concerns assume tremendous significance in the context of the mercantilist mind-set of the trade negotiators and protectionist tendency among the import competing sectors, which is still prevalent in most South Asian countries. The sensitive lists recently prepared by the SAARC member countries bear a testimony to these anomalies, which are antithesis of regional economic integration in South Asia.[9]

Concluding Remarks

The mere fact that there are 230 RTAs, and that the United States, which was the main proponent of multilateralism until a decade ago, has embarked on NAFTA and other RTAs with the enactments of the Trade and Development Act of 2000, clearly indicates that the proponents of an RTA have won the debate. The rationale for a SAARC RTA was the focus of the debate, but as we have pointed out, there is a case for an RTA in South Asia. The problem is the slow progress and the political will to implement it.

While the case for SAFTA is straightforward, the question is a major political problem that cuts across all areas of economic cooperation. Some South Asian nations are recent creations, and a strong rhetoric has been built around the states, which are aided by the powers of state institutions. The mapping of the cartography of the colonial regime has eroded the foundation of regional linking. The division into nation-states is strong. Since the nation-states are themselves in the process of being formed in the region, the concept of a supranational region seems novel and contradictory to the immediate task of nation building. Nation-states are absolutely central and crucial for any project in South Asia. SAARC moves slowly because most nation-states themselves have not been very successful.

In this milieu, the important question is, can SAARC insulate its economic agenda from regional politics? Irrespective of SAARC summits being postponed to accommodate political developments, can the economic agenda have a momentum or life of its own? At present, the answers to all these questions are not very positive. Thus, economic cooperation within a framework of a regional trade arrangement in South Asia will move slowly and depend on the political equation.

Due to the slow progress of SAPTA, a number of SAARC countries have embarked on working out bilateral, subregional, and trans-South Asian regional groupings. SAARC is thus unique because before moving to an FTA, it has bilateral FTAs within the grouping and selective RTAs that include some SAARC countries with neighboring SAARC nonmembers. ASEAN, for instance, did not have bilateral FTAs among ASEAN countries before forming its AFTA, and neither did Mercosur. Thus, SAFTA is being implemented when a "spaghetti bowl" already prevails in the region. The challenge for SAFTA is either to supersede them or to integrate them. Given the SAFTA time frame, this may prove to be difficult. The reviewed debate on regionalism gives little emphasis to such challenges. In this context, the debate on regionalism can be enriched by the experience in South Asia.

After all, if RTAs are to be building blocks for multilateral liberalization efforts, then the vision should be to integrate existing RTAs to three or four major blocs such as the Free Trade Area of Americas, the EU, a proposed African Union, and a contemplated Asian Economic Community. SAFTA, BIMSTEC, ASEAN +3, and so on, are RTAs that can eventually integrate to form the Asian Economic Community. Thus SAFTA has to be repositioned in the pan-Asian context and be considered as a building block of the Asian Economic Community—which will eventually become a major global trading bloc that will in turn be a building block of the multilateral trade liberalization system. Asia has a long way to go and SAFTA needs to be more aggressive in its commitments to becoming that building block for the Asian Economic Community.

Notes

1. However, the initial enthusiasm shown by the Latin American countries to sign the FTAA has waned, of late. At the time of writing, FTAA negotiations were uncertain, at best. See Hornbeck (2006).

2. Based on a personal conversation with Richards Baldwin, January 12, 2002.

3. This article of the GATT provides legal cover to RTAs, which allows for discrimination against nonmembers. However, a major condition to qualify as WTO-compatible is that there be "liberalization of substantially all trade."

4. It took the EU more than forty years to grow from six members to fifteen. The Canada–U.S. free trade agreement has included only one member by converting itself into NAFTA over a decade. Attempts by even a tiny country such as Chile have faced serious resistance. See Panagariya and Arvind (1998, 35).

5. Large-scale foreign direct investment from Japan played a key role in stimulating intra-ASEAN trade via the investment–trade nexus. Further details are given in Kelegama (1996).

6. They are: American Samoa, Bermuda, Channel Islands, Guam, Isle of Man, Monaco, Mongolia, N. Mariana Islands, Palau, Puerto Rico, Timor-Leste, and the Virgin Islands. See World Bank (2004a, 53).

7. The number of RTAs peaked to 285 just before the European Union expanded its membership to 25. However, after the expansion took place a number of inter-regional agreements were subsumed into the EU, which resulted in a reduction in the number of RTAs. See World Bank (2004). As per the latest WTO data (as of 1 March 2006), a total of 193 RTAs have been notified to the WTO. See www.wto.org/english/tratop_e/region_e/summary_e.xls.

8. Officially known as the Decision on Differential and More Favourable Treatment, Reciprocity and Fuller Participation of Developing Countries, 1979 (Tokyo Round).

9. For example, Bangladesh's sensitive list contains 1,254 tariff lines at the six-digit HS code level, India includes 884 tariff lines at the six- to eight-digit level under its sensitive list. Similarly Pakistan maintains a sensitive list of 1,183 tariff lines at the six-digit level, whereas Sri Lankan sensitive list comprises 1,065 tariff lines at the eight-digit level. Details can be obtained from the SAARC Secretariat's Web site, www.saarc-sec.org/main.php.

References

Adhikari, Ratnakar. 2005. "Vulnerability, Trade Integration and Human Development." Background Paper to the Regional Human Development Report on International Trade and Human Development in Asia and the Pacific. Colombo: UNDP Regional Centre.

Baldwin, Richards E. 1997. "The Causes of Regionalism." *World Economy* 20, no. 7: 865–88.

Bergsten, Fred. 1997. "Open Regionalism." Working Paper 97–3, Institute for International Economics, Washington, DC.

Bhagwati, Jagdish. 1998. In *Writings on International Economics*, ed. V.N. Balasubramanium. Oxford: Oxford University Press.

————. 1999. "Regionalism and Multilateralism: An Overview." In *Trading Blocs: Alternative Approaches to Analyzing Preferential Trade Agreements*, ed. Jagdish Bhagwati, Pravin Krishna, and Arvind Panagariya. Cambridge, MA: MIT Press.

Bhagwati, Jagdish; Pravin Krishna; and Arvind Panagariya. 1999. *Trading Blocs: Alternative Approaches to Analyzing Preferential Trade Agreements*. Cambridge, MA: MIT Press.

Cecchini, Paolo, et al. 1988. *The European Challenge 1992: The Benefits of a Single Market*. Aldershot, UK: Gower.

Consumer Unity & Trust Society (CUTS). 1996. "Cost of Non-Cooperation to Consumers in the SAARC Countries: An Illustrative Study." Working Paper, Jaipur, India.

Das, Dilip K. 2001. "Regional Trading Arrangements and the Global Economy: An Asia-Pacific Perspective." Cambridge, MA: Harvard University, Center for International Development.

Ethier, W. 1998. "The New Regionalism." *Economic Journal* 108: 1149–61.

Hornbeck, J.F. 2006. "A Free Trade Area of the Americas: Major Policy Issues and Status of Negotiations." Congressional Research Service (CRS) Report for Congress, updated, January 19, 2006. Washington, DC: Library of Congress.

Jayasekera, Douglas. 2005. "Sri Lanka's Regional and Bilateral Free Trade Agreements: Trends and Characteristics, Asia Pacific Trade and Investment Initiative." Colombo: UNDP Regional Centre.

Kelegama, S. 1996. "SAPTA and Its Future." *South Asian Survey* 3, nos. 1 and 2.

————. 2000a. "Open Regionalism and APEC: Rhetoric and Reality." *Economic and Political Weekly* 35, no. 51.

————. 2000b. "Open Regionalism in the Indian Ocean: How Relevant Is the APEC Model for IOR-ARC?" *Journal of the Asia Pacific Economy* 5, no. 3.

————. 2002. "Indian Ocean Regionalism: Is There a Future?" *Economic and Political Weekly* 37, no. 25: 2422–25.

Kelegama, S. 2003. "Sri Lanka's Exports to India: Impact of the Free Trade Agreement." *Economic and Political Weekly* 38, no. 30 (July 26).

Kelegama, S., and R. Adhikari. 2002. *Regional Integration in the WTO Era: South Asia at Crossroads*. SAWTEE, Kathmandu and CUTS-Centre for International Trade, Economics and Environment (CUTS-CITEE), Jaipur.

Laird, Sam. 1999. "Regional Trade Agreements: Dangerous Liaisons?" *World Economy* 22, no. 9 (December): 1179–200.

Panagariya, Arvind. 1998. "The Regionalism Debate: An Overview." Center for International Development, Harvard University. Published in *World Economy* 22, no. 4 (1999): 477–511.

RIS. 2004. *South Asia Development and Cooperation Report 2004*. "Research and Information System for Non-Aligned and Other Developing Countries." New Delhi, India.

Sapir, Andre. 2001. "Domino Effects in Western European Regional Trade, 1960–92." *European Journal of Political Economy* 17: 377–88.

Srinivasan, T.N. 1996. "Regionalism and the World Trade Organization: Is Non-Discrimination Passe?" Economic Growth Centre Discussion Paper No. 767. New Haven: Yale University.

Summers, Larry. 1991. "Regionalism and the World Trading System." Paper presented to Federal Reserve Bank of Kansas City symposium, www.kansascityfed.org/publicat/sympos/1991/sym91.htm.

World Bank. 2000. *Trade Blocs*. Oxford: Oxford University Press.

———. 2003. "Trade Policies in South Asia: An Overview." Poverty Reduction and Economic Management, South Asia Region, Washington, DC: World Bank.

———. 2004. *Global Economic Prospects 2005: Trade, Regionalism and Development.* Washington, DC: World Bank.

Zissimos, Ben, and David Vines. 2000. "Is the WTO's Article XXIV a Free Trade Barrier?" CSGR Working Paper no. 49/00 (February).

Web Sites

www.saarc-sec.org/main.php
www.unctad.org
www.wto.org/english/tratop_e/region_e/summary_e.xls

13

Market-Oriented Policy Reforms and Export-Led Industrialization

The Sri Lankan Experience

Premachandra Athukorala

It is now widely acknowledged in the economics profession that the industrialization strategy of interventionist import substitution, vigorously pursued by many developing countries during the early postwar period, largely misfired. There is, however, no agreement on the appropriate way forward. The mainstream policy advocacy in the neoclassical tradition of development economics sees the removal of government in direct production activities and a shift toward market forces as the appropriate strategy for achieving rapid, robust, and equitable growth (Bhagwati 1994; Krueger 1997; Little 1994). The economists of the "structuralist" persuasion (the revisionists), however, argue for activist and selective public policies tailored to the circumstances of each individual country, while eschewing indiscriminate state intervention, as the only way to industrialization for latecomers (Amsden 1997; Helleiner 1994; Rodrik 2003). Another way of stating this position is that trade policy must be subservient to the avowed aim of rapid industrialization, thus drawing a contrast between allocation of resources based on neutral policies and those based on selective interventions.

This chapter contributes to this debate through a case study of Sri Lanka. Sri Lanka has experienced a series of changes in its trade regime since attaining independence from British colonial rule in 1948. During the first decade after independence, it continued with a liberal trade regime until growing balance of payment problems induced a policy shift toward protectionist import substitution policies. By the mid-1970s the Sri Lankan economy had become one of the most inward-oriented and regulated outside the group of centrally planned economies, characterized by stringent trade and exchange controls and pervasive state interventions in all areas of economic activity. In 1977, Sri Lanka responded to the dismal economic outcome of this policy stance with a sharp change in policy direction and embarked on an extensive economic liberalization process, becoming the first country in the South Asian region to do so. Despite major macroeconomic problems, political turmoil, and government changes, market-oriented reforms have been sustained and broadened over almost two decades so that Sri Lanka today stands out as one of the most open economies in the developing world. This basic policy orientation looks set to continue for the foreseeable future. Indeed, the most dramatic change in the Sri Lankan political landscape in recent years has been the convergence of broad economic policies among the major political parties and groupings—the achievement of greater openness and liberalization is now a bipartisan policy in Sri Lanka. Given the decisive policy shift in 1977 and policy continuity over the ensuing years, Sri Lanka provides a valuable laboratory for studying the implications of foreign trade policy regimes with respect to the process of industrial adjustment and growth in a developing economy.

A key theme running through this chapter emphasizes the importance of the concomitant liberalization of both trade and investment policy regimes in determining the outcome of liberalization reforms in small trade dependent countries such as Sri Lanka.

The Policy Context

During the first decade after independence in 1948, Sri Lanka (commonly called Ceylon until 1972) continued to remain an open trading nation with only relatively minor trade or exchange rate restrictions and liberal domestic policies.[1] From the late 1950s, a combination of change in political leadership and balance of payments difficulties led to the adoption of a state-led development strategy of import substitution. Trade restrictions, which were initially introduced in response to growing balance of payments difficulties (rather than as part of an ideological commitment to import-substitution industrialization), became transformed into key instruments for directing private sector production activities in line with (perceived) national priorities. Following a hesitant and mild liberalization attempt in 1968–70, the period from 1970 to 1977 saw further government intervention in the economy under the guise of creating a "socialist society." Significant and ever-increasing segments of trade, industry, agriculture, and banking were owned and managed by state-owned enterprises (SOEs).

The policymakers in Sri Lanka, like their counterparts in other developing countries, expected import-substitution industrialization to set the stage for self-sustained growth by reducing the heavy dependence of the economy on imports. The reality was quite different, however. While consumer goods imports were reduced substantially, this was achieved at the expense of increased reliance on imported capital goods and raw materials, resulting, contrary to expectation, in an even more rigid dependence on imports. Given these structural features, the growth dynamism of the newly established industrial sector tended to show a close functional relationship with the fortunes of the traditional export industries. Thus, unanticipated import curtailments brought about by foreign exchange scarcity turned out to be the main constraint on industrial expansion since the late 1960s. In most smaller developing countries, rapid expansion of domestic industry continued until the "easy" import substitution opportunities (i.e., meeting domestic demand in textiles, footwear, some food processing, and other light labor-intensive activities) were used up. It was only then that the cost of additional investment in new import substitution activities begun to rise and growth slowed down (Krueger 1992, 43–44). However, in Sri Lanka, a limit was set on the growth of industry by the balance of payments constraint well before the completion of the easy import substitution phase.

As a reaction to the dismal economic outcome of the inward-looking policy, Sri Lanka embarked on an extensive economic liberalization process in 1977, becoming the first country in the South Asian region to do so. The first round of reforms in 1977–79 included significant trade and financial reforms:

- replacing quantitative restrictions on imports with tariffs and revising the tariff structure to achieve greater uniformity;
- reducing restrictions on foreign investment, with new incentives for export-oriented foreign investment under an attractive free trade zone scheme;
- adjusting interest rates to levels above the rate of inflation, opening the banking sector to foreign banks, and freeing credit markets to determine interest rates;
- placing limits on public sector participation in the economy; and
- creating a program for privatization of public enterprises, exchange rate realignment, and incentives for nontraditional exports.

The reform process lost momentum in the early 1980s, first because of an unfortunate shift in policy priorities toward politically appealing investment projects, and subsequently due to the onset of the ethnic conflict (Athukorala and Jayasuriya 1994, ch. 5). There was, however, no retreat to the old control regime. In a decisive move to infuse momentum into the unfinished reform process, a significant "second wave" liberalization package was implemented in the early 1990s. This included an ambitious privatization program, further tariff cuts and simplification of the tariff structure, the removal of exchange controls on current account transactions, and several important changes to the foreign investment policy in line with the increased outward orientation of the economy.

After seventeen years in government, the reformist United National Party lost power at the 1994 general elections to the People's Alliance. Since then the political climate has become more volatile and receptive to calls for more nationalistic and protectionist policies with the growth of popular disenchantment with the mainstream political parties. However, there has been a convergence in broad economic policies among the major political parties and groupings, maintaining greater openness to trade, and foreign direct investment (FDI) is now a bipartisan policy in Sri Lanka. This policy convergence, coupled with a palpable shift in development thinking in favor of greater outward orientation the world over, makes a sharp reversal to embrace more closed-door policies unlikely in the foreseeable future.

Against this background we now discuss the key elements of trade and foreign investment policy regimes in Sri Lanka as they have evolved since 1977.

Trade Policy

Trade policy reform was the key element of the economic liberalization policy package introduced in 1977. In November 1977 quantitative import restrictions on imports, which were near universal, were supplanted by a revised system of tariffs, retaining only 280 items under license. While many of the tariff changes involved an officially announced increase in the rate, tariffication typically involved a sharp reduction in the degree of protection provided previously by the stringent quantitative restriction regime. Fine-tuning of tariff rates during the next ten years involved some selective tariff increases in response to demand by the domestic protectionist lobby. There were also moderate revenue-oriented across-the-board increases in import duty in some years. These setbacks notwithstanding, overall there was significant rationalization of the tariff structure, in terms of reducing both variability of individual rates and average levels.

As part of the second-wave liberalization reforms initiated in the late 1980s, import tariffs were further reduced with the aim of moving toward a three-band tariff structure involving rates of 10, 20, and 35 percent. In 1997, tariffs on textiles were abolished and tariffs on clothing imports were substantially reduced, with a view to facilitating further expansion of the booming garment industry. Trade liberalization experienced some setbacks because of additional fiscal pressures following the escalation of the civil war in the latter part of the 1990s and the economic downturn during 2001, which infused a new lease on life to the domestic protectionist lobby. A 40 percent across-the-board tariff surcharge (subsequently reduced to 20 percent in 2001) was introduced in 2000. There were also many ad hoc duty exceptions and case-by-case adjustment of duties on many industrial imports that directly compete with domestic production. The tariff structure has also become more complex with the introduction of preferential tariffs under the South Asian Preferential Trade Agreement (SAPTA) and the Indo-Lanka Free Trade Agreement (ILFTA). However, as we will see below, these changes have not resulted in a significant reversal in the trends of economic opening maintained over the past two decades.

The effective duty rate on total imports (duty collection as a percentage of cost, insurance, and freight [CIF] import value) increased from about 14 percent in 1978–80 to 18.6 percent by the mid-1980s, and then declined continuously over the ensuing years, reaching 4.6 percent by 2002 (Table 13.1). The share of dutiable imports in total imports ranged from 52 percent to 77 percent in 1978–90, and declined continuously during the ensuing years. By the late 1990s, only 30 percent of imports (in value terms) were subject to duties.

Interestingly, the sharp reduction in average import duties over the past fifteen years has come predominantly from reductions (or elimination) of tariffs on intermediate goods. During the postreform period until about the mid-1980s, tariffs on intermediate goods were generally higher than those on final goods (consumer goods and investment goods). From then on, tariffs on intermediate goods have declined at a much faster rate as compared with those on final goods. In the early 1990s, consumer goods tariffs were on average about two times higher than tariffs on intermediate goods. Given this pattern of tariff escalation, the effective protection for domestic manufacturing turned out to be much higher than the nominal tariff on final goods. However, as already noted, throughout the postreform period, the trade regime in Sri Lanka continued to provide export producers with free access to intermediate inputs under the export processing zone (EPZ) scheme and an all-encompassing duty rebate scheme for non-EPZ firms. In addition, EPZ firms benefited from a wide range of financial incentives. Therefore, we can reasonably infer that continued high effective protection for domestic market-oriented production may not have been a major deterrent to export expansion.

Foreign Direct Investment Policy

The most important aspect of the FDI policy embodied in the 1977 reform package was the setting up of the Greater Colombo Economic Commission

Table 13.1

Import Duty Collection Rates and the Share of Dutiable Imports, 1978–1995 (%)

	Import duty rate[a]				Share of
	consumer goods	intermediate goods	capital goods	total imports	dutiable imports[b]
1978–80	10.8	17.9	15.0	13.9	76.8
1981–83	12.8	18.6	14.7	15.2	59.4
1984–86	22.8	19.1	17.4	18.6	68.8
1987–89	22.9	8.8	15.9	14.5	58.9
1990	12.5	9.1	18.6	12.3	52.9
1991	16.2	8.0	17.0	12.4	51.5
1992	23.2	7.9	17.5	14.3	45.8
1993	20.0	5.5	15.7	11.1	40.1
1994	13.7	5.2	14.6	9.1	36.5
1995	11.7	4.7	10.2	7.9	39.5
1996	10.3	6.0	7.6	8.5	38.7
1997	11.8	5.9	7.0	7.7	36.4
1998	12.7	4.7	6.0	7.4	35.7
1999	12.8	4.1	4.4	7.0	34.0
2000	11.5	2.9	4.0	4.5	29.3
2001	13.3	1.7	5.3	4.9	25.0
2002	13.3	1.6	5.5	4.6	28.0

Sources: Compiled from Sri Lanka Customs Department, Customs Returns (for the period 1978– 97) and Central Bank of Sri Lanka, *Annual Report* (various years).
[a]Actual import duty (including surcharges and cesses) as a percentage of total import value (c.i.f).
[b]Total dutiable imports as a share of total imports.

(GCEC) in 1978 with wide-ranging power to establish and operate export processing zones.[2] The investment promotion policy package offered by the GCEC to EPZ investors included: allowing complete foreign ownership of investment projects; a tax holiday for up to ten years with complete tax exemption for remuneration of foreign personnel employed, royalties, and dividends of shareholders during that period; duty exemption for the importation of inputs and assistance with customs clearances; industrial services at subsidized rates; unlimited access to foreign currency credit at interest rates prevailing in world financial markets; and access to foreign financing through foreign currency banking units and other incentives. The international news media and the investment community rated the Sri Lankan EPZ incentives highly favorably.[3]

As part of the second-wave liberalization, a new Investment Policy Statement was announced in 1990, activities of the Foreign Investment Advisory Committee and the GCEC were brought together under a new Board of Investment (BOI) in order to facilitate and speed up investment approval within a unified policy framework applicable to both import-substituting and export-oriented investors. Restrictions on the ownership structures of joint-venture projects outside EPZs were abolished. EPZ privileges were extended to local investors who established new export-oriented projects in all parts of the country, and were given free-trade status (in addition to the area demarcated EPZs). This provision, which was initially applicable only to investors who were prepared to implement their projects prior to September 30, 1991, was extended in February 1993 to local investors starting new export ventures as well as existing companies setting up production facilities outside the Western Province. Since then, this has become a permanent feature of the BOI approval procedure.

As an important part of the FDI policy, steps were also taken to enter into Investment Protection Agreements and Double Taxation Relief Agreements with the major investing countries. A guarantee against nationalization of foreign assets without compensation was provided under Article 157 of the new Constitution of Sri Lanka adopted in 1978.

Accompanying Policies and the Investment Climate

It is evident from the foregoing discussion that the liberalization reforms initiated in 1977 have resulted in a significant opening of the Sri Lankan economy. The reform process has been successful in virtually eliminating quantitative restrictions, reinforcing tariffs as the main instruments for regulating import trade. Tariff levels have also come down over the years. Export producers were provided with duty-free access to imported inputs from the very beginning of the reform process. Liberalization of the foreign investment regime has gone hand in hand with trade liberalization. Before proceeding to an assessment of the impact of these significant reforms, it is important to consider the other elements of the reform process that have a bearing on manufacturing performance. While there is no consensus on the timing and sequencing of these accompanying reforms, it is generally believed that the ability of a country to capture the full benefits of trade and investment liberalization depends crucially on the concurrent liberalization of domestic commodity, financial, and labor markets, and the maintenance of macroeconomic stability (Krueger 1994; Michaely, Papageorgiou, and Choksi 1991).

The liberalization reforms in Sri Lanka involved the dismantling of various price controls and state trading monopolies. For political-economic reasons, the proposed privatization/rationalization of state-owned manufacturing enterprises lost much of its rigor in the process of implementation, but it was successfully established as part of the second-wave liberalization.

With the privatization of state-owned enterprises, a major impediment to trade liberalization and a source of pressure policy reversal was weakened. However, the implementation of reforms in other areas fell well short of what was proposed in the original reform package. For instance, in the area of domestic financial sector reforms, the reforms never went beyond some limited opening of the banking sector to the partial entry of foreign banks and permission for domestic banks to operate foreign currency banking units. Proposals to reform labor legislation and the institutional mechanism for wage setting were abandoned in the face of strong resistance and legal challenges by the trade unions (Weerakoon 1996).

The 1997 reform package was formulated with due emphasis on the complementarity between macroeconomic management and the trade liberalization outcome. Thus, trade liberalization was accompanied by significant exchange rate reform. The dual exchange rate system, which had been in operation since 1968, was abolished and the new unified rate was placed under a managed float. The exchange rate was to be adjusted daily to reflect changes in foreign exchange market conditions. The other elements of the macroeconomic policy mix included a significant interest rate reform and a number of measures to ensure fiscal prudence. The latter measures included attempts to reduce the budget deficit, which had been the major source of macroeconomic imbalance, through significant cuts in various consumer and producer subsidies, restraints on budgetary transfers to SOEs, and limits on inflationary financing of the budget deficit.

The policy commitment to sound macroeconomic management was short-lived, however. Government policies soon resulted in the generation of inflationary pressures. The chief source of macroeconomic instability and pressure on the real exchange rate in the early postreform period was a massive public sector investment program that included the Mahaweli scheme, a billion-dollar multipurpose irrigation project, a large public housing program, and an urban development program (Athukorala and Jayasuriya 1994). The Central Bank intensified its intervention in the foreign exchange market and eventually (in November 1982) abandoned the practice of determining the exchange rate daily. From the mid-1980s, the escalation of the civil war begun to hamper the government's attempt to maintain macroeconomic stability. As the widening budget deficit became the major source of macroeconomic instability, the Central Bank naturally succumbed to using the nominal exchange rate as an "anchor" for inflation control. Consequently, the significant real exchange rate depreciation achieved in the immediate aftermath of the economic opening gradually dissipated in the ensuing years, with the exception of a short-lived improvement achieved through greater nominal exchange rate flexibility in 1990–94 (Athukorala and Rajapatirana 2000).

In sum, the preconditions required in order to benefit from trade and investment liberalization were missing during much of the postreform period, except for two subperiods, 1977–82 and 1990–94, because the political stability needed to capture the full benefits of economic liberalization was largely missing for much of the remainder of the postreform period. Thus, Sri Lanka provides us with an interesting case study to examine whether an outward-oriented policy regime can yield a superior industrialization outcome as compared with a controlled regime, even in the absence of required complementary reforms and under the severe strains of the war.

Manufacturing Performance

Growth Trends

The manufacturing sector entered a rapid growth phase following the 1977 reforms (Table 13.2). In the late 1980s the pattern changed; in most years, manufacturing growth surpassed that of other sectors. As a result, the manufacturing share of the gross domestic product (GDP) increased from 11 percent in the early 1980s to over 16 percent by the mid-1990s. In 1978–2000 manufacturing output grew at an average annual rate of 8.5 percent as compared with 4.8 percent during the decade preceding the reforms. Since the mid-1980s, there has been an increasingly close relationship between manufacturing growth and GDP growth.[4]

Manufacturing growth, however, has not been uniform over the past two decades. There was considerable volatility and periodic fluctuation in growth, reflecting policy shifts and changes in the overall investment climate (mostly associated with the course of the protracted civil war). The most impressive growth performance was in the first half of the 1990s when there was firm political commitment to reforms, macroeconomic conditions were relatively favorable, and the debilitating effect of the civil war had been temporarily brought under control through an informal truce. Unfortunately, the resumption of the civil war and its impact on both macroeconomic stability and country-risk perceptions, combined with the lack of clear policy directions and adverse developments in global markets in the aftermath of the 1997–98 East Asian crisis, constrained manufacturing performance in 1995–2001. The average annual manufacturing growth declined from 9.5 percent during 1990–95 to 6.0 percent during 1996–2001.

Table 13.2

Key Indicators of Manufacturing Performance, 1965–1996 (%)

	GDP growth	Growth of value added	Share in GDP	Capacity utilization	Export growth	Export-output ratio
1950–59	3.7	1.3	7.2	n.d.	n.d.	n.d.
1960–64	4.5	7.8	6.2	n.d.	n.d.	n.d.
1965–69	4.9	11.5	10.6	n.d.	n.d.	n.d.
1970–76	2.9	3.6	11.4	54	68.4	4.1
1978–80	6.1	6.3	11.2	72	55.8	18.4
1981–83	5.3	5.2	11.1	75	17.3	27.9
1984–86	4.8	9.3	12.1	75	18.1	35.0
1987–89	2.1	6.3	13.7	79	11.1	41.1
1990–92	5.0	10.4	16.2	82	24.6	50.8
1993–95	6.0	9.2	17.7	84	10.2	62.5
1996	3.8	7.2	16.5	83	18.1	60.3
1997	6.3	10.0	16.6	84	15.0	62.9
1998	4.7	7.5	16.8	84	6.1	63.4
1999	4.3	4.5	16.4	83	–2.2	63.0
2000	6.0	10.0	16.8	85	19.1	70.4
2001	–1.5	–3.8	16.0	80	–11.9	66.6
2002	4.0	2.6	15.9	81	–2.3	63.4
2003	5.5	5.1	15.6	n.d.	n.d.	n.d.

Source: Compiled from Central Bank, *Review of the Economy and Annual Report* (various issues).

Notes: Capacity utilization and export output ratio relate to "organized" manufacturing only. Others are economy-wide indicators.

Manufacturing excluding primary processing of plantation crops.

n.d.—no data available.

At the time of market-oriented policy reforms in 1977, SOEs accounted for over 60 percent of manufacturing output and 50 percent of manufacturing employment. This public sector dominance continued virtually unchanged until about the mid-1980s. From about the mid-1980s, the position of SOEs continuously eroded in the face of rapid output growth in private sector ventures and privatization of an increasing number of SOEs in the 1990s. SOEs accounted for less than 3 percent of total manufacturing output by the turn of the century.[5]

The response of private sector manufacturing to the new policy environment has exhibited rather contrasting patterns across sectors (Table 13.3). As one would expect, labor-intensive, export-oriented sectors—wearing

Table 13.3

Growth and Composition of Manufacturing Output, 1974–2000

		Growth (%)				Composition (%)			
		1974–1981	1981–1988	1988–1995	1995–2000	1981	1988	1995	2000
	Food	6.9	29.5	14.4	4.6	8.1	25.5	15.0	17.4
313	Beverages	-4.1	22.0	29.7	-2.8	1.4	13.1	11.1	9.2
314	Tobacco	1.2	11.4	3.5	3.1	19	1.7	11.2	13.8
321	Textiles	-4.0	10.1	29.2	6.0	8.9	10.3	9.4	11.0
322	Clothing	24.2	11.4	24.2	5.2	21.6	12.9	19.4	19.4
323	Leather goods	-2.5	-5.1	47.4	0.6	0.5	0.3	0.4	0.4
324	Footwear	-2.3	18.8	25.6	3.4	1.2	1.8	2.3	2.0
331	Wood products	7.5	12.0	31.2	-5.0	0.3	1.3	1.1	0.5
332	Furniture	5.9	6.7	23.1	4.8	0.2	0.2	0.2	0.1
341	Paper and paper products	-8.2	11.6	18.1	18.1	1.3	3.3	1.3	2.0
342	Printing and publishing		22.6	10.4	-1.7	1.2	1.9	1.4	0.7
351	Industrial chemicals	-5.3	10.6	30.1	4.8	0.8	0.4	0.8	0.7
352	Other chemicals	5.8	6.9	16.6	-1.1	10.8	3.9	5.2	3.3
355	Rubber goods	16.6	-3.7	38.9	0.7	6.6	5.0	5.7	5.6
356	Plastic goods	5.5	7.8	20.7	4.2	3	1.4	1.7	1.8
361	Pottery	5.2	19.3	6.6	-3.2	0.9	2.3	1.6	1.1

(continued)

278

Table 13.3 *(continued)*

		Growth (%)				Composition (%)			
		1974–1981	1981–1988	1988–1995	1995–2000	1981	1988	1995	2000
361	Pottery	5.2	19.3	6.6	-3.2	0.9	2.3	1.6	1.1
362	Glass and glass products	4.8	6.2	-9.5	13.8	0.9	0.6	0.2	0.5
369	Nonmetallic mineral products	-8.3	34.4	6.8	4.1	0.6	4.8	2.7	2.9
371	Iron and steel basic industries	3.8	9.0	17.4	1.5	0.5	1.1	0.9	0.2
372	Nonferrous metal basic industries				-18.3		0.0	0.3	0.0
381	Fabricated metal products	-3.4	8.3	15.9	-0.3	2.8	1.7	1.2	0.8
382	Nonelectrical machinery	-16.2	-14.0	55.2	12.0	1.5	1.4	1.3	1.8
383	Electrical machinery	-2.5	-0.7	20.4	6.7	4	0.0	1.5	1.7
384	Transport equipment	-14.4	20.1	18.2	-0.7	0.6	1.2	0.7	0.9
	Professional equipment				5.9			0.1	0.1
390	Other manufacturing	8.3	29.4	19.6	-13.9	1.5	4.0	3.3	2.0
	Total manufacturing	4.0	14.0	20.0	3.5	100	100	100	100

Source: Athukorala and Rajapatirana (2000), table 8.2, updated using the same methodology and data sources.
Notes: See Table 13.5.

apparel, footwear, rubber goods, and leather products—indicated impressive growth performance. The only import-substitution production sector that has generally recorded increase in output and employment shares was food and beverages. The share of clothing in total manufacturing value added and employment increased from less than 10 percent in the mid-1980s to over 35 percent by the mid-1990s. In recent years, the production structure has become more diversified as domestic market-oriented industries gradually developed market niches in the new liberalized economy and some new export-oriented industries (in particular natural rubber-based products, ceramics, footwear, and travel goods) gradually expanded.

The overall export orientation of manufacturing tended to increase sharply beginning in the mid-1980s (Table 13.2). The export coefficient (the ratio of exports to gross manufacturing output) increased from a mere 4 percent in the late 1970s to over 50 percent by the late 1980s and over 70 percent by the late 1990s.

Trends and Patterns of Manufactured Exports

By the time of the 1977 policy reforms, the share of manufactures in total merchandise exports was only 5 percent. Since then, manufactured goods have emerged as the most dynamic element in the export structure. Exports of manufactured goods grew (in current U.S. dollar terms) at an annual compound rate of over 30 percent in 1978–2002, lifting their share in total exports to over 70 percent. The value of total manufacturing exports increased from a mere $5 million in the mid-1960s to over $4 billion by the late 1990s. In 1985–2000, Sri Lanka was among the top five low-income countries in terms of both average annual growth in earnings from manufactured exports and increase in manufacturing share in total merchandise exports (UNCTAD 2002).

Manufactured exports of Sri Lanka are heavily concentrated in a single standard labor-intensive consumer good, clothing (Table 13.3). However, from the late 1980s, there has been a noticeable increase in exports of other labor-intensive products such as electronics (included under the commodity category of "machinery"), leather goods, footwear, toys, plastic products, jewelry, and resource-based products related to traditional agricultural exports (tea, rubber, and coconut fiber). Reflecting this ongoing pattern of commodity diversification, the share of clothing in total manufacturing exports declined from 72 percent in the early 1980s to 60 percent in the mid-1990s (Table 13.4). The share of natural rubber (the second largest of the traditional "trio") in total exports has declined sharply, reaching less than 1 percent in 2002, as a result of the rapid growth of rubber-based manufactured products.

Table 13.4

Composition and Growth of Merchandise Exports, 1975–2002

	Composition (%)						Growth (%)		
	1975/76	1980/81	1985/86	1990/91	1995/96	2001/2	1975–1989	1990–2000	1975–2002
Primary products	85.5	67.1	57.1	42.0	29.9	22.8	2.5	3.7	2.7
Tea	46.0	32.7	29.7	23.6	13.9	14.2	1.7	5.5	3.0
Rubber	17.4	14.2	7.3	3.6	2.0	0.5	-1.3	-9.6	-0.5
Coconut products	11.0	6.9	7.2	3.6	2.2	1.7	0.6	3.5	0.1
Manufactured goods including petroleum products	14.5	32.9	42.9	58.0	70.1	77.2	17.2	10.6	15.1
Petroleum products	9.7	16.9	8.9	4.6	2.2	1.5	1.7	0.5	0.5
Manufactured exports excluding petroleum products	4.8	16.1	34.0	53.4	67.9	75.7	25.4	11.1	19.1
Food, excluding fish	0.2	0.4	0.4	0.6	1.3	1.9	12.1	19.7	17.3
Fish products	1.1	1.5	1.5	1.1	0.7	0.8	9.1	1.1	4.7
Textile	0.2	0.4	1.1	1.6	3.8	4.1	25.3	16.4	22.4
Clothing	1.0	12.2	24.1	35.2	40.0	48.1	32.4	10.8	26.6
Footwear	0.1	0.0	0.4	0.5	1.2	0.5	23.8	10.3	20.1
Ceramics	0.4	0.4	0.3	0.7	0.9	0.9		14.2	14.2ᶜ
Rubber goods	0.0	0.0	0.0	2.1	4.1	3.7		11.9	11.9ᶜ

281

Cut/polished diamonds	0.0	0.0	0.0	2.3	4.0	3.8		3.2	3.2[c]
Nonelectrical machinery	0.1	0.2	0.4	0.8	1.3	2.2	16.7	18.8	17.1
Electrical machinery	0.0	0.1	0.1	0.7	1.5	3.2	28.8	23.2	21.0
Travel goods	0.0	0.0	0.0	0.1	1.4	1.7	23.2	38.4	20.8
Toys and sporting goods	0.0	0.0	0.1	0.2	1.0	1.0	30.4	19.6	20.6
Jewelry	0.1	0.1	0.1	0.3	0.7	0.3	19.5	5.5	17.9
Other manufactured goods	1.6	0.8	5.4	11.8	6.0	3.5	38.1	11.9	14.6
Total exports	100	100	100	100	100	100			
Value (US$ millions)	567.5	1,078.8	1,274.5	1,950.1	3,955.1	4,758.8	6.9	8.5	8.6

Source: Compiled from Central Bank of Sri Lanka, Annual Report (various years).
ªComputed for two-year average exports.
ᵇAnnual compound rates estimated by fitting a logarithmic trend.
ᶜEstimates for 1990–2002.

Given the dominance of textiles and clothing in domestic manufacturing and the important role played by "quota-hopping" investors in the expansion of the industry, the likely implications of the abolition of the Multifiber Arrangement (MFA) have become a key concern in Sri Lanka. However, it appears that while some exporting firms are still involved in the production of low-end products for quota-protected markets, overall the Sri Lanka textile and clothing industry appears now to be relatively well positioned to cope with the new challenges.

Employment

In determining the effects of industrial growth on employment in Sri Lanka, one is handicapped by relatively poor data. The coverage of the available employment and wage data is limited to production units in the organized (formal) manufacturing sector. Even for that sector, consistent data series of adequate length (encompassing both pre- and postreform years) are not available. Nevertheless, several interesting facts emerge from the scanty data (Table 13.5).

The postreform years witnessed an impressive increase in manufacturing employment. According to data from the Annual Survey of Industry conducted by the Department of Census and Statistics (CDS), total employment in organized manufacturing (i.e., firms employing more than 5 workers) increased from 142,000 in 1978 to over 500,000 by 2000 (Table 13.5). According to the CDS Labour Force Survey, island-wide manufacturing employment increased from 648,000 in 1985 to 788,000 by the mid-1990s and passed the 1 million mark in 2000. The share of manufacturing employment in total employment increased from around 10 percent in the early 1980s to over 17 percent by the end of the 1990s. The manufacturing sector contributed over 36 percent of the increase in total employment in the economy between 1990–91 and 2001–2. The increase in manufacturing employment has come primarily from private sector manufacturing, in a context where employment in SOEs declined sharply because of output contraction caused by import competition and subsequently closing down and privatization.

Export-oriented manufacturing accounts for the bulk of new employment opportunities. Total local employment in export-oriented BOI firms increased from around 10,000 in the early 1980s to over 416,000 in 2002 (or 40 percent of total manufacturing employment). The export-oriented garment industry contributed to over 35 percent of total employment in organized manufacturing by the mid-1990s. This share declined slowly in subsequent years, reflecting the rapid expansion of other export-oriented industries such as rubber products, ceramics, footwear, and travel goods.

Table 13.5

Manufacturing Employment and Related Data

	Employment (no. of workers)				Real earning per worker	Labor productivity (1980 = 100)	Wage share in value added (%)
	CDS QLS	CDS-MFS	SOE	BOI	RE	RLP	E/Vad
1978		142,347	63,530	261	118.3	96.6	26.6
1979		160,816	75,150	5,876	111.8	85.7	28.01
1980		161,844	70,371	10,538	100.0	100.0	25.7
1981		151,549	66,355	19,727	95.0	112.2	24.2
1982			71,255	24,926	80.9	97.3	19.4
1983		202,100	70,182	27,805	81.1	121.3	17.9
1984		212,332	64,292	32,725	83.6	110.4	17.6
1985	648,000	210,465	58,446	35,786	101.5	135.1	17.3
1986		217,146	54,332	45,047	101.7	131.5	17.2
1987		212,223	54,049	50,743	105.8	130	16.7
1988		219,278	52,050	54,626	105.9	137.3	17.6
1989		243,705	52,611	61,429	100.1	134.2	17.5
1990	669,000	281,114	45,283	71,358	95.0	137.8	17.6
1991	751,000	315,582	40,066	85,457	102.5	142.7	19.5
1992	650,000	289,155	41,394	104,220	100.4	160.1	19.3
1993	684,000	356,950	39,902	122,165	106.6	165.0	20.8
1994	756,000	520,596	36,714	205,660	92.3	149.6	20.5
1995	788,000	514,561	40,436	223,367	94.0	148.0	20.0
1996	807,000	499,052	40,175	241,970	88.6	151.8	19.1
1997	920,000	458,032	38,804	285,663	87.7	165.2	17.7
1998	858,000	462,358	37,698	294,381	88.4	173.6	17.8
1999	902,000	469,132	36,154	327,059	92.5	181.3	17.5
2000	1,045,000	500,366	33,947	367,849	93.6	164.7	19.5
2001	1,057,000		33,513	386,034			
2002	1,092,000		32,614	416,756			

Sources: CDS QLS: Data from the quarterly labor-force survey conducted by the Department of Census and Statistics (cover total manufacturing employment).

CDS ASI: Data from the Annual Survey of Industry conducted by the Department of Census and Statistics (cover employment in firms employing more than five workers).

SOE: Employment in state-owned manufacturing enterprises, from Central Bank *Annual Report* (various issues).

BOI: Employment in firms set up under section 17 of the Board of Investment (BOI) Law. Real earning per worker, real labor productivity, and wage share in value added were compiled using data from the Department of Census and Statistics, *Annual Survey of Industry* (various issues).

The employment impact of new export-oriented industries would look even more impressive if employment in small-scale manufacturing were appropriately accounted for. Many export-oriented firms in the garment, toy, and shoe industries have production subcontracting arrangements with small-scale producers in the unorganized sector.

The increase in manufacturing employment has not been accompanied by an increase in real manufacturing wages. Real wages either declined or stagnated throughout the postreform period. At the same time, labor productivity (real value added per worker) recorded impressive growth over this period. The combined outcome of these developments has somewhat shifted the distribution of total factor income in favor of the employers. The share of employee remuneration (wages and other benefits) in manufacturing value added declined from over 20 percent in the early 1970s to about 17 percent since the mid-1980s. These patterns in the distribution of factor income and the real wage behavior are very much in line with what the theory predicts about the process of industrial adjustment in a labor-surplus economy under export-led industrialization.

Even if the expansion of manufacturing caused relative poverty to worsen through an increased relative share of profits in total factor income as noted above, rapid manufacturing employment growth, coupled with the compositional changes in employment, would have led to a decline in absolute poverty. Reflecting the rapid expansion of export-oriented light manufacturing, the share of female workers in total manufacturing employment increased from 32 percent in the early 1980s to over 60 percent by 1999–2000. There has also been a significant shift in the occupational composition in manufacturing, in favor of unskilled and semiskilled workers. Manual workers (unskilled, semiskilled, and skilled workers) accounted for over 90 percent of total employment in BOI firms in 2002.

The Role of Foreign Direct Investment

Having averaged less than half a million dollars a year in 1970–76, net FDI inflows increased rapidly in the postreform period reaching US$64 million in 1982 (Table 13.6). The outbreak of the war in 1983 severely disrupted this impressive trend and annual flows were in the range of only US$17–$58 million. The second-wave reforms and the temporary cessation of hostilities during the first half of the 1990s witnessed a notable surge in FDI, which increased to an all-time high of US$184 million in 1993. The relative contribution of net FDI inflows to private sector fixed capital formation increased from 0.1 percent during 1970–77 to 5 percent during 1978–89, and to over 12 percent during 1990–94. However, FDI inflows have declined since 1995 both in absolute terms and in relation to fixed capital formation until 2002.

Table 13.6

Net Foreign Direct Investment (NDFI) **Inflow to Sri Lanka**

	NFDI, US$ millions	NFDI as a percentage of gross domestic capital formation
1970–1976	0.4	0.2
1977	1.2	0.3
1978	1.5	0.6
1979	46.9	10.6
1980	43	7.8
1981	49.3	8.6
1982	63.6	9.1
1983	37.8	5.4
1984	32.6	4.5
1985	24.8	3.8
1986	29.2	4.0
1987	58.2	8.2
1988	46.6	5.7
1989	17.6	2.3
1990	42.5	2.9
1991	100	5.6
1992	119.2	9.4
1993	183.8	2.4
1994	158.2	1.8
1995	16.2	1.7
1996	86.3	4.1
1997	129.2	13.6
1998	137.2	5.6
1999	176.8	4.7
2000	172.7	4.3
2001	82.1	5.7
2002	229.8	7.3
2003	225.7	6.3

Source: Compiled from Central Bank of Sri Lanka, *Annual Report* (various years).

Data relating to individual projects set up with FDI participation (henceforth referred to as "foreign firms") points to a clear shift in FDI from domestic market-oriented to export-oriented activities. In 1967–77, a total of 82 foreign manufacturing firms were set up in Sri Lanka. Of these, only 13 were export-oriented ventures (9 garment; 2 gem cutting; 1 ceramics; 1 wall-tiles) (Athukorala 1995). In contrast, out of 2,041 foreign firms set up in 1978–2002,

1,341 received approval under the BOI special incentive scheme for export-oriented firms. These firms accounted for over 90 percent of envisaged investment and employment for all projects. In addition, a considerable number of firms (over 125) approved under general incentive provisions are believed to export a significant share of their output (Athukorala 1995).

Standard labor-intensive manufacturing has been the main attraction to foreign investors, with a heavy concentration in the garment industry. During the early stages, the dominant factor behind the surge of clothing exports through FDI participation was the quota restrictions imposed by the major importing countries on imports from "traditional" developing country producers in East Asia under the Multifiber Arrangement. This was clearly evident from the predominance of firms from Hong Kong, the major developing-country exporter of garments, in Sri Lanka's export-oriented garment industry.

Since the later 1980s, there has been a noticeable increase in the number of foreign firms in other labor-intensive activities, in particular, footwear, travel goods, plastic products, and diamond cutting and jewelry. There has also been an increase in processing of primary products that were previously exported in raw form, notably, rubber-based products (heavy duty tires, rubber bands, and surgical gloves) and ceramics. Initially, the surge of FDI in the garment industry responded to the imposition by developed countries of quota restrictions on garment imports from traditional East Asian developing countries under the MFA. However, by 1983, garment exports from Sri Lanka had also come under quota restrictions, and the BOI stopped approval of new investors in quota-restricted product categories. Since then, new foreign firms in the garment industry, predominantly involved in the production of nonquota garments, have increased. According to BOI firm-level data there were twenty-three nonquota garment-producing foreign firms that accounted for 10 percent of total garment exports by BOI-approved firms. By 2002, these figures had increased to 36 percent and 42 percent, respectively. Another important recent development is the setting up by foreign firms of a number of yarn and textile producing factories to supply input to the garment industry.

There is a close association between the growth of manufactured exports and the share of foreign firms (Table 13.7). The share of foreign firms in total manufacturing exports increased from 24 percent in 1977 to over 65 percent in 1992. Over 80 percent of the total increment in export value (in US$) from 1980–95 came from foreign firms. There has been a decline in the share of foreign earned income in recent years, but by 2002 it was still high at over 47 percent. This decline mostly reflects the success of "pure" local firms in expanding exports of standard light manufactured goods (mostly garments) and benefiting from the market links established though their connections

Table 13.7

**Foreign Firms' Contribution to Manufactured Export Expansion,
1976–1995** (three-year averages)

| | Manufactured exports | | | |
	US$ million	Average annual growth	Manufacturing share in total merchandise exports	Share of foreign firms in manufactured exports
1975–1977	25	14.5	4.0	23.2
1978–1980	103	63.6	10.4	30.2
1981–1983	235	23.0	22.1	43.7
1984–1986	421	24.1	31.9	47.4
1987–1989	654	14.8	44.2	58.2
1990–1992	1,083	32.8	56.6	65.8
1993–1995	2,248	13.5	71.8	62.3
1996–1998	3,269	13.1	72.2	46.1
1999–2001	3,750	1.7	75.6	47.5
2002	3,562	−2.3	75.7	47.0

Source: Athukorala (1995), table 4, updated to 1995 using the same data.

with foreign firms (see below). Foreign firms still dominate "nontraditional" product areas such as travel goods, heavy-duty tires, surgical gloves, and electronics assembly. In 2002, these firms accounted for over 80 percent of total nongarment manufactured exports.[6]

Apart from the "direct" contribution captured in these data, there is evidence that the presence of foreign firms generates significant positive spillover effects on the export success of local export-producing firms (Athukorala 1995). Following the entry of foreign firms into clothing and other light consumer goods industries in Sri Lanka, many international buying groups that had long-established market links with these firms also set up buying offices in the country. These buying offices have subsequently begun to play a crucial role in linking local firms with highly competitive international markets for these products. Furthermore, over 80 percent of export-oriented foreign firms in Sri Lanka operate through joint ventures set up with local entrepreneurs. Local entrepreneurs seem to make use of joint-venture operations with foreign investors as a means of acquiring the production and marketing skills required for the successful operation of their own (independent) production units (Athukorala 1995; Lal and Wignaraja 1992). There are also many cases in which the local partner takes over the entire production operation and continues to thrive in the export business after an initial stage of joint-venture operation. What all this analysis suggests is that the spillover effects of the presence of foreign firms have, to a significant extent, contributed to the export success of local firms.

Athukorala and Rajapatirana (2000) have undertaken an econometric analysis of the determinants of manufactured exports of Sri Lanka, with emphasis on the role of FDI. The results suggest that the significant involvement of foreign firms in export-oriented manufacturing contributed to a considerable weakening of the link between the real exchange rate and export performance. The choices of international production locations by export-oriented foreign firms are governed mainly by the relative attractiveness of the country compared with other investment locations. The nature of the trade and investment regimes and the availability of required inputs (mostly labor) are the key considerations. The domestic incentive structure per se, which determines the relative profitability of exporting compared with selling domestically in a given host country, is not the prime criterion. Given this feature of the behavior of foreign investors and their significant presence in domestic manufacturing, Sri Lanka has been able to achieve rapid export growth despite a less than satisfactory domestic incentive structure.

Conclusions

The liberalization reforms initiated in 1977 resulted in a significant opening of the Sri Lankan economy. The reform process has been successful in virtually eliminating quantitative restrictions and reinforcing tariffs as the main instrument for regulating import trade. Tariff levels have also come down over the years, and export producers have enjoyed duty-free access to imported inputs from the very beginning of the reform process. Liberalization of the foreign investment regime has gone hand in hand with trade liberalization.

These reforms have led to far-reaching changes in the structure and performance of the manufacturing sector in the Sri Lankan economy. The manufacturing sector has become increasingly export oriented, and it is no longer reliant on the fortunes of the traditional primary export industries to obtain required imported inputs. With the gradual erosion of the dominant role of SOEs, the private sector has been largely responsible for the growth of manufacturing in recent years. Despite some output disruption in the immediate aftermath of the removal of trade restrictions, the manufacturing sector has turned in an improved performance in terms of output, productivity, and employment, confounding the predictions of pessimists who expected trade liberalization to set in motion a process of deindustrialization. The gains from export-oriented industrialization have been impressive enough to set the stage for bipartisan acceptance of an outward-oriented policy stance as the centerpiece of national development policy—a landmark development in Sri Lanka's postindependence policy history.

It is important to note that what has been achieved in Sri Lanka under liberalization reforms occurred while civil war had been persisting for much of the period. Quite apart from the direct debilitating effect of political risk on investor perception, the civil war hampered capture of the full benefits of economic opening through delays and inconsistencies in the implementation of the reform process and macroeconomic instability emanating from massive war financing.

In this context, the Sri Lankan experience with export-led industrialization so far can be explained as the joint outcome of trade liberalization, which increased the potential returns to investments that capitalize on the country's comparative advantage, and investment liberalization, which permitted the entry of international firms that have the capacity to take advantage of such profit opportunities. Despite political risk and policy uncertainty, rapid export growth was consistent with this policy configuration as it ensured a handsome profit in labor-intensive export production in a labor-abundant economy, which is usually characterized by a short payback period. Interestingly, the Sri Lankan experience over the past two decades has clearly demonstrated that an outward-oriented policy regime can yield a superior industrial outcome as compared with a closed-economy regime, even under the severe strains of political and macroeconomic instability.

Notes

1. Sri Lanka's postindependence policy history has been well documented. See, for instance, Snodgrass (1966 and 1998), Lal and Rajapatirana (1989), Athukorala and Jayasuriya (1994), Athukorala and Rajapatirana (2000).

2. The first EPZ, at Katunakaye (KEPZ) near the Colombo International Airport was opened in 1978. The remarkable success of the KEPZ paved the way for setting up a second EPZ in Biyagama (BEPZ) in 1982, and a third in Koggala (KGEPZ) in June 1991.

3. The *Asian Wall Street Journal* (September 23, 1980) reported the managing director of Lehman Brothers as saying, "I do not see what more an investor could want than Sri Lanka has to offer." In a comparison of relative labor productivity (which combined both efficiency and wage cost) of Asian workers that appeared in *Business Asia* (June 2, 1978), Sri Lanka (42) was placed ahead of the Philippines (41), Taiwan (34), Korea (21), and India (12), and only next to Singapore (47). The *Far Eastern Economic Review* (October 23, 1978) dubbed Sri Lanka "the new investment centre in Asia."

4. The correlation coefficient between two annual growth rates for the period 1986–2000 is 0.72, compared with 0.35 for 1960–96.

5. The data used in this chapter, unless otherwise indicated, come from the Central Bank of Sri Lanka, Annual Report.

6. Estimated using data provided by the Board of Investment.

References

Amsden, Alice H. 1997. "Editorial: Bringing Production Back in: Understanding Government's Economic Role in Late Industrialization." *World Development* 25 (1997): 469–80.

Athukorala, Premachandra. 1995. "Foreign Direct Investment and Manufacturing for Export in a New Exporting Country: The Case of Sri Lanka." *World Economy* 14, no. 2: 543–64.

Athukorala, Premachandra, and Sisira Jayasuriya. 1994. *Macroeconomic Policies, Crises and Growth in Sri Lanka, 1969–90*. Washington, DC: World Bank.

Athukorala, Premachandra, and S. Rajapatirana. 2000. *Liberalisation and Industrial Transformation: Sri Lanka in International Perspective*. Oxford and New Delhi: Oxford University Press.

Bhagwati, Jagdish. 1994. "Free Trade: Old and New Challenges." *Economic Journal* 104 (1994): 231–46.

Helleiner, Gerald K. 1994. "Introduction." In *Trade Policy and Industrialization in Turbulent Times*, ed. Helleiner. London: Routledge.

Krueger, Anne O. 1992. *Economic Policy Reforms in Developing Countries*. Oxford: Basil Blackwell.

———. 1994. "Problems of Liberalisation." In *World Economic Growth*, ed. Arnold Harberger, 403–23. San Francisco: Institute for Contemporary Studies Press.

———. 1997. "Trade Policy and Economic Development: How We Learn." *American Economic Review* 87: 1–22.

Lal, Deepak, and Sarath Rajapatirana. 1989. "Impediments to Trade Liberalization in Sri Lanka." *Thames Essays* no. 51. Aldershot, UK: Gower.

Lal, Deepak, and G. Wignaraja. 1992. "Foreign Involvement by European Firms and Garment Exports by Developing Countries." *Asian-Pacific Development Journal* 1, no. 2: 21–28.

Little, I.M.D. 1994. "Trade and Industrialization Revisited." *Pakistan Development Review* 33 (1994): 359–81.

Michaely, Michael; D. Papageorgiou; and A. Choksi. 1991. *Liberalizing Foreign Trade: Lessons of Experience in the Developing World*. Oxford: Basil Blackwell.

Rodrik, Dani. 2003. "Introduction: What Do We Learn from Country Narratives." In *In Search of Prosperity: Analytic Narratives on Economic Growth*, ed. Rodrik. Princeton, NJ: Princeton University Press.

Snodgrass, D.R. 1966. *Sri Lanka: An Export Economy in Transition*. Homewood, IL: Richard D. Irwin.

———. 1998. "The Economic Development of Sri Lanka: A Tale of Missed Opportunities." In *Creating Peace in Sri Lanka: Civil War and Reconciliation*, ed. Robert I. Rotberg, 89–107. Washington, DC: Brookings Institution Press.

United Nations Conference on Trade and Development (UNCTAD). 2002. *Trade and Development Report, 2002*. Geneva.

Weerakoon, T.S. 1996. "Organizational Performance—A Stakeholder Concept." In *Proceedings of the First International Research Conference on Quality Management*, Monash University, Melbourne, 80–90.

14

Globalization and Economic Development

Sajid Anwar and Bob Catley

Globalization is transforming the world into a single market that is likely to lead to a more efficient allocation of resources. However, the benefits of globalization are available only if countries give up some measure of independence and autonomy in decision making. The full benefits of globalization cannot be enjoyed unless free movement of goods, services, labor, and capital across borders is supplemented by the development of common economic institutions. The failure of the recent World Trade Organization (WTO) talks in Cancún centered around the fundamental question of equitable distribution of gains from free trade indicates that the aim of efficient allocation of resources worldwide will not be achieved anytime soon. Developing countries believe that trade liberalization is likely to lead to relatively greater benefits to the developed countries. Nonetheless, the form of contemporary opposition to free trade and globalization means that its success would likely result in increasingly nationalist economic policies and politicians. Deteriorating economic conditions may lead to social pressures that might result in protectionism, thereby canceling all steps that have been taken to open up worldwide markets. The opponents of globalization have argued that it can widen inequality, increase poverty, and increase social exclusion. It is therefore necessary for governments to take steps to check the widening gap between the rich and the poor. The Asian financial crisis of 1997–98 suggests that the unregulated free flow of capital can convert an export-led economy into an import-led (and poorer) economy if policy regimes are badly handled.

South Asian economies have, until recently, lagged behind the Southeast Asian economies. South Asian economies have no choice but to fully embrace globalization. India, the economic giant in the region, has attracted significant foreign investment in recent years due to its political stability, well-developed legal system, and the availability of highly skilled workers. There has been a significant increase in trade between India and Pakistan in recent years. However, the continuing border dispute between India and Pakistan is a major obstacle to closer economic cooperation in South Asia. The South Asian region would greatly benefit from a free trade agreement, but this would require the separation of political and economic considerations.

Globalization can be viewed as a shift toward a more integrated and interdependent world economy. Globalization provides opportunities for factors of production such as land, labor, capital, and entrepreneurship to extend beyond domestic markets and thus allows for a greater degree of economies of scale in production and sales potential. This specialization would tend to equalize the returns of these factors of production. They could then operate on a wider dimension, with the possibility of both the opportunity for greater agglomerations of capital and technology (such as the U.S. pursuit of the worldwide cell phone and Internet systems) and a better identification of niche processes (enabling the Finnish economy to pursue a one-corporate model in Nokia).

Globalization is a process by which the world economy is being transformed from a set of national and regional markets into a set of markets that operate with decreasing regard for national boundaries. The trend toward globalization is facilitated by the development of cheaper communication technologies, deregulation, and the declining cost of transport. Globalization creates a competitive drive that weakens nationally established monopolies and protected industries. Rather than a policy option, globalization has become a necessity. Globalization is particularly important for less developed countries because it provides the means of future economic growth for developing countries.[1]

As Adam Smith might have argued, the extent of specialization is extended by the greater size of the market. Globalization is closely linked to economic growth, which is related to the growth of international trade.[2] In one sense, this is merely the extended application of the simple theory of comparative advantage in which the production possibility frontier of each participating economy shifts outward. This extended process of globalization is often masked by the identification of the narrower phenomenon of multinational corporations (MNCs) as being among the main engines of globalization, which is driven, in their case, by capital-seeking profits from operating across national borders. Certainly MNCs are able to establish production operations in different countries, utilize their advanced technologies and hence comparative advantage in production, and then trade within their own company or with other such companies, particularly in high value-added goods to gain market advantage. But stronger economic growth is also driven by the reorganization of factors of production within national economies, thereby enabling capital and labor as a whole to achieve higher productivity, often through greater specialization, not just those sectors attached directly to cross-national economic institutions.

As this process of economic globalization proceeds, certainly, it impacts on other aspects of human organization. Critics charge that globalization will destroy the political power of a community by eroding the capacity of the state to operate as a defender of local customs and laws, as an agency for mitigating the egalitarian impact of an unrestrained market, and as a regulator checking the power of large organizations of capital. They also argue that cherished aspects of society and culture may be homogenized by the conformist-encouraging products and marketing methods of private institutions with a global reach and an interest in creating a more uniform market for their products. Common targets for critics of this process are internationally recognized brand names generated by a combination of quality, astute marketing, and product composition assurance in sectors as diverse as processed food, clothing, and automobiles. Whereas economic theorists may celebrate the consumer confidence and buyer assurance that these relationships generate, critics emphasize the associated destruction of native and localized products and production processes. An early example of this criticism involved the destruction of the indigenous muslin industry in India after the East India Company established and then introduced mass-produced British textiles. More recently, the introduction of MNC-based fast-food outlets has generated criticism, especially of Kentucky Fried Chicken by local Indian food outlets selling chicken. An even more recent phenomenon has involved the adverse identification of some U.S. brand names, such as Coca-Cola and McDonalds, but not all—IBM and Boeing seem exempt—with U.S. foreign policy.

Globalization, for the purposes of this chapter, may be divided into two broad categories: the globalization of markets and the globalization of production. The globalization of markets is the coming together of distinct, segmented and separate national markets into a single global market. Globalization of markets is not the same as standardization. As far as many consumer goods are concerned, at present, due to cultural and other differences, there is still little convergence in taste.[3] This remains true in many areas of processed food, clothing, and cultural output, such as music. However in the area of capital-intensive manufactured products tastes are very similar, as, for example, with microprocessors, cars, and aircraft. The same applies to the market for financial assets. Due to improvements in standards of living, customers are demanding specialized and customized products that draw from worldwide best practice.

Globalization of production refers to the inclination of firms to source goods and services from locations around the globe to take advantage of the availability of cheaper factors of production. This allows firms to reduce the average cost of production per unit of output. This has been enabled by earlier investments in transportation systems that have allowed the cost of transporting each unit of output to fall rapidly. Japanese automobile manufacturers were able to create a world market for their product by investing in specialized bulk carriers, before they began to locate production nearer to foreign markets when their own domestic costs of production became prohibitively high. In addition, firms are able to supply a wider range of goods and services. Consumers benefit from lower costs and greater product diversity.[4] For a firm to have a sustainable long-term competitive advantage, it has to cater to customers' needs in a way that cannot be easily copied or imitated. This must be done across a wide variety of markets. Prahalad and Hamel (1990) were among the first to reveal that managers in coming years would be judged by their ability to identify, cultivate, and exploit core competencies that make growth possible.

Globalization became a euphemism for describing business practices in the 1990s, even when the processes it described were not particularly new. Krueger (2003), among others, has indicated that globalization is not a recent phenomenon. It is a process that has been developing for centuries. It began when west Europeans developed an ocean-crossing galleon of sufficient size, speed, and durability to begin trading with the wider world without having to traverse the formidable obstacle of the Ottoman Empire. Having learned that technology, Europeans constructed a series of global commercial empires based first on the Atlantic littoral and then, by the time of the Seven Years, and Napoleonic Wars, assuming a global reach. The next leap to a more single, globally integrated market took place in the second half of the nineteenth century.

As indicated by O'Rourke and Williamson (1999), by 1914 prices for tradable goods in most domestic markets around the globe were influenced by foreign markets. Nonetheless, and despite the considerable part played by the British in the establishment of a global market based on the pound sterling, the Royal Navy, and British commercial law, by that time the global system was in fact divided into several large imperial economic systems and a myriad of localized economies.

During the period from 1914 to 1945, this fragmentation of the world economy was sustained and arguably deepened. Indeed, after some modest reliberalization in the 1920s, the impact of the depression in the 1930s was to accelerate a tendency toward national self-sufficiency. World War II was then fought between several closed imperial trading and production systems, each based on the currency of the dominant power as the medium of exchange—the sterling area, the dollar bloc, the franc zone, the Greater East Asia Co-prosperity Sphere, the Soviet bloc, and so on—competing, at least in some measure, for access to each others' closed economies.

Despite postwar attempts on the part of the victorious and economically dominant Americans, a wholly globalized economy was not immediately reconstituted. Instead, the world economy was divided into two main economic systems. One was led by the United States, which pursued decolonization through the United Nations, free trade though the General Agreement on Tariffs and Trade (GATT), and freer movement of capital via the Bretton Woods and subsequent agreements. The other, which comprised about half the human race, was committed to some sort of centrally planned economy. In addition, most sovereign states—even those within the U.S. orbit such as its North Atlantic Treaty Organization and Australia, New Zealand, United States Security Treaty allies—were committed to the use of state instrumentalities to regulate markets, production, capital movements, and international trade.

Nonetheless, the movement toward a globalized economy regained considerable momentum during the last few decades of the twentieth century.[5] The collapse of the Soviet Union in 1991 removed a major obstacle, and the realization by previously heavily regulated economies like India and China that import substitution and protectionism are not the right strategies to achieve rapid economic growth resulted in a major push for trade liberalization. As trade became more globalized, even the electorates of the largest economies, such as the United States, realized that they could not go it alone.[6] While much of the U.S. commercial and political elite had been committed to some form of globalization since 1919, during the 1990s their support was considerably widened as President Clinton campaigned for a more open U.S. economy and populist isolationists and opponents of free trade, such as Pat Buchanan, gained less and less electoral traction in a globalizing and prospering U.S. economy.

The process of globalization proceeded and accelerated during the 1990s, although a number of significant developments took place during that decade that enabled critics to point to the continuing risks of deregulation for national economies. These developments included: the massive devaluation of the Mexican peso in 1994; the Asian financial crisis of July 1997; the collapse of the Russian ruble in 1998; the fall of the Brazilian real in 1999; and, more recently, the acute financial problems surrounding currency collapse faced by Argentina. But most of these difficulties can be traced to poor domestic policy regimes constructed in the hope of accessing the benefits of globalization but diverted to other ends. These financial crises and subsequent panics were more the result of inadequate prudential supervision, especially of financial intermediaries, official corruption and consequent erosion of confidence in currencies, and of mismanaged fiscal policies than they were of access to the world market. It is nonetheless the case that a liberalized national economy, when very badly managed, may be more quickly damaged by the withdrawal of support—as was the case in all the situations cited above. Conversely, it may also be more rapidly repaired—as again was the case.

These periodic and critical developments have provided international businesses with new challenges in their operations worldwide. But they have occurred within the context of greater opportunities and economic growth as larger sectors of the globe enter the international economy. Even so, the response of some integrating countries to these crises has been to become more involved in economic integration, but under policy regimes that can be viewed as a compromise between protectionism and globalization (Baldwin et al. 1999; El Kahal 2001). For example, Malaysia successfully negotiated its way out of the 1997–98 crisis by reimposing controls, particularly on capital movements, and Asia-Pacific Economic Cooperation now seems unlikely to achieve its earlier commitment to free trade by the second decade of the twenty-first century. In South Asia, the influence of the economic and strategic partnership with the Soviet Union produced a highly developed state sector in India and its neighbor Bangladesh, socialist theorists brought economic planning to Sri Lanka, while consecutive military regimes favored state controls in Pakistan. As the Soviet bloc collapsed in the 1990s, economic liberalization belatedly took globalization to South Asia. To some extent, of course, this was fostered by the success of economic liberalization in East Asia.

As against these problems, the successful industrialization of the smaller economies of Taiwan, Singapore, South Korea, and Hong Kong convinced countries like China, in the 1980s, and India, in the 1990s, to embrace globalization. After the end of World War II, in East Asia significant progress was made toward globalization, which means that in the areas of trade, production, and finance the world has become much more interconnected and integrated than ever before. Countries that have embraced globalization have enjoyed very high rates of economic growth. It has also been argued that high economic growth has resulted in political freedom. Higher economic growth has also allowed governments to increase social spending, which has resulted in increases in life expectancy and literacy rates (Czinkota and Ronkainen 2001).

But critics argue that globalization has involved both positive and negative consequences. In the sphere of business, Gupta and Govindarajan (2001) argue that globalization has ceased to be an option for firms and has become a strategic necessity for almost all businesses. Growth is a must if a business is to remain viable. Globalization provides new avenues for growth to business firms. However, in the sphere of political relations, the gap between the developed and developing countries is likely to increase if the developing countries do not participate in the process of globalization with appropriate policy regimes. Those that do participate have realized higher growth rates and have narrowed the income gap between them and the developed countries (see World Bank 2002).

On the basis of per capita incomes, the high income sector of the world economy is chiefly divided into the three blocs of North America, the European Union, and Japan (with outriders in Australia and New Zealand). In those areas, strong government regulations and a shared commitment to a commercial civilization has, despite cultural differences, produced a zone of development that can benefit from globalization. Of the world's largest 500 multinational enterprises, 434 are based in that triad, accounting for 90 percent of the world's stock of foreign direct investment (Dunning 1998). Certainly, globalization reduces the effectiveness of national governments in some areas of economic management. For example, it weakens national governments' regulatory capabilities and may reduce their ability to soften the effect of external shocks—although both Malaysia and Australia were able to ride the East Asian financial crisis with few adverse consequences and by vastly different methods. However, globalization cannot erase the differences between countries or render local knowledge, local talent, and local relationships obsolete.

Globalization is facilitated by free trade and investment. Negotiations held under the auspices of WTO, and its predecessor GATT, have resulted in a significant reduction in barriers to trade (Pugel 2004). Recent rounds of negotiations have focused more on indirect barriers such as subsidies. It is well known that in general terms free trade is the optimal policy from the global point of view. However, the gains from trade are rarely equally distributed. Developing countries and in some cases even the developed countries believe that free trade will be harmful to at least some sectors of their respective economies. In order to address the concerns of the less developed countries, a WTO-sponsored conference of trade ministers held in Doha in 2001 developed an agenda. This agenda recognized that there is a close link between trade and development.

The developing countries receive a significant amount of aid from the developed countries on an annual basis. The developed countries believe that aid to less developed countries transfers benefits from free trade to the less developed countries. Developed countries also point out that special and differential treatment for the less developed countries was agreed upon during the WTO's Doha meeting. "Doha represented a watershed for the WTO. It marked the beginning of a new era of negotiations which can and should provide real and lasting opportunities for developing countries to participate in the multilateral trading system," the WTO director-general Mike Moore pointed out. "The new round is underway and we must not lose sight of the win-win scenarios for development and environment that are within our grasp."

Moore referred to the recent Doha Declaration and its emphasis on the major role international trade can play in the promotion of economic development and the alleviation of poverty. He said, "As stated in the Declaration, all WTO member governments 'recognize the need for all our people to benefit from the increased opportunities and welfare gains that the multilateral trading system generates.'"[7]

The negotiating ministers agreed to adopt about fifty decisions clarifying the obligations of developing country member governments with respect to issues including agriculture, subsidies, textiles and clothing, technical barriers to trade, trade-related investment measures, and rules of origin. Agreement on these points required hard bargaining between negotiators over the course of nearly three years. Many other implementation issues of concern to developing countries have not been settled, however. For these issues, the ministers agreed in Doha on a framework program for addressing these matters. In paragraph 12 of the Ministerial Declaration, the ministers underscored that they had made a decision on the fifty or so measures in a separate ministerial document and pointed out that "negotiations on outstanding implementation issues shall be an integral part of the Work Programme" in the coming years.[8]

The ministers established a two-track approach. Issues for which there was an agreed negotiating mandate in the declaration would be dealt with under the terms of that mandate. Implementation issues for which there was no mandate to negotiate would be taken up as "a matter of priority" by relevant WTO councils and committees. These bodies are to report on their progress to the Trade Negotiations Committee by the end of 2002 for "appropriate action." Negotiations on agriculture began in early 2000, under Article 20 of the WTO Agriculture Agreement. By November 2001 and the Doha Ministerial Conference, 121 governments had submitted a large number of negotiating proposals. These negotiations will continue, but now with the mandate given by the Doha Declaration, which also includes a series of deadlines. The declaration builds on the work already undertaken, confirms and elaborates the objectives, and sets a timetable. Agriculture is now part of the single undertaking in which virtually all the linked negotiations were expected to end by Janaury 1, 2005—a target which has only been partially achieved to end by January 1, 2005. However, some of the developing countries believe that the total amount of foreign aid received from the developed countries is only a small fraction of the potential benefits that could be gained from free access to the markets of developed countries.

The so-called Doha Development Agenda was included in the more recent round of ministerial talks held in Cancún in 2003. Although the Cancún ministerial conference ended without any major agreement, it was widely agreed that trade is a vitally important element in any program for development, as it can deliver benefits to developing countries worth many times more than all the development aid they receive. Opening markets for trade in manufactured products, services, and agriculture can provide the key to global economic growth and development. But the negotiations did not deliver more to developing countries than they had received from trade rounds in the past. They had already achieved a historic agreement on access to essential medicines for the poorest countries and agreed on twenty-eight proposals to extend special and differential treatment to developing countries. An initiative to phase out cotton subsidies was advanced but failed at the ministerial conference in Cancún. Nonetheless, the poorest countries took part in the negotiations and succeeded in placing their interests on the trade agenda.

Some progress was also made on agriculture, not as much as many developing countries wanted perhaps, but in a system where all decisions are made by consensus, the political concerns of their trading partners must be addressed. Ministers could not agree on whether to launch negotiations on the so-called Singapore issues of trade and investment, trade and competition, transparency in government procurement, and trade facilitation. The level of political sensitivity varies widely on these issues, but members could not agree on any of them. In the end the ministers could not bridge the gaps that separated them. A more open and equitable trading system would provide them with an important tool in alleviating poverty and raising their levels of economic development.

On the one hand, many governments around the globe, particularly in developed countries, are attempting to speed up the process of globalization. This is broadly the case in North America, in Australia, and now to some extent in Japan where indications of economic revival after the "lost decade" are correspondingly present. On the other hand, individuals residing mostly in developed countries have been regularly organizing demonstrations against globalization, from Seattle to Cancún, and there is a vast body of mostly Western literature that blames globalization for ills as disparate as global warming, the extinction of species, and the September 11, 2001, attack on the United States. The main purpose of this chapter is to examine the reasons for the push toward and the protests against globalization. The chaper also attempts to examine the implications of globalization for South Asia.

Drivers of Globalization

Globalization has resulted in the growing international integration of markets for capital, goods, and services. Politically, globalization is driven by a widespread push toward liberalization of trade and capital markets at first led by the United States but increasingly supported by other state policymakers anxious to access higher growth rates. Economically, increasing internationalization of production and distribution and marketing strategies, on the one hand, and technological progress, on the other, are responsible for the rapid dismantling of barriers to (a) international trade in goods and services, and (b) international capital mobility. In other words, globalization is creating a situation where there is a wider market for trade *and* more commodities, both goods and services, are traded internationally. In addition, there is a relatively high and growing mobility for private capital, which can conglomerate into ever larger concentrations as new forms of funds are created almost annually. Technological advances and free market reforms adopted by developing economies have made significant contributions to the cause of globalization. In addition, firms have commonly attempted to defend their home markets from foreign competitors by entering directly into the competitors' home markets. This has resulted in a significant increase in the size and number of multinational corporations even where in the first instance they were attempting to defend their traditional economic spheres.

The drivers of globalization can, therefore, be divided into two broad categories: (1) the decline of politically and socially constructed barriers to trade and capital mobility; and (2) technological improvements in the means of production, communication, and transportation. Recent trends toward integration such as the formation of the European Union, which offers an ambiguous example, have resulted in significant changes to the world political map. The reduction in barriers to trade and foreign invest-ment and the privatization of industry are speeding up the opening of new markets to multinational firms.[9] Technological advances in computers and communications technology have contributed to an increased flow of ideas and information across international boundaries. Worldwide deregulation of the telecommunications industry has further reduced the marginal cost of computing and communications, which has enabled a massive increase in the flow of information across international boundaries.[10] Consequently, even small firms are able to compete globally.

Regionalization is favored by some nations because it is characterized by preferential trading arrangements among countries. Countries with different levels of economic development may also be involved in regionalization as was the case with members of the North American Free Trade Agreement and has become more recently the case with the European Union as it has embraced the new member states of southern and eastern Europe. Although regionalization and globalization appear to be very different processes, regional and global strategies can in fact complement each other (Mucchielli, Buckley, and Cordell 1998). Many states that would prefer multilateral economic integration pursue regional or bilateral integration when this is the only form available. This was, for example, the stated position of both the U.S. and Australian governments as they embarked on negotiations for a Free Trade Agreement in 2003.[11] Similarly, Morrison, Ricks, and Roth (1998) have argued that at the firm level, regional strategies may often represent a far safer and more manageable option as compared with more costly and more difficult global strategies.

Globalization of the Labor Market

While there are clearly some indicators of the globalization of the labor market, such as the movement of labor from low- to high-wage areas, within and toward the EU, the United States, and Malaysia, for example, political and social barriers have deeply inhibited this process and it is uncertain that labor mobility is now any higher than it was in another period of massive migration, the late nineteenth century. Economic changes often involve winners and losers, particularly when markets are distorted by political interventions. In order to complete the labor-intensive stage of production, MNCs are aggressively looking for production facilities in open, low-wage countries such as China, India, and Mexico. This does not imply that MNCs are necessarily "exploiting" labor in less developed countries—although of course well-documented cases of such behavior do occur. In fact, most often the wages paid by MNCs to workers in less developed countries are higher than the wages paid by domestic firms. In a sense, this is in the form of part of their superior profits won in a high-income foreign market being captured by their domestic labor force. However, the wages paid by MNCs to workers in less developed countries are lower than the wages paid to the workers in developed countries. The origin of these two relationships is to be found in the differences imposed by the political and social barriers to labor mobility and the consequent tendency toward the equalization of wage rates, rather than in the exploitative rapacity of international companies.[12]

Numerous firms whose production facilities were initially based in high-wage countries have relocated to low-wage countries, although their major markets remain in the high-income economies. This has been widely documented in the case of sports shoe manufacturers, including Nike, where the relative costs of advertising, creating brand loyalty, design processes, quality assurance, and rapid model obsolescence take up an unusually high proportion of the fixed costs of production.

This pursuit of cheaper labor, nonetheless, has resulted in a significant decrease in the cost of production, which is a feature of the drive for globalization. However, relocation of production facilities to low-wage countries has also led to a decrease in demand for unskilled or semiskilled workers in developed countries, particularly in labor-intensive manufacturing sectors such as textiles, footwear, and clothing. The disruption to the livelihood of affected workers in high-wage countries has sometimes resulted in labor unions' joining protests against globalization, although they have rarely provided the leadership for these movements in either North America or Europe.

It is interesting to note that these protests against globalization are mainly directed from and are taking place in the developed countries. Capital-poor developing countries usually benefit from foreign investment that creates employment. However, the relocation of resources due to economic integration does generate friction as low-wage, low-productivity industries in developed countries decline in the face of competition from goods produced in low-wage, low-productivity economies. This is likely to result in protectionist pressures within the political system. These pressures are likely to increase if the affected countries cannot facilitate the relocation of resources through the creation of more flexible markets and appropriate reskilling procedures for displaced labor needing to access competitive high productivity industry or—more commonly—service sectors. Part of this is merely the process of relocation of resources, including labor, first from the agricultural to the secondary industry sector and then from the latter to the services sector—the universal trajectory of economic growth and wealth creation.

The international dimension of this process of economic development involves changing patterns of comparative advantage. As early industrial development in Europe displaced labor-intensive trade, Luddism emerged. As industrial exports replaced indigenous handicrafts, nativist ideologies grew. As secondary industry moved to cheaper developing countries, calls for tariff protection grew loud in developed countries. And recently, as service industries have moved to more cost-effective locations—call centers are moving to India, for example—objections to the "export of jobs" have grown. These changes are, in fact, the global dimensions of the processes of specialization, capital intensification, technological change, trade, and economic growth.

Interestingly, there has recently been a decline in the number of workers employed in the manufacturing sector in China (*China Statistical Yearbook* 2005). This reflects not only the increase in the productivity of workers but also the utilization of capital-intensive methods of production. Globalization is going to lead to greater competition in the marketplace, which is likely to result in accelerating product cycles. In such an environment there will be more uncertainty because firms will be permanently vulnerable. This will give rise to mergers that will result in the emergence of large firms specializing in the production of high quality products. China is entering a more mature phase of integrating into the globalized market—a process it embarked on twenty-five years ago.

For a number of years many other developing countries, such as India, relied heavily on less effective development strategies linked to import substitution and protectionism. The failure of these strategies to achieve the desired level of industrialization and growth in per capita incomes—together with the collapse of their Soviet sponsor—resulted in their disbandment in the early 1990s. A decade later, India is attracting capital into even the most sophisticated and high productivity sectors—including interconnection technology (IT) and computer technology—in pursuit of relatively high productivity but lower wage (and English-speaking) labor. Whereas Agiomirgianakis and Zervoycanni (2001) have argued that international labor mobility has a beneficial effect on national employment levels, on the other hand, Minzberg and Quinn (1991) consider globalization to be a success strategy for the comparative advantage of the participant state. They argue that globalization is a strategy that increases profit and market share and, although firms are not subjectively interested in creating jobs and/or improving national welfare, these will be the results of their profit-seeking activities.

Krugman and Venables (1995) have indicated that the rise of manufacturing industries in less developed countries can lead to a decline in the manufacturing industries of the industrialized countries. As we have noted, this occurs anyway as productivity rises in secondary industry and labor moves into the services sector as part of the universal process of development. Adding to this, globalization allows firms to substitute high-wage unskilled local workers with the low-wage unskilled workers overseas. Labor costs continue to affect investment locations, but globalization accentuates this tendency. In the long term, globalization can, theoretically, lead to the convergence of working conditions across countries. This will be more the case where unit costs of transportation are minimized, but less evident where political barriers are constructed to the mobility of factors of production. In other words, the greater the success of the opponents of globalization, the more likely the inequalities they oppose will be sustained.

Of course, if the relative skills, and thus the productivity levels, of workers in developed and developing countries shift to the advantage of the latter, equalization of wages may proceed more rapidly. In this context, Judy and D'Amico (1997) have considered the impact of globalization on American workers. They argue that by 2020, the present labor force, which is very productive, will retire. They further argue that the new workforce is likely to be relatively less productive and hence there is a need for government intervention to ensure that the new workforce is at least as productive as the present one. Edmonds and Pavcnik (2005) have shown that increase in the price of rice in Vietnam is associated with a decline in child labor.

Globalization of Capital Markets

The administrative economic institutions that generate the processes of globalization are, as in all economic processes, of some influence. The emergence of MNCs is one of the most important developments in the history of international trading relations. Their historical origins are in the great companies trading under charter from eighteenth-century Britain and the Netherlands and received considerable sustenance from the invention and strengthening of the joint-stock companies in nineteenth-century Britain and the United States. Contemporary MNCs have both emerged with and created the post-1945 global economy. They are firms that own and/or control value-added activities in two or more—now commonly many—countries. MNCs are major vehicles of foreign direct investment (FDI) programs, which transfer capital and technology between countries.

Some MNCs also engage in foreign production by means of cooperative alliances with foreign firms. As multinational corporations set up subsidiaries around the world, the momentum of globalization is gaining strength. MNCs have become major engines of economic globalization, engaging in foreign direct investment with a view to international production and sales through networks of subsidiaries and in strategic alliances.[13] They are major objects of criticism from antiglobalization critics who object to both their pursuit of efficient labor in the production process and their attempts to create brand loyalty in the marketplace.

Increasingly, international trade and foreign investment have further integrated national economies. It is well known that protectionism is not a guarantee of economic stability. Due to the expansion of international trade, total global output has grown almost every year during the past four decades, which corresponds most closely to the period of heightened globalization. This economic output has recorded enormous growth that has facilitated growth in FDI.[14] Over the past two decades, as more countries have abandoned regulation, FDI flows have grown three times faster than trade flows and almost four times faster than output. Multinationals now control one-third of the world's private sector assets and 30 percent of private gross national product in the major European countries (Hill 2005). In many developing countries, FDI constitutes a major source of foreign capital.

Since the 1980s, there has been a marked liberalization of government policies and attitudes toward foreign investment in both developed and many developing nations, including those that have grown most rapidly, many in East Asia, and the world's two largest nations, India and China. As a result, worldwide production and consumption of goods and services have become increasingly internationalized. The average yearly outflow of FDI increased from US$25 billion in 1975 to US$430 billion in 1998 (Hill 2005). There are at least 45,000 parent firms with 280,000 foreign affiliates, which generated over US$7 trillion in global sales (Hill 2005).[15]

Until the late 1980s, most FDI took place from one developed country to another in the pursuit of high-income market shares. However, during the

1990s a significant proportion of these flows went to the emerging markets such as China, Indonesia, Turkey, Vietnam, and increasingly to India. Some of these countries sought their finance primarily from official sources such as the World Bank and the International Monetary Fund (IMF). Today, almost 50 percent of direct foreign investment and well over 10 percent of portfolio capital flows are directed toward these markets, even though combined they account for less than 25 percent of world GDP. Moreover, these flows are increasingly oriented toward long-term facilities.

Foreign investment brings new ideas and technologies to host countries. Successful industrialization by Singapore, Hong Kong, Taiwan, and South Korea has highlighted the importance and capability of foreign investment in improving living standards. There is little doubt that foreign investment significantly affects the economic performance of host countries. The more widespread recognition of this fact has meant that competition for foreign investment has significantly increased (Thomsen 1999). But without appropriate infrastructure and supporting institutions it is virtually impossible to attract foreign investment, as has been clearly evident in sub-Saharan Africa where economic growth has been among the lowest in the world.[16] The state is still required to provide order, training, and infrastructure rather than direction and regulation.

It is interesting to note that the IMF was created in the mid-1940s under the Bretton Woods agreements, to help countries facing severe balance of payment problems under the regime of fixed exchange rates whereby the main mechanism for changing such imbalances was domestic economic policy rather than currency prices. At the time of the creation of the IMF, capital mobility was limited and imbalances in trade in goods and services were the primary source of balance of payment problems. Liberalization of capital flows and improvements in communications technology have made the transfer of significant funds across international boundaries a simpler task. The primary source of balance of payment problems in the 1990s then became the imbalance in the capital account, not the current account.

Globalization of financial markets influences both financial and physical assets. It is well known that trade in financial assets and debt is much easier to globalize than trade in goods and services, partly because it does not involve an immediate movement of physical resources but a bookkeeping entry. Accordingly, the globalization of trade in financial assets has progressed most rapidly. Financial transactions mainly involve exchanging pieces of paper or making entries in electronic ledgers. Technological progress in the means of communications has made these transactions very easy and cheap.[17]

The theoretical rationale for the globalization of financial markets is that it can assist the movement of productive capital from developed economies to developing countries. The economies of East Asia have been major beneficiaries of foreign investments and a commonly used example of the verity of this theory. However, much of their capital inflow had taken the form of short-term loans of hard currencies to banks located in Indonesia, Malaysia, the Philippines, South Korea, and Thailand. The periods of increasing loans were also periods of increasing growth and investment in those countries receiving the loans (Tobin 2000). The availability of hard currency loans resulted in the overvaluation of national currencies—often fixed in value against a rising U.S. dollar in the early mid-1990s—that then led to growing deficits in the current account.[18] Financial crises resulted in the late 1990s, when the lenders refused to renew the loans after they lost confidence in the management of the Asian financial intermediaries that were their recipients. Obviously, financial globalization is only worthwhile if the expected benefits are likely to outweigh the expected costs. But the crises of 1997–98 could have been averted by better prudential supervision of the financial sector—or often, more simply, by floating and deregulating their currencies.

The Asian financial crisis of 1997–98 followed quickly on the heels of the East Asian Economic Miracle and was a consequence of some of the characteristics of that state-sponsored period of hypergrowth. As production costs rose in Japan in the 1970s, Japanese firms invested heavily in offshore production plants located in cheaper neighboring countries. This sparked a generation of accelerated economic growth in the region that was assisted by favorable state interventionist policies in most East and Southeast Asian countries. In search of greater returns, capital flowed into these economies as both loans and direct investment.

Most of these economies, however, had not been liberalized, nor their states democratized. This resulted in a situation where most regional currencies were at fixed rates against the U.S. dollar and few governments practiced appropriate supervision of their financial institutions. In 1996 the appreciation of these currencies against a falling U.S. currency produced trade problems. It then became apparent that much capital inflow had been poorly supervised and invested by badly managed financial institutions. The resulting flight of investors out of these economies produced currency crises and induced economic recessions. A lengthy process of economic and governmental reform was then undertaken by most of them with serious and adverse short-term impacts on economic growth and living standards. The economic miracle that globalization can generate has to be appropriately managed.

Not so long ago, the greater part of a country's savings could circulate only within its domestic financial institutions. Integration of capital markets has significantly changed the situation. At present, international financial institutions operate on a worldwide scale and handle national saving centrally. Globalization has increased the competition between policy regimes seeking to attract the attention of managers of such funds. National savings increasingly flow to locations where profits are likely to be higher. Prospects of higher profit are the major inducement. But higher profits are generally associated with higher risk. Global capital-market integration combined with the volatility of capital flows is making macroeconomic management more complex (Kim and Singal 2000).

At the microeconomic level, international financial markets allow residents of different countries to pool various risks. This implies that investors can achieve more effective insurance than purely domestic arrangements would allow. At the macroeconomic level, a country suffering from a recession can borrow from the international capital market. In simple words, the international capital market channels the world's savings to its most productive uses, irrespective of location.[19] International capital markets are capable of disciplining national policymakers seeking to exploit a captive domestic capital market. Inward foreign direct investment almost always reduces the overall unemployment rate. Markets are becoming increasingly international in scope while governments remain national. Accordingly, the gains from globalization depend heavily on the response, structure, and flexibility of national economies and policy regimes. In general terms, globalization enhances production efficiency. But national governments through their power of taxation also have to ensure that efficiency is not achieved at the expense of equity.

As the World Bank (1995) report on the impact of globalization on the international labor market argued, wage rates are determined by both the occupation and sector within which the worker is located, and by the country within which the work is undertaken. Wage rates for highly skilled workers in efficient multinational companies operating in developing countries in some cases may have already overtaken those of low-skilled workers in labor-intensive sectors in developed countries. An international hierarchy of labor has emerged, which stretches from low-skilled agricultural laborers in low-growth, nonglobalized economies through to high-skilled workers in technology-intensive sectors in high-growth, globalized economies. This hierarchy is not static, however, and will develop dynamically and differentially as capital moves to areas and sectors of most recent opportunity. In turn, this will be determined by government policy regimes, technological change, and the efficiency of labor and capital. Protests against this process are not only unlikely to be effective, but, paradoxically, if successful in changing policy regimes, result in a deterioration of the conditions under which local labor operates. Hence, the most recent World Bank study (2002) found that the states that had least committed to globalization had the worst economic growth rates and the correspondingly lowest rates of growth of labor remuneration.

Developments in international capital markets are driving a convergence of economic policy across more and more countries—often termed in the 1990s "the Washington Consensus." This term was coined to describe the policy consensus generated in the major Washington-based institutions—the World Bank, the IMF, and the U.S. Treasury Department—on appropriate state policy in a globalizing world. Its characteristics included: a free floating currency; little restraint on trade such as tariffs or quotas; a very small state sector with no state-owned enterprises; a deregulated labor market; low money supply growth; a balanced budget; and clearly defined property rights. After the Asian financial crisis, a representative and stable system of government was often added.

Economies that are viewed by investors as fiscally responsible and politically committed to free-market policies attract a significant amount of foreign capital. This capital is often utilized to develop the local production infrastructure. In order to attract foreign investment, countries offer incentives including tax holidays, preferential access to credit, and reduction of import duties on raw material (Fortanier and Maher 2001). Investment liberalization significantly increased during the 1990s. As a result of this liberalization, some developing countries such as China have been able to accumulate capital much more rapidly than their counterparts among the developed countries. This situation has resulted in the narrowing of the per capita income gap with the already developed countries. While it is generally agreed that free capital flow leads to efficiency, the 1997–98 Asian financial crisis demonstrated that uncontrolled capital flows can be risky and destabilizing, particularly when accompanied by fixed exchange rate regimes and incompetent policymakers. Increasing integration of capital markets, on the one hand, combined with administered exchange rates, on the other, have resulted in significant deviations of exchange rates from their long-term sustainable levels. This phenomenon is known as exchange rate misalignment.[20]

The Case Against Globalization

Globalization offers significant benefits but at the same time creates serious hazards. The presence of asymmetric information and imperfect contract enforcement in the real world complicates the situation further (Razin and Sadka 1999). Rapid globalization in tastes, production, and labor markets has resulted in a sharp increase in the level of international competition. Rising international competition has forced business firms to reduce the cost of production. As a result, growth in employment and real wages within the industrialized countries has been minimal where productivity gains have not occurred. Restructuring, downsizing, and utilization of improved technologies has allowed firms to compete vigorously in the international marketplace. In most developed countries, at least some sections of the society consider globalization as a threat to employment, particularly in low-productivity sectors.

But due to a higher level of poverty, resistance to globalization is not strong within the developing countries. Nevertheless, increasing competition for foreign capital can force the governments of less developed countries to make structural adjustments at the expense of the long-term interests of domestic capital tied to local economies (Dunning 1998). It has been argued that globalization can increase wage inequality within a country. By making use of a Vector Autoregressive Model, Dutt and Mukhopadhyay (2006) have shown that globalization can contribute to income inequality among nations.

Globalization can also result in cultural changes, which critics decry. Czinkota and Kotabe (1998) have considered cultural issues in the context of one of the most challenging markets, Japan, where the interlocking relationships among suppliers and manufacturers make market entry and development a daunting task to outsiders. But without such competition and associated liberalization, the Japanese economy faces the continuation of the stagnation it has experienced since 1990. Competition for foreign investment can force governments to spend large amounts on production infrastructure that may not be directly productive for the country's domestic economy. This can result in excess capacity. Excessive investment in production infrastructure may be funded at the expense of social welfare programs, which can lower a country's standard of living. In the absence of restrictions on capital flows, capital can move to locations where the tax rate is relatively low. Consequently, small countries lose some of their autonomy with respect to capital tax rates. This situation gives rise to international competition to create a capital tax regime most attractive to financial markets. Over $1.5 trillion is exchanged every day in currency markets around the world. About 95 percent of this total represents "speculative" transactions that fail to benefit directly the world's poorest countries. It is also claimed that economic development resulting from globalization has increased the level of pollution in developing economies like Hong Kong, China, and India (Chan 2001).

The globalization of financial markets with their volatile effects on national economic management has destabilized and weakened the capacity of all countries to autonomously pursue economic policy regimes. It has been argued that the global market represents a concentration of power capable of influencing the macroeconomic policies of countries. Globalization has the potential to result in a borderless world. Opponents of globalization argue that it is a process of suppressing state influence on the economy and of giving private capital authority over any investment decision. The link between globalization and cross-border pollution has been recently explored by Hatzipanayotou, Lahiri and Michael (2005).

It is becoming increasingly difficult to distinguish domestic economic activity from international events. Decisions made elsewhere in the world are already significantly influencing domestic economies.[21] Given the benefits to be derived from globalization, governments are eager to take advantage of the opportunities, but may at the same time also have to accept the negative consequences of increased competition. Prasad and colleagues (2003) have suggested that financial globalization should be approached cautiously. They further argue that the benefits from financial globalization to the developing countries will be limited unless sound macroeconomic policies are adopted. Luo (2005) has argued that globalization can also affect corporate governance and accountability. Finally, it is interesting to note that Clark and Themudo (2005) have argued that there is a link between Internet-based networks and transnational protest movements against globalization.

Implications of Globalization for South Asia

The experience of the Asian region in this respect is instructive, since it contains such a broad range of experiences. The first Asian economy to achieve developed country per capita incomes was Japan in the 1970s. It did this by developing an efficient secondary industry sector on which its extraordinary export performance was based. This was achieved with almost no foreign investment being permitted in the domestic economy. This economic structure was sufficiently robust to survive two severe oil price shocks in 1974 and 1981, and to evolve into a major source of international investment funds in its own right as its currency appreciated to stellar levels in the 1980s. Nonetheless, this structure produced seemingly intractable economic stagnation—at high levels of income—for twelve years after 1990. This was the product of a dual economy: efficient secondary industry coexisted with illiberal policy regimes in the primary and tertiary sectors. Stagnant domestic levels resisted public sector stimulants while product innovation stalled. Japan was never a globalized economy and until it moved toward one, stagnation would continue.

The export-oriented nature of the successful Japanese economy did excite interest elsewhere in the region. The "Four Tigers" of South Korea, Hong Kong, Singapore, and Taiwan emulated export-oriented industrialization in various ways, to produce diverse policy regimes sharing successful development trajectories by the 1980s. Although their growth began to slow in the 1990s, they had generated incomes to developed country levels. Their success led economic managers in neighboring countries toward globalizing policies.

Among the other countries of the Association of Southeast Asian Nations, export-oriented industrialization with open economies and freedom of capital movement became more common. Malaysia and Thailand were beneficiaries of such growth regimes. Indonesia, under the Suharto dictatorship, had compound economic growth of 6 percent from 1966 to 1998. With a lag, the communist economies of Vietnam and Laos, postcommunist Cambodia, and post-Marcos Philippines also undertook some liberalization with more limited success. Even the military junta in Burma tried to produce growth by entering the world market.

The Chinese communist leadership took these developments sufficiently seriously for them to be a central issue in the economic and political debates that followed the death of Mao in 1976. Taiwan was widely cited by the reformers as an example of what could be done with a liberalized economy but authoritarian state. From the early 1980s, China increasingly embarked on a process of successful globalization that has generated arguably the most profound transformation in the economic life of the most people over the past 2,000 years. Needless to say, during the same period, the unreformed centrally planned economy of North Korea shrank as the withdrawal of Soviet subsidies impacted on a structure lacking the flexibility to accommodate this.

The East Asian financial crisis of 1997–98 threatened the broad success of the globalizing Asian economies. Economic growth stalled in almost all of them and political regimes were faced with considerable pressures, and in several cases—including Indonesia, Thailand, and South Korea—they collapsed. But the source of the crisis was not in the process of globalization. It was in the policies that the states brought to globalization. These often included corruption, inflexible economic structures, and nepotistic financial markets, also known as crony capitalism. Where these practices were less common, as in Taiwan, Singapore, and even Malaysia, the crisis was more easily managed. In any case, after appropriate adjustments, most of the regional economies resumed growth within a few years.[22]

South Asian economies have only recently started taking advantage of the opportunities presented by globalization. India is the most vibrant of the South Asian economies. From its independence to the mid-1980s, India pursued an inward-looking trade and industrial policy whereby imports were actively discouraged. Pakistan's economy has never taken off, not the least because it inherited relatively less developed areas with little industrial infrastructure. Among the main factors hindering economic growth in Pakistan is political instability, which has resulted in frequent interventions by the military. Continued conflict with India is used to justify huge spending on national defense. Pakistan's industrial base remains weak. The Sri Lankan economy has suffered from internal conflicts, and Bangladesh's economic record is dismal. Real GDP growth rates of South Asian economies are shown in Figure 14.1. Economic cooperation among the South Asian economies is highly desirable, but this would require political concessions.

It is clear from Figure 14.1 that growth rates of the Bangladesh and Indian economies are quite stable, whereas there is significant fluctuation in the growth

Figure 14.1   **Real GDP Growth in Percentage** (1985–2004)

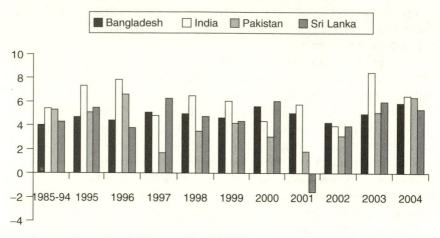

Source: International Monetary Fund (2005)

Figure 14.2   **Foreign Exchange Reserves minus Gold in Billions of U.S. Dollars**

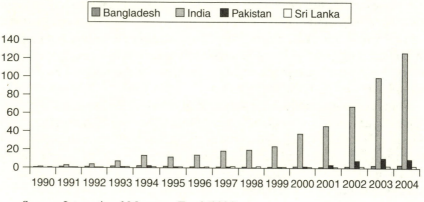

Source: International Monetary Fund (2004)

rates of Pakistan and Sri Lanka. The Sri Lankan economy relies heavily on the export of tea but, unlike Pakistan, it has been able to control its population growth rate. Globalization offers huge opportunities to South Asia, but India is likely to be the major beneficiary due to its well-developed political and legal system. In addition, there is no shortage of well-educated and highly skilled workers in India.

Figure 14.2 shows the foreign reserves (excluding gold) of South Asian economies. Indian reserves have grown steadily, while Pakistan's reserves

Figure 14.3   **Index of Industrial Production** (1995 = 100)

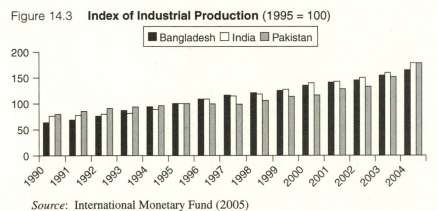

Source: International Monetary Fund (2005)

Figure 14.4   **Exports in Billions of U.S. Dollars**

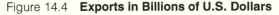

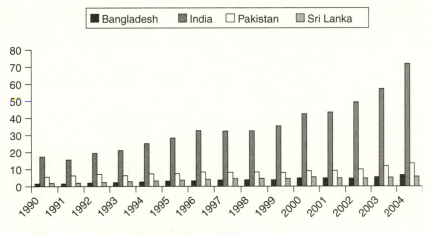

Source: International Monetary Fund (2005)

have fluctuated significantly. Due to considerable aid received by the United States since late 2001, Pakistan's foreign reserves have increased.

Figure 14.3 shows the trend in the index of industrial production in some South Asian economies. There is a steady increase in industrial production in Bangladesh, India, and Pakistan. India, however, is the most efficient producer of most manufactured goods.

The era of increasing globalization has witnessed a steady increase in exports of South Asian economies. Figure 14.4 shows that all four countries have done well in this area. However, the smaller ones (i.e., Bangladesh, Pakistan, and Sri Lanka) are reluctant to engage in freer trade with India, which is a more efficient and larger economic power.

Free and equitable trade can benefit all South Asian economies (Nasim 2001). Because of the large size of the South Asian market, free trade would better exploit economies of scale. Free trade is likely to lead to economic interdependence; however, close economic interdependence is unlikely until the regional disputes are resolved.

Political instability, the threat of military conflict, and the rigidity of economic policies can be attributed to South Asia's poor growth record as compared to Southeast Asia. In a recent study Hassan, Waheeduzzaman, and Rahman (2003) examined the economic growth record of five South Asian countries over the 1980–99 period. They also attempted to examine the impact of military spending on economic growth and FDI. They argue that defense spending can lead to the crowding out of investment; however, such spending also increases aggregate demand. In some cases increased defense spending can result in technology transfer that can also be used in the production of nondefense goods. A decrease in defense spending would greatly benefit both India and Pakistan. Given its relatively poor economic record and continued political instability, Pakistan has much to gain by reducing spending on defense. Despite rising prosperity in some urban centers, most of the Indian population remains well below the poverty line. Sri Lankan economic growth, which has been stifled by ethnic disputes, is likely to slow down due to destruction caused by the Asian tsunami of December 2004.

Conclusions

Globalization is transforming the world into a single market that is likely to lead to more efficient allocation of resources. But the benefits of globalization are available only if countries give up some measure of independence and autonomy in decision making. The full benefits of globalization cannot be enjoyed unless free movement of goods, services, labor, and capital across borders is supplemented by the development of common economic institutions. In other words, unless a single authority rules the world operating under a single law, it will be difficult to achieve an equitable outcome. The failure of the recent WTO talks in Cancún indicates that the aim of efficient allocation of resources worldwide will not be achieved any time soon. The failure of these talks centers around the fundamental question of equitable distribution of gains from free trade. Developing countries believe that trade liberalization is likely to lead to relatively greater benefits to the developed countries.

Nonetheless, the form of contemporary opposition to free trade and globalization means that its success would likely result in increasingly nationalist economic policies and politicians. Deteriorating economic conditions may lead to social pressures that might result in protectionism, thereby canceling all steps that have been taken to open up worldwide markets. The opponents of globalization have argued that it can widen inequality, and increase poverty and social exclusion. It is therefore necessary for governments to take steps to check the widening gap between the rich and the poor.

Globalization presents many opportunities and challenges. During the past decade there has been a significant decrease in barriers to free trade and capital mobility. However, impediments such as domestically oriented business practices continue to test businesses globally. In other words, while governmental controls are weakening, cultural barriers are still strong. Globalization is likely to increase the interaction between economies with diverse cultures and standards of living.

The process of globalization has been under way for a very long time. International conflicts in the first half of the twentieth century slowed it down. However, the increasing availability of global capital, coupled with advances in computing and communications technology in the early 1990s, served to accelerate the processes of globalization. The protests against globalization are meant to slow down that process.

The opponents of globalization argue that it has resulted in an increase in unemployment among the unskilled and semiskilled workers in developed countries, an argument that ignores the increasing availability of higher productivity jobs with higher wage levels. The impact of globalization on the employment level of unskilled workers in less developed countries, on the other hand, has been positive. Yet opponents of globalization consider the relocation of production facilities to less developed countries as exploitation of labor. As far as the free flow of capital is concerned, the Asian financial crisis of 1997–98 has suggested that unregulated capital inflow can convert an export-led economy into an import-led (and poorer) economy if policy regimes are badly handled.

Arguments in favor of globalization essentially revolve around the core issue of its generating faster economic growth. Since the relationship between economic growth and the expansion of both market size and its freedom of operation is among the core beliefs of the intellectual structure of modern economic theory, economists generally support this development. Since this process has the capacity to undermine the sovereign power of the state and the unique characteristics of localized cultures, supporters of these more traditional features of human society are likely to object to the process. Economic theory and technological change suggest that for the foreseeable future, the economic process of globalization will remain ascendant. In a recent study, Teitel (2005) has suggested some policy measures that may help to alleviate certain negative aspects of increased globalization.

South Asian economies have no choice but to fully embrace globalization. India is the economic giant in the region that has attracted significant foreign investment in recent years. It has become a favored destination for foreign investment due to its political stability, well-developed legal system, and the availability of highly skilled workers. There has been a significant increase in trade between India and Pakistan in recent years. Pakistan, for example, is still importing some goods from other countries that can be imported more cheaply from India. Recent improvement in relations between India and Pakistan is likely to further increase the volume of trade between the two countries. The South Asian region would greatly benefit from a free trade agreement, but this would require the separation of political and economic considerations.

Notes

1. See Anwar (2002) and references therein.
2. The link between trade and economic growth was implicitly established by Adam Smith. Persuasive arguments have been presented by Jagdesh Bhagwati (e.g., Bhagwati, Panagariya, and Srinivasan 1998), among others. See also Feenstra (2004), Van Den Berg (2004), and Wong (1995).
3. Consumer products that are almost universally accepted include, for example, McDonald's, Coca-Cola, Gillette razors, Levi jeans, and Toyota cars.
4. Globalization in production is associated with the rise of MNCs that are managed by an international team of managers. Multinational corporations purchase raw material from the cheapest sources around the world and produce in the lowest cost locations to lock into the highest price markets. Examples include automobiles, steel, aircraft, consumer electronics, and pharmaceutical products.
5. The East India Company established foreign branches in 1600. Colt Fire Arms had an English plant before the American Civil War. By 1914, there were thirty-seven American firms with production facilities in two or more overseas locations. National Cash Register, Burroughs, Parke-Davis, and Ford were some of the first firms to have overseas plants. European firms were also going overseas at the same time (see Hill 2005).
6. It is now well recognized that the world marketplace is too large and the competition too strong for even the largest multinationals to do everything independently. Because of the free flow of information, technologies are converging, making the cost and the risk of both goods and market development even greater. In order to exploit the available opportunities, management in firms has become more pragmatic about what it takes to be successful in global markets. For further discussion, see Catley and Mosler (2000) and Catley (1996).
7. See www.wto.org/english/tratop_e/dda_e/symp_devagenda_02_e.htm.
8. See www.wto.org/english/tratop_e/dda_e/dohaexplained_e.htm.
9. Since the end of World War II, negotiations under the auspices of GATT and, since 1995, the WTO, have resulted in significant reductions in barriers to international trade and capital mobility. This can also be attributed to lobbying by representatives of multinational firms that have much to gain from free trade.
10. The number of Internet hosts grew from 9 million in 1993 to 72 million in 2000. A total of 304 million people were estimated to be online in 2000 with explosive growth

expected from new, and increasingly more affordable, computer and telecommunication technologies. Advances in transportation and ease of travel allow consumers to experience new markets and products in person (Czinkota and Ronkainen 2001).

11. The Australia–U.S. free trade agreement came into effect on January 1, 2005. It is worth mentioning Krueger's (2000) finding that the United States has gained relatively little from its free trade deal with Canada and Mexico.

12. It is perhaps worth mentioning that international trade theory suggests that under some conditions, free trade in goods can lead to factor price equalization.

13. Greider (1998) has argued that the global capital markets are linked with global labor markets. This implies that the negative impact of globalization on capital markets is transmitted to global labor markets.

14. The largest 500 MNCs account for 90 percent of the world's stock of foreign direct investment. They also carry out half of all trade, often in the form of intracompany sales between subsidiaries.

15. More than 60 percent of U.S. foreign investment takes place in Europe. At the same time, approximately 50 percent of European foreign investment takes place in the United States (Appleyard, Field and Cobb 2006). Prasad and colleagues (2003) report that less developed countries still receive a very small fraction of worldwide capital inflow.

16. One of the myths of the critics of globalization is that local firms will lose to large multinationals. It has been argued that local firms can compete with foreign multinationals if they focus on the areas ignored by the multinationals (Ger 2001; Obstfeld 1998).

17. The only barriers to financial transactions are national regulations (Tobin 2000).

18. The worldwide gross volume of foreign exchange transactions is worth approximately US$1.5 trillion per business day. However, most of these transactions are reversed within a week, 40 percent within a day. This suggests that most of the transactions are speculative and do not contribute much directly toward national economic growth (Tobin 2000).

19. It is estimated that the world economy that was open to global competitors in product, service, or asset ownership markets has risen from approximately $4 trillion in 1995 to well over $21 trillion in 2000 (Czinkota and Ronainken 2001).

20. Misalignment is defined in terms of the deviation of the level of the real exchange rate under price (that is, administered exchange rate) rigidity from its equilibrium real level under perfect price flexibility.

21. A simple example is the currency exchange rates. The Australian dollar significantly depreciated against the U.S. dollar in the early 2000s despite the fact that the Australian economy was strong. Indeed, its devaluation permitted the maintenance of domestic growth. In the second quarter of 2006, the Australian dollar has sharply appreciated against the U.S. dollar.

22. The neighboring economies of Australia and New Zealand are also instructive in this respect. Although among the world's richest economies in 1945, both slipped down the world per capita income tables from 1950 to the early 1980s. In the 1980s both undertook reform programs of economic liberalization designed to reinvigorate growth (Catley 1996, 2001). In the more successful and larger Australian economy, after twelve years of world-standard-setting growth per capita, income levels again surpassed those of Germany, France, Britain, Japan, and Singapore by 2003. A Productivity Commission report in 2002 showed that most of this multifactor productivity growth was the result of the more efficient reallocation of the factors of production that was the outcome of liberalization and globalization (Barnes and Kennard 2002). A political science perspective of globalization can also be found in Smith (2006).

References

Agiomirgianakis, G., and A. Zervoycanni. 2001. "Globalization of Labor Market and Macroeconomic Equilibrium." *International Review of Economics and Finance* 10: 109–33.

Anwar, S. 2002. "Globalization and National Economic Development: Analyzing Benefits and Costs." *Journal of Business and Management* 8, no. 4: 411–23.

Appleyard, D.; A. Field; and S. Cobb. 2006. *International Economics*. 5th ed. Boston: McGraw-Hill/Irwin.

Baldwin, R.; D. Cohen; A. Sapir; and A. Venables. 1999. *Market Integration, Regionalism and the Global Economy*. Cambridge: Cambridge University Press.

Barnes, P., and S. Kennard. 2002. "Skill and Australia's Productivity Surge." *Staff Research Paper,* Productivity Commission, Canberra.

Bhagwati, J.; A. Panagariya; and T.N. Srinivasan. 1998. *Lectures on International Trade*. 2d ed. Cambridge, MA: MIT Press.

Catley, B. 1996. *Globalizing Australian Capitalism*. Cambridge: Cambridge University Press.

———. 2001. *Waltzing with Matilda: Should New Zealand Join Australia?* Wellington: Dark Horse Publications.

Catley, B., and D. Mosler. 2000. *Global America: Imposing Liberalism on a Recalcitrant World*. New York: Praeger.

Chan, Y.K. 2001. "An Emerging Green Market in China: Myth or Reality?" In *Best Practices in International Business*, ed. M. Czinkota and I. Ronkainen, 110–19. Orlando, FL: Harcourt.

China Statistical Yearbook. 2005. Beijing: China Statistics Press.

Clark, J.D., and N.S. Themudo. 2005. "Linking the Web and the Street: Internet-Based 'Doctcauses' and the "Anti-Globalization." *World Development* 34: 50–74.

Czinkota, M., and M. Kotabe. 1998. *Trends in International Business*. Orlando, FL: Harcourt.

Czinkota, M., and I. Ronkainen. 2001. "Globalization: An Introduction and Assessment of Realities and Strategies," In *Best Practices in International Business*, ed. Czinkota and Ronkainen, 1–7. Orlando, FL: Harcourt.

Dunning, J.H. 1998. *Globalization, Trade and Foreign Direct Investment*. Oxford: Elsevier.

Dutt, A.K., and K. Mukhopadhyay. 2006. "Globalization and the Inequality Among Nations: A VAR Approach." *Economics Letters* 88: 295–299.

Edmonds, E.V., and N. Pavcnik. 2005. "The Effect of Trade Liberalization on Child Labour." *Journal of International Economics* 65: 401–19.

El Kahal, S. 2001. *Business in Asia Pacific*. New York: Oxford University Press.

Feenstra, R.C. 2004. *Advanced International Trade: Theory and Evidence*. Princeton, NJ: Princeton University Press.

Fortanier, M., and M. Maher. 2001. "Foreign Direct Investment and Sustainable Development." *Financial Market Trends* 79: 107–30.

Ger, G. 2001. "Localizing in the Global Village: Local Firms Competing in Global Markets." In *Best Practices in International Business*, ed. M. Czinkota and I. Ronkainen, 159–78. Orlando, FL: Harcourt.

Greider, W. 1998. *One World, Ready or Not: The Manic Logic of Global Capitalism*. New York: Touchstone Books.

Gupta, A.K., and V. Govindarajan. 2001., *Managing Global Expansion: A Conceptual Framework.*" In *Best Practices in International Business*, ed. M. Czinkota and I. Ronkainen, 123–41. Orlando, FL: Harcourt.

Hassan, M.K.; M. Waheeduzzaman; and A. Rahman. 2003. "Defense Expenditure and Economic Growth in the SAARC Countries." *Journal of Social, Political and Economic Studies* 28, no. 3: 275–93.

Hatzipanayotou, P.; S. Lahiri; and M. Michael. 2005. "Globalization, Cross-Border Pollution and Welfare." *CESifo Working Paper No. 1479* (www.cesifo.de/wp).

Hill, C. 2005. *International Business*. 5th ed. Boston: McGraw-Hill/Irwin.

International Monetary Fund. 2005. *Yearbook of Statistics 2005*. Washington, DC.

Judy, R.W., and C. D'Amico. 1997. *Workforce 2020: Work & Workers in the 21st Century*. Indianapolis, IN: Hudson Institute.

Kim, E.H., and V. Singal. 2000. " The Fear of Globalizing Markets." *Emerging Market Review* 1: 183–98.

Krueger, A. 2000. "NAFTA's Effects: A Preliminary Assessment." *World Economy* 23, no. 6: 761–76.

———. 2003. "Globalisation: Preserving the Benefits." *OECD Observer* 240/241: 21–22.

Krugman, P., and A.J. Venables. 1995. "Globalization and the Inequality of Nations." *Quarterly Journal of Economics* 110, no. 4 (November): 857–80.

Luo, Y. 2005. "How Does Globalization Affect Corporate Governance and Acountability? A Perspective from MNEs." *Journal of International Management* 11: 19–41.

Minzberg, H., and J.B. Quinn. 1991. *The Strategy Process*. 2d ed. Englewood Cliffs, NJ: Prentice Hall.

Morrison, A.; D. Ricks; and K. Roth. 1998. "Globalization versus Regionalization: Which Way for the Multinational?" In *Trends in International Business: Critical Perspectives*, ed. M. Czinkota and M. Kotabe, 271–82. Malden, MA: Blackwell.

Mucchielli, J.; P. Buckley; and V. Cordell. 1998. *Globalization and Regionalization: Strategies, Policies, and Economic Environments*. London: International Business Press.

Nasim, A. 2001. "Trading with the Enemy: A Case for Liberalizing Pakistan-India Trade." In *Regionalism and Globalization: Theory and Practice*, ed. S. Lahiri, 170–198. London: Routledge.

Obstfeld, M. 1998. "The Global Capital Markets: Benefactor or Menace?" *Journal of Economic Perspectives* 12, no. 4: 9–30.

O'Rourke, K., and J. Williamson. 1999. *Globalization and History.* Cambridge, MA: MIT Press.

Prahalad, C.K., and G. Hamel. 1990. "The Core Competence of the Corporation." *Harvard Business Review* 68, no. 3: 79–91.

Prasad, E.K.; K.S. Rogoff; S. Wei; and M. Kose. 2003. *Effects of Financial Globalization on Developing Countries*. Washington, DC: International Monetary Fund.

Pugel, T. 2004. *International Economics*. 12th ed. New York: McGraw-Hill/Irwin.

Razin, A., and E. Sadka. 1999. *The Economics of Globalization: Policy Perspectives from Public Economics*. Cambridge: Cambridge University Press.

Smith, N. 2006. "The Endgame of Globalization." *Political Geography* 25: 1–14.

Teitel, S. 2005. "Globalization and Its Disconnects." *Journal of Socio-Economics* 34: 444–70.

Thomsen, S. 1999. "Southeast Asia: The Role of Foreign Direct Investment Policies in Development." Working papers on international investment. Paris: Organization for Economic Cooperation and Development.

Tobin, J. 2000. "Financial Globalization." *World Development* 28, no. 6: 1101–4.

Van Den Berg, H. 2004. *International Economics*. Boston: McGraw-Hill/Irwin.

Wong, K. 1995. *International Trade in Goods and Factor Mobility*. Cambridge, MA: MIT Press.

World Bank. 1995. *World Development Report: Workers in an Integrating World*. Washington, DC: World Bank.

———. 2002. *Globalization, Growth and Poverty*. Washington, DC: World Bank.

Part IV

Corruption in Governance
and Its Effects

15

Decentralization of Governance and Development

Pranab Bardhan

All around the world in matters of governance, decentralization is the rage. Even apart from the widely debated issues of subsidiarity and devolution in the European Union and states' rights in the United States, decentralization has been on the center stage of policy experiments in the past two decades in a large number of developing and transition economies in Latin America, Africa, and Asia. The World Bank, for example, has embraced it as one of the major governance reforms on its agenda (many *World Development Reports* of recent years as well as other bank documents give the matter a great deal of prominence) (e.g., see World Bank 1999, 2000). Taking just the two most populous countries in the world, China and India, decentralization has been regarded as the major institutional framework for China's phenomenal industrial growth in the past two decades (taking place largely in the nonstate, nonprivate sector); and India ushered in a fundamental constitutional reform in favor of decentralization around the same time that it launched a major program of economic reform.

On account of its many failures, the centralized state everywhere has lost a great deal of legitimacy and decentralization is widely believed to promise a range of benefits. It is often suggested as a way of reducing the role of the state in general, by fragmenting central authority and introducing more intergovernmental competition and checks and balances. It is viewed as a way to make government more responsive and efficient. Technological changes have also made it somewhat easier than before to provide public services (such as electricity and water supply) relatively efficiently in smaller market areas, and the lower levels of government now have a greater ability to handle certain tasks. In a world of rampant ethnic conflicts and separatist movements, decentralization is also regarded as a way of defusing social and political tensions and ensuring local cultural and political autonomy.

These potential benefits of decentralization have attracted a very diverse range of supporters. For example, free-market economists tend to emphasize the benefits of reducing the power of the overextended or predatory state. In some international organizations pushing structural adjustment and transitional reform, decentralization has sometimes been used almost as a synonym for privatization; similarly, in the literature on mechanism design an informationally decentralized system of individual decisions coordinated by a price mechanism is pitted against a system of central commands and plans. Even those who are still convinced of the pervasiveness of market failures are increasingly turning for their resolution to the government at the local level, where the transaction costs are relatively low and the information problems that can contribute to central government failures are less acute. They are joined by a diverse array of social thinkers: post-modernists, multicultural advocates, grassroots environmental activists, and supporters of the cause of indigenous peoples and technologies. In the absence of a better unifying name, I would describe this latter group as "anarcho-communitarians." They are usually both anti-market and anti–centralized state, and they energetically support assignment of control to local self–governing communities.

As is usually the case when a subject draws advocates from sharply different viewpoints, different people mean different things by decentralization. But in this chapter, we focus on a particular kind of decentralization in developing (and transition) economies, the devolution of political decision-making power to local-level small-scale entities. In countries with a long history of centralized control (as in the old imperial states of Russia, China, or India), by decentralization, public administrators often mean the dispersion of some responsibilities to regional branch offices at the local level of implementation on a particular project. For the purpose of discussion here we distinguish decentralization in the sense of devolution of political decision-making power from such mere administrative delegation of functions of the central government to their local branches. We should also separate the political and administrative aspects of decentralization from those of fiscal decentralization, and in the latter, the more numerous cases of decentralization of public expenditure from those involving decentralization of both tax and expenditure assignments. We include cases where local community organizations get formally involved in the implementation of some centrally directed or funded projects. Not all these aspects of decentralization operate simultaneously in any particular case and it is quite possible that a given economy may be decentralized in some respects but not in others. It should also be made clear that the effects of a policy of deliberate decentralization—which is our concern here—can be qualitatively different from those following from an anarchic erosion of central control (either due to the collapse of the state, as has happened in some countries in Africa, or a lack of administrative or fiscal capacity on the part of the central authority leading to abandonment of social protection functions, as has happened in some transition economies).

The territorial domain of subnational governments, of course, varies enormously from country to country. A typical province in India or China is larger (in population) than most countries in the world, and so federalism in the sense of devolution of power to the provincial state governments may still retain fairly centralized power over people. Unfortunately, data below the provincial government level are often very scarce, and most quantitative studies of decentralization (e.g., those based on the share of the central government in total expenditure or revenues) do not pertain to issues at the local community level (even apart from the fact that the share of expenditure or revenues is not a good index of decision-making authority). Even at the latter level, the units are diverse (ranging from megacities to small villages) and the boundaries are often determined by accidents of history and geography, not by concerns of decentralization of administration. In this chapter, we generally confine the analytical focus of decentralization to the governing authority at the local community level (say, village, municipality, or county levels of administration).

Our chapter begins with a description of why decentralization poses some different issues in the institutional context of developing (and transition) countries, and thus why it may sometimes be hazardous to draw lessons for them from, say, the experiences of U.S. states and city governments. We attempt to give a sense of some new theoretical models that extend the discussion to political agency problems that may resonate more in the context of developing and transition economies. We discuss some of the ongoing empirical work in evaluating the impact of decentralization on delivery of public services and local business development.

Decentralization has undoubted merits and strengths. However, the idea of decentralization may need some protection against its own enthusiasts, both from free-market advocates who see it as an opportunity to cripple the state and from those anarcho-communitarians who ignore the "community failures" that may be as serious as the market failures or government failures that economists commonly analyze.

Departures from the Fiscal Federalism Literature

There is a large literature on decentralization, often referred to as "fiscal federalism," mostly relating to the case of the United States.[1] The principles discussed in this literature have been effectively applied to national-provincial relations in developing countries such as Argentina, Brazil, Colombia, South Africa, India, and China, but in this chapter we go beyond this to stress the special issues that arise in decentralization in developing (and transitional) economies, primarily because the institutional contexts (and therefore the structure of incentives and organization) are in some respects qualitatively different from those in the classical case of the United States (or the recent case of the European Union).

Much of the fiscal federalism literature focuses on the economic efficiency of intergovernmental competition, which often starts with a market metaphor that is rationalized by the well-worn Tiebout (1956) model. In this approach, different local governments offer different public tax-expenditure bundles and mobile individuals are supposed to allocate themselves according to their preferences. The assumptions required for the Tiebout model are, however, much too stringent, particularly for poor countries.[2] The crucial assumption of population mobility (fully informed citizens "voting with their feet" in response to differential public performance), which enables governments in the Tiebout framework to overcome the well-known problem of inducing citizens to reveal their preferences for public goods, largely fails in poor countries. In any case, many of the public goods in question are community—and site—specific, and it is often possible to exclude nonresidents. In rural communities of poor countries, social norms sharply distinguish "outsiders" from "insiders," especially with respect to entitlement to community services.

Also, the information and accounting systems and mechanisms of monitoring public bureaucrats are much weaker in low-income countries. In the standard literature on decentralization and "fiscal federalism," the focus is on allocation of funds and it is implicitly assumed that allocated funds automatically reach their intended beneficiaries. This assumption needs to be drastically qualified in developing countries, where attention must be paid to special incentives and devices to check bureaucratic corruption—and thus the differential efficacy of such mechanisms under centralization and decentralization.

Third, even in the relatively few democratic developing countries, the institutions of local democracy and mechanisms of political accountability are often weak. Thus, any discussion of delivery of public services has to grapple more seriously with issues of capture of governments at different tiers by elite groups than is the custom in the traditional decentralization literature.

Fourth, the traditional literature on decentralization, even though not impervious to issues of distribution, is usually preoccupied with issues of efficiency in public provision. When a major goal of decentralization in developing countries is to effectively reach out to the poor (or to defuse unrest among disadvantaged minority groups), often in remote backward areas, targeting success in poverty alleviation programs is a more important performance criterion than the efficiency of interregional resource allocation.

In the traditional discussion of decentralization and federalism, the focus is on checks and balances, on how to restrain the central government's power, whereas in many situations in developing countries, the poor and the minorities, oppressed by the local power groups, may be looking to the central state for protection and relief. Stepan and Linz (forthcoming) make a useful distinction between "coming-together federalism," such as in the United States, where previously sovereign polities gave up part of their sovereignty for efficiency gains from resource pooling and a common market, and "holding-together federalism," such as in the multinational democracies of India, Belgium, and Spain, where the emphasis is on redistributive or compensating transfers to keep the contending polities together. In heterogeneous societies, such redistributive pressures sometimes lead fiscal decentralization to allow for state and local borrowing that may be large enough to cause problems of macroeconomic stabilization, as has happened in South Africa, Brazil, and Argentina.[3] Not all state-mandated redistribution, however, is inflationary or unproductive rent creation, as is usually presumed in the traditional literature. Some redistribution to disadvantaged groups or regions (say, in the form of decentralized delivery of health, education, or infrastructural services) need not be at the expense of efficiency, and may even improve the potential for productive investment, innovation, and human resource development on the part of communities long bypassed by the elite or the mainstream.

Fifth, the fiscal federalism literature typically assumes that lower levels of government both collect taxes and spend funds, so localities can be classified as low-tax/low-service or high-tax/high-service. This connection between local revenues and spending is rather tenuous. In most countries, much of the more elastic (and progressive) sources of tax revenue lie with the central government, and there is a built-in tendency toward vertical fiscal imbalance. Income is often geographically concentrated, both because of agglomeration economies and initial endowments of natural resources and infrastructural facilities. Thus, certain local areas will find it much easier to raise significant tax revenue than others do. In addition, there are limits to interregional tax competition. In many low-income countries, the decentralization issues discussed there are primarily about providing centrally collected tax revenue to lower levels of government, rather than seeking to empower lower levels of government to collect taxes. The focus is on public expenditure assignments, unaccompanied by any significant financial devolution.

Sixth, the decentralization literature typically assumes that different levels of government all have similar levels of technical and administrative capacity. This assumption is questionable for all countries. With respect to the attraction of qualified people by agglomeration economies, in most countries central bureaucracies attract better talent. But the problem is especially severe in many developing countries, where the quality of staff in local bureaucracies—including those performing basic tasks such as accounting and recordkeeping—is very low. Even their more professional and technical people suffer from the disadvantages of isolation, poor training, and low interaction with other professionals. As Bird (1995) puts it, information asymmetry thus works both ways: the central government may not know *what* to do, the local government may not know *how* to do it.[4] Of course, this problem is of differential importance in different services. Providing for street cleaning or garbage collection may not require sophisticated expertise, but power production and transmission, bulk supply of clean water, and public sanitation do. Decentralization to the local level will often work better in the former kind of services than in the latter.

In our subsequent discussion we consider the issues of decentralization in developing countries, keeping in mind these points of difference with the traditional literature.

Adapting the Theory of Decentralization for Developing Countries

The conventional wisdom in the fiscal federalism literature, as in Oates (1972), is that decentralization is to be preferred when tastes are heterogeneous and there are no spillovers across jurisdictions. With spillovers and no heterogeneity, a central government providing a common level of public goods and services for all localities is more efficient; with spillovers decentralization leads to underprovision of local public goods, as local decision makers do not take into account benefits going to other districts. The issue of spillovers is relevant to investment in highway transport and communication, public research and extension, control of pollution and epidemics, and so on. It is less relevant when the public goods are more local, as in local roads or minor irrigation, village health clinics and sanitation, identification of beneficiaries of public transfer programs, and so forth.

Centralization can also exploit economies of scale better in the construction of overhead facilities, but these economies of scale are less important in local management and maintenance. In a canal irrigation system, for example, the one in South Korea described by Wade (1997), construction was in the hands of central authority, but maintenance was devolved to local communities. Similarly, in primary education, while the local government may run the day-to-day functioning of schools, the upper-tier government may have the economies of scale in designing curricula, and prescribing and enforcing minimum quality standards. In the public delivery of electricity, economies of scale in generation and transmission may be the responsibility of centralized power plants and grids, while the distribution may be decentralized to local governments.

The traditional theory of fiscal federalism is now being extended to a political economy setting, with the introduction of transaction costs in the political markets, or political agency problems between the ruler and the ruled, between the politicians/bureaucrats and the electorate; and, for reasons mentioned above, these transaction and agency costs may be much more serious in the context of developing countries. It is usually argued that the local government has an information advantage over the upper-tier governments. But it may be asked why a central government cannot procure for itself the same information advantage of proximity through local agents. In some countries, the central government uses such representatives at the local level (e.g., the *préfets* in France and Italy or the *intendentes* in Chile) for this purpose. It may even be argued that the central government can have economies of scope in the collection of information. But the main reason why in practice the local government still retains the informational advantage has to do with political accountability. In democratic countries, the local politicians may have more incentive to use local information than national or provincial politicians, since the former are answerable to the local electorate while the latter have wider constituencies (where the local issues may get diluted).

Focusing on accountability, rather than information per se, leads to considering how the public can monitor and affect elected officials at different levels of government. Seabright (1996) discusses the problem of political accountability theoretically in terms of allocation of control rights in the context of incomplete contracts, where breaches of contract are observable—though not verifiable in administrative or judicial review—and are subject to periodic electoral review. His model has both central and local elected officials. In his framework, centralization allows benefits from policy coordination, which is especially important if there are spillovers across jurisdictions. However, centralization has costs in terms of diminished accountability, in the sense of reduced probability that the welfare of a given locality can determine the reelection of the government. Elections are, of course, extremely blunt instruments of political accountability, and other institutional devices and unelected community organizations (such as nongovernmental organizations) may be deployed to strengthen local accountability.

The mechanism of accountability may also be strengthened by "yardstick competition," where jurisdictions are compared with each other (e.g., see Besley and Case 1995). The effort or competence of public officials is not directly observable by citizens, and if poor results occur, public officials can always plead that they did the best that was possible under the circumstances. However, if the shocks that create a wedge between effort and outcomes are correlated across jurisdictions, then yardstick competition can act as an indicator of relative effort on the part of agents. As Seabright (1996) points out, this argument of yardstick competition under decentralization, which may help voters to know whether they should seek to replace their governments, is to be distinguished from his own argument that decentralization may increase their ability to do so.

The combination of decentralization and yardstick competition allows the possibility of experimentation in the way a given public service is provided, and then demonstration and learning from other jurisdictions. In China in the early years of its market reforms, decentralization with jurisdictional competition allowed some coastal areas to experiment with institutional reform, the success of which showed the way for the rest of the country. Economic historians have pointed to the fragmentation and decentralization of early modern Europe—sometimes called "parcelized sovereignty" (e.g., see North and Thomas 1973)—as a source of strength, in enabling experimentation and competition, leading to technological and institutional innovations that helped Europe ultimately to overtake the more centralized empire-states of Asia.

In comparing centralization and decentralization, Tommasi and Weinschelbaum (1999) pose the political agency problem in terms of the number of principals (relative to agents). Citizens are viewed as principals and their elected representatives as agents. The local government has better means (in the form of information) to be responsive, also better (electoral) incentives. In the case of centralization the number of principals is very large while the number of agents is few, whereas in the case of decentralization there is one agent per locality. The larger the number of principals, the more serious the problem of lack of coordination in contracting with agents. Decentralization is preferable to centralization when the problem of interjurisdictional externality is less important than the coordination effect.[5]

Besley and Coate (2000) focus on the importance of political aggregation mechanisms in the trade-off between centralized and decentralized provision of local public goods. Under decentralization public goods are selected by locally elected representatives, while under a centralized system policy choices are determined by a legislature consisting of elected representatives from each district (so that conflicts of interest between citizens of different jurisdictions play out in the legislature). They then reconsider the traditional questions of the fiscal federalism literature in terms of alternative models of legislative behavior (one in which decisions are made by a minimum winning coalition of representatives and the other where legislators reach a bargaining solution). They show that the familiar presumption that larger spillovers across jurisdictions help the case for centralization is not so clear under such political economy considerations.

Political accountability in poor countries is particularly affected by the likelihood of corruption or capture by interest groups. While local governments may have better local information and accountability pressure, they may be more vulnerable to capture by local elites, who will then receive a disproportionate share of spending on public goods.[6] This is in contrast to the Seabright (1996) model, in which political accountability is always greater at the local level. On the other hand, the central bureaucrat who is in charge of the delivery of, for example, an infrastructural service such as electricity, telecommunication, or canal irrigation may be corrupt in a way that leads to cost-padding, targeting failures, and generally inefficient and inequitable service delivery. The problem for the central government employing the bureaucrat is that it has very little information on the local needs, delivery costs, and the amount actually delivered. Many programs in developing countries thus have a large gap between the commitment of resources at the central level and the delivery of services at the local level. For a particularly egregious example, see Reinikka and Svensson (2001), who study leakage in the flow of educational funds from the central government to schools in Uganda in the period 1991–95. They found that only 13 percent of the total grant transferred from the central government for nonwage expenditures in schools (on items such as textbooks, instructional materials, and on other expenses) actually reached the schools. The majority of schools actually received no money at all from the central transfers for non-wage expenditures.

Bardhan and Mookherjee (2000a) develop a simple analytical framework that formalizes the trade-off between these conflicting aspects of centralized and decentralized delivery systems. Decentralization, by shifting control rights from the central bureaucrat (who otherwise acts as an unregulated monopolist) to a local government, typically tends to expand service deliveries as authority goes to those more responsive to user needs. But with capture of the local government (in the sense of elites receiving a larger weight in the local government's allocation of a weighted sum of welfare), there is a tendency for the service to be overprovided to local elites at the expense of the nonelite. The extent of such inefficient and inequitable cross-subsidization will depend on the extent of local capture and on the degree of fiscal autonomy of the local government. On the latter question, three different financing mechanisms for local governments are considered: local taxes, user fees, and central grants. With local tax financing there is the risk that the captured local government may resort to a regressive financing pattern whereby the nonelite bear the tax burden of providing services to the elite. Restrictions on the ability of local governments to levy taxes may then be desirable, even at the cost of reducing the flexibility of service provision for local needs.

User charges may be a convenient compromise between the need to match provision with local needs and to avoid an unduly heavy burden on the local poor. Since no user is compelled to use the service, this imposes a limit on the extent of cross-subsidization foisted on the poor. So with user-fee financing, decentralization as well as local tax-financed decentralization unambiguously dominate centralization in terms of welfare, irrespective of the extent of local capture. Central grant financing, on the other hand, may encourage local governments to claim higher local need or cost, leading to a restriction of the level of service delivery; the welfare implications are ambiguous, depending on a range of relevant political and financing parameters. User charges cannot, however, be used to finance antipoverty programs (such as targeted public distribution of food, education, or health services) that by their very nature are targeted at groups that do not have the ability to pay for the service (or to pay bribes to the central bureaucrats). In such cases, as is shown in Bardhan and Mookherjee (2000b), the extent of capture of local governments relative to that of the central government is a critical determinant of the welfare impact of decentralization. If local governments are equally or less vulnerable to capture than the central government, decentralization is then likely to improve both efficiency and equity. But the opposite may be the case when capture at the local level is much greater than at the central level.

Even though the extent of relative capture of governments at different levels is crucial in understanding the likely impact of decentralization initiatives, there has been very little work on the subject, either theoretical or empirical.[7] The extent of capture of local governments by local elites depends on levels of social and economic inequality within communities, traditions of political participation and voter awareness, fairness and regularity of elections, transparency in local decision-making processes and government accounts, media attention, and so on. These vary widely across communities and countries, as documented in numerous case studies (e.g., see Conning and Kevane 2000; Crook and Manor 1998). Of course, central governments are also subject to capture, and perhaps at more than the local level because of the larger importance of campaign funds in national elections and better information about candidates and issues in local elections based on informal sources. On the other hand, particularly in large heterogeneous societies, the elites are usually more divided at the national level, with more competing and heterogeneous groups neutralizing one another. At the local level in situations of high inequality, collusion may be easier to organize and enforce in small proximate groups (involving officials, politicians, contractors, and interest groups); the risks of being caught and reported are easier to manage, and the multiplex interlocking social and economic relationships among the local influential people may act as formidable barriers to entry into these cozy rental havens. At the central level in democratic countries, more institutional mechanisms for checks and balances are usually in place: these include various constitutional forms of separation of powers and adjudicatory systems in some countries, more regular auditing of public accounts, more vigilance by national media, and so forth, most of which are often absent or highly ineffective at the local level.

Even in undemocratic but largely egalitarian societies, the problem of local capture may be less acute. It is generally overlooked in the widely noted success story of decentralized rural-industrial development of China over the past two decades that the decollectivization of agriculture since 1978 represented one of the world's most egalitarian distributions of land cultivation rights (with the size of land cultivated by a household assigned almost always strictly in terms of its demographic size), and this may have substantially mitigated the problem of capture of local governments and other institutions by the oligarchic owners of immobile factors of production (such as land), which afflicts other rural economies (for example, India).

When the potential for capture of local governments is serious, decentralization programs have to focus a great deal of attention on strengthening local accountability mechanisms. In fact, in policy debates when we consider the costs and benefits of redistributive policies (e.g., land reforms, public health campaigns, and literacy movements), we often ignore their substantial positive spillover effects in terms of enlarging the stake of large numbers of the poor in the system and strengthening the institutions of local democracy. Comparing across the various states in India, it is clear that local democracy and institutions of decentralization are more effective in the states (such as Kerala and West Bengal) where land reforms and mass movements for raising political awareness have been more active. The 1996 National Election Survey data in India suggest that in West Bengal, 51 percent of the respondent voters expressed a high level of trust in their local government (Mitra and Singh 1999), whereas in the adjoining state of Bihar (where both land reform and local democratic institutions have been very weak) the corresponding figure is 30 percent. Near-universal literacy in Kerala has helped sustain widespread newspaper readership, which has encouraged a vigilant press on issues like corruption in local governments.

In both Kerala and West Bengal, it has also been observed that theft and corruption at the local level are more effectively resisted if regular local elections to select representatives in the local bodies are supplemented by an institutionalized system of periodic public hearings on items of major public expenditure. But even that is inadequate if the complaints made in public are not acted upon by the ruling party. There is evidence that sometimes the opposition parties or minority factions stop attending the village council meetings or the public hearings, as they perceive that they cannot do much about the ruling party's spending of public funds that takes the form of widespread distribution of patronage (e.g., "jobs for the boys" or what Italians call *lottizzazione*), which sometimes consolidates its electoral advantage. It is important to install public accounts committees at the local legislative level with their leading members taken from the opposition party (as is the case on the central parliamentary committees in India or Britain). In general the auditing process at the local level is extremely deficient, not always by design, but by the sheer dearth in the villages of technical capacity for accounting, record-keeping, and auditing.

In sum, in considering the theory of decentralization in developing countries, it is important to move beyond the traditional trade-off that centralization is better for dealing with spillovers and decentralization is better for dealing with heterogeneity. It is necessary to delve into political economy issues of institutional process and accountability at both the local and the central levels.

Empirical Evaluation of Decentralized Delivery of Public Services

In this section we shall briefly indicate some of the attempts that have been made to empirically evaluate the impact of decentralization on the delivery of social services in developing countries. Even though decentralization experiments are being conducted in many of these countries, hard quantitative evidence on their impact is rather scarce. There are a number of scattered studies that we will try to arrange in terms of the nature of their empirical methodology.

In two successful cases of decentralization in Latin America, there is some evidence available on the "before and after" comparison of service delivery outcomes. One is the widely noted case of participatory budgeting in municipal government in the city of Porto Alegre in Brazil, and the other is the less well-known but quite dramatic success of the post-1994 decentralization initiative in Bolivia. In Porto Alegre, where assembly meetings of local citizens and neighborhood associations in different regions discuss investment priorities, review accounts and elect representatives to a citywide council (COP) that allocates available resources across wards, impressive results have followed: between 1989 and 1996, access to basic sanitation (water and sewage) as well as enrollment in elementary or secondary schools nearly doubled, while revenue collection increased by 48 percent (see Santos 1998). Although it is difficult from this study to isolate the impact of participatory budgeting reforms from those of other ongoing changes, it seems likely that there has been a substantial impact on the pattern of resource allocation across localities, particularly to poor ones, and in the lessening of the misappropriation of resources compared with the past and with other areas in Brazil.

In Bolivia in 1994, the number of municipalities as well as the share of national tax revenue allocated to municipalities doubled, along with devolution to the municipalities of administrative authority, investment responsibility, and title to local infrastructural facilities. This has been associated with a massive shift of public resources in favor of the smaller and poorer municipalities and from large-scale production to social sectors. Faguet (2001) finds that public investment in education, water, and sanitation rose significantly in three-quarters of all municipalities, and investments responded to measures of local need; for example, expanded public education spending was larger on average in municipalities with a lower literacy rate or with fewer private schools. Faguet's analysis is in terms of levels of public spending rather than outcome variables such as school enrollments or school performance, or access to water and sanitation services. In the studies of Porto Allegre and Bolivia there is not much information available on the allocation of resources within a community across households in different socioeconomic classes. This means that issues like the cost effectiveness of programs, targeting performance, or the extent of capture of local governments cannot be addressed. Without household-level data on access to public services, these crucial aspects of the impact of decentralization cannot be properly assessed.

There is hardly any household-level analysis in the literature on the comparative effects of centralized versus decentralized delivery. One detailed study of targeting performance of a decentralized program using household-level information in a developing country is that of Galasso and Ravallion (2001), who studied a decentralized food-for-education program in Bangladesh. In this central government program, in which 2 million children participated in 1995–96, the identification of beneficiary households within a selected community was made typically by a local school management committee (consisting of parents, teachers, education specialists, and school donors). Galasso and Ravallion use data from a 1995–96 Household Expenditure Survey to assess the targeting performance of the program. They find that the program was mildly pro-poor (i.e., taking all villages, a somewhat larger fraction of the poor than the nonpoor received benefits from the program). But they also find some evidence of local capture. For example, within the set of participating villages, targeting performance was worse in communities with greater land inequality or in remote locations. But the targeting improved as the program expanded, suggesting that the program shifted the balance of power in favor of the poor. It is also clearly that the level of targeting *within* communities was superior to that achieved *across* communities by central allocation, thus offering little support for the view that the central government is more accountable to the poor than local communities. This contrasts somewhat to the experience of the widely acclaimed antipoverty transfer program PROGRESA (Programa de Educación, Salud y Alimentación) in Mexico. The program follows a two-stage targeting process. Coady (2001) finds that most of PROGRESA's targeting effectiveness is achieved at the first stage when poor localities are selected, rather than at the second stage when households are selected within localities, not on the basis of identification of beneficiaries by local communities as in the food-for-education program in Bangladesh, but on the basis of information collected from a census undertaken for this purpose.

Alderman (1998) examines, on the basis of a household survey conducted in 1996, a targeted social assistance program (Ndihme Ekonomika) in Albania that was decentralized in 1995. He finds that there have been modest gains in targeting efficiency and cost effectiveness following decentralization, that local authorities use some additional information in allocating program benefits among households, and that the central allocation of social assistance funds to local authorities is ad hoc and not strongly correlated with the level of poverty in the local communities. He does not find evidence that the decentralization initiative caused the benefits of the program to be captured by the well-off members of the community.

There is some quantitative evidence on the impact of mandated representations of historically disadvantaged groups like women in leadership positions in local governance in India. Since 1998, one-third of all positions of chief of the village councils in India have been reserved for women: only women may be candidates for the position of chief in a reserved village council and the latter is selected randomly. Taking advantage of this random assignment (thus avoiding an econometric problem in usual cross-sectional studies of this question, whereby communities that are more likely to take women's needs into account may also be more willing to let them be in leadership positions), Chattopadhyay and Duflo (2001) measure the impact of this political reservation policy on outcomes of decentralization with data collected from a survey of all investments in local public goods made by village councils in one district in West Bengal. They find that the women leaders of village councils invest more in infrastructure that is directly relevant to the needs of rural women (drinking water, fuel, and roads), and that village women are more likely to participate in the policymaking process if the leader of their village council is a woman. However, without direct evidence on the nature of women's preferences relative to men's, and since women's reserved leadership positions in local government were not linked to the distribution of women in the village, this study does not quite address how local democracy affects the ability of underrepresented groups in the village to implement their desired outcomes.

Foster and Rosenzweig (2001) use a panel data set of villages across India to examine the consequences of democratization and fiscal decentralization. They find that an increase in the demographic weight of the landless households in a village under democratic decentralization has a positive effect on allocation of public resources to road construction (which, according to them, primarily benefits the landless workers) and a negative effect on resources to irrigation facilities (which primarily benefit the landed). But their data set does not contain the many severe institutional lapses in the implementation of decentralization across India, particularly in manipulations of the local electoral process and in the range of authority and finances devolved to local governments, making democratic decentralization not yet a reality in most parts of India. It is not clear, for example, how much leeway elected local village councils have in matters of allocation to projects like road construction, which are often centrally sponsored and quite bureaucratically controlled from above; at most, the local government gets involved only in deciding where to locate the road and to identifying the beneficiary workers.

There are also some case studies on the effects of decentralization in different parts of the world that provide some descriptive and suggestive correlations, but not enough to clinch any hypothesis. Azfar, Kahkonen, and Meagher (2000) surveyed households and government officials at municipal and provincial levels in the Philippines with respect to the stated public investment priorities in a given locality. It turned out that the stated priorities of officials at the municipal level weakly matched those of local residents, while those of officials at the provincial level did not, suggesting that decentralization may improve the quality of information used in public investment decisions. There is also some evidence in the survey of more perceived corruption at the central level than at the local level. Azfar, Kahkonen, and Meagher (2000) carried out a similar survey in Uganda with qualitatively similar results. In Uganda they also found a greater reliance on community leaders for news concerning local corruption and local elections than for national news, which they interpret as evidence of greater potential for local capture.

In the 1990s, Nicaragua started a program of transferring key management tasks in public schools from central authorities to local councils involving parents. An evaluation of this program by King and Ozler (1998) on the basis of school and household surveys and student achievement tests suggests that de facto autonomy has not yet been given to many of the councils, but where it has been, there is a significant positive effect on student performance.

The *World Development Report 1994* on infrastructure cited several cases of quality improvement and cost savings in infrastructure projects after local communities were given part of the responsibility of management. A review of World Bank data for forty-two developing countries found that where road maintenance was decentralized, backlogs were lower and the condition of roads better. Data for a group of developing countries revealed that per capita costs of water in World Bank–funded water projects were four times higher in centralized than in fully decentralized systems. A study of 121 completed rural water supply projects, financed by various agencies, showed that projects with high participation in project selection and design were much more likely to have the water supply maintained in good condition than would be the case with more centralized decision making.

Wade's (1997) contrasting account of the operations of irrigation bureaucracy in South Korea and in South India brings out the importance of local accountability in delivery of infrastructural services. The Indian canal systems are large, centralized hierarchies in charge of all functions (operations and maintenance as well as design and construction). Their methods of operation (including the promotion and transfer rules for officials, rules designed to minimize identification between the irrigation patrollers and the local farmers, and the frequent use of low-trust management and supervision methods) and source of finance (most of the irrigation department's budget comes in the form of a grant from the state treasury) are insensitive to the need for developing local trust and cooperation. In Korea, on the other hand, according to this account, there are functionally separate organizations in the canal systems. The implementation and routine maintenance tasks (as opposed to policymaking and technical design work) are delegated to the Farmland Improvement Associations, one per catchment area, which are staffed by local part-time farmers (selected by the village chiefs), knowledgeable about changing local conditions, dependent for their salary and operational budget largely on the user fees paid by the farmers, and continually drawing upon local trust relationships. At the time of the study, Korea did not have a democratic political regime or a free press, but farmers were better informed about, and had better access to, the local irrigation organization. In this example there is no one-to-one relationship between the strength of democracy at the national political level and that of institutions of accountability at the local level.

A similar story on accountability can be told in the field of education and health, comparing North India with some authoritarian countries. Institutions of local accountability are rather weak in large parts of North India, and it is common to observe, for example, a serious problem of absenteeism of salaried teachers in village public schools and of doctors in rural public health clinics.[8] The villagers are usually aware of the problem but do not have the institutional means of correcting it, as the state-funded teachers and doctors are not answerable to the villagers in the insufficiently decentralized system. On the other hand, in nondemocratic China, the local Communist Party officials have sometimes been quite responsive to local needs (at least as long as they are not in conflict with the party's program), as the comparative study of two villages in China and India by DrPze and Saran (1995) shows in the context of China's far better performance in the provision of primary education at the local level. (Similar accounts are available of more effective public pressure in rural basic education and health services in Cuba as compared with some of the more democratic regimes in Latin America.) There are, of course, many authoritarian countries where local accountability is completely absent and the situation is much worse than in North India.

Taken as a group, these studies suggest generally positive effects of decentralization, but it is hard to draw conclusive lessons. Many of the studies are largely descriptive, not analytical, and often they suggest correlations rather than causal processes. Most of them are not based on household survey data, making the comparative impact of centralized versus decentralized programs on different socioeconomic groups of households difficult to assess.

Decentralization and Local Business Development

Most of the cases of decentralization in developing countries examined in the theoretical and empirical literature relate to the delivery of social services. But in recent years there has been an extension of the traditional literature on federalism to the case of the role of local government in promoting local business development, particularly in the context of transition economies, especially China, and this has potential implications for developing countries where public delivery issues have so far been more prominent. In Qian and Weingast (1997) and Qian and Roland (1998), for example, decentralization of information and authority and interjurisdictional competition are considered as commitment devices on the part of the central or provincial government to provide market incentives, both the "positive" incentive rewarding economic success at the local level and the "negative" incentive in terms of punishing economic failure. The local government-run township and village enterprises (TVEs), which served as the engine of growth in China over the past two decades, are cited as a major example of the outcome of a successful "market-preserving federalism." In terms of "positive" market incentives, the TVEs had full control over their assets and they were largely left alone (as a residual claimant) to "get rich gloriously," and the limited knowledge of the upper-tier governments about the "extra-budget" and "off-budget" accounts of local governments acted as a check on the formers' interventionism. In contrast, as we can see from an econometric study of the fiscal relations between local and regional governments in Russia by Zhuravskaya (2001) on the basis of a panel data set for thirty-five large cities, local governments could retain only about 10 percent of their revenues at the margin, thus providing only weak incentives to foster local business development and thereby to increase their tax base. In terms of the "negative" incentive, Chinese upper-tier governments enforced a dynamic commitment in denying bailout to many failing TVEs. Having no access to state banks and facing the mobility of capital across jurisdictions raised the opportunity costs of local governments for rescuing inefficient firms, thus leading to the endogenous emergence of a hard budget constraint.

Without denying the importance of these market incentives, it is possible to argue, however, that the case of market-preserving federalism is institutionally underspecified in these studies. Depending on the political-institutional complex in different countries, the same market incentives may have different efficacy. As Rodden and Rose-Ackerman (1997) have pointed out in a critique of market-preserving federalism, whether political leaders of a local government respond to highly mobile investors or instead pay more attention to the demands of strong distributive coalitions dominated by owners of less mobile factors depends on the institutional milieu. Owners of capital vary widely in the specificity of their assets, and institutional incentives confronting political leaders may vary even for the same jurisdictional competitive pressure. Even in a democracy, not to mention authoritarian systems, electoral competition does not necessarily punish local leaders who fail to respond to exit threats of mobile asset owners and are instead more responsive to coalition building and the "voice" of well-organized lobbies. We have pointed out earlier the problem of local capture by the oligarchic owners of immobile factors of production such as land in rural India, and how in the Chinese case the lack of such strong rural lobbies (owing largely to the egalitarian land distribution) may have made a difference in the local governments' vigorous pursuit of rural industrialization.[9] In Russia many have pointed out that over much of the 1990s, local governments have shown features of being captured by erstwhile rent-holders and old firms that sometimes blocked the rise of new firms that could compete away their rents.[10] Of course, even in China by some accounts (e.g., Shirk 1993), local officials have often used their financial authority under decentralization to build political machines, collecting rents in exchange for selective benefits and patronage distribution, and federalism may not always have been that market-preserving.

It seems that jurisdictional competition is not enough to explain the emergence of endogenous hard budget constraints for local governments without much more specification of the local political process. Even ignoring the lobbies of land oligarchies, in some countries (democratic or otherwise) if a local business fails, threatening the livelihood of thousands of poor people, it is difficult for the local government (or if the latter is bankrupt, upper-tier governments) to ignore the political pressure that will be generated in favor of bailing them out. Wildasin (1997) has rightly pointed out that federal grants to local governments may be less "soft" in the small jurisdictions than the large (which are "too big to fail"), but even small jurisdictions may have key politicians representing (or lobbying for) them, and, in any case, it is cheaper to come to their rescue.

Conclusion

It is quite plausible to argue that in the matter of service delivery as well as in local business development, control rights in governance structures should be assigned to people who have the requisite information and incentives, and, at the same time, will bear responsibility for the (political and economic) consequences of their decisions. In many situations this calls for more devolution of power to local authorities and communities. But it is also important to keep in mind that structures of local accountability are not in place in many developing countries, and local governments are often at the mercy of local power elites, who may frustrate the goal of achieving public delivery to the general populace of social services, infrastructural facilities, and conditions conducive to local business development. This means that to be really effective, decentralization has to be accompanied by serious attempts to change the existing structures of power within communities and to improve the opportunities for participation and voice, and to engage the hitherto disadvantaged or disenfranchised in the political process. After all, the logic behind decentralization is not just about weakening the central authority or about preferring local elites to central authority, it is fundamentally about making governance at the local level more responsive to the felt needs of the large majority of the population. To facilitate this the state, far from retreating into the minimalist role of classical liberalism, may sometimes have to play an activist role in enabling (if only as a "catalyst") the mobilization of people in local participatory development, in neutralizing the power of local oligarchs, and in providing supralocal support in the form of pump-priming local finance, supplying technical and professional services toward building local capacity, acting as a watchdog for service quality standards, evaluation, and auditing, investing in larger infrastructure, and providing some coordination in the face of externalities across localities.

The literature on decentralization in the context of development is still in its infancy. On the theoretical side, perhaps the key challenge is to find better ways to model the complex organizational and incentive problems that are involved, in a situation with pervasive problems of monitoring and enforcement. On the empirical side, there is a great deal of scope for rigorous work in evaluating the impact of ongoing decentralization initiatives, using detailed household and community surveys, comparing it with the experience of centralization or some other counterfactual. In such empirical work, one has to be particularly wary of several econometric problems. One issue is that some of the data involved in evaluating community participation and project performance may be subjective. For instance, some investigators start with the prior belief that participation is good, which creates a "halo effect"

in their observations. A second problem involves simultaneity: better beneficiary participation may cause improved project performance, but improved
project performance often also encourages higher participation.[11] Finally,
there is the commonly encountered endogeneity problem. Before being too
quick to claim that decentralization has brought about certain outcomes, it
is worth considering that decentralization may have resulted from ongoing
political and economic changes that have also affected these same outcomes.
Separating decentralization from its political and economic causes, so that
decentralization is not just a proxy for an ill-defined broad package of social
and economic reforms, is a delicate problem.

Notes

I am grateful to Brad de Long, Timothy Taylor, and Michael Waldman for editorial suggestions and to Dilip Mookherjee for substantive discussion (and joint research) on issues
relating to this chapter.

1. Many of the issues have been well surveyed in the *JEP* "Symposium on Fiscal
Federalism," *Journal of Economic Perspectives* 11, no. 4 (Fall 1997).

2. There are doubts about just how the Tiebout mechanism operates even in relatively
mobile societies like that of the United States. For instance, very few poor people move
from state to state in search of higher welfare benefits (Hanson and Hartman 1994).

3. This chapter will not address the impact of decentralization on macroeconomic
stabilization. For a game-theoretic model of how decentralization or local democratization may increase the level of central redistribution to prevent spirals of regional revolt
and how the macroeconomic consequences depend on the initial levels of cultural division and decentralization, see Treisman (1999).

4. Occasionally, however, the local people come up with ingenious low-cost solutions, whereas centralized systems use the unnecessarily expensive services of specialized technicians. For some of the basic needs for poor people, local youths with some
minimum training as primary health workers or primary school teachers can be adequate.
In other, more technical, projects there is much scope for improving access to engineering, project design, and skills. Organizations such as AGETIP (Agence d'Exécution des
Travaux d'Intérêt Public) in Africa or the Brazil-based IBAM (Instituto Brasileiro de Ad-
ministração Municipal) have in recent years been helpful in developing local technical
capacity.

5. The idea of fewer principals in smaller jurisdictions having more political control
clearly resembles the relationship between group size and free riding in the voluntary
provision of a public good first discussed by Olson (1965). As is well known, this relationship can be ambiguous.

6. In the *Federalist Papers* (no. 10) James Madison comments on the notion that local governments are more prone to capture by elites and special interests: "The smaller
the society, the fewer probably will be the distinct parties and interests composing it; the
fewer the distinct parties and interests, the more frequently will a majority be found of
the same party, and the smaller the number of individuals composing a majority; and the
smaller the compass within which they are placed, the more easily will they concert and
execute their plans of oppression. Extend the sphere and you take in a greater variety of

parties and interests; you make it less probable that a majority of the whole will have a common motive to invade the rights of other citizens; or if such a common motive exists, it will be more difficult for all who feel it to discover their own strength and to act in unison with each other" (available at www.constitution.org/fed/federa10.htm).

7. For a theoretical analysis of the problem, see Bardhan and Mookherjee (2000c). We argue that the overall comparison of capture at central and local levels in a democracy would depend on the interplay of a large number of underlying institutional factors, such as relative degrees of voter awareness and cohesiveness of special interest groups, the extent of heterogeneity across districts, and the nature of the national electoral system, and so the issue is ultimately context- and system-specific.

8. See, for example, *PROBE* (1999), on the basis of an intensive survey of 234 randomly selected villages in North India carried out in 1996.

9. Even in India, in areas where land distribution is relatively egalitarian and local democracy is more solidaristic, as in Kerala, there are now some instances of municipal governments taking a leading role, in collaboration with bankers and social groups, in local business development. For some examples, see Das (2000).

10. The explanation of China's relative success attributed to political centralization in Blanchard and Shleifer (2000) does not seem very plausible. A strong central political authority can punish local governments (reducing the risk of their capture and the scope of their rent-seeking), but one needs a plausible story of a benevolent nonrentier central authority to go with it.

11. For an attempt to take this latter set of econometric problems into account in an evaluation of 121 rural water projects, see Isham, Narayan, and Pritchett (1995).

References

Alderman, H. 1998. "Social Assistance in Albania: Decentralization and Targeted Transfers." LSMS Working Paper no. 134, World Bank, Washington, DC.

Azfar, O.; S. Kahkonen; and P. Meagher. 2000. "Conditions for Effective Decentralized Governance: A Synthesis of Research Findings." IRIS Center Working Paper, University of Maryland.

Bardhan, P., and D. Mookherjee. 2000a. "Corruption and Decentralization of Infrastructure Delivery in Developing Countries." University of California, Berkeley.

———. 2000b. "Decentralizing Anti-Poverty Program Delivery in Developing Countries." University of California, Berkeley.

———. 2000c. "Relative Capture of Government at Local and National Levels." *American Economic Review* 90, no. 2: 135–39.

Besley, T., and A. Case. 1995. "Incumbent Behavior: Vote-Seeking, Tax-Setting and Yardstick Competition." *American Economic Review* 85, no. 1: 25–45.

Besley, T., and S. Coate. 2000. "Centralized Versus Decentralized Provision of Local Public Goods: A Political Economy Analysis." London School of Economics.

Bird, R.M. 1995. "Decentralizing Infrastructure: For Good or for Ill?" In *Decentralizing Infrastructure: Advantages and Limitations*. World Bank Discussion Papers 290, ed. A. Estache. Washington, DC.

Blanchard, O., and A. Shleifer. "Federalism with and Without Political Centralization: China Versus Russia." NBER Working Paper no. 7616, Cambridge, MA.

Chattopadhyay, R., and E. Duflo. 2001. "Women as Policy Makers: Evidence from an India-Wide Randomized Policy Experiment." Massachusetts Institute of Technology, Cambridge, MA.

Coady, D. 2001. "An Evaluation of the Distributional Power of Progresa's Cash Transfers in Mexico." International Food Policy Research Institute Working Paper, Washington, DC.

Conning, J., and M. Kevane. 2000. "Community Based Targeting Mechanisms for Social Safety Nets." World Bank, Washington, DC.

Crook, R., and J. Manor. 1998. *Democracy and Decentralization in South Asia and West Africa*. Cambridge: Cambridge University Press.

Das, M.K. 2000. "Kerala's Decentralized Planning." *Economic and Political Weekly* 35, no. 49: 4300–303.

DrPze, J., and M. Saran. 1995. "Primary Education and Economic Development in China and India: Overview and Two Case Studies." In *Choice, Welfare, and Development: A Festschrift in Honour of Amartya K. Sen*, ed. K. Basu et al. Oxford: Clarendon Press.

Faguet, J.P. 2001. "Does Decentralisation Increase Government Responsiveness to Local Needs? Decentralisation and Public Investment in Bolivia." Centre for Economic Performance Working Paper, London School of Economics.

Foster, J.D., and M.R. Rosenzweig. 2001. "Democratization, Decentralization and the Distribution of Local Public Goods in a Poor Rural Economy." University of Pennsylvania, Philadelphia.

Galasso, E., and M. Ravallion. 2001. "Decentralized Targeting of an Anti-Poverty Program." Development Research Group Working Paper, World Bank, Washington, DC.

Hanson, R.L., and J.T. Hartman. 1994. "Do Welfare Magnets Attract?" Institute for Research on Poverty, University of Wisconsin, Madison.

Isham, J.; D. Narayan; and L. Pritchett. 1995. "Does Participation Improve Performance? Establishing Causality with Subjective Data." *World Bank Economic Review* 9, no. 2: 175–200.

King, E., and B. Ozler. 1998. "What's Decentralization Got to Do with Learning? The Case of Nicaragua's School Autonomy Reform." Development Research Group Working Paper, World Bank, Washington, DC.

Mitra, S.K., and V.B. Singh. 1999. *Democracy and Social Change in India: A Cross-Sectional Analysis of the National Electorate*. New Delhi: Sage.

North, D.C., and R. Thomas. 1973. *The Rise of the Western World*. Cambridge: Cambridge University Press.

Oates, W. 1972. *Fiscal Federalism*. New York: Harcourt Brace Jovanovich.

Olson, M. 1965. *The Logic of Collective Action*. Cambridge, MA: Harvard University Press.

PROBE: Public Report on Basic Education for India. 1999. New Delhi: Oxford University Press.

Qian, Y., and G. Roland. 1998. "Federalism and the Soft Budget Constraint." *American Economic Review* 88, no. 5: 1143–62.

Qian, Y., and B.R. Weingast. 1997. "Federalism as a Commitment to Preserving Market Incentives." *Journal of Economic Perspectives* 11, no. 4: 83–92.

Reinikka, R., and J. Svensson. 2001. "Explaining Leakage of Public Funds." Development Research Group Working Paper, World Bank, Washington, DC.

Rodden, J., and S. Rose-Ackerman. 1997. "Does Federalism Preserve Markets?" *Virginia Law Review* 83, no. 7: 1521–72.

Santos, B.D.S. 1998. "Participatory Budgeting in Porto Alegre: Toward a Redistributive Democracy." *Politics and Society* 26, no. 4: 461–509.

Seabright, P. 1996. "Accountability and Decentralization in Government: An Incomplete Contracts Model." *European Economic Review* 40, no. 1: 61–89.

Shirk, S. 1993. *The Political Logic of Economic Reform in China.* Berkeley: University of California Press.

Stepan, A., and J.J. Linz. Forthcoming. *Federalism, Democracy, and Nation.*

Tiebout, C.M. 1956. "A Pure Theory of Local Expenditures." *Journal of Political Economy* 64, no. 5: 416–24.

Tommasi, M., and F. Weinschelbaum. 1999. "A Principal-Agent Building Block for the Study of Decentralization and Integration." University of San Andrés, Argentina.

Treisman, D. 1999. "Political Decentralization and Economic Reform: A Game-Theoretic Analysis." *American Journal of Political Science* 43, no. 2: 488–517.

Wade, R. 1997. "How Infrastructure Agencies Motivate Staff: Canal Irrigation in India and the Republic of Korea." In *Infrastructure Strategies in East Asia*, ed. A. Mody. Washington, DC: World Bank Economic Development Institute.

Wildasin, D.E. 1997. "Externalities and Bailouts: Hard and Soft Budget Constraints in Inter-Governmental Fiscal Relations." Vanderbilt University, Nashville.

World Bank. 1999. *Beyond the Center: Decentralizing the State.* Washington, DC.

———. 2000. *Entering the 21st Century.* Washington, DC.

Zhuravskaya, E.V. 2000. "Incentives to Provide Local Public Goods: Fiscal Federalism, Russian Style." *Journal of Public Economics* 76, no. 3: 337–68.

16

Governance Issues in India

Desh Gupta and Bhagwan Dahiya

"Good governance is perhaps the single most important factor in eradicating poverty and promoting development."

UN Secretary-General Kofi Annan

Governance is defined as the traditions and institutions by which authority is exercised in a country.

(Kaufmann, Kraay, and Zoido-Lobaton 2002, 4)

Despite the enormous costs of conducting and managing elections in the context of a poor country facing problems of vote-rigging, ballot-stuffing, difficulties of terrain and terrorism, over time and to its credit India has improved the quality and fairness of the elections and the robustness and independence of the Indian Election Commission. At the same time, the losing parties have accepted election outcomes at both the state and center levels. The independence of the judiciary and its judgments are accepted by all political parties. Despite its poverty, India is emerging as a mature democracy. In addition, in purchasing power parity (PPP), after more than two decades of average growth of nearly 6 percent per annum, it has emerged as the fourth largest global economy, with nearly 5 percent of global output. Its market is thus increasingly attractive to international business, including Australian business.

Because governance in India affects business, it is likely to interest those participating in business there. Using various sources, this chapter presents a mixed picture of governance issues in India, including discussions of: (a) perceived corruption and (b) general governance indicators. It addresses changes that have already taken place and those being planned as compared with the situation in China. Comparisons with China are important because of that country's significant role in global and Indian discourse (see, for instance, *Economist* 2003a). The chapter attempts to answer questions relating to the issue of whether Australian business should continue to avoid engaging in bribery in India.

Table 16.1

Corruption Perceptions Index (CPI) and Rank

Country	CPI* (maximum 10)	Rank (lowest 102)	High-low range	90% confidence range
Singapore	9.3	5	8.9–9.6	9.2–9.4
China	3.5	59	2.0–5.6	3.1–4.1
India	2.7	71	2.4–3.6	2.5–2.9
Indonesia	1.9	96	0.8–3.0	1.7–2.2

Sources: Transparency International (2003b).
*The CPI score ranges from 10 (highly clean) to 0 (highly corrupt).

A caveat is necessary to start with: intercountry comparisons, though used here, are problematic, because differences in cultural and socioeconomic backgrounds may lead respondents to interpret identical questions differently.

Corruption Perception Index

Corruption is one of the most damaging consequences of poor governance, which is characterized by a lack of both transparency and accountability. The adverse effects of corruption on growth have been statistically corroborated based on cross-country data (Bardhan 1997).

The 2002 *Corruption Perceptions Index* published by Transparency International (2003a) (its eighth), based on a survey of businesspeople and risk analysts, presents a rather unflattering picture of India relative to most of the 113 countries surveyed (see Table 16.1).

In 2002, India, with a low corruption perception index (CPI) of 2.7 and a rank of 71 out of 102, was perceived to be among the most corrupt in the world. The CPI in India has hovered around the 2.7–2.8 level, reflecting the lack of improvement in perceptions of the level of corruption (Table 16.2).

A higher CPI for China, meaning lower perception of corruption relative to India, may lead some to question whether or not perceptions and reality are the same. It may be that India's relatively open and more highly scrutinized system leads to greater reporting of corruption and therefore to the perception of higher levels of corruption. Certainly there is a much greater level of awareness of corruption in India. Such awareness has been furthered by the establishment of Transparency International India and its ongoing activities, including the publication (with Org-Marg Research) of its 2002 report titled "Corruption in India: An Empirical Study." It may also be that "gift giving" by the large proportion of "overseas Chinese" investors in China is considered a norm

Table 16.2

Corruption Perceptions Index (CPI) and Rank of India, 1995–2002

Year	No. of countries	CPI	Rank
1995	41	2.78	35
1996	54	2.63	46
1997	52	2.75	45
1998	85	2.90	66
1999	99	2.90	72
2000	90	2.80	69
2001	91	2.70	71
2002	102	2.70	71

Source: Transparency International India (2002).
Note: Yearly variations in rank do not reflect improvement or deterioration in level of corruption.

and therefore may not be perceived as corruption by them or the recipients. Another reason may be that the sharp erosion in the share of bureaucratic positions of the upper castes in India, since 1991, has reduced net working strength and therefore reduced opportunities based on the exchange of favors (as against the exchange of money) and heightened their dissatisfaction with the situation on the ground. At the same time, appointments based on caste and quotas have strengthened the power of government ministers, who have found it easier to get the now less secure bureaucrats to do their bidding. In the process, they are able to extract much larger payments as rent from potential and new appointees to certain bureaucratic positions than was the case before. In turn, such bureaucrats attempt to make a return on this investment.

Nevertheless, to the extent that greater regulations and controls in the hands of bureaucrats in a situation of significant scarcity lead to increased corruption, the reduction of such regulations in the post-1991 period should have reduced the actual level of corruption. The abolition of import quotas and the opening of motor vehicle, telephone, and aviation markets to private competition have virtually eliminated the need to offer bribes for such products and services. Similarly, the introduction of competition in banking made it unnecessary to bribe bank staff to get a loan approved. In fact, in the current situation, bank personnel pursue individuals and businesses to offer them loans. While it is true that these developments have helped only a very small segment of the population, this is nevertheless a growing segment that has the capacity to bribe officials. The poor do not have this capacity, and thus, unfortunately, they suffer from a lack of services.

At the same time, if the perception and reality are the same, then it reflects the ineffectiveness of India's Prevention of Corruption Act of 1988, which is aimed at dealing severely with public servants and those abetting them in criminal misconduct. The definition of a public servant is quite broad and covers any person in the service or pay of the government or remunerated by the government by fees or commission for the performance of any public duty.

Per Capita Relationship

The lower perception of corruption may also be because China's per capita income has increased much more rapidly than that of India since 1980. Even though in terms of PPP China overtook India only in 1992, by 2001 it had a 70 percent larger PPP per capita (World Bank source quoted in the *Economist* 2003a). Per capita income and the quality of governance are strongly and positively correlated across countries (Kaufman, Kraay, and Mastruzz 2003). This is not surprising, given that high-income countries are more open societies and have a greater capacity not only to enact appropriate laws but also, and more important, to enforce them. In addition, individuals are much more aware of their rights and are more likely to get recourse for them. In India, one of the most galling aspects of the system is that individual legal cases can drag on for ten to twenty years, and there is a huge backlog of cases. The legal system simply does not have the capacity to handle the cases assigned to it, which forces individuals to seek nonjudicial alternatives.

We now turn to India's performance relative to that of other poor countries using broad governance indicators.

Broad Governance Indicators

Court and Hyden (2003) have attempted governance assessments of sixteen developing and transitional societies, representing 51 percent of the world's population. The methodology involved interviewing a panel of thirty-five persons with extensive experience of the governance realm in each of the countries to complete assessments of indicators of good governance: participation, fairness, decency, accountability, transparency, and efficiency. Respondents were asked to score each indicator on a scale of 1 to 5; the higher the score, the better. In addition, respondents also provided qualitative comments.

Table 16.3 shows the median rating for ten indicators that relate particularly to accountability and transparency.

India's total governance score of 98 is much better than China's 82. This is not surprising, given that India is a liberal democracy with freedom of expression and processes that are open to challenge by opposition groups. Though civil servants in general in most countries were not seen to be accountable

Table 16.3

Selected Governance Indicators for Transition Societies, 2001

Country	Pakistan	Russia	Philippines	Indonesia	China	Argentina	Bulgaria	Jordan	India	Chile	Thailand	Average
Total governance score (min = 30)	65	73	75	80	82	83	83	97.5	98	99	100	83.25
Accountability of judicial	2	2	3	2	3	2	2	3	3	3	4	2.56
Transparency in judicial process	2	2	3	2	2	2	2	4	3	3	4	2.56
Access to justice	2	2	2	2	3	2	3	4	3	3	3	2.50
Equal application of regulations	3	2	1	2	3	2	2	4	3	4	3	2.69
Respect for property rights	3	2	3	2	3	3	3	4	3	4	3	3.00

												Average
Transparency in the Civil Service	2	2	2	2	2	2	2	3	3	3	3	2.38
Accountability of civil servants	2	2	2	2	2	2	2	3	3	3	3	2.38
Accountability of legislators	1	2	2	2	3	2	2	2	3	2	3	2.19
Government open to public input	2	2	2	3	2	2	2	3	3	3	4	2.50
Freedom of expression	3	3	4	4	3	4	3	3	4	4	4	3.31

Sources: Court and Hyden (2003); Transparency International (2003b).

and their processes were seen as lacking in transparency, India was viewed as an exception. Qualitative comments were favorable to the bureaucracy, confirming it as the backbone of the country. At the same time, transactions between the private sector and the government were seen to be marked by cronyism and corruption. Viewed as the number one problem in India, this could be linked to the country's low CPI, as discussed earlier. In terms of trend, a comparison of 1996 and 2001 showed that total governance scores had improved for all Asian countries, with the exception of the Philippines, where they dropped from 90 in 1996 to 75 in 2001. The improvement was much greater for China than for India: from 70 to 82 and from 96 to 98, respectively. The latter reflects the slow pace of reforms in India and the difficulties of getting reforms through the system, often because the opposition parties support groups that might be adversely affected by reform to heighten opposition to reforms, which forces the ruling United Progressive Alliance (UPA), a multiparty coalition, to postpone their introduction (discussed further below).

Kaufman, Kraay, and Zoido-Lobaton (2002) use six indicators to capture three aspects of governance or three clusters that are part of their definition (see Table 16.4).

The first two indicators "voice and accountability" (which concern the political process, civil liberties, and political rights) and "political stability" (which measures perceptions of the likelihood that the government in power will be destabilized or overthrown by possibly unconstitutional means) focus on the processes by which governments are selected, monitored, and replaced. While foreign business may evince interest in the first of these two indicators, in general they are not too concerned about whether or not the regime is authoritarian or suppresses human rights. Political stability is obviously important; here long-lasting authoritarian regimes may be seen as more stable than democratically elected coalitions, which in poor countries are seen as somewhat unstable.

The next two indicators "government effectiveness" (which combines the quality, competence, and independence of the civil service from political pressure and the credibility of government's commitment to policies) and "regulatory quality" (which measures the perceptions of excessive regulation and market-unfriendly policies) concern the ability of government to formulate and implement sound policies. These two indicators are probably the most significant from the standpoint of business in general because they represent the prospects for growth of the economy in general and of the private sector in particular.

The next two indicators "rule of law" (which measures the extent to which agents abide by and have confidence in the rules of society) and "control of corruption" (which measures perceptions of corruption) concern the respect

Table 16.4

Estimates of Governance

	(1) Voice and accountability				(2) Political stability				(3) Government effectiveness			
	2000/2001		1997/1998		2000/2001		1997/1998		2000/2001		1997/1998	
Country	Est.	S.E.	Est.	S.E.	Est.	S.E.	Est.	S.E.	Est.	S.E.	Est.	S.E.
China	-1.11	0.24	-1.29	0.25	0.39	0.22	0.48	0.26	0.14	0.18	0.02	0.25
India	0.66	0.24	0.36	0.25	-0.05	0.22	-0.04	0.25	-0.17	0.18	-0.26	0.23

	(4) Regulatory quality				(5) Rule of law				(6) Control of corruption			
	2000/2001		1997/1998		2000/2001		1997/1998		2000/2001		1997/1998	
Country	Est.	S.E.	Est.	S.E.	Est.	S.E.	Est.	S.E.	Est.	S.E.	Est.	S.E.
China	-0.13	0.27	-0.07	0.23	-0.19	0.18	-0.04	0.22	-0.30	0.16	-0.29	0.16
India	-0.16	0.27	-0.04	0.23	0.23	0.18	0.16	0.21	-0.39	0.16	-0.31	0.15

Source: Kaufmann, Kraay, and Zoido-Lobaton (2002, table 2).
Notes: Est. = estimate; S.E. = standard error.

of citizens and the state for the institutions that govern economic and social interactions. These two indicators are at least as important for foreign business as the preceding two because they affect the sanctity of contracts and the extent to which rules can be changed to the disadvantage of a foreign business without the latter's having recourse to due process and an independent judiciary in a timely manner.

Table 16.4 presents data for 1997/98 (based on an earlier study) and for 2000/2001 on the above indicators. Kaufman, Kraay and Zoida-Lobaton use a scale of –2.5 to 2.5, with higher values representing better outcomes. Their ratings, based on subjective assessments from a variety of sources and subject to substantial margins of error, should be interpreted with some caution.

1. Voice and accountability. As expected, India, as a liberal democracy, does much better than China. While voice and liberal democracy—by providing a safety valve—should be seen to provide a degree of political stability, there does not appear to be such a link.

2. Political stability. China's long-ruling Communist Party is firmly in the saddle and has been willing to suppress any dissent with an iron hand, even as liberalization of the economy continues at a steady pace. Therefore, even though Indian democracy is a stable and more resilient political system, India is viewed as considerably less politically stable than China! Obviously, India's coalition governments and fractured mandates are seen as creating a high degree of political instability at both the center and state levels. In practice, the previous National Democratic Alliance (NDA) government (led by Prime Minister Atal Behari Vajpayee) was in power for six years at the center, which is a reasonably long time for a government in a democratic country. Therefore, India should be regarded at least as politically stable as is China. There is no threat of a coup or a sudden change in policy, which would adversely affect foreign business. There is a need to revise this index upward for India.

3. Government effectiveness. Less surprisingly, China appears to be much better than India in this regard. This is despite Court and Hyden's (2003) argument that Indian bureaucracy was highly respected. The results may reflect China's twelve-year lead in starting economic reforms and somewhat greater commitment and effectiveness in bringing about reforms as compared with India between 1979 and the present. In India reforms remain hostage to lobby groups and the policy of opposition parties to be against reforms they may have advocated when in power. As an example of the former, the introduction of value-added tax because of pressure from Delhi's trading community was postponed by the NDA government, when it was in power. As an example of the latter, at the state level the governments have difficulty in increasing charges for electricity supply, because of opposition parties,

even though both recognize that the appalling state of finances of the State Electricity Boards makes it difficult for them to invest in improving supply and access to electricity for the poor. Some necessary reforms, such as reservations of certain industries for the small-scale sector, labor laws, and bankruptcy legislation, seem stuck in the "too-hard basket" in India.

4. Regulatory quality. Both India and China appear to perform poorly and there even appears to be some deterioration. This does not accord with the removal of quantitative import restrictions in India and the freeing up of a number of markets, most significantly in the telecommunications industry and the establishment of an independent effective telecommunications regulator and with respect to improvements in corporate governance, including in the important prudential regulation of banks by the central bank, the Reserve Bank of India. There has also been enhancement in the regulatory powers and increased effectiveness of the corporate watchdog, the Securities and Exchange Bureau of India. In a number of industries investment caps on foreign direct investment have been significantly relaxed. Therefore, the data on regulatory quality are dated for India and do not reflect improvements that have taken place more recently. The same applies to China, with its entry into the World Trade Organization and the related requirements to scale back barriers to the entry of foreign products and foreign firms. Because a number of these changes have taken place since 2000, the picture today is better than it was in 2000 for both of these Asian giants.

In this context, Naushad Forbes (2002) presents data for India to show where changes have taken place and where changes have not. In brief the "license raj" or "permit raj" has essentially been eliminated, although the "inspector raj" remains and heavily affects the activities of small and medium business. It is likely though to have less impact on foreign business. Again, the regulatory quality index should be raised and moved into positive territory for India (and China).

5. Rule of law. Not surprisingly, with its recognized independence of judiciary from the executive and parliament, India does much better than China in terms of rule of law. More important, the backlog of cases pending before the Supreme Court was reduced from 104,936 in 1991 to 23,012 in 2002, although the situation in both the high courts and the lower courts is as bad as ever. In 2002, more than 3.6 million cases were pending in the high courts, while 2 million were pending in the lower courts all over the country. The former is more relevant to foreign business.

6. Control of corruption. This indicator was addressed earlier and there is little to add here.

Table 16.5

Bribe Payers Index

Rank	Country	Score (0 = high; 10 = low)
1	Australia	8.5
2	Sweden	8.4
3	Switzerland	8.4
4	Austria	8.2
5	Canada	8.1
6	Netherlands	7.8
7	Belgium	7.8
8	Britain	6.9
9	Singapore	6.3
10	Germany	6.3
11	Spain	5.8
12	France	5.5
13	United States	5.3
14	Japan	5.3
15	Malaysia	4.3
16	Hong Kong	4.3
17	Italy	4.1
18	South Korea	3.9
19	Taiwan	3.8
20	China (excluding Hong Kong)	3.5
21	Russia	3.2
	Domestic companies	1.9

Sources: Galtung (2003); Transparency International (2003b).

Note: Respondents were asked: "In the business sectors with which you are familiar, please indicate whether companies from the following countries are very likely or unlikely to pay bribes to win or retain business in this country." The standard error in the results was 0.2 or less.

Bribe Payers Index

Given the high level of perceived corruption in India, the issue is whether or not Australian exporters and investors need to change their behavior. Companies from Australia were regarded as relatively clean among twenty-one leading exporting nations in an interview-based survey of about fifty-five private sector leaders based in fifteen major emerging economies, including India but excluding China. On a scale of 1 to 10, where 10 reflects low bribery, Australia had the top score of 8.5 (see Table 16.5).

There are a number of reasons why Australian companies do not need to pay bribes in order to compete with companies from other countries to get contracts in India. They obviously do not have the resources of the larger multinationals based in the EU, United States, and Japan. They also do not have comparative advantage in arms and defense industries, in which bribery is perceived to occur frequently. In construction, where bribery is perceived to occur most frequently, they are unlikely to be able to compete with the large U.S. companies, such as Bechtel. Most of the public works contracts, which are also prone to high levels of bribery, end up with local companies.

More important, a number of developments are likely to help Australian companies because of their relatively clean image. Bureaucrats are more wary in entering into contracts in view of the exposure of corruption linked to foreign contracts, for example, the defense industry's purchase of expensive coffins; Indian Airlines' 1985 purchase from Airbus of relatively more expensive aircraft than those being offered by Boeing (*Economist* 2003b); and the exposure of corruption by Tehlka.com in the Indian defense establishment. Airbus is unlikely to sell aircraft to Air India and Indian Airlines, because of the Indian Supreme Court's 2000 ruling that Indian government should not approve further purchases from Airbus until the matter of Airbus has been cleared by the French government. This matter was brought before the Supreme Court by an individual on grounds of "public interest." There are also the problems faced by the highly unethical Enron company, which was involved through Dabhol in the power project in Maharashtra. Though kickbacks have not been proved, nevertheless, Dabhol's contract to supply electricity at inflated prices to the Maharashtra Electricity Board is suspicious for such kickbacks. Enron had subsequent difficulties in selling electricity at such inflated prices and has had to settle for prices received by other suppliers.

In addition, Transparency International India has been pressing, among other things, for (1) the appointment of Lok Pal (federal ombudsman), (2) forfeiture of illegally acquired property by erring politicians, and (3) declaration of assets by ministers, members of parliament, and members of legislative assemblies. It has also set up new chapters in a number of Indian states, beginning with Kerala and including Uttar Pradesh. All of these are relatively recent or post-2000 developments.

Under such intense pressure, the Indian government has introduced the Lok Pal legislation, under which it will be the role of the Lok Pal to expose corruption among high-ranking legislatures and bureaucrats. The Congress Party, which because of its monopoly of power has not talked about improving governance in the past, has increasingly recognized the importance of good governance as a means of securing and retaining power.

Good governance is becoming an important election plank for the two major parties in India, Congress and the Bharatiya Janata Party (BJP). Even in the Gujarat State elections, where "Hindutva" was used to mobilize support, the election victory of the Narendra Modi government was attributed by the BJP to good governance.

Competition among media firms has increased and as a consequence corrupt practices among the political class, among the administrators, police, business, and even the judiciary are being increasingly exposed.

Australian companies have been awarded road construction BOT (build, operate, and transfer) contracts in the major highway construction project to link the four metros through a dual carriage-way.

In addition, export data clearly suggest that Australian exports to India have grown more rapidly than those of any other major economy, though more recently China, not unsurprisingly, given its highly competitive position in a number of manufacturing industries is rapidly expanding its exports to India. The lower transport costs, partly because of more balanced trade resulting in fuller use of capacity of ships, also helps. In this regard, the imbalance in trade between Australia and India combined with distance adds to transport costs.

Conclusion

India offers a mixed picture of governance indicators. On corruption, as measured by the CPI, it performs poorly. Australia has a relatively clean image as an exporter. It should not tarnish it by competing with businesses from other countries offering bribes to Indian officials. The degree of vigilance about corrupt practices has increased and there is a risk of being caught. In fact, having a clean image may help and has certainly helped in some major road construction contracts.

The Indian market will continue to expand and Australian business should thus be actively engaged with India. This is because competition from neighboring countries, particularly from China, is likely to increase. Lowering transport costs would help, and this requires increased trade intensity, including import intensity.

References

Annan, Kofi. 1998. *Partnerships for Global Community: Annual Report of the Organisation.* New York: United Nations.
Bardhan, P. 1997. "Corruption and Development: A Review of Issues." *Journal of Economic Literature* 35, no. 3 (September): 1320–46.
Court, Julius, and Goran Hyden. 2003. "World Governance Survey: A New Approach to Assessing Governance." www.transparency.org.

Economist. 2003a. "Special Report on India and China: Two Systems, One Grand Rivalry." June 21: 21–23.

Economist. 2003b. "Airbus's Secret Past." June 14: 53–56.

Forbes, Naushad. 2002. "Doing Business in India: What Has Liberalization Changed?" In *Economic Policy, Reforms, and the Indian Economy*, ed. Anne Krueger. Chicago: University of Chicago Press.

Galtung, Fredrik. 2003. "2002 Bribe Payers Index." www.profor.info/pdf/TI%20Tools. pdf.

Kaufman, Daniel; Aart Kraay; and Massimo Mastruzz. 2003. "Governance Matters III: Governance Indicators for 1996–2002." World Bank, June 30, 2003. www. worldbank.org/wbi/governance/pubs/govmatters3.html.

Kaufmann, Daniel; Aart Kraay; and Pablo Zoido-Lobaton. 2002. "Governance Matters II: Updated Indicators for 2000–2001." World Bank, January. www. worldbank. org/wbi/governance/govdata2001.htm.

Transparency International. 2003a. *Corruption Perceptions Index*. www.transparency. org.

———. 2003b. *Global Corruption Report 2003*. www.transparency.org.

Transparency International India with Org-Marg Research. 2002. "Corruption in India: An Empirical Study." www.transparency.org.

17

Corruption in South Asia

Causes and Consequences

Johann Graf Lambsdorff

Many South Asian countries do not perform well with respect to their perceived levels of corruption. Included in the 2005 Transparency International Corruption Perceptions Index are Afghanistan, Bangladesh, India, Nepal, Pakistan, and Sri Lanka. On a scale ranging from 0 (very corrupt) to 10 (not corrupt), Sri Lanka performs best, with a score of 3.2, followed by India, with 2.9. Nepal and Afghanistan are rated with 2.5, Pakistan receives a score of 2.1, and Bangladesh, with a score of 1.7, is currently the worst-performing country among 146 included on the list. Other South Asian countries were not included due to lack of data and to the rule that at least three independent sources be available so as to report the assessment with a satisfactory degree of reliability. Dropping this rule, Bhutan would receive a score of 6.9, and the Maldives 4.2. These data might be indicative but measured with less precision.

These perceptions are commonly regarded as a good proxy for real levels of corruption. Indicators such as the Transparency International Corruption Perceptions Index have been widely used in cross-country research on the causes and consequences of corruption. Results obtained from a cross-section of countries can also be applied to South Asian countries. These can provide us with an idea of the existing welfare losses and may encourage reform.

This chapter briefly reviews the theoretical literature on the links between corruption and welfare and provides empirical evidence. It shows that an increase in corruption by 1 point on a scale from 10 (highly clean) to 0 (highly corrupt) lowers productivity by 4 percent of the gross domestic product (GDP) and decreases net annual capital inflows by 0.5 percent of GDP. An improvement with regard to corruption by 6 points on the Transparency International Corruption Perceptions Index—for example, India improving to the level of the United Kingdom—increases GDP by more than 20 percent and increases net annual capital inflows by 3 percent of GDP. A variety of explanatory variables that were tested in cross-country regressions can encourage reform.

Corrupt Agents

Traditional economic writers have argued that corruption may facilitate economic exchange, helping to overcome cumbersome regulation. This argument has been commonly countered by observing that cumbersome regulation and corruption are often two sides of the same coin. For example, Kaufmann and Wei (1999) prove that high levels of corruption are positively associated with the time that managers waste with bureaucrats. A more detailed discussion of this issue can be found in Aidt (2003). This suggests that regulation should not commonly be regarded as exogenous in an analysis of corruption (Lambsdorff 2002b). The argument of corruption "greasing the wheels" can thus no longer be upheld.

There is an important adverse impact of corruption on the quality of goods. Corruption distorts public procurement, tax assessments, and the issuing of permits and licenses. Decisions are biased in favor of those who pay the largest bribe, instead of those who provide high quality, and who would be legally eligible. Those who are most inclined to bribe and are best connected for arranging a corrupt transaction are preferred to those who act in the public interest.

Not only might the wrong competitors be chosen, corrupt income may also induce a misallocation of resources. Customized goods present better opportunities to arrange for hidden payments than do off-the-shelf products. Shleifer and Vishny (1993) report on a bottle-making factory in Mozambique that needed a new machine for attaching paper labels to the bottles. A simple machine could have been bought for US$10,000, but the manager wanted a more sophisticated version for ten times that price. Because there was only one supplier of this machine, this provided sufficient room to overinvoice and pay a kickback to the manager. The loss to the factory would in this case have been substantial. Winston (1979, 840–41) argues that the risk associated with corruption increases with the number of transactions, the number of people involved, the duration of the transaction, and the simplicity and standardization of the procedure. Because the risk does not clearly increase with the value of a transaction, large, one-shot purchases create a more efficient base for a kickback. This biases the decisions made by corrupt public servants in favor of capital-intensive, technologically sophisticated, and custom-built products and technologies.

Furthermore, it can be the explicit goal of collusion between agents and clients to create distortions. When clients pay agents for restricting competition by harassing their competitors, distortions are a straightforward consequence of the corrupt dealings (Bardhan 1997, 1322). It may not help in this context that their competitors do the same and that the most efficient firms may win the battle, because the level of competition suffers. Another example is when clients pay supervisors for turning a blind eye to the use of substandard material (Frisch 1999, 92–94; Klitgaard 1988, 36–48). The creation of a distortion becomes the actual intention of the corrupt inducement.

When public servants cannot credibly promise to reject bribes, they are no longer trustworthy. This loss of trust is another reason for decreased welfare. For example, it may be thought worthwhile to construct good-quality roads, but bad quality is expected to result from corrupt behavior. The project is therefore canceled and the potential benefits for all parties cannot be achieved. Or imagine that a fair and efficient tax system is about to be established, but tax collectors cannot be kept from taking bribes in exchange for turning a blind eye to underreporting; the project may fall into disfavor and be terminated. Or if a supervisor cannot guarantee that he will not fake reports in exchange for a bribe, his contribution loses value and he may not be hired in the first place—even though an honest exchange would have been favorable to all.

Empirical evidence sheds light on these theoretical arguments. Some studies report a significant adverse impact of corruption on the growth of GDP (Knack and Keefer 1995; Mauro 1997; Poirson 1998, 16; Tanzi and Davoodi 2001). Yet, the corruption variable they use is from the Political Risk Services/*International Country Risk Guide* (PRS/ICRG), which does not measure corruption but the political risks associated with high levels of and high intolerance toward corruption. The PRS/ICRG data have been misinterpreted up to now. The results are also questionable in light of insignificant findings by others (Brunetti, Kisunko, and Weder 1997, 23, 25; Mauro 1995).[1] Wedeman (1997) carried out a simple cross-tabulation of growth and corruption, and observed that many corrupt countries exhibit high growth rates. More recent studies are again more suggestive of the adverse impact of corruption on growth (Méon and Sekkat 2003; Mo 2001). Whether we should feel comfortable with this recent evidence is beyond the scope of this chapter. One reason for insignificant results may be that the growth of GDP is not adversely affected by corruption but by increases in corruption.

Another line of research argues that corruption is a factor for production, impacting primarily on levels of GDP and not its growth (Hall and Jones 1999; Kaufmann, Kraay, and Zoido-Lobaton 1999, 15). But other authors claim that the causality runs from income per capita to corruption, because poorer countries lack the resources to fight corruption effectively (Husted 1999, 341–42; Paldam 2002). The quality of the argument lies significantly with the variables used for instrumentalizing corruption. Such variables have to carry a heavy burden, because corruption and income per capita are highly interrelated and correlated and their causes and consequences are difficult to separate. Thus, the instruments used may not be above criticism.

Tanzi and Davoodi (1997) claim that corruption lowers the quality of the infrastructure as measured by the condition of paved roads and power outages. Yet, their regressions are again based on PRS/ICRG data. Based on my own regressions for a cross-section of countries using the Transparency International Corruption Perceptions Index for 1998 it was not possible to reproduce their significant results. Mauro (1997) also obtained insignificant results.

Given the many unconvincing results, let us turn to more significant findings. Gupta, Davoodi, and Tiongson (2001) show that countries with high levels of corruption are associated with high child and infant mortality and high percentages of low-birth-weight babies. Their results are tested for a variety of corruption indicators and turn out to be robust. Mauro (1998, 1997) finds that corruption lowers expenditure on education, arguing that other expenditures offer public servants better opportunities to collect bribes. His results hold for various specifications. Other researchers show that countries with high levels of corruption cut spending for health care, and overinvest in public infrastructure or the military (Esty and Porter 2002; Gupta, de Mello, and Sharan 2001).

Recently, Lambsdorff (2003b) has shown that corruption reduces macroeconomic productivity, measured as the ratio of output (i.e., GDP) to capital stock. These results were robust to various specifications, controlling for different explanatory variables. The investigation was carried out on a sample of sixty-nine countries. Figure 17.1 depicts the relationship.

Corruption can include different types of institutional malfunctioning; the above focus on corrupt agents may depict only one of them. Which aspect of corruption is most relevant for lowering productivity? This can be tested by adding further governance indicators to the regressions. These indicators are often closely related to the level of corruption. If they dominate the regression, the impact of corruption can be attributed to this particular type of governance. Various data from the *International Country Risk Guide*[2] have been employed. Most interesting is the impact of bureaucratic quality. Bureaucratic quality signals an administration that is independent of political pressure, that uses established mechanisms for recruiting and training, and that has government services characterized by strength and expertise. If such characteristics are missing, public servants may create artificial bottlenecks to increase their corrupt income. Once corruption becomes embedded, the bureaucracy is less concerned with expertise and more open to political pressure. As a result, corruption can go along with low bureaucratic quality.

Figure 17.1   **Corruption and Productivity**

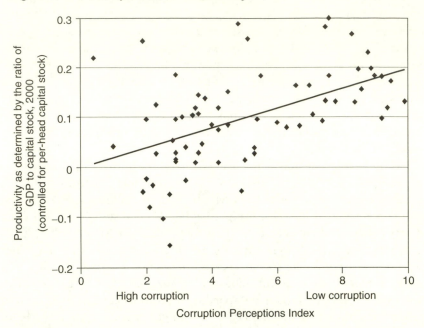

In 1998 the assessment for bureaucratic quality in India was 3 and in Sri Lanka, Bangladesh, and Pakistan it was 2 on a scale of 0 (low quality) to 4 (high quality). A one-point increase in bureaucratic quality increases productivity by almost 5 percent. Bureaucratic quality exerts a significant impact on productivity. Once included in the regression it captures a significant portion of the former impact of corruption, rendering this variable insignificant. This suggests that the adverse impact of corruption on productivity is due to its association with low bureaucratic quality.

Corrupt Governments

Another type of corruption emerges when it is not primarily low-level bureaucrats who misuse their position but governments themselves. Corruption is commonly defined as the misuse of public power for private benefit. But the term "misuse" is open to different interpretations. With respect to low-level bureaucrats it involves the rules set up by a benevolent government, which are trespassed upon by a self-serving official. But a corrupt government may create an environment where laws do not prohibit either its own self-enrichment or that of a ruling class. In this case "misuse" is not clearly related to trespassing on rules (in the legal sense). Instead, it relates to acts that the general public regards as illegitimate, or acts that contradict the public interest. See Heidenheimer, Johnston, and LeVine (1989, 3–14), for a review of various approaches to defining corruption.

A government, self-serving or benevolent, always dislikes welfare losses because they absorb what it otherwise regards as its own property or that of the public. A corrupt government will thus attempt to organize a corrupt system to operate as smoothly as a tax. If a corrupt government is particularly strong it is sometimes referred to as a "stationary bandit" or a "kleptocrat" (McGuire and Olson 1996; Grossman 1995). Such a government is in a prime position to acquire large bribes. But it is arduous to prove a negative effect on public welfare. Quite the contrary, McGuire and Olson argue that self-serving rulers with complete coercive power have an incentive to exercise their power consistently with the interests of society.

An illustrative example of this consistency took place in Indonesia. One of the grandchildren of President Suharto attempted to take a cut from the taxes on beer that were collected by his private company. But as a result, tourism in Bali suffered from a shortage of beer and inflated prices, forcing President Suharto to withdraw the tax (*Economist* 1996). The *Economist* presumed that some of his relatives were probably strong in the hotel business. This argument well illustrates the "encompassing interest" of a strong ruler, who comes to consider how inefficient solutions in one sector spill over to other parts of the economy. If provided with sufficient power a ruler will avoid such consequences. He will keep subordinates from overgrazing the market by taxing excessively and even provide public goods so as to increase future tax income.

But a serious adverse problem concerning a strong self-serving government arises due to its lack of capacity to credibly commit to long-term policies (Lambsdorff 2003a). This may not hurt industries that can quickly relocate, but seriously deters those who must sink costs. For example, in a survey of businesspeople in Karnataka, India, it was found that the high level of corruption among the local administration strongly affected most sectors but had little impact on the software industry, as a result of the minor role of this industry's site-specific investments. Their potential to relocate production seems to have reduced extortionate demands for bribes among public officials (*Hindu* 2000; *Times of India* 2001). But many other investments are often sunk and cannot be redeployed if investors are disillusioned about the institutional environment of a country. Railroads cannot be moved, pipelines cannot be relocated, and real estate cannot possibly be used in a different region. Politicians and bureaucrats may misuse their position once investments are sunk. They can delay necessary permits and hold up investors until offered a bribe. Thus, investors become locked into a particular usage of resources, and, being limited in their power to protect their property against rival attacks, they must fear for the expropriation of their rents. Investors are particularly vulnerable where there is corruption because self-serving rulers are not motivated to honor their commitments, nor are they sufficiently constrained to do so (Ades and Di Tella 1997; Mauro 1995). In order for commitments to be credible the respective person must be motivated or forced to honor them (North 1993, 13). But a corrupt ruler is devoted primarily to personal enrichment and lacks the motivation to honor commitments (Rose-Ackerman 1999, 118). Governments with a reputation for corruption find it difficult to commit to effective policies and to convince investors of their achievements.

As a result investments will suffer from corruption. One theme of the literature significantly relates corruption with the ratio of investment to GDP (Brunetti and Weder 1998a; Brunetti, Kisunko, and Weder 1997, 23, 25; Campos, Lien, and Pradhan 1999; Knack and Keefer 1995; Mauro 1995). Another line of research focuses on foreign direct investments (FDI). Recent studies provide significant evidence that corruption reduces incoming (net and gross) FDI (Habib and Zurawicki 2001 and 2002; Lambsdorff and Cornelius 2000; Smarzynska and Wei 2000; Wei 2000a; Wei 2000b; Wei and Wu 2001).

The reasons for this are manifold. On the one hand, corruption deters total capital inflows and FDI suffers by being part of these. On the other hand, FDI may be more sensitive to corruption than other forms of capital inflows, such as portfolio investments and bank loans. The reason is that FDI is accompanied by long-term commitments that can be more easily exploited by corrupt public servants (Wei and Wu 2001).

Lambsdorff (2003a) investigated the impact of corruption on total net capital inflows, which embrace FDI, portfolio investments, and bank loans. Corruption was shown to significantly reduce capital inflows throughout various specifications of the regressions for a sample of sixty-four countries. This relationship is illustrated in Figure 17.2.

This impact can be further investigated by introducing additional governance indicators into the regression. One significant variable is "law and order." Law and order indicates that a country has sound and accepted political institutions, a strong court system, and provisions for an orderly succession of power. These conditions can be seriously violated in case of corruption. If judicial decisions and laws can be bought for a price, a country cannot develop a tradition of law and order. An orderly succession of power is replaced by a system where power can be bought. The resulting insecurity of property rights is likely to alienate investors.

If law and order is introduced into the regression, the impact of corruption is lower. This indicates that corruption lowers capital inflows partly because it is associated with the absence of law and order. The data for this indicator

Figure 17.2   **Corruption and Capital Inflows**

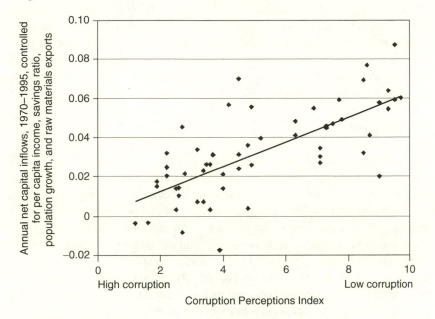

in 1998 reveal that India and Bangladesh scored a reasonable 4, Sri Lanka and Pakistan a 3 on a scale of 1 (low quality) to 6 (high quality). A one-point increase in law and order increases annual capital inflows by more than 0.5 percent of GDP.

These results suggest that anticorruption reform strategies should be fine-tuned, depending on whether countries are concerned primarily with increasing productivity or with attracting foreign capital. Public-sector reform aimed at increasing bureaucratic quality should be given priority if countries are to increase productivity. Legal reform should be addressed with the primary aim of improving law and order and the security of property rights if countries want to attract foreign capital. Tying politicians' hands by the rule of law is important in attracting foreign capital, but it does little to increase productivity. Reforming the public sector improves productivity, but it is less central to the calculations of foreign investors.

Reform in Empirical Research

Reform is difficult to trace over time due to a lack of time-series data on corruption. The common approach to empirical research is cross-country observations on the occurrence of corruption.

Government involvement in private markets is commonly seen as a source of corruption. It has been suggested that the overall size of the government budget relative to GDP may therefore be positively correlated with levels of corruption. But this line of research has produced largely inconsistent results and has equally been the subject of theoretical criticism. I will focus here on more promising avenues of research: entry regulation, competition, freedom of the press and the judiciary, and some additional variables.

Policy Distortions

Using a sample of transition economies in Europe and Central Asia, Broadmann and Recanatini (1999) show that higher barriers to market entry lead to higher corruption. Djankov and colleagues (2000, 40, 47), in a study of the nature of entry regulation, determine the number of procedures required for starting a new business for a cross-section of seventy-one countries, along with the necessary time and official costs. The authors find a strong correlation of these variables with a country's level of corruption for a variety of specifications and control variables. This impact of corruption supports the conclusion that entry regulation does not correct market failure, but rather is an instrument by which corrupt politicians and bureaucrats pursue their goals.

A similar conclusion is drawn by Gatti (1999), who argues that a highly diversified trade tariff schedule fuels bribe-taking behavior, whereas uniform trade tariffs limit public officials' ability to extract bribes from importers. She reports a positive association between the standard deviation of trade tariffs and the level of corruption for a small sample of thirty-four countries. This result is robust to tests for endogeneity, where the Gini coefficient was used as an instrument.

Another analysis of policy distortions is presented by Ades and Di Tella (1997, 1999). The authors use an index measuring "the extent to which public procurement is open to foreign bidders" and another index measuring "the extent to which there is equal fiscal treatment of all enterprises." These two variables as well as a corruption variable are taken from the survey by the Institute for Management Development, Lausanne, Switzerland. In explaining the level of corruption, these variables enter significantly into the regressions, even when controlling for other explanatory variables. This leads the authors to assume that policy intervention causes corruption. But they acknowledge that corruption may cause policy distortions and not vice versa, bringing about problems of a simultaneity bias.[3] It is quite often the case that policy distortions and corruption are just two sides of the same coin. As pointed out previously, other studies had focused on corruption as a cause of policy distortions. Whether causality can therefore be established might be questionable on theoretical grounds. But disregarding this problem, a correlation between political distortions and corruption is an important result, clearly giving direction to policy reform.

Lack of Competition

Concerning the causes of corruption, studies have been carried out on the extent to which corruption can be explained by a low level of competition. It is commonly assumed that competition lowers the rents of economic activities and consequently reduces the motivation for public servants and politicians to seize part of these rents by means of extortion and corruption.

Government restrictions on economic freedom are likely to reduce competition and thus encourage corruption. A negative correlation between corruption and different indicators of economic freedom is shown by Goldsmith (1999, 878) for a sample of sixty-six countries. This result is robust to the inclusion of GDP per capita. The same finding is reported by Paldam (2002) in multivariate regressions that include further explanatory variables for a sample of seventy-seven countries. Such arguments, however, may be tautological. Freedom House's civil liberties index, for example, includes corruption in government among its criteria.

Countries that are exposed to global competition tend to exhibit lower levels of corruption. This can be measured by the degree of openness. Wei (2000a) provides an approach to disentangling the various ways in which openness affects corruption. He determines a measure of "natural openness" as the extent of openness that is caused by a country's total population and its remoteness from world trading centers. Both of these measures tend to lower a country's openness, the former because large countries tend to trade less with the outside world and the latter because transport costs make foreign trade less attractive. These indicators are independent of a country's trade regime and thus exogenous to a regression. Wei finds that natural openness significantly lowers a country's level of corruption, pointing to the helpful role of competition in reducing corruption.[4] Residual openness (i.e., the part that is not explained by country size and geography) is a measure of a country's trade regime and its policy decision in favor of global competition. Yet, Wei does not find a significant impact of this variable, casting doubt on trade policy as a cause of corruption.

Another valid measure of the extent of competition existing in a country can be derived from the number of years it has been open to trade, as assessed by Sachs and Warner (1995). Treisman (2000) and Leite and Weidmann (1999) provide evidence that this variable negatively and significantly affects the level of corruption.

Ades and Di Tella (1995) test for the influence of two other indicators of competition taken from the survey by the Institute for Management Development. A subjective index of "market dominance" measures the extent to which dominance by a limited number of firms is detrimental to new business development. Another index of "antitrust laws" measures the effectiveness of these laws in checking noncompetitive practices. The authors conclude that the less competitive a market environment, the higher the amount of corruption due to the incentive for public servants to extract some of the monopoly rents through bribes.

Freedom of the Press, the Judiciary, and Democracy

By regressing various measures of corruption on indicators of freedom of the press, Brunetti and Weder (1998b) show that a free press effectively deters corruption. The latter variables consist of "laws and regulations that influence media content," "political influence over media content," "economic influence over media content," and "repressive actions" as compiled by Freedom House. These four separate indexes and an aggregate index of freedom of the press all impact negatively on the level of corruption in various specifications.

An approach by the World Bank (1997, 104, 168) focuses on the quality of the judiciary. While controlling for other explanatory variables, an index of the predictability of the judiciary taken from a survey by the World Bank and the University of Basel significantly influences the level of corruption in fifty-nine countries. A similar correlation between corruption and the independence of the judicial system is proposed in Ades and Di Tella (1996). Voigt, Feld, and van Aaken (2004) investigate the impact of prosecutorial independence on corruption. Data on independence have been produced with the help of a questionnaire sent to supreme court judges, law professors, lawyers, and anticorruption activists. The authors distinguish between de jure independence (e.g., life tenure, appointment and promotion by other than politicians, lacking executive power to substitute prosecutors working on a specific case) and de facto independence (e.g., dependence would be relevant in the case of forced retirement, frequent changes in legal foundations, and decreasing income and budget of prosecutors). They relate their finding that de facto independence decreases corruption to the disciplining effect on the executive branch and influential politicians. Interestingly, de jure independence increases corruption. This surprising finding may be related to endogeneity: the more corruption in the executive branch the more willingness to pay lip service to procedural independence. De facto politicians would make sure that prosecutors do not investigate corruption in the executive branch itself.

There is an ongoing debate on the link between democracy and corruption. Without going into detail here, there seems to be consensus that it takes many years of democracy before it reduces levels of corruption. Only in countries with a longer democratic tradition can the expected impact on reduced corruption be observed, while during transition and during the early years of democracy, corruption may even increase.

There are a variety of additional studies on parliamentary versus presidential systems and on voting systems. These results are still somewhat inconsistent, and thus will not be discussed in this chapter.

Recruitment and Salaries

The impact of merit-based recruitment on corruption in thirty-five developing countries has been investigated by Evans and Rauch (2000). Higher values in the merit-based recruitment index are associated with a greater proportion of higher-level officials in the core economic agencies who either possess a university degree or who enter the civil service through a formal examination system. While controlling for income, this index is negatively associated with corruption.

The extent to which the level of public-sector salaries is linked to the amount of corruption was examined by Rijckeghem and Weder (2001). They argue that low salaries force public servants to supplement their incomes illicitly while high salaries mean higher losses if a public servant gets caught. In a small sample of thirty-one developing countries, they find a significant negative influence on the level of corruption of civil service wages relative to manufacturing wages. However, they employ the corruption data of the PRS/ICRG. Given the methodological problems of the ICRG data, the findings remain questionable. The authors also point out that the association may be driven by reverse causality: Corrupt countries tend to have poor budgetary performance or may subscribe to the view that civil servants earn sufficient income from corruption, and thus reduce civil service pay as a consequence. Even when disregarding these issues, it becomes apparent that pay increases turn out to be a costly approach to fighting corruption.

Other studies by Swamy and colleagues (2001) and Treisman (2000) investigated inter alia the impact on corruption of the average government wage as a multiple of per capita GDP, controlling for a variety of other influences. The results are ambiguous and mostly insignificant, depending on the indicator for corruption employed and the inclusion of control variables. Manow (2005) even reports a positive, albeit insignificant, association between public-sector wages (relative to average local wages) and corruption.

Cultural Determinants

Some societies are characterized by a high level of trust among its people, while others may lack trust. Data from the World Values Survey, which surveys 1,000 randomly selected people since the 1980s in an increasing number of countries, have made it possible to investigate the consequences of such forms of "social capital." One of the questions is: "Generally speaking, would you say that most people can be trusted or that you can't be too careful in dealing with people?" La Porta and colleagues (1997, 336) argue that trust can be helpful in fighting corruption because it helps bureaucrats to better cooperate with each other and with private citizens. In a sample of thirty-three countries, the authors show that trust has a significant negative impact on corruption, while controlling for GDP per capita. Uslaner (2004) finds support for the positive association between trust and corruption. Focusing on causality, he claims that trust lowers corruption while the opposite causality cannot be proved. Björnskov and Paldam (2004) undertake a first attempt to construct valid time series data with the Transparency International data on corruption. Seeking explanatory variables, they find that trust has a significant impact.

The role of religion as a contributor to the level of corruption was examined by La Porta and colleagues (1997, 337). The authors consider the Catholic, Eastern Orthodox, and Muslim religions to be particularly hierarchical—and that such hierarchical forms of religion are detrimental to civic engagement, a factor that should help reduce corruption. For the same sample of thirty-three countries mentioned above, the authors report a positive association between the percentage of the population belonging to a hierarchical religion and corruption, controlling for other influences. This relationship is reproduced by La Porta and colleagues (1999, 251–52) for a larger sample of 114 countries, but here the relationship becomes rather weak as soon as GDP per capita is included. A strong association between religion and corruption is obtained by Treisman (2000). He regresses corruption on the percentage of Protestants in the total population in a sample of up to sixty-four countries and obtains a highly significant negative impact of this index on corruption, controlling for other variables such as GDP per capita. A more in-depth analysis of the impact of religion is provided by Paldam (2001). He identifies eleven different groups of religions and tests their impact on corruption, controlling for other variables. While corruption is lower in countries with a large proportion of Reform Christianity and tribal religion, higher levels of corruption can be found in countries with a large influence of Pre-Reform Christianity, Islam, Buddhism, and Hinduism. However, the impact is only significant for Reform Christians (Protestants and Anglicans).

In line with the argument by La Porta and colleagues, the idea that hierarchies contribute to corruption has been supported by Husted (1999), who uses a totally different set of data. He uses data on cultural values based on surveys by Hofstede (1997). One variable is called "power distance," which measures "the extent to which the less powerful members of institutions and organizations within a country expect and accept that power is distributed unequally" (Husted 1999, 343). This variable is shown to have a positive impact on the level of corruption in a sample of forty-four countries in various regressions, while controlling for other explanatory variables. Concomitant with this indicator, two further cultural variables positively and significantly affect the level of corruption: first, the extent to which the quest for material success dominates over a concern for the quality of life,[5] and second, the extent to which members of a culture feel threatened by uncertainty or unknown situations. The latter variable must clearly be distinguished from risk avoidance, which might be expected to lower corruption. The idea is that corruption may give its beneficiaries the hope of reducing the level of uncertainty they face.

Tracing the level of corruption to cultural determinants should not suggest that levels of corruption are largely inevitable. Culture can explain only a certain portion of the level of corruption and there remains sufficient room for improvements in a country's integrity. Moreover, cultural attitudes can also be a reflection of the organizational patterns that led to their formation. The extent to which these organizational patterns can be the subject of policy reflects the scope for reform. But a clear conclusion drawn by Husted (1999) is that effective measures to fight corruption are dependent on culture. Countries with a large power distance or a strong desire for material wealth will require different treatment than others.

But trust can also be a facilitator of corrupt transactions. Because corrupt deals cannot be legally enforced, it may require trust among the partners that their favors will be reciprocated. This resembles a strategic type of trust that clearly differs from "generalized trust" as assessed by the World Values Survey. This is investigated in Lambsdorff (2002a). Throughout various specifications and different indexes of corruption it is shown that opportunism among corrupt partners, although potentially troublesome to investors, reduces a country's level of corruption. Instrumental variable technique ascertains the hypothesized causality. It is concluded that the adverse effects of corruption cannot be avoided by divesting it of its unpredictability.[6] The term "trust," on the other hand, requires a precise definition before sound conclusions vis-à-vis its impact on levels of corruption can be derived.

Additional Variables

The impact of gender on corruption has been investigated recently by Swamy and colleagues (2001) and by Dollar, Fisman, and Gatti (2001). The authors determine the percentage of women in the labor force and in parliament. Both indicators negatively affect the level of corruption in a cross-section of up to sixty-six countries. The influence is large in magnitude, highly significant, and robust throughout a large variety of regressions, controlling for a range of variables. These findings are in line with some microevidence reported by Swamy and colleagues and suggest that policies designed to increase the role of women may help in lowering the level of corruption. On the other hand, there is reason for the reverse causality. Low levels of corruption may impose restrictions on male-dominated networks, providing women with legal recourse and improved access to higher positions.

There are still no full-fledged studies on the impact of colonialism on the level of corruption. But indicators of colonial heritage sometimes enter as control variables in some studies investigating the causes of corruption (e.g., Swamy et al. 2001; Treisman 2000). According to Treisman, former British colonies exhibit lower levels of corruption than other countries, controlling for the level of income per capita and several other variables, for example, the existence of a common-law legal system. This result is reproduced by Swamy and colleagues (2001). Surprisingly, anecdotal evidence suggests that colonialism does not increase the level of corruption. To arrive at sound conclusions further analysis is required that goes beyond the use of dummy variables and takes into consideration certain characteristics of colonial rule.

Ades and Di Tella (1999) and Leite and Weidmann (1999) argue that an abundance of natural resources creates opportunities for rent-seeking behavior and gives rise to corruption. Both studies measure the first variable as a country's exports of fuels and minerals as a share of gross national product. Throughout several specifications this variable is found to significantly increase the level of corruption. These results are robust to the inclusion of various explanatory variables, different samples of countries, and the use of different indicators of corruption. Montinola and Jackman (2002) argue similarly, but instead employ a dummy variable for OPEC member states that relates to abundance of oil. This variable also significantly increases a country's level of corruption.

Conclusions

This chapter provides evidence that an increase in corruption by one point on a scale of 10 (highly clean) to 0 (highly corrupt) lowers productivity by 4 percent of GDP and decreases net annual capital inflows by 0.5 percent of GDP. An improvement with regard to corruption by 6 points on the Transparency International Corruption Perceptions Index—for example, India improving to the level of the United Kingdom—increases GDP by more than 10 percent of the capital stock (roughly 20 percent of GDP) and increases net annual capital inflows by 3 percent of GDP.

The crucial means by which corruption adversely affects capital inflows is through an absence of law and order. The impact on productivity is related to an association of corruption with low bureaucratic quality. Anticorruption reform strategies should therefore be fine-tuned, depending on whether countries are primarily concerned with increasing productivity or attracting foreign capital. The rather poor performance of South Asian countries with respect to law and order suggests that this might be a promising avenue for reform. Tying politicians' hands by the rule of law might help to attract foreign capital.

A variety of detailed reform proposals have been investigated. Some causes of corruption provide little scope for reform, such as the abundance of natural resources, colonial history, religion, and the extent to which less powerful members of institutions and organizations within a country expect and accept that power is distributed unequally. Other issues are the direct outcome of policy. Decentralization, public-sector wages, and democracy have only a limited impact. But a free press, high-quality independent judiciary, avoidance of political veto players, reduced entry regulation, and increased economic competition are promising avenues for reform.

The role of the international community deserves equal recognition. In a global market, corruption often takes place in cross-border activities. This idea was investigated in various studies, suggesting that some exporters and donors tend to favor countries perceived to be corrupt. This suggests that some global players contribute to high levels of corruption more than others. An effective reform strategy must not forget these actors and involve them in coordinated efforts to reduce corruption.

Notes

1. Mauro (1995) found a slightly significant impact only in a bivariate regression. But as soon as the ratio of investment to GDP was included as an explanatory variable, this impact disappeared.

2. The data used are from the *International Country Risk Guide*, Political Risk Services, East Syracuse, New York, May 1998.

3. Whether this problem can be adequately solved by the instrumental variables applied by Ades and Di Tella (1997) is not addressed here.

4. The trade distance to major exporters has also been shown by Ades and Di Tella (1999) to increase corruption.

5. While this variable is called masculinity-femininity, I avoid the term because it might mislead some readers.

6. This conclusion is in contrast to Wei (1997) and Campos, Lien, and Pradhan (1999) and other researchers who consider the lack of predictability of corrupt deals to add to its adverse welfare effects.

References

Ades, A., and R. Di Tella. 1995. "Competition and Corruption." Keble College, Oxford University.
———. 1996. "The Causes and Consequences of Corruption: A Review of Recent Empirical Contributions." *Institute of Development Studies Bulletin* (Brighton) 27, no. 2: 6–11.

————. 1997. "National Champions and Corruption: Some Unpleasant Interventionist Arithmetic." *Economic Journal* 107: 1023–42.

————. 1999. "Rents, Competition, and Corruption." *American Economic Review* 89: 982–94.

Aidt, Toke S. 2003. "Economic Analysis of Corruption: A Survey." *Economic Journal* 113: 632–52.

Bardhan, Pranab. 1997. "Corruption and Development: A Review of Issues." *Journal of Economic Literature* 35: 1320–46.

Björnskov, C., and M. Paldam. 2004. "Corruption Trends." In *New Institutional Economics of Corruption: Norms, Trust, and Reciprocity*, ed. J. Graf Lambsdorff, M. Schramm, and M. Taube, 59–75. London: Routledge.

Broadman, H.G., and F. Recanatini. 1999. "Seeds of Corruption: Do Market Institutions Matter?" World Bank Policy Research Working Paper 2368. Washington, DC: World Bank.

Brunetti, A., and B. Weder. 1998a. "Explaining Corruption." University of Saarland and University of Basel.

————. 1998b. "A Free Press Is Bad News for Corruption." *Wirtschaftswissenschaftliches Zentrum der Universität Basel Discussion Paper*, no. 9809.

Brunetti, A.; G. Kisunko; and B. Weder. 1997. "Credibility of Rules and Economic Growth: Evidence from a World Wide Private Sector Survey." Background paper for the *World Development Report 1997*. Washington, DC: World Bank.

Campos, J.E.; D. Lien; and S. Pradhan. 1999. "The Impact of Corruption on Investment: Predictability Matters." *World Development* 27, no. 6: 1059–67.

Djankov, S.; R. La Porta; F. Lopez-de-Silanes; and A. Shleifer. 2000. "The Regulation of Entry." National Bureau of Economic Research Working Paper 7892.

Dollar, D.; R. Fisman; and R. Gatti. 2001. "Are Women Really the 'Fairer' Sex? Corruption and Women in Government." *Journal of Economic Behavior and Organization* 46, no. 4: 423–29.

Economist. 1996. "Indonesia. When Trouble Brewed." February 10: 37.

Esty, D., and M. Porter. 2002. "National Environmental Performance Measurement and Determinants." In *Environmental Performance Measurement: The Global Report 2001–2002*, ed. D. Esty and P. Cornelius, 78–100. New York: Oxford University Press.

Evans, P.B., and J.E. Rauch. 2000. "Bureaucratic Structures and Economic Performance in Less Developed Countries." *Journal of Public Economics* 75: 49–71.

Frisch, D. 1999. "Entwicklungspolitische Gesichtspunkte der Korruption." In *Korruption im internationalen Geschäftsverkehr: Bestandsaufnahme, Bekämpfung, Prävention*, ed. M. Pieth and P. Eigen, 169–190. Basel, Frankfurt am Main: Luchterhand.

Gatti, R. 1999. "Corruption and Trade Tariffs, or a Case for Uniform Tariffs." World Bank Policy Research Working Paper no. 2216. Washington, DC: World Bank.

Goldsmith, A.A. 1999. "Slapping the Grasping Hand: Correlates of Political Corruption in Emerging Markets." *American Journal of Economics and Sociology* 58, no. 4: 866–83.

Grossman, H.I. 1995. "Rival Kleptocrats: The Mafia Versus the State." In *The Economics of Organized Crime*, ed. G. Fiorentini and S. Peltzman, 143–56. Cambridge: Cambridge University Press.

Gupta, S.; L. de Mello; and R. Sharan. 2001. "Corruption and Military Spending." *European Journal of Political Economy* 17, no. 4: 749–77.

Gupta, S.; H. Davoodi; and E.R. Tiongson. 2001. "Corruption and the Provision of Health Care and Education Services." In *The Political Economy of Corruption*, ed. A.K. Jain, 111–41. London: Routledge.

Habib, M., and L. Zurawicki. 2001. "Country-Level Investments and the Effect of Corruption: Some Empirical Evidence." *International Business Review* 10, no. 6: 687–700.

———. 2002. "Corruption and Foreign Direct Investment." *Journal of International Business Studies* 33, no. 2: 291–308.

Hall, R., and C. Jones. 1999. "Why Do Some Countries Produce So Much More Output per Worker Than Others." *Quarterly Journal of Economics* 114: 83–116.

Heidenheimer, A.; M. Johnston; and V. LeVine. 1989. *Political Corruption: A Handbook*, 2d ed. New Brunswick, NJ: Transaction.

Hindu. 2000. "Investors See Red in Karnataka." January 10.

Hofstede, G. 1997. *Cultures and Organizations: Software of the Mind*. New York: McGraw-Hill.

Husted, B. 1999. "Wealth, Culture, and Corruption." *Journal of International Business Studies* 30, no. 2: 339–60.

Kaufmann, D., and S.J. Wei. 1999. "Does 'Grease Money' Speed Up the Wheels of Commerce?" National Bureau of Economic Research Working Paper 7093. Cambridge, MA: NBER.

Kaufmann, D.; A. Kraay; and P. Zoido-Lobaton. 1999. "Governance Matters." World Bank Policy Research Working Paper no. 2196. Washington, DC: World Bank.

Klitgaard, R. 1988. *Controlling Corruption*. Berkeley: University of California Press.

Knack, Stephen, and P. Keefer. 1995. "Institutions and Economic Performance: Cross-Country Tests Using Alternative Institutional Measures." *Economics and Politics* 7 (November): 207–27.

La Porta, R.; F. Lopez-De-Silanes; A. Shleifer; and R.W. Vishny. 1997. "Trust in Large Organizations." *American Economic Review, Papers and Proceedings* 137, no. 2: 333–38.

———. 1999. "The Quality of Government." *Journal of Law, Economics and Organization* 15, no. 1: 222–79.

Lambsdorff, J. Graf. 2002a. "How Confidence Facilitates Illegal Transactions." *American Journal of Economics and Sociology* 61, no. 4: 829–54.

———. 2002b. "Corruption and Rent-Seeking." *Public Choice* 113, nos. 1/2: 97–125.

———. 2003a. "How Corruption Affects Persistent Capital Flows." *Economics of Governance* 4, no. 3: 229–44.

———. 2003b. "How Corruption Affects Productivity." *Kyklos* 56, no. 4: 459–76.

Lambsdorff, J. Graf, and P. Cornelius. 2000. "Corruption, Foreign Investment and Growth." The Africa Competitiveness Report 2000/2001, ed. K. Schwab, L. Cook, P. Cornelius, J.D. Sachs, S. Sievers, and A. Warner, 70–78. A joint publication of the World Economic Forum and the Institute for International Development, Harvard University. Oxford University Press.

Leite, C., and J. Weidmann. 1999. "Does Mother Nature Corrupt? Natural Resources, Corruption, and Economic Growth." International Monetary Fund Working Paper, 99/85 (July).

Manow, P. 2005. "Politische Korruption und politischer Wettbewerb: Probleme der quantitativen Analyse." In *Dimensionen politischer Korruption*, ed. U. von Alemann, 249–266. Sonderheft 35. PVS–Politische Vierteljahresschrift, VS Verlag für Sozialwissenschaften.

Mauro, P. 1995. "Corruption and Growth." *Quarterly Journal of Economics* 110, no. 3: 681–712.

———. 1997. "The Effects of Corruption on Growth, Investment, and Government Expenditure: A Cross-Country Analysis." In *Corruption and the Global Economy*, 83–107. Washington, DC: Institute for International Economics.

———. 1998. "Corruption and the Composition of Government Expenditure." *Journal of Public Economics* 69: 263–79.

McGuire, M.C., and M. Olson. 1996. "The Economics of Autocracy and Majority Rule: The Invisible Hand and the Use of Force." *Journal of Economic Literature* 34: 72–96.

Méon, P.-G., and K. Sekkat. 2003. "Corruption, Growth and Governance: Testing the 'Grease the Wheels' Hypothesis." Paper presented at the annual meeting of the European Public Choice Society, Aarhus, Denmark, April 26–28.

Mo, P.H. 2001. "Corruption and Economic Growth." *Journal of Comparative Economics* 29: 66–79.

Montinola, G., and R.W. Jackman. 2002. "Sources of Corruption: A Cross-Country Study." *British Journal of Political Science* 32: 147–70.

North, D.C. 1993. "Institutions and Credible Commitment." *Journal of Institutional and Theoretical Economics* 149: 11–23.

Paldam, M. 2001. "Corruption and Religion. Adding to the Economic Model." *Kyklos* 54, nos. 2/3: 383–414.

———. 2002. "The Big Pattern of Corruption. Economics, Culture and the Seesaw Dynamics." *European Journal of Political Economy* 18: 215–40.

Poirson, H. 1998. "Economic Security, Private Investment, and Growth in Developing Countries." International Monetary Fund Working Paper, 98/4 (January).

Rijckeghem, C. van, and B. Weder. 2001. "Bureaucratic Corruption and the Rate of Temptation: Do Wages in the Civil Service Affect Corruption, and by How Much?" *Journal of Development Economics* 65, no. 2: 307–31.

Rose-Ackerman, Susan. 1999. *Corruption and Government: Causes, Consequences and Reform.* Cambridge: Cambridge University Press.

Sachs, J., and A. Warner. 1995. "Economic Reform and the Process of Global Integration." *Brookings Papers on Economic Activity* 1: 1–118.

Shleifer, Andrei, and Robert W. Vishny. 1993. "Corruption." *Quarterly Journal of Economics* 108: 599–617.

Smarzynska, B.K., and S. Wei. 2000. "Corruption and the Composition of Foreign Direct Investment: Firm-Level Evidence." World Bank Discussion Paper Series no. 2360. Washington, DC: World Bank.

Swamy, A.; S. Knack; Y. Lee; and O. Azfar. 2001. "Gender and Corruption." *Journal of Development Economics* 64: 25–55.

Tanzi, Vito, and Hamid Davoodi. 1997. "Corruption, Public Investment, and Growth." International Monetary Fund Working Paper, 97/139.

———. 2001. "Corruption, Growth, and Public Finances." In *Political Economy of Corruption*, ed. A.K. Jain, 89–110. London: Routledge.

Times of India. 2001. "Bribes Are a Big Barrier for Investors." March 28.

Treisman, Daniel. 2000. "The Causes of Corruption: A Cross-National Study." *Journal of Public Economics* 76: 399–457.

Uslaner, E. 2004. "Trust and Corruption." In *The New Institutional Economics of Corruption: Norms, Trust, and Reciprocity*, ed. J. Graf Lambsdorff, M. Schramm, and M. Taube, 76–92. London: Routledge.

Voigt, S.; L. Feld; and A. van Aaken. 2004. "Power over Prosecutors Corrupts Politicians: Cross-Country Evidence Using a New Indicator." Economics Faculty, University of Kassel, Germany.

Wedeman, A. 1997. "Looters, Rent-scrapers, and Dividend-Collectors: Corruption and Growth in Zaire, South Korea, and the Philippines." *Journal of Developing Areas* 31: 457–78.

Wei, S.-J. 1997. "Why Is Corruption So Much More Taxing Than Tax? Arbitrariness Kills." National Bureau of Economic Research Working Paper 6255.

———. 2000a. "Natural Openness and Good Government." World Bank Policy Research Working Paper no. 2411 and NBER Working Paper 7765.

———. 2000b. "How Taxing Is Corruption on International Investors?" *Review of Economics and Statistics* 82, no. 1: 1–11.

Wei, S.-J., and Y. Wu. 2001. "Negative Alchemy? Corruption, Composition of Capital Flows, and Currency Crises." NBER Working Paper Series 8187 (March).

Winston, G.C. 1979. "The Appeal of Inappropriate Technologies: Self-Inflicted Wages, Ethnic Price and Corruption." *World Development* 7, nos. 8/9: 835–45.

World Bank. 1997. *World Development Report 1997*. Washington, DC.

18

Military Expenditure in South Asia

A Case Study of Economic Irrationality

Geoff Harris

The purpose of this chapter is to examine military expenditure (milex) in South Asia since the early 1990s and in doing so to demonstrate the use of relevant economic concepts, tools, and ways of reasoning.

Governments are justified in engaging in activities where the free market "fails," that is, where the free market would provide inadequate amounts of the relevant goods and services, not provide them at all, or provide them only at an excessive price. The aspect of market failure that justifies government military expenditure is that the military is a public good. This has two aspects, the first of which is nonexcludability. That is, the benefits of defense are available to all residents of the country, whether they want these benefits or not and whether they pay for them or not. No one can be excluded. The second is the practical impossibility of collecting revenue from residents as and when they benefit from defense. For these reasons, defense is financed by general taxation payable by all residents.

The military has a number of potential benefits (see Table 18.1). Many of these benefits are subject to debate in particular contexts, but each has no doubt applied to some country at some point in time. The fundamental benefit is military protection from external attack. The potential benefit of most interest to economists is the possibility that it promotes economic growth, and we examine this in detail.

A point worth noting is that a number of the potential benefits are the result of "mission creep"—the taking on of additional tasks by the military, sometimes as a way of justifying sustained military expenditure in the absence of an external threat. Here the economist should employ the tool of cost effectiveness: that is, how effectively does the military carry out tasks, for

Table 18.1

Potential Benefits of the Military

Security	Security from external threat
	Security from internal threat
	Reduced likelihood of war
Economic	Secure environment promotes economic growth
	Employment
Attitudinal	Modernization via training and discipline
	National pride
Broad social	Civil defense/disaster relief
International	Peacekeeping
	International prestige

example, the protection of natural resources from poaching, and at what cost does it do so compared with a nonmilitary provider? Generally speaking, the military is not particularly effective in providing a number of these noncore activities and it is also a high-cost provider. At the same time, it might be argued that while the military is waiting for an external threat to emerge, it makes sense for it to be used in socially useful activities. The economist's response to this argument is neither yes nor no, but "Do the cost effectiveness calculations."

In several important respects, milex differs from other government expenditure categories such as education and health. These expenditures may be regarded as investments in that they result in a stream of quantifiable benefits over time. Education and health expenditures make adults more productive during their working lives. It is thus possible to calculate a rate of return to society from education and health expenditures. The core function of milex, however, does not yield such benefits over time (although it may provide a secure environment where other expenditures can result in such benefits). Milex is a consumption expenditure and has a zero social rate of return. This point is well made by Dumas:

> Military expenditure is one of the most important types of non-contributive activity in the modern world. Whatever else can be said for it, military activity does not grow food, it does not produce clothing, it does not build housing, and it does not keep people amused. . . . Military activity may have other kinds of value, but it has no *economic* value because it does not directly contribute to material well-being, to the material standard of living. (2002, 16–17)

The Changed Security Environment

Three important changes to the environment in which milex is applied have occurred over the past two decades. The first is the nature of warfare. The vast majority of "major armed conflicts"—defined by the Stockholm International Peace Research Institute (SIPRI) as involving the military forces of two parties, at least one of which is the government of a state, and resulting in at least 1,000 battle-related deaths in any single year—occur within nation-states rather than between them. The SIPRI *Yearbook 2003*, for example, records twenty-one armed conflicts in 2002, of which twenty were within countries and one was between countries (India and Pakistan). For the period 1990–2002, there were fifty-eight major armed conflicts of which only three were interstate—Iraq versus Kuwait, India versus Pakistan, and Ethiopia versus Eritrea. The point is well illustrated by the fact that twenty-five of the Indian Army's thirty-five divisions are engaged in internal security maintenance, particularly in Assam, the Northeast, and Kashmir. A similar situation applies to Pakistan in the Sind and Baluchistan. Internal conflicts are typically motivated by the desire to take over government or to secede. This change in the nature of warfare has important implications for the nature and size of military expenditures. The "war on terror" declared after the September 11, 2001, attacks also has important implications for milex, because a conventional military is of little use in combating terrorist attacks.

Second, the nature of security has changed. This recognition dates from the early 1980s, when writers such as Buzan (1983) showed that the threat of external attack was only one of a number of security issues. The United Nations Development Programme's (UNDP) *Human Development Report 1994* identified seven types of security: economic, food, health, environmental, personal, community, and political (1994, 24–35). Most commentators would regard the lack of these as far greater threats to residents of developing countries than war. Indeed, the UNDP estimates that people in the developing world are thirty-three times more likely to die of "social neglect" (e.g., failure to prevent preventable disease) by government than in a war of external aggression (1994, 50).

Third, there are increasing attempts by bodies such as the World Bank and the International Monetary Fund to encourage greater rationality in public expenditure decisions. We return to consider how an appropriate level of milex may be determined later in the chapter.

Having dealt with these preliminaries, we now proceed to examine the levels and trends of milex in South Asia.

Table 18.2

Military Expenditure in South Asia, 1993 and 2002 (US$ billions, in 2000 prices and exchange rates)

	1993	2002
Bangladesh	453	622
India	8,137	12,882
Nepal	41	87
Pakistan	2,993	3,176
Sri Lanka	361	524
Total	11,985	17,297

Source: SIPRI (2003).

Milex in South Asia

This section presents data on the level and trends of various milex indicators. Table 18.2 shows milex in constant price terms over a ten-year period, 1993–2002. India and Pakistan dominate the subcontinent's milex, making up 93 percent of the total in 2002. India spent four times more than Pakistan in 2002, compared with 2.7 times in 1993. Over the ten years, India's real milex rose progressively by a total of 58.3 percent while Pakistan's milex was virtually constant in real terms. Rises in 2001 and 2002 resulted in a 6.1 percent increase over the decade.

Table 18.3 (column 1) shows the "military burden" for South Asia, that is, milex, as a proportion of the gross domestic product (GDP). In the late 1990s, India's military burden was 2.5 percent (equal to the average figure for developing countries) while Pakistan's figure was much higher at 4.5 percent. The military burden of both countries fell during the 1990s. Columns 2 and 3 list education and health expenditures as proportions of GDP. One rule of thumb by which to guide the level of milex is that it should not exceed health and education expenditures combined; we discuss these data in more detail below. The other entry in Table 18.3 is debt service. Adding milex and debt service together provides an indicator of unproductive expenditure, although this is not to say that the use made of the funds was necessarily unproductive. These expenditures were twice as high in Pakistan (9.5 percent of GDP) than in India (4.4 percent). In 2001, India's debt service was equivalent to 12.6 percent of its export earnings while for Pakistan the figure was 21.2 (UNDP 2003).

It may seem to be an indirect approach to relate milex to GDP. Why not relate it directly to total central government expenditure (CGE)? One reason

Table 18.3

Public Expenditure on Various Categories, as a Percentage of Gross Domestic Product

	Military	Education	Health	Total debt service
Bangladesh				
1990	1.0	1.5	0.7	2.5
1998–2000	1.3		1.4	1.4
Bhutan				
1990	na	na	1.7	1.8
1998–2000	na	5.2	3.7	1.2
India				
1990	2.7	3.9	0.9	2.6
1998–2000	2.5	4.1	0.9	1.9
Nepal				
1990	0.9	2.0	0.8	1.9
1998–2000	0.9	2.0	0.8	1.9
Pakistan				
1990	5.8	2.6	1.1	4.8
1998–2000	4.5	1.8	0.9	5.0
Sri Lanka				
1990	2.1	2.6	1.5	4.8
1998–2000	3.9	3.1	1.8	4.5

Source: United Nations Development Programme (2003, various tables).

is that the CGE/GDP ratio varies considerably between countries. Another is that education and health expenditures, for example, are frequently carried out by state or provincial governments, so that national expenditures on these categories will be higher than that indicated by CGE (see the note to Table 18.4). With these caveats in mind, Table 18.4 presents milex, education, and health expenditures as a proportion of total CGE. Both India and Pakistan allocate high proportions of their CGE (15.6 and 18.0 percent, respectively) to defense.

Current economic orthodoxy urges government to restrict the size of its budget deficits. Any expenditure by government adds to the potential size of its deficit, and the levels of milex in relation to the size of its budget deficits are presented in Table 18.5. At a very simplistic level of reasoning, if milex fell to zero, the budget deficit for Pakistan would virtually disappear, while those of Sri Lanka and India would be halved.

Table 18.4

Selected Government Expenditure Categories as a Proportion of Central Government Expenditure (CGE)

	Year	Defense	Education	Health
India	2001	15.6	2.2	1.8
Nepal	2002	7.6	16.9	5.8
Pakistan	2002	18.0	1.3	6.8
Sri Lanka	2001	14.7	7.7	5.1

Source: International Monetary Fund (2002).
Note: The United Nations Development Programme (2003) reports respective education expenditures between 1998 and 2000 for India, Nepal, and Pakistan as averaging 12.7, 14.1, and 7.8 percent of CGE, respectively.

Table 18.5

Defense Expenditure as a Proportion of Budget Deficit (%)

	Average, 1992–1994	Average, 1999–2001
India	39.8	50.4
Nepal	22.5[a]	27.5[b]
Pakistan	74.1[b]	93.7
Sri Lanka	47.8	46.5

Source: International Monetary Fund (2002).
[a] 1993–1995.
[b] 2000–2002.

We have examined milex over the past decade in real terms and as a proportion of GDP, CGE, and budget deficits. How does this expenditure translate into military personnel and weaponry? We should note that milex consists predominantly of recurrent expenditures. A typical developing country allocates about three-quarters of its milex to personnel and operating costs and a quarter to capital expenditures. The last of these may include imported weapons. Table 18.6 presents data on armed forces personnel and numbers of heavy weapons. India and Pakistan totally dominate the subcontinent, with India having roughly twice the personnel and heavy weapons of Pakistan. Between 1985 and 2001, India's armed forces personnel have increased by 50 percent and those of Pakistan by 28 percent. Sri Lanka's armed forces have increased more than sevenfold in response to the civil war. In terms of heavy weapons, India increased its holdings by 22 percent between 1991 and 2001; the corresponding figure for Pakistan was 4 percent.

Table 18.6

Armed Forces Personnel and Heavy Weapons, 2001

	Personnel	Heavy weapons*
Bangladesh	137,000	550
India	1,163,000	10,540
Nepal	46,000	10
Pakistan	620,000	5,410
Sri Lanka	120,000	380

Source: BICC (2003).
*Includes armored vehicles, artillery, combat aircraft, and major fighting ships.

Table 18.7

Imports of Major Conventional Weapons, 1998–2002
(US$ millions, 1990)

	Value	World ranking
Bangladesh	611	34
India	4,824	3
Pakistan	2,992	11
Sri Lanka	490	42

Source: SIPRI (2003, 466–69).
Note: Includes combat aircraft, armored vehicles, artillery, radar systems, missiles, and naval vessels.

It is very difficult to place a value on arms imports, given the complexity of pricing and payment arrangements in the arms trade. The best source (SIPRI 2003) provides estimates for the five years 1998–2002 (a five-year period is used to account for considerable fluctuations between years) and these are reported in Table 18.7. The estimates are in 1990 U.S. dollar prices and therefore cannot easily be compared with the milex figures in Table 18.2. India was the world's third-largest weapons importer over the period and imported 61 percent more than Pakistan. In addition to imports, India has one of the largest defense industries in the world, largely government owned. About 60 percent of the expenditure by the Indian military on capital acquisition, weapons systems, defense equipment, and stores in 1999 came from the domestic public sector arms industry. This was twice that procured from foreign sources (BICC 2003, 136).

We can summarize the foregoing data as follows:

- Pakistan and India dominate the subcontinent's milex.
- India spends much more than Pakistan on the military and the India/ Pakistan milex ratio increased significantly during the 1990s. Similar remarks may be made concerning numbers of military personnel and heavy weapons.
- The opportunity costs of milex are very high for both countries, given the very high proportions of their populations living on less than $1 per day.
- Given the respective size of the countries' GDP, the arms race has much higher opportunity costs to Pakistan.

Some Economic and Social Consequences of Arms Races

There are few more obvious examples of classic arms race behavior than that of India and Pakistan. Leaving aside the competitive development of nuclear weapons and missiles to deliver them since 1998, a recent illustration is the Indian order in 2001 of 310 T-90 main battle tanks from Russia (at a cost of $600–700 million) in response to Pakistan's acquisition of 320 T-80UB tanks (SIPRI 2003, 497). This section considers some of the economic and social consequences of this military rivalry. For an overview of this rivalry since the advent of nuclear weapons in 1998, see Ramana and Mian (2003).

Milex and Economic Growth

Table 18.1 noted reduced economic growth as one of the costs of milex. The first major study of the relationship between the military burden (milex/GDP) in developing countries and their rates of economic growth was carried out for forty-four developing countries between 1950 and 1965 (Benoit 1978). The Spearman rank correlation coefficient between average values of these two variables was positive and significant. Benoit ascertained that no other variable (e.g., foreign aid) was affecting both variables so as to make them appear to be correlated. He then examined the direction of causality and concluded that it ran from milex to growth. (A country's military burden was determined very largely by threat and perceived threat.) How might milex cause growth? Benoit focused on its potential effects on developing human capital, and the involvement of the military in public works, in modernizing the way people think, and in nation building. Milex was thus, according to this reasoning, desirable for developing countries.

Benoit's research stimulated a large number of subsequent studies. One of the main criticisms of his work was that he used a single equation model and therefore failed to consider all of the effects, direct and indirect, that milex might have on growth. A representative response is that of Saadet Deger (1986a, 1986b), who studied fifty developing countries between 1965 and 1973. Deger employed a simultaneous equation model involving four equations, one each for growth, saving, trade, and milex. In brief, she found that milex did produce positive spinoffs but that the large negative effect of milex on growth as a result of reduced savings meant that the overall impact was strongly negative. Deger estimated the savings multiplier (ds/dm) to be 2.56; that is, a 1 percent reduction in the military burden would increase savings two and a half times (Deger 1986b, 356). She estimated the growth multiplier (dg/dm) at 0.217 (1986a) and 0.36 (1986b); that is, a 1 percent reduction in the military burden would raise growth by between one-fifth and one-third of a percentage point.

Many other studies, of increasing degrees of econometric sophistication, have confirmed that, at best, milex has no effect on economic growth and in most cases has a negative effect. For a comprehensive review of such studies, see Dunne (1996).

Milex and Poverty

Economic growth is not an end in itself. It is a means to achieve a higher standard of living for the population and/or to reduce the numbers living in poverty and the degree of that poverty. Milex works against the achievement of higher standards of living in at least two ways. First, as we have seen, it depresses economic growth, which is generally accepted as the major prerequisite for raising standards of life. Second, milex may divert the government from other government expenditures that may directly raise living standards. Tables 18.3 and 18.4 give some indication of this possibility. It is worth noting at this point that more than a third of the population of India and Pakistan live on less than $1 a day (UNDP 2003) and that under age five mortality rates are 93 and 109 per 1,000 live births, respectively.

Studies of possible trade-offs between milex and other CGE categories, usually education and health, have been largely unsuccessful in demonstrating a trade-off (see Dunne 1996). This is despite the obvious fact that if financial resources are allocated to the military then they cannot be spent elsewhere. What might account for this apparent lack of trade-offs? The answer seems to lie in the government budgetary processes, which are not particularly well understood by economists. The decision to spend on the military, it seems, is made independently of decisions to spend on poverty reduction. If more is spent on the military in any year, it does not mean that other CGE categories are cut in order to finance this. And the converse applies: increased allocations to the poverty-reducing categories of CGE would not normally be financed by milex cuts. There may be, in the minds of budget decision makers, an appropriate amount to spend on each category so that, normally, the issue of trade-offs does not arise. We discuss the importance of rational decision making by governments in the next section.

This is not to say that resources from reduced milex cannot be channeled into poverty-reduction expenditures. The Delhi Declaration of November 1986, signed by Mikhail Gorbachev and Rajiv Gandhi, included the following statement: "The resources spent on arms should be channelled to ensuring social and economic growth; only disarmament can release the enormous resources required for fighting economic backwardness and poverty" (quoted in Volkov 1988, 216). These words have been echoed many times but have rarely been acted upon. That the government can play a decisive role in poverty reduction is beyond dispute. Sri Lankan government initiatives in the past mean that only 6.6 percent of its population lives on less than $1 a day and its under age five mortality rate per 1,000 live births is about one-fifth that of India and Pakistan (UNDP 2003).

As the 2001 purchase of main battle tanks by India and Pakistan illustrates, countries that engage in arms races do not become more secure, but they do become poorer. The fact that Pakistan finds the arms race so much more costly than India has an obvious parallel with the rivalry between the United States and the Soviet Union, which ended in the economic collapse of the Soviet Union. The acquisition of nuclear weapons and delivery systems by both countries means that India could take little comfort in an economic collapse of Pakistan. As Pervaz Hoodbhoy has noted, "if Pakistan was to collapse, India will find . . . that it has created a South Asian nuclear Somalia for a neighbour" (quoted in Kumar 1999, 21). There have, incidentally, been no savings on conventional milex since the two countries acquired nuclear weapons.

Is Milex Decision Making Economically Rational?

Following Pareto optimality reasoning, we can imagine the nation as a mountain that represents potential total welfare, given the nation's resources, broadly defined. Exactly where a nation is located on the mountain depends on how well these resources are allocated. If resources are allocated to those sectors where social rates of return are highest, there will be movement up the mountain toward the summit. If resources are misallocated, there will be slower progress, no progress, or decline. As we saw above, milex is a non-contributive activity with a zero social rate of return. Excessive milex, then, will hinder progress up the mountain. The question that must be answered, then, is what is an appropriate level of milex for any country?

As noted earlier, a common rule of thumb is that milex should not exceed the amount spent on education plus health, and this can provide an upper boundary to milex. More generally, reference to what other countries allocate as a proportion of GDP or CGE is not an appropriate criterion. For example, the average proportion of GDP devoted to milex in developing countries is around 2.5 percent. For constitutional reasons, Japan is limited to 1 percent. Nonetheless, the size of its GDP means that Japan's milex is second highest in the world. Given that countries differ in the size of their CGE and GDP, the ratio of milex to either of these is irrelevant as a guide to the appropriate level of milex.

It makes sense to consider what neighboring countries are spending with respect to milex, but only if there is some possibility that their forces may be used to invade. As we have seen, interstate wars are now very rare events and many countries have developed such harmonious relations with their neighbors that invasion is unthinkable. If such harmony does not exist, it can be built (see below). Small countries like Bangladesh and Bhutan, which border countries with huge militaries, cannot hope to effectively defend themselves militarily and should focus on nonmilitary ways of achieving security.

The short answer to how much to allocate to the military is that this should be based on an objective assessment of the realistic external threats facing the country. If there is no realistic external threat, then there may be no need for a military at all, and some countries have made that decision (e.g., Costa Rica in 1947, Panama in 1990, and Haiti in 1994). If there is a significant external threat, then the economist would argue for milex just sufficient to effectively deter an invasion. (We are assuming here that similar milex results in similar effectiveness in terms of military capability.) On the other hand, the presence of large military forces may encourage countries to deal with their disputes by force rather than by less costly, more effective nonmilitary means.

The foregoing leads us to consider the case of demilitarization in the next section, but it is important to admit that government decision making does not necessarily follow the rational logic of neoclassical economists. The public-choice school of economists recognizes that decision makers are influenced by interest groups. In the case of milex, the interest group will include senior military personnel, senior personnel within the Ministry of Defense, domestic arms producers, and foreign arms producers. These can be expected to exert pressure on governments to increase milex and the capability of the military. They can be expected to emphasize that "if you want peace, you must prepare for war"; that the country faces realistic external threats or, if none exist now, that they may appear at some time in the future; and that security is fundamentally a matter for the military. Such interest groups are extremely well organized and funded and very effective in achieving their objectives even in the absence of realistic external threats.

There are considerable efforts, using instruments such as the World Bank's Public Expenditure Reviews, to make public expenditures more efficient and effective. These have not been applied to milex to any extent because it has been regarded as a political decision of the government concerned. Nonetheless, pressure from international lending and donor bodies will be applied, and there may be pressure from within countries to increase the transparency of military budgeting so that, like other expenditures, its efficiency and effectiveness may be measured and improved. Two aspects of efficiency are relevant here. Allocative efficiency involves deciding how much milex should receive compared with other CGE categories, and this should be based on transparent political priorities and an objective analysis of a country's security situation. Operational efficiency, on the other hand, refers to how efficiently and effectively the budget allocation received by the military is used to achieve its purposes; again, these purposes need to be politically decided and transparent.

The remainder of this chapter examines the effectiveness of the military in achieving its fundamental purpose—protection from external attack. A number of potentially more effective ways of achieving security are proposed.

The Case for Demilitarization

Demilitarization does not necessarily mean no military forces. It does mean at least two things—a significant and sustained reduction in milex, military personnel, and weaponry; and a change of mindset toward dealing with disputes by nonmilitary means.

The case for demilitarization is fourfold:

- The use of force and violence to deal with disputes is morally/spiritually/ethically unacceptable.
- The military is a very costly way of dealing with disputes.
- The military is not very effective in dealing with disputes in terms of achieving a sustainable peace.
- There are cost-effective, nonmilitary ways of dealing with disputes.

While the first of these is of great importance, we shall focus on the other three in this chapter. We have already seen that very large proportions of CGE and GDP (Tables 18.3 and 18.4) are allocated to what is economically a noncontributive activity.

We have not discussed the costs of armed conflict, which, it has to be accepted, may be encouraged by the existence of military forces. These costs are:

- Human—deaths, injuries, and displacement;
- Physical—destruction, damage, and the consequences of nonmaintenance;
- Financial—the additional milex incurred as a result of war; plus deferred and lost output; and
- Societal—the social capital (many kinds of voluntary human interactions that are built on trust).

One estimate of the costs of the civil war in Sri Lanka between 1983 and 1996 (Arunatilake, Jayasuriya, and Kelegama 2001) is $20.6 billion, about 1.7 times the country's GDP in 1996. The seventy-four-day Kargil conflict between India and Pakistan in 1999 cost each country some $2 million a day ($300 million in total), excluding losses of weaponry, plus 1,100 military deaths and the deaths of an unknown number of mujahideen guerrilla fighters (Kumar 1999, 24).

Milex and actual warfare, then, are very costly. Are they effective in achieving their outcome—which is presumably a sustainable peace? The simmering India–Pakistan conflict over Kashmir, now over fifty years old, and the twenty-year-old Sri Lankan civil war suggest not. Two recent studies of U.S. military interventions support the contention that force does not result in sustainable peace. Pei and Kasper (2003) studied the sixteen forced regime changes in which significant numbers of U.S. ground troops were involved in the twentieth century. These were designed either to prevent a regime collapse or to bring about a regime change. Of the sixteen, four were judged success-ful in terms of the establishment of a democracy ten years or more after the U.S, withdrawal, namely, Germany, Japan, Grenada, and Panama. In a related study, Dobbins (2003) examined six major nation-building operations since 1990 in which U.S. military forces helped to build a transition to democracy. Of the six, two (Somalia and Haiti) were clear failures, while Bosnia, Kosovo, Afghanistan, and Iraq are still pending, but do not look promising. In terms of civil wars, Collier and Hoeffler's (2002) comprehensive study found that high milex on the part of developing countries does not deter internal rebellion and that low milex does not encourage it. In short, military solutions seem likely to have limited effectiveness.

If milex is costly and its effectiveness limited, are there alternative ways of achieving security? Table 18.8 suggests a number of alternatives under three headings: transforming the military, reducing the incidence of disputes, and

Table 18.8

Alternate Ways of Achieving Security

	Cost	Effectiveness
Traditional military	High	Low-moderate
Transforming the military		
Nonoffensive defense[a]	Lower	Increased
Privatizing or civilianizing noncore activities	Lower	Increased
Social defense[b]	Lower	Moderate
Reducing the incidence of disputes	Moderate	Moderate-high
Befriending the neighbors	Moderate	High
Democracy development	High	High
Developing dispute-resolution capacity	Moderate	High
Peace education; conflict-resolving institutions	Low	Moderate
Developing dispute-resolution capacity	Moderate	High
Peace education; conflict-resolving institutions	Low	Moderate

Source: Harris (2004).
[a]Removing offensive weapons and changing the posture and mindset of the military to defense only.
[b]Training the population to resist nonviolently or not to cooperate with an invader.

developing dispute-resolution capacity. I have included a personal assessment of the costs and effectiveness of each as compared with the traditional military. This will not be examined here in detail (see Harris 2004): suffice it to say that all of them appear to be potentially less costly and/or more effective than the conventional military approach.

Is demilitarization feasible? One striking affirmation is the experience of Costa Rica, which did away with its military over fifty years ago. In a region that has been beset by civil wars and human rights abuse for decades, it has prospered in terms of democratic governance and social indicators. What, then, impedes the adoption of such an approach, with its obvious benefits, by other countries? At the risk of oversimplification, there are several possible answers. First, there is a widespread belief that the military is an effective means of achieving security. The evidence suggests otherwise. Second, there is a widespread belief that nonviolence does not work. The evidence suggests otherwise (for detailed examinations of the success of well-planned and carefully implemented nonviolent campaigns in achieving major social change, see Ackerman and Duval 2000; Galtung 1996; Zunes, Kurtz, and Asher 1999). The major "limitation" of nonviolent methods is that they have not been adequately used. Third, there is the power of military interest groups, both domestic and international, in whose interests it is to promote military thinking and military solutions. The power of the interest groups representing the poor is weak by comparison. Fourth, there is the inertia that always impedes new ways of thinking and acting.

Economists have an important role in increasing the rationality of milex allocations. In particular, they can examine the cost effectiveness of the traditional military approach for specific countries, as opposed to that of the various alternative ways of achieving security. The failure thus far to seriously consider alternative ways of building security has had very heavy costs for India and Pakistan and only generated less security.

References

Ackerman, P., and J. Duvall. 2000. *A Force More Powerful: A Century of Nonviolent Conflict*. New York: St. Martin's Press.

Arunatilake, N.; S. Jayasuriya; and S. Kelegama. 2001. "The Economic Cost of the War in Sri Lanka." *World Development* 29, no. 9: 1483–1500.

Benoit, E. 1978. "Growth and Defense in Developing Countries. *Economic Development and Cultural Change* 26, no. 2: 271–80.

Bonn International Centre for Conversion (BICC). 2003. *Conversion Survey 2003*. Baden-Baden: Nomos Verlagsgesellschaft.

Buzan, B. 1983. *People, States and Fear*. Hemel Hempstead, UK: Wheatsheaf.

Collier, P., and A. Hoeffler. 2002. "Military Expenditure, Threats, Aid, and Arms Races." Policy Research Working Paper 2927. Washington, DC, World Bank.

Deger, S. 1986a. "Economic Development and Defense Expenditure." *Economic Development and Cultural Change* 35, no. 1: 179–96.

———. 1986b. *Military Expenditure in Third World Countries*. London: Routledge and Kegan Paul.

Dobbins, James, et al. 2003. *America's Role in Nation-Building: From Germany to Iraq*. Santa Monica, CA: Rand.

Dumas L. 2002. "The Role of Demilitarization in Promoting Democracy and Prosperity in Africa." In *Arming the South. The Economics of Military Expenditure, Arms Production and Arms Trade in Developing Countries*, ed. J. Brauer and J. Dunne, 15–34. London: Macmillan.

Dunne, J. 1996. "Economic Effects of Military Expenditure in Developing Countries." In *The Peace Dividend*, ed. N.P. Gleditsch, 439–64. Amsterdam: North-Holland.

Galtung, J. 1996. *Peace by Peaceful Means*. London: Sage.

Harris, G., ed. 2004. *Demilitarising Sub-Saharan Africa*. Pretoria: Institute for Security Studies.

International Monetary Fund (IMF). 2002. *Government Finance Statistics Yearbook*. Washington, DC.

Kumar, D. 1999. "South Asia After the Nuclear Tests: Securing Insecurity." Centre for Nepal and Asian Studies, Tribhuvan University, Occasional Paper (September).

Pei, M. and S. Kasper. 2003. *Lessons from the Past: The American Record in Nation Building*. Washington, DC: Carnegie Endowment for International Peace, www.ceip. org/files/publications/HTMLBriefs-WP/24_May_2003_Policy_Brief/20009539v01. html.

Ramana, M., and Z. Mian. 2003. "The Nuclear Confrontation in South Asia." In Stockholm International Peace Research Institute, *SIPRI Yearbook 2003*, 195–212. Oxford: Oxford University Press.

Stockholm International Peace Research Institute (SIPRI). 2003. *SIPRI Yearbook 2003*. Oxford: Oxford University Press.

United Nations Development Programme (UNDP). 1994. *Human Development Report 1994*. Washington, DC: Oxford University Press.

Volkov, M. 1988. "Interrelations Between Militarism, Arms Race and Economic Development." *Development and Peace* 9, no. 2: 207–17.

Zunes, S.; L. Kurtz; and S. Asher. 1999. *Non-violent Social Movements: A Geographical Perspective*. Malden, MA: Blackwell.

About the Editor and Contributors

The Editor

Anjum Siddiqui is the author of international publications in the areas of monetary policy, finance, debt and deficits, and energy economics. His interests in business competitiveness and governance have led to publications on leadership and restructuring issues. He has been senior executive vice president and chief economist of the National Bank of Pakistan. He was consultant to the Reserve Bank of New Zealand and the State Bank of Pakistan and taught for many years at the University of Auckland, New Zealand, and also at the University of Toronto and the Schulich School of Business at York University, Canada. He is the founder and coordinator of the Canadian Center for South Asian Studies.

The Contributors

Ratnakar Adhikari is a member of the South Asia Watch on Trade Economics and Environment (SAWTEEE) and has published a number of articles on the environment, agriculture, and World Trade Organization issues facing South Asia.

Sajid Anwar is senior lecturer at the University of Adelaide (Australia). He has published a number of papers in the area of international trade and economic development.

Premachandra Athukorala's major areas of research include international capital mobility and financial crisis, structural adjustment and stabilization reforms, international production and trade patterns, international labor migration, and global trade issues. He has served as a consultant to the World Bank, the Asian Development Bank, the International Labor Organization, the United Nation Industrial Development Organization, and the Economic Commission for Asia and the Pacific.

Pranab Bardhan is professor of economics at the University of California, Berkeley. He is the author of numerous journal articles and several books in the areas of institutional and political economy of development and international trade. His most recent books include *Scarcity, Conflicts, and Cooperation* (2005) and *Poverty, Agrarian Structure and Political Economy in India* (2003).

Parikshit K. Basu is a lecturer in finance and economics. Before joining CSU, he taught macroeconomics, finance and microeconomics at Griffith University (Brisbane), University of Queensland (Brisbane) and a number of management and professional institutions in India. He has extensive experience in the corporate sector in Australia, Papua New Guinea, and India, and has worked with financial institutions and national and regional tourism bodies in senior management positions. His research interests include corporate governance, financial markets, economic impact studies, cost-benefit analysis, and tourism policy and planning issues.

Bob Catley is professor of management at the University of Newcastle, Australia. He is the author of fourteen books—most recently *The (Strange, Recent but Understandable) Triumph of Liberalism in Australia* (Sydney, 2005)—and around two hundred papers/academic articles/chapters. He was a member of the Australian House of Representatives and consultant to a number of Australian ministers.

Bhagwan Dahiya is Director, Institute of Development Studies and Professor of Economics at M.D. University, Rohtak. He has been Executive Director of Jan Tinbergen Institute of Development Planning and the Chief Editor of a number of journals and has published widely. In 1999 he edited and published five titled books on *The Current State of Economic Science* and in 2000, he edited and published six titled books on *The Current State of Business Disciplines*. With Desh Gupta, he is also the co-author of *India in a Globalising World*.

Desh Gupta holds a Ph.D. from the University of London. He is the author of six books and several articles and book chapters. His latest book (with Bhagwan Dahiya), *India in a Globalising World*, was published in 2005. He retired as senior lecturer in economics from the University of Canberra in July 2005 and currently has an adjunct position at that university.

Geoff Harris is a development economist with particular interest in the military expenditure of developing countries. He also directs the Conflict Resolution

and Peace Studies Program at the University of KwaZulu–Natal, Durban, South
Africa. He studies cost effectiveness of alternate ways to achieve security and
the determinants of military expenditure.

Raghbendra Jha analyzes public finance and macroeconomic issues with particular reference to developing countries. His current work includes village economy
in semi-arid agriculture, determinants of poverty, undernutrition, and inequality
in India, the behavior of retail prices for food grains in India, the sustainability of
the public debt in developing countries, and the linkage between macroeconomic
stabilization and banking crises in semi-open developing countries.

Saman Kelegama is executive director of the Institute of Policy Studies of Sri
Lanka. He is the editor of the *South Asia Economic Journal* and serves on the
editorial boards of a number of other journals. He has published extensively on
Sri Lankan economic issues in both local and international journals and delivered
many lectures on the subject in both domestic and international forums.

Ahmed M. Khalid is associate professor of economics and finance at Bond
University in Australia. He previously taught at the National University of
Singapore. He specializes in applied macro and monetary economics, econometrics, and financial sector reforms. He has worked with the U.S. Agency
for International Development and has been engaged as a consultant by the
Asian Development Bank, the UNDP, and the Haans Seidel Foundation and
as a visiting consultant at the World Bank (2000).

Umer Khalid is presently working as poverty economist in the Ministry
of Finance in Pakistan. He has experience working in economic and policy
research with well-known national organizations in Pakistan, including the
Mahbub ul Haq Human Development Centre (a renowned policy research
institute and think tank) and the State Bank of Pakistan (the central bank of
the country). His research interests include poverty, globalization, employment and labor markets, and the social sector in Pakistan.

Johann Graf Lambsdorff is chair of economic theory at the University of
Passau and director of statistical work for Transparency International. He has
published on institutional economics and corruption. His work has appeared
in *Kyklos*, *Public Choice*, the *Journal of Economic Behavior and Organization*, and *Economics of Governance*.

Edelgard Mahant studies regional economic integration and comparative foreign policy. Her publications include works on European and North

American economic integration as well as comparisons of European and Asian economic integration.

Baldev Raj is professor emeritus of economics at the School of Business and Economics, Wilfrid Laurier University, Ontario, Canada, and editor of the journal *Empirical Economics*. His research specializations include development and growth economics, technology and economic policies, public economics, and econometrics.

Abdul Waheed holds a masters degree in applied economics from the Applied Economics Research Centre, University of Karachi, Pakistan, and a Ph.D. in the field of international development from Nagoya University, Japan, where he is currently a postdoctoral researcher under the Japan Society for the Promotion of Science (JSPS) fellowship program. He is a faculty member in the Department of Economics, University of Karachi, Pakistan.

Dushni Weerakoon is deputy director of the Institute of Policy Studies of Sri Lanka (IPS). She holds a Ph.D. in economics from the University of Manchester, UK. Her research and publications are in the areas of international trade, regional integration, and macroeconomic policy management.

Ann Weston is vice president and research coordinator of the North-South Institute (NSI), Ottawa, Canada. Her research focuses on Canada's trade relations with developing countries and the development dimensions of the World Trade Organization. Before joining NSI, she worked at the Commonwealth Secretariat and the Overseas Development Institute. She was educated at the University of Sussex and the School of African and Asian Studies at London University.

Index

Italic page references indicate charts, maps, and graphs.